The Baby Boom

AMERICANS
BORN 1946 to 1964

7th EDITION

The Baby Boom

AMERICANS BORN 1946 to 1964

7th EDITION

The American
Generations Series

New Strategist Publications, Inc.
Ithaca, New York

New Strategist Publications, Inc.
P.O. Box 242, Ithaca, New York 14851
800/848-0842; 607/273-0913
www.newstrategist.com

ISBN 978-1-937737-06-1 (hardcover)
ISBN 978-1-937737-07-8 (paper)

Printed in the United States of America

Table of Contents

Introduction 1

Chapter 1. Attitudes

Highlights 3
Boomers Are Most Likely to Say They Are Not Too Happy 4
Belief in Hard Work Is Strong Across Generations 7
Older Americans Are Doing Far Better than Middle-Aged or Younger Ones 9
The American Standard of Living Is Falling 12
Two Children Are Most Popular. 15
Religious Diversity Is on the Rise 19
Growing Tolerance of Sexual Behavior 23
Television News Is Most Important 26
Most Support Abortion if a Mother's Health Is Endangered 29

Chapter 2. Education

Highlights 33
Boomers Now Rank Third in Educational Attainment 34
Most Boomers Have Been to College. 36
Older Boomer Men Are among the Best Educated 38
Most Boomer Women Have Been to College. 40
Among Boomer Men, Asians Are the Best Educated 42
Among Boomer Women, Hispanics Are the Least Educated 44
Few Boomers Are Still in School 46
Nearly 1.4 Million Boomers Are Still in College 48

Chapter 3. Health

Highlights 51
Most 45-to-54-Year-Olds Feel Excellent or Very good 52
Weight Problems Are the Norm for Boomers 54
Nearly One in Five 45-to-54-Year-Olds Smoke Cigarettes 57
Many Middle-Aged Americans Lack Health Insurance 61
Health Problems Increase in the 45-to-64 Age Group 67
Prescription Drug Use Is Increasing 73
Millions of Middle-Aged Americans Are Disabled 77
Boomers Are Filling Physician Waiting Rooms 80
Boomers Account for One in Five Deaths 85

Chapter 4. Housing

Highlights 89
Homeownership Rate Has Declined. 90
Homeownership Rises with Age 92
Married Couples Are Most Likely to Be Homeowners 94
Most Middle-Aged Blacks and Hispanics Are Homeowners 96
The Middle Aged Are Most Likely to Live in Single-Family Homes 98
Mobility Rates Are Low in Middle Age 100

Chapter 5. Income

Highlights 103
Median Income Is Declining for Households Headed by the Middle Aged 104
Household Income Peaks in Late Forties 106
Among Boomers, Asians and Non-Hispanic Whites Have the Highest Incomes 108
Married Couples Have the Highest Incomes 113
The Median Income of Middle-Aged Men Has Declined 120
Men Aged 45 to 54 Have the Highest Incomes 123
Women's Incomes Are Flat through Middle Age 129
Earnings Rise with Education 135
Poverty Rate among Boomers Is below Average 140

Chapter 6. Labor Force

Highlights 143
Labor Force Participation Rose among Older Boomers 144
Boomers Are a Large Share of Workers 146
Among Boomer Men, Hispanics Have the Highest Labor Force Rate 148
Most Boomer Women Are in the Labor Force 151
Most Couples under Age 55 Are Dual Earners 154
Boomers Are Almost Half of Nation's Managers 156
Many Workers Have Part-Time Jobs 165
Few Boomers Are Self-Employed 168
Job Tenure among Younger Boomers Has Decreased 170
Most Minimum-Wage Workers Are Young Adults 173
Union Representation Peaks among Workers Aged 55 to 64 175
Number of Workers Aged 65 or Older Will Soar during the Decade 177

Chapter 7. Living Arrangements

Highlights 181
Most Boomer Households Are Headed by Married Couples 182
Few Black Households Are Headed by Married Couples 184
Boomer Households Are Shrinking 189
Most Boomers Are Empty-Nesters 191
Boomers Account for More than One-Third of People Who Live Alone 198
Divorced Population Peaks in Middle Age 200
Regardless of Race, the Middle Aged Are Most Likely to Be Married 202
Divorce Is Highest among Men and Women in Their Fifties 207

Chapter 8. Population

Highlights 209
Boomers Are Still the Largest Generation 210
Boomers Are Less Diverse than Younger Americans 214
Many Boomers Live in Their State of Birth 218
The Middle Aged Are a Substantial Share of Immigrants 221
Many Working-Age Adults Do Not Speak English at Home 223
Largest Share of Baby Boomers Lives in the South 225

Chapter 9. Spending

Highlights 265
Boomer Spending Has Declined 266
Householders Aged 45 to 54 Are the Biggest Spenders 276
Householders Aged 55 to 64 Spend Slightly More than Average 280

Chapter 10. Time Use

Highlights 285
The Middle Aged Spend More Time at Work than at Play 286

Chapter 11. Wealth

Highlights 299
Net Worth Fell Sharply during the Great Recession 300
Financial Asset Value Declined in Most Age Groups 302
Nonfinancial Assets Are the Basis of Household Wealth 307
Most Households Are in Debt 311
Retirement Worries Are Growing 315

Glossary 320

Bibliography 325

Index 329

Tables

Chapter 1. Attitudes

1.1	General Happiness, 2010	5
1.2	Happiness of Marriage, 2010	5
1.3	Is Life Exciting, Routine, or Dull, 2010	6
1.4	Trust in Others, 2010	6
1.5	How People Get Ahead, 2010	8
1.6	Geographic Mobility Since Age 16, 2010	8
1.7	Social Class Membership, 2010	10
1.8	Family Income Relative to Others, 2010	10
1.9	Satisfaction with Financial Situation, 2010	11
1.10	Job Satisfaction, 2010	11
1.11	Parents' Standard of Living, 2010	13
1.12	Standard of Living Will Improve, 2010	13
1.13	Children's Standard of Living, 2010	14
1.14	Ideal Number of Children, 2010	16
1.15	Spanking Children, 2010	16
1.16	Better for Man to Work, Woman to Tend Home, 2010	17
1.17	Working Mother's Relationship with Children, 2010	17
1.18	Should Government Help the Sick, 2010	18
1.19	Attitude toward Science, 2010	20
1.20	Attitude toward Evolution, 2010	20
1.21	Religious Preference, 2010	21
1.22	Degree of Religiosity, 2010	21
1.23	Belief in the Bible, 2010	22
1.24	Bible in the Public Schools, 2010	22
1.25	Premarital Sex, 2010	24
1.26	Homosexual Relations, 2010	24
1.27	Gay Marriage, 2010	25
1.28	Main Source of Information about Events in the News, 2010	27
1.29	Political Leanings, 2010	27
1.30	Political Party Affiliation, 2010	28
1.31	Favor or Oppose Death Penalty for Murder, 2010	30
1.32	Favor or Oppose Gun Permits, 2010	30
1.33	Legalization of Marijuana, 2010	31
1.34	Support for Legal Abortion by Reason, 2010	31
1.35	Doctor-Assisted Suicide, 2010	32

Chapter 2. Education

2.1.	Educational Attainment by Generation, 2010	35
2.2	Educational Attainment of Baby Boomers, 2010	37
2.3	Educational Attainment of Baby-Boom Men, 2010	39
2.4	Educational Attainment of Baby-Boom Women, 2010	41
2.5	Educational Attainment of Baby-Boom Men by Race and Hispanic Origin, 2010	43
2.6	Educational Attainment of Baby-Boom Women by Race and Hispanic Origin, 2010	45
2.7	School Enrollment by Sex and Age, 2010	47
2.8	College Students by Age and Enrollment Level, 2010	49

Chapter 3. Health

3.1	Health Status by Age, 2010	53
3.2	Average Measured Weight by Age and Sex, 2003–06	55
3.3	Weight Status by Sex and Age, 2007–10	55

3.4   Leisure-Time Physical Activity Level by Sex and Age, 2010 56
3.5   Cigarette Smoking Status by Age, 2010 58
3.6   Alcohol Use by Age, 2010 58
3.7   Illicit Drug Use by People Aged 12 or Older, 2010 59
3.8   Marijuana Use by People Aged 12 or Older, 2010 60
3.9   Health Insurance Coverage by Age, 2010 62
3.10   Private Health Insurance Coverage by Age, 2010 63
3.11   Government Health Insurance Coverage by Age, 2010 64
3.12   Spending on Health Care by Age, 2009 65
3.13   Spending on Health Care by Generation, 2009 66
3.14   Number of Adults with Health Conditions by Age, 2010 68
3.15   Distribution of Health Conditions among Adults by Age, 2010 69
3.16   Percent of Adults with Health Conditions by Age, 2010 70
3.17   Hypertension by Sex and Age, 1988–94 to 2007–10 71
3.18   High Cholesterol by Sex and Age, 1988–94 to 2007–10 72
3.19   Diabetes Diagnosis by Age, 2010 72
3.20   Prescription Drug Use by Sex and Age, 1988–94 to 2005–08 74
3.21   Spending on Prescription Medications by Age, 2009 75
3.22   Spending on Prescription Medications by Generation, 2009 76
3.23   Difficulties in Physical Functioning among Adults by Age, 2010 78
3.24   Cumulative Number of AIDS Cases by Sex and Age, through 2009 79
3.25   Physician Office Visits by Sex and Age, 2009 81
3.26   Hospital Outpatient Department Visits by Age and Reason, 2008 82
3.27   Emergency Department Visits by Age and Urgency of Problem, 2008 82
3.28   Number of Overnight Hospital Stays by Age, 2010 83
3.29   Rating of Health Care Received from Doctor's Office or Clinic by Age, 2009 83
3.30   Rating of Health Care Received from Doctor's Office or Clinic by Generation, 2009 84
3.31   Adults Who Use Complementary and Alternative Medicine by Age, 2007 84
3.32   Leading Causes of Death among People Aged 45 to 64, 2010 86
3.33   Life Expectancy by Age and Sex, 2010 87

Chapter 4. Housing

4.1   Homeownership by Age of Householder, 2000 to 2011 91
4.2   Owners and Renters by Age of Householder, 2011 93
4.3   Homeownership Rate by Age of Householder and Type of Household, 2011 .95
4.4   Homeownership Rate by Age of Householder and Region, 2011 95
4.5   Homeownership Rate by Age, Race, and Hispanic Origin, 2010 97
4.6   Number of Units in Structure by Age of Householder and Homeownership Status, 2010 99
4.7   Geographical Mobility by Age and Type of Move, 2010–11 101
4.8   Reason for Moving among People Aged 45 to 64, 2010–11 102

Chapter 5. Income

5.1   Median Income of Households Headed by People Aged 45 to 64, 1990 to 2010 105
5.2   Income of Households Headed by People Aged 45 to 64, 2010: Total Households 107
5.3   Income of Households Headed by People Aged 45 to 64, 2010: Asian Households 109
5.4   Income of Households Headed by People Aged 45 to 64, 2010: Black Households 110
5.5   Income of Households Headed by People Aged 45 to 64, 2010: Hispanic Households 111
5.6   Income of Households Headed by People Aged 45 to 64, 2010:
       Non-Hispanic White Households 112
5.7   Income of Households by Household Type, 2010: Aged 45 to 54 114
5.8   Income of Households by Household Type, 2010: Aged 45 to 49 115
5.9   Income of Households by Household Type, 2010: Aged 50 to 54 116
5.10   Income of Households by Household Type, 2010: Aged 55 to 64 117
5.11   Income of Households by Household Type, 2010: Aged 55 to 59 118
5.12   Income of Households by Household Type, 2010: Aged 60 to 64 119
5.13   Median Income of Men Aged 45 to 64, 1990 to 2010 121
5.14   Median Income of Women Aged 45 to 64, 1990 to 2010 122

5.15   Income of Men Aged 45 to 64, 2010: Total Men 124
5.16   Income of Men Aged 45 to 64, 2010: Asian Men 125
5.17   Income of Men Aged 45 to 64, 2010: Black Men...126
5.18   Income of Men Aged 45 to 64, 2010: Hispanic Men 127
5.19   Income of Men Aged 45 to 64, 2010: Non-Hispanic White Men 128
5.20   Income of Women Aged 45 to 64, 2010: Total Women 130
5.21   Income of Women Aged 45 to 64, 2010: Asian Women 131
5.22   Income of Women Aged 45 to 64, 2010: Black Women...............................132
5.23   Income of Women Aged 45 to 64, 2010: Hispanic Women 133
5.24   Income of Women Aged 45 to 64, 2010: Non-Hispanic White Women 134
5.25   Earnings of Men by Education, 2010: Aged 45 to 54 136
5.26   Earnings of Men by Education, 2010: Aged 55 to 64 137
5.27   Earnings of Women by Education, 2010: Aged 45 to 54...............................138
5.28   Earnings of Women by Education, 2010: Aged 55 to 64...............................139
5.29   People below Poverty Level by Age, Race, and Hispanic Origin, 2010 141

Chapter 6. Labor Force

6.1   Labor Force Participation Rate by Sex and Age, 2000 to 2011.........................145
6.2   Employment Status by Sex and Age, 2011 147
6.3   Employment Status of Men by Race, Hispanic Origin, and Age, 2011 149
6.4   Employment Status of Women by Race, Hispanic Origin, and Age, 2011 152
6.5   Labor Force Status of Married-Couple Family Groups by Age, 2011 155
6.6.   Occupations of Workers Aged 45 to 64, 2011 157
6.7   Share of Workers Aged 45 to 64 by Occupation, 2011 158
6.8   Distribution of Workers Aged 45 to 64 by Occupation, 2011 159
6.9   Workers Aged 45 to 64 by Detailed Occupation, 2011 160
6.10   Full- and Part-Time Workers by Age and Sex, 2011 166
6.11   Part-Time Workers by Sex, Age, and Reason, 2011 167
6.12   Self-Employed Workers by Sex and Age, 2011 169
6.13   Job Tenure by Sex and Age, 2000 and 2010 171
6.14   Long-Term Employment by Sex and Age, 2000 and 2010 172
6.15   Workers Earning Minimum Wage by Age, 2011 174
6.16   Union Representation by Sex and Age, 2011 176
6.17   Projections of the Labor Force by Sex and Age, 2010 and 2020......................178
6.18   Projections of Labor Force Participation by Sex and Age, 2010 and 2020...........179

Chapter 7. Living Arrangements

7.1   Households Headed by People Aged 45 to 64 by Household Type, 2011: Total Households...........183
7.2   Households Headed by People Aged 45 to 64 by Household Type, 2011: Asian Households 185
7.3   Households Headed by People Aged 45 to 64 by Household Type, 2011: Black Households 186
7.4   Households Headed by People Aged 45 to 64 by Household Type, 2011: Hispanic Households.......187
7.5   Households Headed by People Aged 45 to 64 by Household Type, 2011:
        Non-Hispanic White Households 188
7.6   Average Size of Household by Age of Householder, 2011 190
7.7   Households by Type, Age of Householder, and Presence of Children, 2011: Total Households 192
7.8   Households by Type, Age of Householder, and Presence of Children, 2011: Asian Households 193
7.9.   Households by Type, Age of Householder, and Presence of Children, 2011: Black Households 194
7.10   Households by Type, Age of Householder, and Presence of Children, 2011: Hispanic Households 195
7.11   Households by Type, Age of Householder, and Presence of Children, 2011:
        Non-Hispanic White Households 196
7.12   Households by Presence and Age of Children and Age of Householder, 2011 197
7.13   People Who Live Alone by Age, 2011 199
7.14   Marital Status by Sex and Age, 2011: Total People 201
7.15   Marital Status by Sex and Age, 2011: Asians 203
7.16   Marital Status by Sex and Age, 2011: Blacks 204
7.17   Marital Status by Sex and Age, 2011: Hispanics 205

7.18   Marital Status by Sex and Age, 2011: Non-Hispanic Whites 206
7.19   Marital History of Men by Age, 2009 208
7.20   Marital History of Women by Age, 2009..208

Chapter 8. Population

8.1   Population by Age and Generation, 2010 211
8.2   Population by Age and Sex, 2010 212
8.3   Population by Age, 2000 and 2010 213
8.4   Number of People by Age, Race Alone, and Hispanic Origin, 2010...........................215
8.5   Number of People by Age, Race Alone or in Combination, and Hispanic Origin, 2010 216
8.6   Population by Generation, Race Alone or in Combination, and Hispanic Origin, 2010..........217
8.7   Population by Age and Place of Birth, 2010 219
8.8   Foreign-Born Population by Age and World Region of Birth, 2010...........................220
8.9   Immigrants by Age, 2011..222
8.10   Language Spoken at Home by People Aged 18 to 64, 2010 224
8.11   Population by Age and Region, 2010 226
8.12   Regional Distribution of Population by Age, 2010 227
8.13   Age Distribution of Population by Region, 2010 228
8.14   Population by Generation and Region, 2010 229
8.15   State Populations by Age, 2010 230
8.16   Distribution of State Populations by Age, 2010 232
8.17   State Populations by Generation, 2010 234
8.18   Distribution of State Populations by Generation, 2010 236
8.19   State Populations by Age, Race Alone or in Combination, and Hispanic Origin, 2010 238

Chapter 9. Spending

9.1   Average Household Spending, 2000 to 2010...267
9.2   Average Spending by Householders Aged 45 to 54, 2000 to 2010 270
9.3   Average Spending by Householders Aged 55 to 64, 2000 to 2010 273
9.4   Average, Indexed, and Market Share of Spending by Householders Aged 45 to 54, 2010 277
9.5   Average, Indexed, and Market Share of Spending by Householders Aged 55 to 64, 2010............281

Chapter 10. Time Use

10.1   Detailed Time Use of People Aged 45 to 54, 2010 287
10.2   Detailed Time Use of People Aged 55 to 64, 2010 289
10.3   Detailed Time Use of Men Aged 45 to 54, 2010..291
10.4   Detailed Time Use of Men Aged 55 to 64, 2010..293
10.5   Detailed Time Use of Women Aged 45 to 54, 2010 295
10.6   Detailed Time Use of Women Aged 55 to 64, 2010 297

Chapter 11. Wealth

11.1   Net Worth of Households, 2007 and 2009...301
11.2   Ownership and Value of Financial Assets, 2007 and 2009 303
11.3   Households Owning Transaction Accounts, Life Insurance, and CDs, 2007 and 2009 304
11.4   Households Owning Retirement Accounts and Stocks, 2007 and 2009 305
11.5   Households Owning Pooled Investment Funds and Bonds, 2007 and 2009......................306
11.6   Ownership and Value of Nonfinancial Assets, 2007 and 2009 308
11.7   Households Owning Primary Residence, Other Residential Property, and
       Nonresidential Property, 2007 and 2009 309
11.8   Households Owning Vehicles and Business Equity, 2007 and 2009............................310
11.9   Debt of Households, 2007 and 2009 312
11.10 Households with Residential Debt, 2007 and 2009...313
11.11 Households with Credit Card Debt, Vehicle Loans, and Education Loans, 2007 and 2009 314
11.12 Retirement Confidence, 2002 and 2012..316
11.13 Expected Age of Retirement, 2002 and 2012 317
11.14 Retirement Savings by Age, 2012 318

Illustrations

Chapter 1. Attitudes

Few Millennials trust others 4
Many Americans live in the same city as they did when a teenager. 7
Older Americans are least likely to be dissatisfied with their finances. 9
Most still believe their children will be better off. 12
Even among older Americans, a minority thinks traditional sex roles are best 15
Younger generations are less likely to be Protestant. 19
Most Millennials support gay marriage 23
News sources differ dramatically by generation. 26
Fewer than half of Americans in every generation favor allowing abortion for any reason 29

Chapter 2. Education

People aged 25 to 44 have the highest level of educational attainment 34
More than half the Baby-Boom generation has college experience 36
Men aged 60 to 64 are the best educated Boomers. 38
The youngest Boomer women are most likely to have at least some college experience 40
Half of Asian Baby-Boom men have a bachelor's degree 42
Among Boomer Women, Asians are the best educated 44
Women outnumber men in school 46
Boomers account for 14 percent of graduate students 48

Chapter 3. Health

More than half of 55-to-64-year-olds say their health is excellent or very good 52
Middle-aged Americans weigh more than they should. 54
As Boomers fill the 65-or-older age group, lifetime marijuana use will rise sharply in the oldest age group 57
Many Americans under age 65 do not have health insurance coverage 61
The percentage of people with diabetes rises with age 67
Most Boomers have prescription drug expenses 73
Disabilities rise in middle age 77
Doctor visits rise with advancing age. 80
Baby Boomers have lived more years than they have remaining. 85

Chapter 4. Housing

After peaking in 2004, homeownership has fallen among householders aged 45 to 64. 90
Homeowners greatly outnumber renters among 45-to-64-year-olds 92
Ninety percent of couples aged 55 or older own their home 94
Most Boomers are homeowners, regardless of race or Hispanic origin 96
Most of the middle aged are in single-family homes 98
Few of the middle aged move. 100

Chapter 5. Income

Households headed by Boomers lost ground during the past decade. 104
The middle aged have the highest incomes 106
Median household income varies by race and Hispanic origin 108
Incomes peak among married couples aged 45 to 54 113
Boomer men and women aged 45 to 54 saw their incomes fall 120
Median income tops $60,000 for men aged 60 to 64 who work full-time 123
Among women who work full-time, median income tops $40,000 129
College bonus is big for Boomers. 135
Black Boomers are most likely to be poor 140

Chapter 6. Labor Force

A growing share of 60-to-64-year-olds is in the labor force. 144
Labor force participation rate falls with age among Boomer men 146
Labor force participation rate varies by race and Hispanic origin 148
Labor force participation rates are similar among women by race and Hispanic origin .151
Dual earners are the norm among Boomers aged 45 to 54 154
People aged 45 to 64 account for more than half of workers in some occupations 156
Many part-time workers want full-time jobs 165
Self-employment rises with age 168
Older Boomer men are staying on the job longer 170
Boomers account for few minimum-wage workers 173
Few workers are represented by a union 175
Expect more older workers in the labor force 177

Chapter 7. Living Arrangements

In middle age, a growing share of households are headed by women who live alone 182
Married couples head a minority of households among blacks 184
The nest is emptying for householders in their forties and fifties 189
Many Boomer households include children of any age 191
Women are increasingly likely to live alone as they age 198
Most Boomers are married 200
Among the middle aged, men are much more likely than women to be married 202
More than one in five adults have experienced divorce 207

Chapter 8. Population

Boomers slightly outnumber Millennials 210
Nearly three of four Baby Boomers are non-Hispanic white 214
Among the foreign-born, those from Mexico are the youngest 218
Immigrants aged 45 to 64 account for 19 percent of the 2011 total 221
Half of adults who speak Spanish at home cannot speak English very well 223
The Northeast is home to just 19 percent of Boomers 225

Chapter 9. Spending

Household spending peaks in the 45-to-54 age group 266
Householders aged 45 to 54 spend nearly twice as much as the average household on education 276
Householders aged 55 to 64 spend 47 percent more than average on other lodging 280

Chapter 10. Time Use

Time at work peaks in middle age 286

Chapter 11. Wealth

Net worth peaks among householders aged 55 to 64 300
The value of retirement accounts is modest, even in the older age groups 302
Median housing value peaks in the 45-to-54 age group 307
Education loans are common among young and middle-aged householders 311
Most workers are not planning on an early retirement 315

Introduction

The mood of the nation—its problems and concerns, hopes and fears—are influenced by the age structure of the population. For more than 50 years, the Baby-Boom generation has been one of the most important factors shaping the age structure. The enormous size of the Baby-Boom generation ensures that when it sneezes the nation catches a cold. Today, the United States has pneumonia, struggling to recover from the worst economic downturn since the Great Depression. The collapse and subsequent paralysis of the housing market has decimated the net worth of Boomers, millions of them on the brink of retirement. The seventh edition of *The Baby Boom: Americans Born 1946 to 1964* is your strategic guide to the changing socioeconomic status of this important generation of Americans.

The oldest Boomers have crossed the threshold into old age, turning 65 in 2011 and now being eligible for Medicare. Few have saved much money, and those who managed to save are watching their housing wealth shrink and their financial assets barely stay even. The priorities of Baby Boomers have changed. *The Baby Boom: Americans Born 1946 to 1964* details the status of the Baby-Boom generation today and reveals the direction in which their new priorities may steer the nation in the future.

It is not easy to study the nation's 77 million Boomers. Few government surveys focus solely on the generation, and the age span of the generation often does not fit neatly into traditional five- or 10-year age categories. This time around, however, we got lucky. The Baby-Boom generation—which spanned the ages of 46 to 64 in 2010 (the date for most of the data in this book)—fits almost perfectly into the 45-to-64 age group. Consequently, *The Baby Boom: Americans Born 1946 to 1964* provides real insight into the status of the Baby-Boom generation as it embarks on one of the most important life transitions—retirement.

Many of the oldest Boomers are already retired. Others are postponing retirement as they try to make up for the losses of the Great Recession. Rising labor force participation rates are changing the lifestyles of many older Americans—a group that is increasingly dominated by Boomers. It looks like the Golden Years of the Baby-Boom generation are going to be busy. *The Baby Boom: Americans Born 1946 to 1964* is your guide to the dynamic and unfolding story of the fate of the Baby-Boom generation and the future of the nation itself.

How to use this book

The Baby Boom: Americans Born 1946 to 1964 is designed for easy use. It is divided into 11 chapters, organized alphabetically: Attitudes, Education, Health, Housing, Income, Labor Force, Living Arrangements, Population, Spending, Time Use, and Wealth.

The seventh edition of *The Baby Boom* includes the latest data on the changing demographics of homeownership, based on the Census Bureau's 2011 Housing Vacancies and Homeownership Survey. The Income chapter, with 2010 income statistics, reveals the struggle of so many Americans to stay afloat. The Spending chapter reveals trends in Boomer spending through 2010 and examines how their spending changed after the Great Recession. *The Baby Boom* includes the latest labor force numbers, including the government's projections that show rising participation among older Boomers. The Wealth chapter presents data from the Survey of Consumer Finances revealing the impact of the Great Recession on household wealth, with a look at 2007-to-2009 trends. The Health chapter includes up-to-date statistics on health insurance coverage, chronic conditions, and prescription drug use. The Attitudes chapter, based on New Strategist's analysis of the 2010 General Social Survey, compares and contrasts the perspectives of the generations.

Most of the tables in *The Baby Boom* are based on data collected by the federal government, in particular the Bureau of the Census, the Bureau of Labor Statistics, the National Center for Education Statistics, the National Center for Health Statistics, and the Federal Reserve Board. The federal government is the best source of up-to-date, reliable information on the changing characteristics of Americans. By having *The Baby Boom* on your bookshelf, you can get the answers to your questions faster than you can online. Even better, visit newstrategist.com and download the PDF version of *The Baby Boom* with links to each table in Excel.

The chapters of *The Baby Boom* present the demographic and lifestyle data most important to researchers. Within each chapter, most of the tables are based on data collected by the federal government, but they are not simple reproductions of government spreadsheets—as is the case in many reference books. Instead, each table is compiled and created by New Strategist's editors with calculations designed to reveal the trends. The task of extracting and processing data from the government's web sites to create a single table can require hours of effort. New Strategist has done the work for you, with each table telling a story about Boomers—a story explained by the accompanying text and chart, which analyze the data and highlight future trends. If you need more information than the tables and text provide, you can plumb the original source listed at the bottom of each table.

The book contains a comprehensive table list to help you locate the information you need. For a more detailed search, see the index at the back of the book. Also at the back of the book is the glossary, which defines the terms commonly used and describes the many surveys referenced in the tables and text.

Although most Americans are now younger than the youngest Boomer, the Baby Boom continues to be the most influential of all the generations. With *The Baby Boom: Americans Born 1946 to 1964* in your hands, you have a guide not only to Boomers but to the likely course of our nation as well.

1

Attitudes

■ The 55 percent majority of Boomers think you can't be too careful in life, exceeding the 40 percent who think most people can be trusted.

■ Only 20 percent of Boomers are satisfied with their financial situation. They are more likely to call themselves "working" than "middle" class.

■ Despite their financial struggles, the majority of Boomers think they are better off than their parents were at the same age. Most also think their children will be better off than they themselves are today.

■ The majority of Gen Xers, Boomers, and older Americans think two children are ideal. Among Millennials, only 39 percent think two is ideal and a larger 48 percent think three, four, or more children are ideal.

■ The 53 percent majority of Boomers identify themselves as Protestant compared with only 33 percent of Millennials.

■ In 2010, only 41 percent of Boomers thought gays and lesbians should have the right to marry. Because attitudes are changing rapidly on this issue, the figure is probably higher today.

■ Boomers are more likely to identify themselves as conservative than liberal. Thirty-six percent say they are slightly to extremely conservative, and 27 percent say they are slightly to extremely liberal.

■ Most Boomers and Millennials favor legalizing marijuana.

Boomers Are Most Likely to Say They Are Not Too Happy

Fewer than one in three Americans is very happy.

When asked how happy they are, only 29 percent of Americans aged 18 or older say they are very happy. The majority says it feels only pretty happy. The Millennial generation is least likely to report being very happy (25 percent), but Boomers are most likely to report being not too happy (17 percent).

The 63 percent majority of married Americans say they are very happily married. Interestingly, older Americans are least likely to report being very happily married (59 percent), while Gen Xers are most likely (66 percent).

The majority of the public thinks life is exciting (52 percent). The only generation that does not feel this way is older Americans, with only 42 percent finding life exciting and the 53 percent majority finding it pretty routine.

Few believe most people can be trusted. Only 32 percent of the public says most can be trusted. Younger generations are far less trusting than older Americans. Only 18 percent of Millennials believe most people can be trusted compared with 44 percent of people aged 65 or older.

■ Younger generations of Americans are struggling with a deteriorating economy, which reduces their happiness and increases their distrust.

Few Millennials trust others

(percent of people aged 18 or older who think most people can be trusted, by generation, 2010)

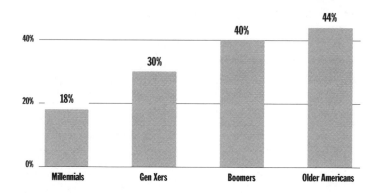

Table 1.1 General Happiness, 2010

"Taken all together, how would you say things are these days—
would you say that you are very happy, pretty happy, or not too happy?"

(percent of people aged 18 or older responding by generation, 2010)

	very happy	pretty happy	not too happy
Total people	**28.8%**	**57.0%**	**14.2%**
Millennial generation (18 to 33)	25.0	62.8	12.2
Generation X (34 to 45)	32.9	54.2	13.0
Baby Boom (46 to 64)	27.2	55.5	17.4
Older Americans (65 or older)	32.8	54.5	12.7

Source: Survey Documentation and Analysis, Computer-assisted Survey Methods Program, University of California, Berkeley, General Social Surveys, 1972–2010 Cumulative Data Files, Internet site http://sda.berkeley.edu/cgi-bin32/ hsda?harcsda+gss10; calculations by New Strategist

Table 1.2 Happiness of Marriage, 2010

"Taking all things together, how would you describe your marriage?"

(percent of currently married people aged 18 or older responding by generation, 2010)

	very happy	pretty happy	not too happy
Total married people	**63.0%**	**34.3%**	**2.6%**
Millennial generation (18 to 33)	60.3	37.2	2.5
Generation X (34 to 45)	66.2	30.8	3.0
Baby Boom (46 to 64)	63.9	33.6	2.5
Older Americans (65 or older)	58.9	38.4	2.7

Source: Survey Documentation and Analysis, Computer-assisted Survey Methods Program, University of California, Berkeley, General Social Surveys, 1972–2010 Cumulative Data Files, Internet site http://sda.berkeley.edu/cgi-bin32/ hsda?harcsda+gss10; calculations by New Strategist

Table 1.3 Is Life Exciting, Routine, or Dull, 2010

"In general, do you find life exciting, pretty routine, or dull?"

(percent of people aged 18 or older responding by generation, 2010)

	exciting	pretty routine	dull
Total people	**52.1%**	**43.3%**	**4.6%**
Millennial generation (18 to 33)	56.2	40.3	3.5
Generation X (34 to 45)	50.1	43.7	6.2
Baby Boom (46 to 64)	54.6	40.7	4.7
Older Americans (65 or older)	42.5	53.2	4.3

Note: Numbers do not sum to total because "don't know" is not shown.
Source: Survey Documentation and Analysis, Computer-assisted Survey Methods Program, University of California, Berkeley, General Social Surveys, 1972–2010 Cumulative Data Files, Internet site http://sda.berkeley.edu/cgi-bin32/hsda?harcsda+gss10; calculations by New Strategist

Table 1.4 Trust in Others, 2010

"Generally speaking, would you say that most people can be trusted or that you can't be too careful in life?"

(percent of people aged 18 or older responding by generation, 2010)

	can trust	cannot trust	depends
Total people	**32.2%**	**62.5%**	**5.3%**
Millennial generation (18 to 33)	17.8	76.9	5.3
Generation X (34 to 45)	30.4	64.4	5.2
Baby Boom (46 to 64)	40.2	54.8	5.1
Older Americans (65 or older)	43.7	50.6	5.7

Source: Survey Documentation and Analysis, Computer-assisted Survey Methods Program, University of California, Berkeley, General Social Surveys, 1972–2010 Cumulative Data Files, Internet site http://sda.berkeley.edu/cgi-bin32/hsda?harcsda+gss10; calculations by New Strategist

Belief in Hard Work Is Strong Across Generations

Millennials are most likely to believe hard work is the key to success.

How do people get ahead? More than two-thirds of Americans say it is by hard work. Only 10 percent believe luck alone gets people ahead. Millennials (73 percent) believe most strongly in hard work to get ahead.

Not surprisingly, Millennials are most likely to live in the same city as they did when they were 16 (48 percent), mostly because they have had less time to move than older generations. Older Americans are most likely to live in a different state (43 percent).

■ Older Americans are most likely to say (24 percent) that people get ahead through hard work and luck equally.

Many Americans live in the same city as they did when a teenager

(percent of people aged 18 or older who live in the same city/town/county as they did at age 16, by generation, 2010)

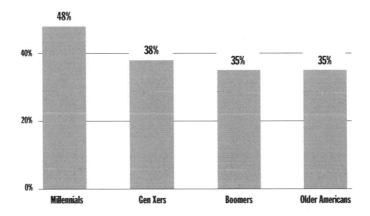

Table 1.5 How People Get Ahead, 2010

"Some people say that people get ahead by their own hard work; others say that lucky breaks or help from other people are more important. Which do you think is most important?"

(percent of people aged 18 or older responding by generation, 2010)

	hard work	both equally	luck
Total people	**69.6%**	**20.4%**	**10.0%**
Millennial generation (18 to 33)	72.7	17.4	9.9
Generation X (34 to 45)	68.4	19.8	11.8
Baby Boom (46 to 64)	69.4	21.6	9.1
Older Americans (65 or older)	67.0	24.0	9.0

Source: Survey Documentation and Analysis, Computer-assisted Survey Methods Program, University of California, Berkeley, General Social Surveys, 1972–2010 Cumulative Data Files, Internet site http://sda.berkeley.edu/cgi-bin32/ hsda?harcsda+gss10; calculations by New Strategist

Table 1.6 Geographic Mobility since Age 16, 2010

"When you were 16 years old, were you living in this same (city/town/county)?"

(percent of people aged 18 or older responding by generation, 2010)

	same city	same state, different city	different state
Total people	**39.4%**	**25.7%**	**34.9%**
Millennial generation (18 to 33)	48.3	23.9	27.9
Generation X (34 to 45)	38.1	26.5	35.3
Baby Boom (46 to 64)	35.0	28.8	36.2
Older Americans (65 or older)	34.8	21.8	43.3

Source: Survey Documentation and Analysis, Computer-assisted Survey Methods Program, University of California, Berkeley, General Social Surveys, 1972–2010 Cumulative Data Files, Internet site http://sda.berkeley.edu/cgi-bin32/ hsda?harcsda+gss10; calculations by New Strategist

Older Americans Are Doing Far Better than Middle-Aged or Younger Ones

People aged 65 or older are the only ones likely to say they are middle class.

The 60 percent majority of Americans aged 65 or older call themselves middle class compared with only 36 to 41 percent of younger generations, who are more likely to label themselves working class than middle class. Is the preference of younger generations for the label working class simply a matter of semantics or does it record a slippage in the standard of living among people under age 65?

Only 43 percent of Americans believe their family's income is average, down from 49 percent in 2000. Fully 36 percent say they make less than average, up from 26 percent in 2000. Older Americans are the ones least likely to say they have below average incomes and (along with Baby Boomers) most likely to say they have above average incomes.

The share of people who are satisfied with their financial situation fell to 23 percent in 2010, down from 31 percent in 2000. Satisfaction with personal finances is greatest among older Americans, only 18 percent of whom are not at all satisfied. The dissatisfied share is a much larger 32 to 35 percent among the younger generations.

When asked whether they are satisfied with the work they do—either at a job or at home, older Americans are much more likely than middle-aged or younger people to say they are very satisfied. Seventy percent of Americans aged 65 or older are very satisfied, as are the majority of Boomers and Gen Xers. Only 36 percent of Millennials are very satisfied with their work.

■ Older Americans, buoyed by the security of Medicare and Social Security, are the only ones who have managed to hold on to their middle-class status as the Great Recession swept through the economy.

Older Americans are least likely to be dissatisfied with their finances

(percent of people aged 18 or older who say they are not at all satisfied with their financial situation, by generation, 2010)

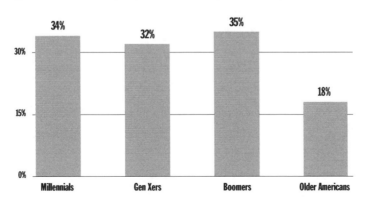

Table 1.7 Social Class Membership, 2010

"If you were asked to use one of four names for your social class,
which would you say you belong in: the lower class,
the working class, the middle class, or the upper class?"

(percent of people aged 18 or older responding by generation, 2010)

	lower	working	middle	upper
Total people	**8.2%**	**46.8%**	**42.4%**	**2.5%**
Millennial generation (18 to 33)	9.8	52.7	35.6	2.0
Generation X (34 to 45)	7.9	51.8	39.7	0.6
Baby Boom (46 to 64)	8.6	46.8	41.0	3.6
Older Americans (65 or older)	5.0	31.1	60.1	3.8

Source: Survey Documentation and Analysis, Computer-assisted Survey Methods Program, University of California, Berkeley, General Social Surveys, 1972–2010 Cumulative Data Files, Internet site http://sda.berkeley.edu/cgi-bin32/hsda?harcsda+gss10; calculations by New Strategist

Table 1.8 Family Income Relative to Others, 2010

"Compared with American families in general, would you say
your family income is far below average, below average,
average, above average, or far above average?"

(percent of people aged 18 or older responding by generation, 2010)

	far below average	below average	average	above average	far above average
Total people	**6.8%**	**28.8%**	**43.5%**	**18.4%**	**2.5%**
Millennial generation (18 to 33)	7.0	30.6	46.6	13.7	2.0
Generation X (34 to 45)	7.9	27.4	44.2	17.8	2.7
Baby Boom (46 to 64)	8.0	30.8	37.3	20.6	3.3
Older Americans (65 or older)	2.6	23.6	49.4	23.1	1.2

Source: Survey Documentation and Analysis, Computer-assisted Survey Methods Program, University of California, Berkeley, General Social Surveys, 1972–2010 Cumulative Data Files, Internet site http://sda.berkeley.edu/cgi-bin32/hsda?harcsda+gss10; calculations by New Strategist

Table 1.9 Satisfaction with Financial Situation, 2010

"So far as you and your family are concerned, would you say
that you are pretty well satisfied with your present financial
situation, more or less satisfied, or not satisfied at all?"

(percent of people aged 18 or older responding by generation, 2010)

	satisfied	more or less satisfied	not at all satisfied
Total people	**23.3%**	**45.2%**	**31.5%**
Millennial generation (18 to 33)	20.3	45.4	34.3
Generation X (34 to 45)	19.8	47.8	32.4
Baby Boom (46 to 64)	19.9	44.8	35.3
Older Americans (65 or older)	39.9	41.9	18.1

Source: Survey Documentation and Analysis, Computer-assisted Survey Methods Program, University of California, Berkeley, General Social Surveys, 1972–2010 Cumulative Data Files, Internet site http://sda.berkeley.edu/cgi-bin32/ hsda?harcsda+gss10; calculations by New Strategist

Table 1.10 Job Satisfaction, 2010

"On the whole, how satisfied are you with the work you do—would you say you
are very satisfied, moderately satisfied, a little dissatisfied, or very dissatisfied?"

(percent of people aged 18 or older responding by generation, 2010)

	very satisfied	moderately satisfied	a little dissatisfied	very dissatisfied
Total people	**49.8%**	**36.2%**	**10.3%**	**3.7%**
Millennial generation (18 to 33)	36.2	45.6	14.9	3.3
Generation X (34 to 45)	52.4	33.8	10.0	3.8
Baby Boom (46 to 64)	54.6	32.8	8.4	4.3
Older Americans (65 or older)	69.9	24.5	3.8	1.8

Note: Question refers to job or housework.
Source: Survey Documentation and Analysis, Computer-assisted Survey Methods Program, University of California, Berkeley, General Social Surveys, 1972–2010 Cumulative Data Files, Internet site http://sda.berkeley.edu/cgi-bin32/ hsda?harcsda+gss10; calculations by New Strategist

The American Standard of Living Is Falling

Fewer Americans believe they are better off than their parents.

When comparing their own standard of living now with that of their parents when they were the same age, 59 percent of respondents say they are better off. The figure was 67 percent 10 years earlier. Older Americans are by far most likely to think they are better off than their parents were at the same age (73 percent). Generation Xers are least likely to feel that way (52 percent).

When asked whether they think they have a good chance of improving their standard of living, 58 percent of Americans say yes. This is down sharply from 77 percent a decade earlier. Not surprisingly, Millennials—with most of their life ahead of them—are most hopeful (65 percent). Disturbingly, Boomers are least hopeful (52 percent).

Fifty-nine percent of parents believe their children will have a better standard of living when they reach the respondent's present age. The share is 73 percent among Millennials, 60 percent among Xers, 53 percent among Boomers, and just 47 percent among older Americans. Apparently, many older Americans are aware of the declining standard of living among the younger generations. A substantial 27 percent of older Americans believe their children will be worse off in the years ahead.

■ The Americans who now have the least (Millennials) are most likely to believe things will be better in the future.

Most still believe their children will be better off

(percent of people aged 18 or older with children who think their children's standard of living will be somewhat or much better than theirs is now, by generation, 2010)

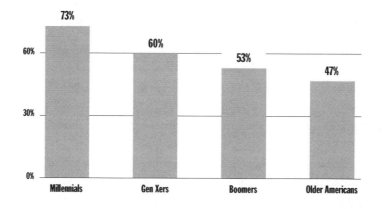

Table 1.11 Parents' Standard of Living, 2010

"Compared to your parents when they were the age you are now, do you think your own standard of living now is much better, somewhat better, about the same, somewhat worse, or much worse than theirs was?"

(percent of people aged 18 or older responding by generation, 2010)

	much better	somewhat better	about the same	somewhat worse	much worse
Total people	**29.2%**	**29.7%**	**24.8%**	**12.1%**	**4.2%**
Millennial generation (18 to 33)	27.6	32.3	25.6	10.4	4.0
Generation X (34 to 45)	25.6	26.0	29.1	16.5	2.9
Baby Boom (46 to 64)	27.8	27.7	23.7	14.9	5.9
Older Americans (65 or older)	39.2	34.0	19.6	4.6	2.6

Source: Survey Documentation and Analysis, Computer-assisted Survey Methods Program, University of California, Berkeley, General Social Surveys, 1972–2010 Cumulative Data Files, Internet site http://sda.berkeley.edu/cgi-bin32/hsda?harcsda+gss10; calculations by New Strategist

Table 1.12 Standard of Living Will Improve, 2010

"The way things are in America, people like me and my family have a good chance of improving our standard of living. Do you agree or disagree?"

(percent of people aged 18 or older responding by generation, 2010)

	strongly agree	agree	neither	disagree	strongly disagree
Total people	**13.1%**	**44.9%**	**16.2%**	**21.6%**	**4.2%**
Millennial generation (18 to 33)	15.5	49.7	16.9	15.9	2.0
Generation X (34 to 45)	18.5	38.4	16.3	22.4	4.4
Baby Boom (46 to 64)	10.7	41.6	16.4	25.0	6.2
Older Americans (65 or older)	7.4	50.8	14.1	23.5	4.2

Source: Survey Documentation and Analysis, Computer-assisted Survey Methods Program, University of California, Berkeley, General Social Surveys, 1972–2010 Cumulative Data Files, Internet site http://sda.berkeley.edu/cgi-bin32/hsda?harcsda+gss10; calculations by New Strategist

Table 1.13 Children's Standard of Living, 2010

"When your children are at the age you are now, do you think their
standard of living will be much better, somewhat better, about
the same, somewhat worse, or much worse than yours is now?"

(percent of people aged 18 or older with children responding by generation, 2010)

	much better	somewhat better	about the same	somewhat worse	much worse
Total people with children	**27.4%**	**32.0%**	**20.6%**	**15.0%**	**5.1%**
Millennial generation (18 to 33)	38.0	34.6	16.6	9.0	1.8
Generation X (34 to 45)	32.4	27.7	19.1	14.7	6.1
Baby Boom (46 to 64)	19.8	33.1	22.4	18.5	6.2
Older Americans (65 or older)	17.0	30.3	25.9	19.2	7.8

*Source: Survey Documentation and Analysis, Computer-assisted Survey Methods Program, University of California,
Berkeley, General Social Surveys, 1972–2010 Cumulative Data Files, Internet site http://sda.berkeley.edu/cgi-bin32/
hsda?harcsda+gss10; calculations by New Strategist*

Two Children Are Most Popular

Many Millennials think three children is the ideal number, however.

Across generations a plurality of Americans thinks two is the ideal number of children. The majority of Gen Xers, Boomers, and older Americans say two is ideal. Among Millennials, a smaller 39 percent think two is the ideal number, and a hefty 48 percent think three, four, or more is best. With a new baby bust in force because of the Great Recession, it is doubtful that Millennials will act on their larger family ideal.

Regardless of their number, most children are subject to a good, hard spanking when they misbehave. Sixty-nine percent of Americans believe children sometimes must be spanked, with little difference by generation.

As older Americans exit the stage, the preference for traditional sex roles has fallen below 50 percent even among people aged 65 or older. Only 48 percent of older Americans believe it is better for everyone involved if the man is the achiever outside the home and the woman takes care of the home and family. Among younger generations, the figure is just 31 to 35 percent. Most of the oldest generation now agrees with young and middle-aged adults that a working mother can have just as warm and secure a relationship with her children as a mother who does not work.

Support for the view that government should help people who are sick and in need is strongest among Millennials (58 percent). Ironically, those least likely to feel this way are older Americans—the only age group with government-provided health insurance. Just 35 percent believe government should help.

■ Many older Americans may not understand that Medicare is a government-provided health insurance program.

Even among older Americans, a minority thinks traditional sex roles are best

(percent of people aged 18 or older who think traditional sex roles are best, by generation, 2010)

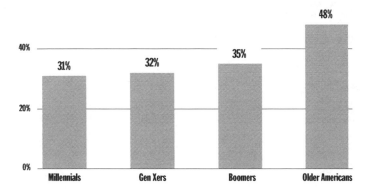

Table 1.14 Ideal Number of Children, 2010

"What do you think is the ideal number of children for a family to have?"

(percent of people aged 18 or older responding by generation, 2010)

	none	one	two	three	four or more	as many as want
Total people	**0.3%**	**2.5%**	**48.4%**	**26.3%**	**12.0%**	**10.5%**
Millennial generation (18 to 33)	0.1	2.1	39.3	32.4	15.8	10.3
Generation X (34 to 45)	0.3	1.2	54.0	23.9	11.1	9.5
Baby Boom (46 to 64)	0.5	3.4	51.7	22.1	11.3	11.0
Older Americans (65 or older)	0.2	3.0	51.7	26.3	8.0	10.8

Source: Survey Documentation and Analysis, Computer-assisted Survey Methods Program, University of California, Berkeley, General Social Surveys, 1972–2010 Cumulative Data Files, Internet site http://sda.berkeley.edu/cgi-bin32/hsda?harcsda+gss10; calculations by New Strategist

Table 1.15 Spanking Children, 2010

"Do you strongly agree, agree, disagree, or strongly disagree that it is sometimes necessary to discipline a child with a good, hard, spanking?"

(percent of people aged 18 or older responding by generation, 2010)

	strongly agree	agree	disagree	strongly disagree
Total people	**23.6%**	**45.4%**	**23.5%**	**7.5%**
Millennial generation (18 to 33)	21.3	48.1	24.0	6.7
Generation X (34 to 45)	26.6	43.9	22.6	6.8
Baby Boom (46 to 64)	22.2	45.1	23.6	9.0
Older Americans (65 or older)	25.7	43.4	23.6	7.3

Source: Survey Documentation and Analysis, Computer-assisted Survey Methods Program, University of California, Berkeley, General Social Surveys, 1972–2010 Cumulative Data Files, Internet site http://sda.berkeley.edu/cgi-bin32/hsda?harcsda+gss10; calculations by New Strategist

Table 1.16 Better for Man to Work, Woman to Tend Home, 2010

"Do you strongly agree, agree, disagree, or strongly disagree with the statement:
It is much better for everyone involved if the man is the achiever outside the
home and the woman takes care of the home and family?"

(percent of people aged 18 or older responding by generation, 2010)

	agree			disagree		
	total	strongly agree	agree	total	disagree	strongly disagree
Total people	**35.4%**	**6.8%**	**28.6%**	**64.7%**	**43.5%**	**21.2%**
Millennial generation (18 to 33)	31.1	5.5	25.6	68.9	42.7	26.2
Generation X (34 to 45)	31.6	5.9	25.7	68.4	42.9	25.5
Baby Boom (46 to 64)	34.8	5.5	29.3	65.2	46.5	18.7
Older Americans (65 or older)	48.5	12.8	35.7	51.5	40.0	11.5

*Source: Survey Documentation and Analysis, Computer-assisted Survey Methods Program, University of California,
Berkeley, General Social Surveys, 1972–2010 Cumulative Data Files, Internet site http://sda.berkeley.edu/cgi-bin32/*

Table 1.17 Working Mother's Relationship with Children, 2010

"Do you strongly agree, agree, disagree, or strongly disagree with the statement:
A working mother can establish just as warm and secure a relationship
with her children as a mother who does not work?"

(percent of people aged 18 or older responding by generation, 2010)

	agree			disagree		
	total	strongly agree	agree	total	disagree	strongly disagree
Total people	**74.7%**	**28.8%**	**45.9%**	**25.2%**	**20.1%**	**5.1%**
Millennial generation (18 to 33)	76.0	30.2	45.8	24.0	19.5	4.5
Generation X (34 to 45)	78.4	32.6	45.8	21.6	17.0	4.6
Baby Boom (46 to 64)	74.7	28.5	46.2	25.3	19.7	5.6
Older Americans (65 or older)	68.9	22.4	46.5	31.1	25.4	5.7

*Source: Survey Documentation and Analysis, Computer-assisted Survey Methods Program, University of California,
Berkeley, General Social Surveys, 1972–2010 Cumulative Data Files, Internet site http://sda.berkeley.edu/cgi-bin32/
hsda?harcsda+gss10; calculations by New Strategist*

Table 1.18 Should Government Help the Sick, 2010

"Some people think that it is the responsibility of the government in Washington to see to it that people have help in paying for doctors and hospital bills; they are at point 1. Others think that these matters are not the responsibility of the federal government and that people should take care of these things themselves; they are at point 5. Where would you place yourself on this scale?"

(percent of people aged 18 or older responding by generation, 2010)

	1 government should help	2	3 agree with both	4	5 people should help themselves
Total people	**30.5%**	**16.4%**	**31.9%**	**11.1%**	**10.1%**
Millennial generation (18 to 33)	35.7	21.9	27.2	9.7	5.5
Generation X (34 to 45)	27.3	12.1	37.1	15.5	8.0
Baby Boom (46 to 64)	31.6	16.6	30.3	10.0	11.6
Older Americans (65 or older)	23.3	11.7	37.1	10.1	17.7

Source: Survey Documentation and Analysis, Computer-assisted Survey Methods Program, University of California, Berkeley, General Social Surveys, 1972–2010 Cumulative Data Files, Internet site http://sda.berkeley.edu/cgi-bin32/hsda?harcsda+gss10; calculations by New Strategist

Religious Diversity Is on the Rise

Share of Protestants dwindles with each successive generation.

Asked whether science makes our way of life change too fast, the 51 percent majority of Americans disagrees with the statement. Most Millennials, Gen Xers, and Boomers disagree. But among Americans aged 65 or older, the 56 percent majority agrees that things are changing too fast.

The 56 percent majority of Americans now believes in evolution, up from an even split in 2006. The majority in every generation believes in evolution, the proportion being highest among Millennials.

Among older Americans, 59 percent are Protestants. Among Baby Boomers, the figure is 53 percent. The figure falls to 44 percent among Generation Xers and to just 33 percent among Millennials. Conversely, the share of people with no religious preference climbs from a mere 9 percent among older Americans to a substantial 27 percent among Millennials. Older Americans are twice as likely as members of younger generations to describe themselves as very religious and they are more likely to see the Bible as the word of God.

The majority of Americans disapproves of the Supreme Court decision barring local governments from requiring religious readings in public schools. While the slight majority of Millennials and nearly half the Generation Xers support the decision, only 39 percent of Baby Boomers and just 37 percent of older Americans back the Supreme Court's decision.

■ Along with the growing racial and ethnic diversity of the American population, religious preferences are also growing more diverse.

Younger generations are less likely to be Protestant

(percent of people aged 18 or older whose religious preference is Protestant, by generation, 2010)

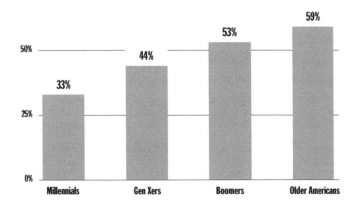

Table 1.19 Attitude toward Science, 2010

"Do you strongly agree, agree, disagree, or strongly disagree with the statement:
Science makes our way of life change too fast?"

(percent of people aged 18 or older responding by generation, 2010)

	strongly agree	agree	disagree	strongly disagree
Total people	**7.2%**	**41.5%**	**43.2%**	**8.1%**
Millennial generation (18 to 33)	8.5	40.5	45.4	5.5
Generation X (34 to 45)	8.7	39.0	47.4	5.0
Baby Boom (46 to 64)	6.3	39.4	41.1	13.2
Older Americans (65 or older)	4.7	51.4	38.7	5.2

Source: Survey Documentation and Analysis, Computer-assisted Survey Methods Program, University of California, Berkeley, General Social Surveys, 1972–2010 Cumulative Data Files, Internet site http://sda.berkeley.edu/cgi-bin32/hsda?harcsda+gss10; calculations by New Strategist

Table 1.20 Attitude toward Evolution, 2010

"True or false: Human beings, as we know them today,
developed from earlier species of animals?"

(percent of people aged 18 or older responding by generation, 2010)

	true	false
Total people	**55.7%**	**44.3%**
Millennial generation (18 to 33)	59.5	40.5
Generation X (34 to 45)	57.7	42.3
Baby Boom (46 to 64)	52.7	47.3
Older Americans (65 or older)	52.7	47.3

Source: Survey Documentation and Analysis, Computer-assisted Survey Methods Program, University of California, Berkeley, General Social Surveys, 1972–2010 Cumulative Data Files, Internet site http://sda.berkeley.edu/cgi-bin32/hsda?harcsda+gss10; calculations by New Strategist

Table 1.21 Religious Preference, 2010

"What is your religious preference?"

(percent of people aged 18 or older responding by generation, 2010)

	Protestant	Catholic	Jewish	none	other
Total people	**46.7%**	**25.2%**	**1.6%**	**17.8%**	**8.7%**
Millennial generation (18 to 33)	33.3	26.7	0.5	26.7	12.8
Generation X (34 to 45)	44.4	26.9	1.6	18.0	9.1
Baby Boom (46 to 64)	53.3	22.7	2.1	15.0	6.9
Older Americans (65 or older)	59.1	25.4	2.6	9.4	3.5

Source: Survey Documentation and Analysis, Computer-assisted Survey Methods Program, University of California, Berkeley, General Social Surveys, 1972–2010 Cumulative Data Files, Internet site http://sda.berkeley.edu/cgi-bin32/ hsda?harcsda+gss10; calculations by New Strategist

Table 1.22 Degree of Religiosity, 2010

"To what extent do you consider yourself a religious person?"

(percent of people aged 18 or older responding by generation, 2010)

	very religious	moderately relgious	slightly religious	not religious
Total people	**16.8%**	**41.5%**	**23.6%**	**18.1%**
Millennial generation (18 to 33)	10.8	35.8	27.8	25.6
Generation X (34 to 45)	15.0	41.0	25.9	18.1
Baby Boom (46 to 64)	20.1	42.0	22.3	15.6
Older Americans (65 or older)	22.2	51.0	16.1	10.7

Source: Survey Documentation and Analysis, Computer-assisted Survey Methods Program, University of California, Berkeley, General Social Surveys, 1972–2010 Cumulative Data Files, Internet site http://sda.berkeley.edu/cgi-bin32/ hsda?harcsda+gss10; calculations by New Strategist

Table 1.23 Belief in the Bible, 2010

"Which of these statements comes closest to describing your feelings about the Bible? 1) The Bible is the actual word of God and is to be taken literally, word for word; 2) The Bible is the inspired word of God but not everything in it should be taken literally, word for word; 3) The Bible is an ancient book of fables, legends, history, and moral precepts recorded by men."

(percent of people aged 18 or older responding by generation, 2010)

	word of God	inspired word	book of fables	other
Total people	**34.1%**	**43.6%**	**20.6%**	**1.7%**
Millennial generation (18 to 33)	30.7	44.3	23.3	1.7
Generation X (34 to 45)	31.8	45.6	21.3	1.3
Baby Boom (46 to 64)	35.3	42.7	19.9	2.1
Older Americans (65 or older)	39.9	42.0	16.5	1.6

Source: Survey Documentation and Analysis, Computer-assisted Survey Methods Program, University of California, Berkeley, General Social Surveys, 1972–2010 Cumulative Data Files, Internet site http://sda.berkeley.edu/cgi-bin32/hsda?harcsda+gss10; calculations by New Strategist

Table 1.24 Bible in the Public Schools, 2010

"The United States Supreme Court has ruled that no state or local government may require the reading of the Lord's Prayer or Bible verses in public schools. What are your views on this? Do you approve or disapprove of the court ruling?"

(percent of people aged 18 or older responding by generation, 2010)

	approve	disapprove
Total people	**44.1%**	**55.9%**
Millennial generation (18 to 33)	52.4	47.6
Generation X (34 to 45)	47.0	53.0
Baby Boom (46 to 64)	39.1	60.9
Older Americans (65 or older)	37.0	63.0

Source: Survey Documentation and Analysis, Computer-assisted Survey Methods Program, University of California, Berkeley, General Social Surveys, 1972–2010 Cumulative Data Files, Internet site http://sda.berkeley.edu/cgi-bin32/hsda?harcsda+gss10; calculations by New Strategist

Growing Tolerance of Sexual Behavior

Americans are more accepting of homosexuality.

The share of Americans who believe premarital sex is not wrong at all grew from 42 percent in 2000 to 53 percent in 2010. While the majority of Boomers and younger generations see nothing wrong with premarital sex, the share is just 37 percent among older Americans.

When it comes to sexual relations between adults of the same sex, the trend of growing tolerance is apparent as well. Each successive generation is less likely to condemn homosexuality. The 54 percent majority of Millennials sees nothing wrong with same-sex sexual relations, but support dwindles to 43 percent among Xers, 39 percent among Boomers, and a mere 30 percent among older Americans. Millennials are the only generation in which the majority (62 percent) believes gays and lesbians should have the right to marry.

■ Acceptance of gays and lesbians will grow as tolerant Millennials replace older, less tolerant generations in the population.

Most Millennials support gay marriage

(percent of people aged 18 or older who think gays and lesbians should have the right to marry, by generation, 2010)

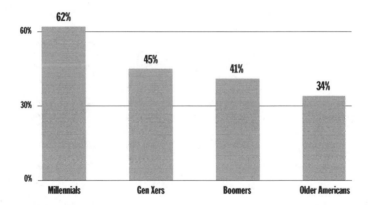

Table 1.25 Premarital Sex, 2010

"If a man and woman have sex relations before marriage,
do you think it is always wrong, almost always wrong,
wrong only sometimes, or not wrong at all?"

(percent of people aged 18 or older responding by generation, 2010)

	always wrong	almost always wrong	sometimes wrong	not wrong at all
Total people	**21.3%**	**7.8%**	**17.8%**	**53.1%**
Millennial generation (18 to 33)	15.0	5.3	20.1	59.6
Generation X (34 to 45)	16.7	8.5	17.9	56.8
Baby Boom (46 to 64)	25.0	5.3	16.4	53.4
Older Americans (65 or older)	30.9	15.7	16.5	36.9

Source: Survey Documentation and Analysis, Computer-assisted Survey Methods Program, University of California, Berkeley, General Social Surveys, 1972–2010 Cumulative Data Files, Internet site http://sda.berkeley.edu/cgi-bin32/hsda?harcsda+gss10; calculations by New Strategist

Table 1.26 Homosexual Relations, 2010

"What about sexual relations between two adults of the same sex?"

(percent of people aged 18 or older responding by generation, 2010)

	always wrong	almost always wrong	sometimes wrong	not wrong at all
Total people	**45.7%**	**3.7%**	**7.9%**	**42.7%**
Millennial generation (18 to 33)	29.6	4.6	11.5	54.3
Generation X (34 to 45)	48.1	2.5	6.1	43.3
Baby Boom (46 to 64)	50.4	3.0	7.2	39.4
Older Americans (65 or older)	58.5	5.4	6.0	30.1

Source: Survey Documentation and Analysis, Computer-assisted Survey Methods Program, University of California, Berkeley, General Social Surveys, 1972–2010 Cumulative Data Files, Internet site http://sda.berkeley.edu/cgi-bin32/hsda?harcsda+gss10; calculations by New Strategist

Table 1.27 Gay Marriage, 2010

"Do you agree or disagree: Homosexual couples should have the right to marry one another?"

(percent of people aged 18 or older responding by generation, 2010)

	agree				disagree		
	total	strongly agree	agree	neither	total	disagree	strongly disagree
Total people	**46.5%**	**21.1%**	**25.4%**	**12.8%**	**40.7%**	**15.6%**	**25.1%**
Millennial generation (18 to 33)	62.2	30.8	31.4	19.7	18.0	10.2	7.8
Generation X (34 to 45)	45.0	20.7	24.3	13.6	41.4	14.2	27.2
Baby Boom (46 to 64)	41.1	17.1	24.0	7.6	51.3	17.3	34.0
Older Americans (65 or older)	34.4	14.5	19.9	11.8	53.8	22.7	31.1

Source: Survey Documentation and Analysis, Computer-assisted Survey Methods Program, University of California, Berkeley, General Social Surveys, 1972–2010 Cumulative Data Files, Internet site http://sda.berkeley.edu/cgi-bin32/ hsda?harcsda+gss10; calculations by New Strategist

Television News Is Most Important

The Internet ranks second in importance.

Nearly half of Americans get most of their news from television, 22 percent from the Internet, and 18 percent from newspapers. Together these three news outlets are the main source of news for 88 percent of the public. But there are big differences by generation. Millennials and Gen Xers are far more likely than older generations to depend on the Internet. Twenty-eight percent of Millennials and 33 percent of Gen Xers say the Internet is their most important source of news. This compares with 20 percent of Boomers and just 2 percent of older Americans. Millennials and Gen Xers are more likely to get their news from radio than newspapers.

When asked about their political leanings, the largest share of Americans likes to point to the moderate middle (38 percent). A smaller 29 percent say they are liberal, and 34 percent identify themselves as conservative. Millennials are the only generation in which liberals outnumber conservatives (31 versus 27 percent). An examination of Americans by political party identification shows that self-identified Democrats far outnumber Republicans (46 versus 33 percent). This is the case in every generation.

■ Television remains the primary source of news for every generation of Americans.

News sources differ dramatically by generation

(percent of people aged 18 or older who identify medium as their primary source for news, by generation, 2010)

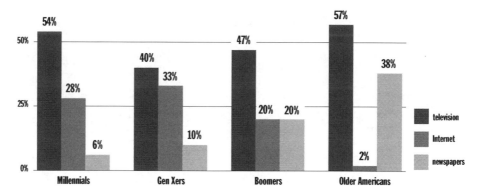

Table 1.28 Main Source of Information about Events in the News, 2010

"We are interested in how people get information about events in the news. Where do you get most of your information about current news events?"

(percent of people aged 18 or older responding by generation, 2010)

	television	Internet	newspapers	radio	family, friends, colleagues	books, magazines, other
Total people	**49.1%**	**21.6%**	**17.7%**	**7.7%**	**2.2%**	**1.7%**
Millennial generation (18 to 33)	54.3	28.3	5.7	8.4	3.3	0.0
Generation X (34 to 45)	40.2	33.5	9.8	12.2	2.9	1.4
Baby Boom (46 to 64)	47.2	19.7	20.2	6.7	2.2	4.0
Older Americans (65 or older)	56.7	1.8	38.4	3.2	0.0	0.0

Source: Survey Documentation and Analysis, Computer-assisted Survey Methods Program, University of California, Berkeley, General Social Surveys, 1972–2010 Cumulative Data Files, Internet site http://sda.berkeley.edu/cgi-bin32/hsda?harcsda+gss10; calculations by New Strategist

Table 1.29 Political Leanings, 2010

"We hear a lot of talk these days about liberals and conservatives. On a seven-point scale from extremely liberal (1) to extremely conservative (7), where would you place yourself?"

(percent of people aged 18 or older responding by generation, 2010)

	1 extremely liberal	2 liberal	3 slightly liberal	4 moderate	5 slightly conservative	6 conservative	7 extremely conservative
Total people	**3.8%**	**12.9%**	**11.9%**	**37.6%**	**12.8%**	**16.6%**	**4.4%**
Millennial generation (18 to 33)	4.0	15.7	11.1	42.0	11.5	13.2	2.6
Generation X (34 to 45)	1.4	14.6	12.7	37.1	13.8	15.0	5.5
Baby Boom (46 to 64)	4.6	10.4	11.9	37.3	12.5	18.0	5.2
Older Americans (65 or older)	4.8	10.8	12.2	31.8	14.4	21.6	4.4

Source: Survey Documentation and Analysis, Computer-assisted Survey Methods Program, University of California, Berkeley, General Social Surveys, 1972–2010 Cumulative Data Files, Internet site http://sda.berkeley.edu/cgi-bin32/hsda?harcsda+gss10; calculations by New Strategist

Table 1.30 Political Party Affiliation, 2010

"Generally speaking, do you usually think of yourself as
a Republican, Democrat, independent, or what?"

(percent of people aged 18 or older responding by generation, 2010)

	strong Democrat	not strong Democrat	independent, near Democrat	independent	independent, near Republican	not strong Republican	strong Republican	other
Total people	**16.5%**	**15.7%**	**13.5%**	**18.8%**	**10.0%**	**13.4%**	**9.6%**	**2.6%**
Millennial generation (18 to 33)	12.1	18.2	15.3	23.9	10.3	12.1	5.1	3.1
Generation X (34 to 45)	13.1	15.9	13.6	19.5	10.0	15.1	9.4	3.3
Baby Boom (46 to 64)	17.7	13.2	14.6	16.7	10.0	13.4	12.2	2.3
Older Americans (65 or older)	25.3	16.3	8.0	13.4	9.7	13.2	12.2	1.8

Source: Survey Documentation and Analysis, Computer-assisted Survey Methods Program, University of California, Berkeley, General Social Surveys, 1972–2010 Cumulative Data Files, Internet site http://sda.berkeley.edu/cgi-bin32/ hsda?harcsda+gss10; calculations by New Strategist

Most Support Abortion if a Mother's Health Is Endangered

The majority of Millennials and Boomers favor legalizing marijuana.

Although opposition to capital punishment has grown slightly over the past decade, the great majority still supports the death penalty. In 2000, 30 percent of the public opposed the death penalty for persons convicted of murder. In 2010, the figure had increased slightly to 32 percent. The majority in every generation favors the death penalty.

Most Americans support requiring a permit for gun ownership, and there is little variation by generation. Nearly half the public supports legalizing marijuana—48 percent are for it and 52 percent are against it. More than 50 percent of Millennials and Boomers want to legalize marijuana compared with 43 percent of Gen Xers and 32 percent of older Americans.

Support for legal abortion under certain circumstances is overwhelming. Nearly 9 out of 10 Americans want abortion to be legal if a women's health is in serious danger, and three-quarters want it legal if a pregnancy is the result of rape or there is a chance of serious defect in the baby. Economic and lifestyle reasons garner substantially lower approval ratings.

The two-thirds majority of Americans favor the right of the terminally ill to die with a doctor's assistance. Support is strongest in the younger generations and weakest among Boomers and older Americans.

■ Attitudinal differences between older and younger generations have become more complex, with Gen Xers standing apart on some issues such as the legalization of marijuana.

Fewer than half of Americans in every generation favor allowing abortion for any reason

(percent of people aged 18 or older who favor legal abortion for any reason, by generation, 2010)

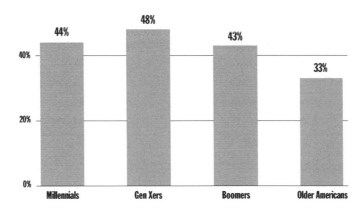

Table 1.31 Favor or Oppose Death Penalty for Murder, 2010

"Do you favor or oppose the death penalty for persons convicted of murder?"

(percent of people aged 18 or older responding by generation, 2010)

	favor	oppose
Total people	**67.8%**	**32.2%**
Millennial generation (18 to 33)	63.6	36.4
Generation X (34 to 45)	69.5	30.5
Baby Boom (46 to 64)	69.2	30.8
Older Americans (65 or older)	70.3	29.7

Source: Survey Documentation and Analysis, Computer-assisted Survey Methods Program, University of California, Berkeley, General Social Surveys, 1972–2010 Cumulative Data Files, Internet site http://sda.berkeley.edu/cgi-bin32/hsda?harcsda+gss10; calculations by New Strategist

Table 1.32 Favor or Oppose Gun Permits, 2010

"Would you favor or oppose a law which would require a person to obtain a police permit before he or she could buy a gun?"

(percent of people aged 18 or older responding by generation, 2010)

	favor	oppose
Total people	**74.3%**	**25.7%**
Millennial generation (18 to 33)	76.4	23.6
Generation X (34 to 45)	68.8	31.2
Baby Boom (46 to 64)	73.8	26.2
Older Americans (65 or older)	79.4	20.6

Source: Survey Documentation and Analysis, Computer-assisted Survey Methods Program, University of California, Berkeley, General Social Surveys, 1972–2010 Cumulative Data Files, Internet site http://sda.berkeley.edu/cgi-bin32/hsda?harcsda+gss10; calculations by New Strategist

Table 1.33 Legalization of Marijuana, 2010

"Do you think the use of marijuana should be made legal or not?"

(percent of people aged 18 or older responding by generation, 2010)

	made legal	not legal
Total people	**48.4%**	**51.6%**
Millennial generation (18 to 33)	55.6	44.4
Generation X (34 to 45)	43.5	56.5
Baby Boom (46 to 64)	53.9	46.1
Older Americans (65 or older)	31.9	68.1

Source: Survey Documentation and Analysis, Computer-assisted Survey Methods Program, University of California, Berkeley, General Social Surveys, 1972–2010 Cumulative Data Files, Internet site http://sda.berkeley.edu/cgi-bin32/hsda?harcsda+gss10; calculations by New Strategist

Table 1.34 Support for Legal Abortion by Reason, 2010

"Please tell me whether or not you think it should be possible for a pregnant woman to obtain a legal abortion if..."

(percent of people aged 18 or older responding by generation, 2010)

	her health is seriously endangered	pregnancy is the result of rape	there is a serious defect in the baby	she cannot afford more children	she does not want more children	she is single and does not want to marry the man	she wants it for any reason
Total people	**86.4%**	**79.1%**	**73.9%**	**47.7%**	**44.9%**	**41.9%**	**42.9%**
Millennial generation (18 to 33)	84.7	82.3	70.9	44.2	47.3	41.2	44.4
Generation X (34 to 45)	86.4	80.9	74.1	46.2	52.1	46.6	48.2
Baby Boom (46 to 64)	87.7	75.7	74.0	46.7	50.0	44.1	42.6
Older Americans (65 or older)	86.2	78.6	78.2	39.5	36.7	31.0	33.4

Source: Survey Documentation and Analysis, Computer-assisted Survey Methods Program, University of California, Berkeley, General Social Surveys, 1972–2010 Cumulative Data Files, Internet site http://sda.berkeley.edu/cgi-bin32/hsda?harcsda+gss10; calculations by New Strategist

Table 1.35 Doctor-Assisted Suicide, 2010

"When a person has a disease that cannot be cured, do you think doctors should be allowed by law to end the patient's life by some painless means if the patient and his family request it?"

(percent of people aged 18 or older responding by generation, 2010)

	yes	no
Total people	**68.4%**	**31.6%**
Millennial generation (18 to 33)	71.5	28.5
Generation X (34 to 45)	73.0	27.0
Baby Boom (46 to 64)	64.6	35.4
Older Americans (65 or older)	64.9	35.1

Source: Survey Documentation and Analysis, Computer-assisted Survey Methods Program, University of California, Berkeley, General Social Surveys, 1972–2010 Cumulative Data Files, Internet site http://sda.berkeley.edu/cgi-bin32/hsda?harcsda+gss10; calculations by New Strategist

2

Education

■ The Baby-Boom generation was the first to go to college in significant numbers. Overall, the 57 percent majority of Boomers have college experience and 30 percent have at least a bachelor's degree.

■ Men aged 60 to 64—an age group now entirely filled with the oldest Boomers—are among the most highly educated of all Americans. Nearly 37 percent have a bachelor's degree, and 15 percent have an advanced degree.

■ Women aged 45 to 64 are less educated than their male counterparts. Among people aged 60 to 64, for example, 30 percent of women and 37 percent of men have a college degree.

■ Asians are by far the best-educated Americans in every generation. Among Boomers, half of Asian men and 46 percent of Asian women have a bachelor's degree or more education.

Boomers Now Rank Third in Educational Attainment

Generation X and Millennials are better educated than Boomers.

Boomers were once the best educated generation. They are still far better educated than older Americans, but the younger generations have surpassed them in educational attainment.

Thirty percent of Boomers had a bachelor's degree in 2010. An even higher 33 percent of Gen Xers and Millennials aged 25 or older had a bachelor's degree. The two younger generations are also more likely than Boomers to have at least some college experience—57 percent of Boomers versus 60 percent of Gen Xers and 61 percent of Millennials. Among older Americans (aged 65 or older), only 23 percent are college graduates and a 43 percent minority have college experience.

■ Generation X and Millennial women are far better educated than Boomer women, boosting the educational attainment of younger generations above that of Boomers.

People aged 25 to 44 have the highest level of educational attainment

(percent of people aged 25 or older with a bachelor's degree, by age, 2010)

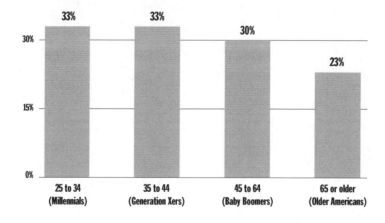

33%	33%	30%	23%
25 to 34 (Millennials)	35 to 44 (Generation Xers)	45 to 64 (Baby Boomers)	65 or older (Older Americans)

Table 2.1 Educational Attainment by Generation, 2010

(number and percent distribution of people aged 25 or older by highest level of education, by generation, 2010; numbers in thousands)

	total 25 or older	Millennials (25 to 34)	Generation X (35 to 44)	Boomers (45 to 64)	Older Americans (65 or older)
Total people	**199,928**	**41,085**	**40,447**	**79,782**	**38,613**
Not a high school graduate	25,711	4,763	4,715	8,316	7,917
High school graduate	62,456	11,186	11,582	25,632	14,057
Some college, no degree	33,662	7,752	6,593	13,569	5,748
Associate's degree	18,259	3,903	4,180	7,975	2,201
Bachelor's degree	38,784	9,840	8,857	15,022	5,066
Master's degree	15,203	2,773	3,298	6,730	2,402
Professional degree	3,074	494	649	1,297	635
Doctoral degree	2,779	373	575	1,243	588
High school graduate or more	174,217	36,321	35,734	71,468	30,697
Some college or more	111,761	25,135	24,152	45,836	16,640
Associate's degree or more	78,099	17,383	17,559	32,267	10,892
Bachelor's degree or more	59,840	13,480	13,379	24,292	8,691
Total people	**100.0%**	**100.0%**	**100.0%**	**100.0%**	**100.0%**
Not a high school graduate	12.9	11.6	11.7	10.4	20.5
High school graduate	31.2	27.2	28.6	32.1	36.4
Some college, no degree	16.8	18.9	16.3	17.0	14.9
Associate's degree	9.1	9.5	10.3	10.0	5.7
Bachelor's degree	19.4	24.0	21.9	18.8	13.1
Master's degree	7.6	6.7	8.2	8.4	6.2
Professional degree	1.5	1.2	1.6	1.6	1.6
Doctoral degree	1.4	0.9	1.4	1.6	1.5
High school graduate or more	87.1	88.4	88.3	89.6	79.5
Some college or more	55.9	61.2	59.7	57.5	43.1
Associate's degree or more	39.1	42.3	43.4	40.4	28.2
Bachelor's degree or more	29.9	32.8	33.1	30.4	22.5

*Source: Bureau of the Census, Educational Attainment in the United States: 2010, detailed tables, Internet site http://www
.census.gov/hhes/socdemo/education/data/cps/2010/tables.html; calculations by New Strategist*

Most Boomers Have Been to College

Three of 10 are college graduates.

The Baby-Boom generation was the first to go to college in significant numbers. Overall, the 57 percent majority have been to college—17 percent have college experience but no degree, 10 percent have an associate's degree, 19 percent have a bachelor's degree, and 12 percent have a graduate degree.

The oldest Boomer men were once the most educated Americans, but no longer. Thirty-seven percent of men aged 60 to 64 have a college degree, thanks to draft deferments offered to college students during the Vietnam War. Boomer women are significantly less likely than Boomer men to have a college degree, lowering the overall educational attainment of the Baby-Boom generation. The percentage of the oldest Boomer men with a bachelor's degree is slightly below the 38 percent of Millennial women aged 30 to 34 who are college graduates.

■ Because most Boomers have college experience, they have been eager to see their children go to college as well, boosting enrollments.

More than half the Baby-Boom generation has college experience

(percent distribution of people aged 45 to 64 by educational attainment, 2010)

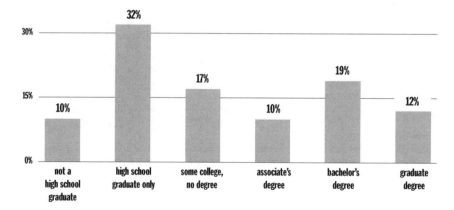

Table 2.2 Educational Attainment of Baby Boomers, 2010

(number and percent distribution of people aged 25 or older, aged 45 to 64, and aged 45 to 64 in five-year age groups, by highest level of education, 2010; numbers in thousands)

		aged 45 to 64				
	total 25 or older	total	45 to 49	50 to 54	55 to 59	60 to 64
Total people	**199,928**	**79,782**	**22,527**	**21,860**	**19,172**	**16,223**
Not a high school graduate	25,711	8,316	2,411	2,212	1,980	1,712
High school graduate	62,456	25,632	7,348	7,215	5,979	5,089
Some college, no degree	33,662	13,569	3,659	3,773	3,482	2,654
Associate's degree	18,259	7,975	2,422	2,284	1,861	1,408
Bachelor's degree	38,784	15,022	4,359	4,070	3,565	3,028
Master's degree	15,203	6,730	1,677	1,648	1,721	1,684
Professional degree	3,074	1,297	318	328	300	351
Doctoral degree	2,779	1,243	333	329	284	297
High school graduate or more	174,217	71,468	20,116	19,647	17,192	14,511
Some college or more	111,761	45,836	12,768	12,432	11,213	9,422
Associate's degree or more	78,099	32,267	9,109	8,659	7,731	6,768
Bachelor's degree or more	59,840	24,292	6,687	6,375	5,870	5,360
Total people	**100.0%**	**100.0%**	**100.0%**	**100.0%**	**100.0%**	**100.0%**
Not a high school graduate	12.9	10.4	10.7	10.1	10.3	10.6
High school graduate	31.2	32.1	32.6	33.0	31.2	31.4
Some college, no degree	16.8	17.0	16.2	17.3	18.2	16.4
Associate's degree	9.1	10.0	10.8	10.4	9.7	8.7
Bachelor's degree	19.4	18.8	19.4	18.6	18.6	18.7
Master's degree	7.6	8.4	7.4	7.5	9.0	10.4
Professional degree	1.5	1.6	1.4	1.5	1.6	2.2
Doctoral degree	1.4	1.6	1.5	1.5	1.5	1.8
High school graduate or more	87.1	89.6	89.3	89.9	89.7	89.4
Some college or more	55.9	57.5	56.7	56.9	58.5	58.1
Associate's degree or more	39.1	40.4	40.4	39.6	40.3	41.7
Bachelor's degree or more	29.9	30.4	29.7	29.2	30.6	33.0

Source: Bureau of the Census, Educational Attainment in the United States: 2010, detailed tables, Internet site http://www .census.gov/hhes/socdemo/education/data/cps/2010/tables.html; calculations by New Strategist

Older Boomer Men Are among the Best Educated

More than one-third of men aged 60 to 64 have a bachelor's degree.

Men aged 60 to 64—an age group now entirely filled with the oldest Boomers—are among the most highly educated of all Americans. Nearly 37 percent have a bachelor's degree, and 15 percent have an advanced degree. Behind this high level of education is the Vietnam War. To avoid being drafted during the 1960s and early 1970s, many young men opted for college deferments. Most of those men are now in their late fifties and early sixties.

When the war ended, so did the incentive to stay in school. Consequently, younger Boomer men are less educated than their older counterparts. Still, more than half of men between the ages of 45 and 59 have college experience and 29 to 32 percent have at least a bachelor's degree.

■ The high educational attainment of Baby-Boom men transformed American society, driving the demand for technology and creating the service economy.

Men aged 60 to 64 are the best educated Boomers

(percent of men aged 45 to 64 with a bachelor's degree, 2010)

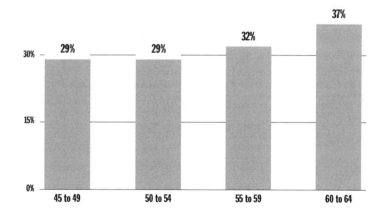

Table 2.3 Educational Attainment of Baby-Boom Men, 2010

(number and percent distribution of men aged 25 or older, aged 45 to 64, and aged 45 to 64 in five-year age groups, by highest level of education, 2010; numbers in thousands)

		aged 45 to 64				
	total 25 or older	total	45 to 49	50 to 54	55 to 59	60 to 64
Total men	**96,325**	**38,769**	**11,092**	**10,692**	**9,318**	**7,667**
Not a high school graduate	12,914	4,313	1,331	1,144	989	849
High school graduate	30,682	12,585	3,842	3,713	2,890	2,140
Some college, no degree	15,908	6,421	1,712	1,824	1,666	1,219
Associate's degree	7,662	3,400	981	947	830	642
Bachelor's degree	18,674	7,358	2,045	1,898	1,758	1,657
Master's degree	6,859	3,066	796	738	798	734
Professional degree	1,861	868	198	208	197	265
Doctoral degree	1,763	756	185	220	190	161
High school graduate or more	83,409	34,454	9,759	9,548	8,329	6,818
Some college or more	52,727	21,869	5,917	5,835	5,439	4,678
Associate's degree or more	36,819	15,448	4,205	4,011	3,773	3,459
Bachelor's degree or more	29,157	12,048	3,224	3,064	2,943	2,817
Total men	**100.0%**	**100.0%**	**100.0%**	**100.0%**	**100.0%**	**100.0%**
Not a high school graduate	13.4	11.1	12.0	10.7	10.6	11.1
High school graduate	31.9	32.5	34.6	34.7	31.0	27.9
Some college, no degree	16.5	16.6	15.4	17.1	17.9	15.9
Associate's degree	8.0	8.8	8.8	8.9	8.9	8.4
Bachelor's degree	19.4	19.0	18.4	17.8	18.9	21.6
Master's degree	7.1	7.9	7.2	6.9	8.6	9.6
Professional degree	1.9	2.2	1.8	1.9	2.1	3.5
Doctoral degree	1.8	2.0	1.7	2.1	2.0	2.1
High school graduate or more	86.6	88.9	88.0	89.3	89.4	88.9
Some college or more	54.7	56.4	53.3	54.6	58.4	61.0
Associate's degree or more	38.2	39.8	37.9	37.5	40.5	45.1
Bachelor's degree or more	30.3	31.1	29.1	28.7	31.6	36.7

Source: Bureau of the Census, Educational Attainment in the United States: 2010, detailed tables, Internet site http://www .census.gov/hhes/socdemo/education/data/cps/2010/tables.html; calculations by New Strategist

Most Boomer Women Have Been to College

Nearly 30 percent have a bachelor's degree.

Unlike their male counterparts, Boomer women were not threatened by the Vietnam War draft. They did not have as much incentive as their male counterparts to stay in college. Consequently, women aged 45 to 64 are less educated than men in the age group. Among 60-to-64-year-olds, for example, 30 percent of women and 37 percent of men have a bachelor's degree.

Baby-Boom women are much more educated than older generations of women, however. The 30 percent of Baby-Boom women with a bachelor's degree is much higher than the 18 percent of women aged 65 or older who are college graduates. Millennial women have the highest level of educational attainment in the nation. Thirty-eight percent of women aged 30 to 34 have a bachelor's degree.

■ Because people marry those with similar educational backgrounds, college-educated Boomers tended to marry one another. As those couples entered their peak-earning years in the 1990s, affluence in the United States peaked.

The youngest Boomer women are most likely to have at least some college experience

(percent of women aged 45 to 64 with some college or more, 2010)

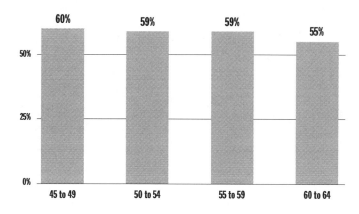

Table 2.4 Educational Attainment of Baby-Boom Women, 2010

(number and percent distribution of women aged 25 or older, aged 45 to 64, and aged 45 to 64 in five-year age groups, by highest level of education, 2010; numbers in thousands)

	total 25 or older	aged 45 to 64				
		total	45 to 49	50 to 54	55 to 59	60 to 64
Total women	**103,603**	**41,014**	**11,435**	**11,169**	**9,854**	**8,556**
Not a high school graduate	12,797	4,001	1,081	1,067	990	863
High school graduate	31,774	13,046	3,506	3,502	3,089	2,949
Some college, no degree	17,753	7,148	1,946	1,949	1,817	1,436
Associate's degree	10,597	4,575	1,441	1,337	1,031	766
Bachelor's degree	20,110	7,665	2,314	2,172	1,808	1,371
Master's degree	8,344	3,663	880	910	923	950
Professional degree	1,213	429	120	120	103	86
Doctoral degree	1,015	486	147	109	94	136
High school graduate or more	90,806	37,012	10,354	10,099	8,865	7,694
Some college or more	59,032	23,966	6,848	6,597	5,776	4,745
Associate's degree or more	41,279	16,818	4,902	4,648	3,959	3,309
Bachelor's degree or more	30,682	12,243	3,461	3,311	2,928	2,543
Total women	**100.0%**	**100.0%**	**100.0%**	**100.0%**	**100.0%**	**100.0%**
Not a high school graduate	12.4	9.8	9.5	9.6	10.0	10.1
High school graduate	30.7	31.8	30.7	31.4	31.3	34.5
Some college, no degree	17.1	17.4	17.0	17.5	18.4	16.8
Associate's degree	10.2	11.2	12.6	12.0	10.5	9.0
Bachelor's degree	19.4	18.7	20.2	19.4	18.3	16.0
Master's degree	8.1	8.9	7.7	8.1	9.4	11.1
Professional degree	1.2	1.0	1.0	1.1	1.0	1.0
Doctoral degree	1.0	1.2	1.3	1.0	1.0	1.6
High school graduate or more	87.6	90.2	90.5	90.4	90.0	89.9
Some college or more	57.0	58.4	59.9	59.1	58.6	55.5
Associate's degree or more	39.8	41.0	42.9	41.6	40.2	38.7
Bachelor's degree or more	29.6	29.9	30.3	29.6	29.7	29.7

Source: Bureau of the Census, Educational Attainment in the United States: 2010, detailed tables, Internet site http://www .census.gov/hhes/socdemo/education/data/cps/2010/tables.html; calculations by New Strategist

Among Boomer Men, Asians Are the Best Educated

Hispanics are the least educated.

Asians are by far the best-educated men in every generation, including the Baby Boom. Sixty-eight percent of Asian men aged 45 to 64 have college experience and more than half have a bachelor's degree. Among non-Hispanic white men, the figures are 61 and 34 percent, respectively.

Black men are much better educated than Hispanics. Eighty-four percent are high school graduates, 45 percent have college experience, and 18 percent have a bachelor's degree. Only 61 percent of Hispanic men of the Baby-Boom generation are high school graduates. Just 33 percent have college experience, and 14 percent have a bachelor's degree. One reason for the low educational level of Hispanics is that many are immigrants from countries that offer little educational opportunity.

■ Educational attainment is directly linked to income. The gap in the education of men by race and Hispanic origin translates into occupational and income differences.

Half of Asian Baby-Boom men have a bachelor's degree

(percent of men aged 45 to 64 with a bachelor's degree, 2010)

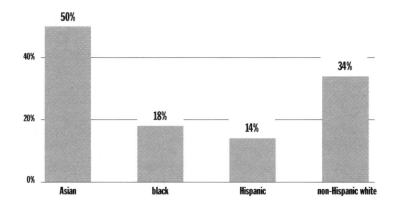

Table 2.5 Educational Attainment of Baby-Boom Men by Race and Hispanic Origin, 2010

(number and percent distribution of men aged 45 to 64 by educational attainment, race, and Hispanic origin, 2010; numbers in thousands)

	total	Asian	black	Hispanic	non-Hispanic white
Total men aged 45 to 64	**38,769**	**1,645**	**4,148**	**4,217**	**28,422**
Not a high school graduate	4,313	148	650	1,634	1,859
High school graduate	12,585	374	1,625	1,207	9,268
Some college, no degree	6,421	159	755	546	4,876
Associate's degree	3,400	141	352	241	2,627
Bachelor's degree	7,358	474	473	381	5,980
Master's degree	3,066	193	224	136	2,490
Professional degree	868	66	37	33	731
Doctoral degree	756	86	32	42	595
High school graduate or more	34,454	1,493	3,498	2,586	26,567
Some college or more	21,869	1,119	1,873	1,379	17,299
Associate's degree or more	15,448	960	1,118	833	12,423
Bachelor's degree or more	12,048	819	766	592	9,796
Total men aged 45 to 64	**100.0%**	**100.0%**	**100.0%**	**100.0%**	**100.0%**
Not a high school graduate	11.1	9.0	15.7	38.7	6.5
High school graduate	32.5	22.7	39.2	28.6	32.6
Some college, no degree	16.6	9.7	18.2	12.9	17.2
Associate's degree	8.8	8.6	8.5	5.7	9.2
Bachelor's degree	19.0	28.8	11.4	9.0	21.0
Master's degree	7.9	11.7	5.4	3.2	8.8
Professional degree	2.2	4.0	0.9	0.8	2.6
Doctoral degree	2.0	5.2	0.8	1.0	2.1
High school graduate or more	88.9	90.8	84.3	61.3	93.5
Some college or more	56.4	68.0	45.2	32.7	60.9
Associate's degree or more	39.8	58.4	27.0	19.8	43.7
Bachelor's degree or more	31.1	49.8	18.5	14.0	34.5

Note: Asians and blacks are those who identify themselves as being of the race alone and those who identify themselves as being of the race in combination with other races. Non-Hispanic whites are those who identify themselves as being white alone and not Hispanic. Numbers do not add to total because not all races are shown and Hispanics may be of any race.
Source: Bureau of the Census, Educational Attainment in the United States: 2010, detailed tables, Internet site http://www .census.gov/hhes/socdemo/education/data/cps/2010/tables.html; calculations by New Strategist

Among Boomer Women, Hispanics Are the Least Educated

Asian women have the highest level of education.

Among women aged 45 to 64 in 2010, Asians are by far the best educated. Sixty-two percent of Asians have college experience and 46 percent have a bachelor's degree. Interestingly, however, Asian women are less likely than non-Hispanic white women to have a high school diploma. The explanation lies in the socioeconomic differences within the Asian-American community itself, some being immigrants from countries with little educational opportunity.

Sixty-three percent of non-Hispanic white women of the Baby-Boom generation have college experience, while 33 percent have a bachelor's degree. Among black women in the age group, the figures are 53 and 21 percent, respectively. Hispanics are the least educated. Only 63 percent have a high school diploma and just 15 percent have a bachelor's degree.

■ The incomes of Asian women reflect their higher level of education.

Among Boomer women, Asians are the best educated

(percent of women aged 45 to 64 with a bachelor's degree, 2010)

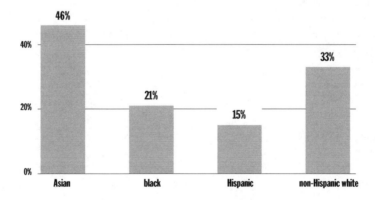

Table 2.6 Educational Attainment of Baby-Boom Women by Race and Hispanic Origin, 2010

(number and percent distribution of women aged 45 to 64 by educational attainment, race, and Hispanic origin, 2010; numbers in thousands)

	total	Asian	black	Hispanic	non-Hispanic white
Total women aged 45 to 64	**41,014**	**1,876**	**5,098**	**4,189**	**29,497**
Not a high school graduate	4,001	235	660	1,541	1,542
High school graduate	13,046	483	1,762	1,188	9,473
Some college, no degree	7,148	161	1,030	516	5,349
Associate's degree	4,575	140	584	329	3,498
Bachelor's degree	7,665	611	678	452	5,881
Master's degree	3,663	169	329	124	3,020
Professional degree	429	38	33	13	342
Doctoral degree	486	37	23	25	393
High school graduate or more	37,012	1,639	4,439	2,647	27,956
Some college or more	23,966	1,156	2,677	1,459	18,483
Associate's degree or more	16,818	995	1,647	943	13,134
Bachelor's degree or more	12,243	855	1,063	614	9,636
Total women aged 45 to 64	**100.0%**	**100.0%**	**100.0%**	**100.0%**	**100.0%**
Not a high school graduate	9.8	12.5	12.9	36.8	5.2
High school graduate	31.8	25.7	34.6	28.4	32.1
Some college, no degree	17.4	8.6	20.2	12.3	18.1
Associate's degree	11.2	7.5	11.5	7.9	11.9
Bachelor's degree	18.7	32.6	13.3	10.8	19.9
Master's degree	8.9	9.0	6.5	3.0	10.2
Professional degree	1.0	2.0	0.6	0.3	1.2
Doctoral degree	1.2	2.0	0.5	0.6	1.3
High school graduate or more	90.2	87.4	87.1	63.2	94.8
Some college or more	58.4	61.6	52.5	34.8	62.7
Associate's degree or more	41.0	53.0	32.3	22.5	44.5
Bachelor's degree or more	29.9	45.6	20.9	14.7	32.7

Note: Asians and blacks are those who identify themselves as being of the race alone and those who identify themselves as being of the race in combination with other races. Non-Hispanic whites are those who identify themselves as being white alone and not Hispanic. Numbers do not add to total because not all races are shown and Hispanics may be of any race.
Source: Bureau of the Census, Educational Attainment in the United States: 2010, detailed tables, Internet site http://www.census.gov/hhes/socdemo/education/data/cps/2010/tables.html; calculations by New Strategist

Few Boomers Are Still in School

The number of Boomers in school surpasses 1 million, however.

Just 1.8 percent of people aged 45 to 64 were enrolled in school in 2010. Although the proportion is small, the numbers add up because the generation is so large. In 2010, 1.4 million people aged 45 to 64 were in school.

Among Boomers in school, women outnumber men by a wide margin. While 1.3 percent of men aged 45 to 64 are in school, the proportion is 2.2 percent among women in the age group.

■ The economic downturn has boosted the percentage of Americans in school, including middle-aged Boomers.

Women outnumber men in school

(number of people aged 45 to 64 enrolled in school, by sex, 2010)

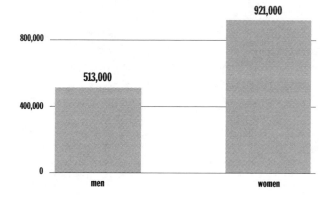

Table 2.7 School Enrollment by Sex and Age, 2010

(total number of people aged 3 or older, and number and percent enrolled in school by sex and age, 2010; numbers in thousands)

		enrolled	
	total	number	percent
Total people	**292,233**	**78,519**	**26.9%**
Under age 45	172,729	77,035	44.6
Aged 45 to 64	80,593	1,435	1.8
Aged 45 to 49	22,270	610	2.7
Aged 50 to 54	22,060	480	2.2
Aged 55 to 59	19,457	247	1.3
Aged 60 to 64	16,806	98	0.6
Aged 65 or older	38,910	51	0.1
Total females	**149,234**	**39,778**	**26.7**
Under age 45	85,816	38,831	45.2
Aged 45 to 64	41,381	921	2.2
Aged 45 to 49	11,324	385	3.4
Aged 50 to 54	11,270	306	2.7
Aged 55 to 59	10,084	158	1.6
Aged 60 to 64	8,703	72	0.8
Aged 65 or older	22,039	25	0.1
Total males	**142,999**	**38,741**	**27.1**
Under age 45	86,915	38,199	43.9
Aged 45 to 64	39,212	513	1.3
Aged 45 to 49	10,946	225	2.1
Aged 50 to 54	10,791	174	1.6
Aged 55 to 59	9,373	88	0.9
Aged 60 to 64	8,102	26	0.3
Aged 65 or older	16,871	26	0.2

Source: Bureau of the Census, School Enrollment—Social and Economic Characteristics of Students: October 2010, Internet site http://www.census.gov/hhes/school/data/cps/2010/tables.html; calculations by New Strategist

Nearly 1.4 Million Boomers Are Still in College

They are a substantial share of graduate students.

The number of older college students has been growing, but their share of total enrollment remains small. Fewer than 7 percent of people enrolled in institutions of higher education in 2010 were aged 45 to 64. The Boomer share of those attending graduate school, however, was a larger 14 percent.

Within the Baby-Boomer age groups, the number of students declines steadily with age. More than half a million 45-to-49-year-olds are in college, but fewer than 100,000 people aged 60 to 64.

■ As Boomers enter the 65-plus age group, they will boost the number of elderly college students.

Boomers account for 14 percent of graduate students

(students aged 45 to 64 as a percentage of total students, by level of study, 2010)

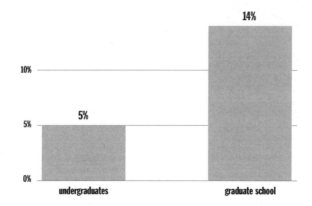

Table 2.8 College Students by Age and Enrollment Level, 2010

(number and percent distribution of people aged 15 or older enrolled in institutions of higher education by age and level of enrollment, 2010; numbers in thousands)

	total	undergraduate	graduate school
Total enrolled	**20,275**	**16,354**	**3,921**
Under age 45	18,867	15,538	3,329
Aged 45 to 64	1,361	805	556
Aged 45 to 49	589	375	214
Aged 50 to 54	449	259	190
Aged 55 to 59	236	130	106
Aged 60 to 64	87	41	46
Aged 65 or older	48	12	36
PERCENT DISTRIBUTION BY AGE			
Total enrolled	**100.0%**	**100.0%**	**100.0%**
Under age 45	93.1	95.0	84.9
Aged 45 to 64	6.7	4.9	14.2
Aged 45 to 49	2.9	2.3	5.5
Aged 50 to 54	2.2	1.6	4.8
Aged 55 to 59	1.2	0.8	2.7
Aged 60 to 64	0.4	0.3	1.2
Aged 65 or older	0.2	0.1	0.9
PERCENT DISTRIBUTION BY LEVEL OF ENROLLMENT			
Total enrolled	**100.0%**	**80.7%**	**19.3%**
Under age 45	100.0	82.4	17.6
Aged 45 to 64	100.0	59.1	40.9
Aged 45 to 49	100.0	63.7	36.3
Aged 50 to 54	100.0	57.7	42.3
Aged 55 to 59	100.0	55.1	44.9
Aged 60 to 64	100.0	47.1	52.9
Aged 65 or older	100.0	25.0	75.0

Source: Bureau of the Census, School Enrollment—Social and Economic Characteristics of Students: October 2010, Internet site http://www.census.gov/hhes/school/data/cps/2010/tables.html; calculations by New Strategist

3

Health

■ The percentage of Americans reporting excellent or very good health declines from 52 to 54 percent in the 45-to-64 age group to 41 percent among people aged 65 or older as chronic conditions become common.

■ Most Baby Boomers are overweight. The average Boomer man weighs nearly 200 pounds. The average Boomer woman weighs more than 170 pounds.

■ Among all Americans, 16 percent do not have health insurance. The figure ranges from 14 to 18 percent among 45-to-64-year-olds.

■ Thirty-eight percent of Americans aged 45 to 64 have experienced joint pain lasting longer than three months, making it the most common health condition in the age group.

■ Sixty-five percent of people aged 45 to 64 have taken at least one prescription drug in the past month, and 34 percent have taken three or more.

■ Heart disease and cancer are the two leading causes of death in the United States. Among 45-to-64-year-olds, however, cancer is the number-one cause of death.

Most 45-to-54-Year-Olds Feel Excellent or Very Good

The proportion falls below 50 percent only in the 65-or-older age group.

Overall, the 55 percent majority of Americans aged 18 or older say their health is "excellent" or "very good." The figure peaks at 63 percent in the 25-to-34 age group, then declines with age. The percentage of Americans who report excellent or very good health falls substantially as people age into their sixties and beyond.

Fewer than half of people aged 65 or older report that their health is excellent or very good. Nevertheless, the proportion of those who say their health is excellent or very good (41 percent) far surpasses the proportion of those who say their health is only fair or poor (25 percent).

■ Medical advances that allow people to better manage chronic conditions may continue to boost the proportion of older Americans who report excellent or very good health in the years ahead.

More than half of 55-to-64-year-olds say their health is excellent or very good

(percent of people aged 18 or older who say their health is excellent or very good, by age, 2010)

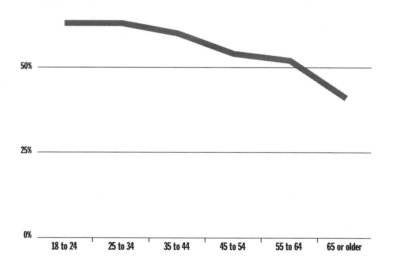

Table 3.1 Health Status by Age, 2010

(percent distribution of people aged 18 or older by self-reported health status, by age, 2010)

	total	excellent or very good			good	fair or poor		
		total	excellent	very good		total	fair	poor
Total people	**100.0%**	**54.8%**	**20.2%**	**34.6%**	**29.8%**	**14.9%**	**10.9%**	**4.0%**
Aged 18 to 24	100.0	62.6	25.0	37.6	27.5	6.7	5.6	1.1
Aged 25 to 34	100.0	62.9	25.0	37.9	28.8	9.0	7.5	1.5
Aged 35 to 44	100.0	60.2	23.0	37.2	28.6	10.6	8.2	2.4
Aged 45 to 54	100.0	54.4	20.0	34.4	29.0	15.1	10.7	4.4
Aged 55 to 64	100.0	51.7	17.6	34.1	30.3	19.0	13.2	5.8
Aged 65 or older	100.0	40.7	12.1	28.6	33.9	24.7	17.7	7.0

Source: Centers for Disease Control and Prevention, Behavioral Risk Factor Surveillance System Prevalence Data, 2010, Internet site http://apps.nccd.cdc.gov/brfss/

Weight Problems Are the Norm for Boomers

Most men and women are overweight.

Americans have a weight problem, and Boomers are no exception. The average Boomer man weighs nearly 200 pounds. The average Boomer woman weighs more than 170 pounds. More than 70 percent of Boomer men and women are overweight, and more than one-third are obese.

Although many people say they exercise, only 20 percent of adults meet federal physical activity guidelines. The proportion that meets the guidelines falls with age to fewer than 10 percent of people aged 65 or older. The guidelines are complex and demanding, however, which might explain why so few can meet them.

■ As Boomers retire, they may gain more free time to be physically active.

Middle-aged Americans weigh more than they should

(percent distribution of people aged 55 to 64 by weight status, by sex, 2007–10)

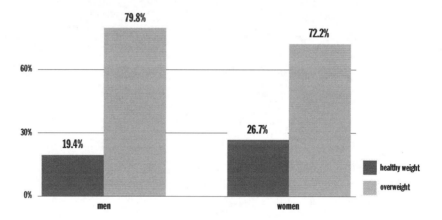

Table 3.2 Average Measured Weight by Age and Sex, 2003–06

(average weight in pounds of people aged 20 or older by age and sex, 2003–06)

	men	women
Total aged 20 or older	**194.7**	**164.7**
Aged 20 to 29	188.3	155.9
Aged 30 to 39	194.1	164.7
Aged 40 to 49	202.3	171.3
Aged 50 to 59	198.8	172.1
Aged 60 to 69	198.3	170.5
Aged 70 to 79	187.4	155.6
Aged 80 or older	168.1	142.2

Note: Data are based on measured weight of a sample of the civilian noninstitutionalized population.
Source: National Center for Health Statistics, Anthropometric Reference Data for Children and Adults: United States, 2003–2006, National Health Statistics Reports, Number 10, 2008, Internet site http://www.cdc.gov/nchs/products/pubs/pubd/nhsr/nhsr.htm; calculations by New Strategist

Table 3.3 Weight Status by Sex and Age, 2007–10

(percent distribution of people aged 20 or older by weight status, sex, and age, 2007–10)

	total	healthy weight	overweight total	overweight obese
Total people	**100.0%**	**29.6%**	**68.7%**	**34.9%**
Total men	**100.0**	**25.8**	**73.2**	**33.9**
Aged 20 to 34	100.0	37.5	61.1	27.1
Aged 35 to 44	100.0	19.8	80.2	37.2
Aged 45 to 54	100.0	21.8	76.8	36.6
Aged 55 to 64	100.0	19.4	79.8	37.3
Aged 65 to 74	100.0	21.6	77.5	41.5
Aged 75 or older	100.0	25.4	73.2	26.6
Total women	**100.0**	**33.2**	**64.5**	**35.9**
Aged 20 to 34	100.0	41.1	55.4	30.4
Aged 35 to 44	100.0	34.4	63.9	37.1
Aged 45 to 54	100.0	30.7	66.2	36.9
Aged 55 to 64	100.0	26.7	72.2	43.4
Aged 65 to 74	100.0	23.9	74.2	40.3
Aged 75 or older	100.0	35.4	63.2	28.7

Note: Data are based on measured height and weight of a sample of the civilian noninstitutionalized population. "Overweight" is defined as a body mass index of 25 or higher. "Obese" is defined as a body mass index of 30 or higher. Body mass index is calculated by dividing weight in kilograms by height in meters squared. Percentages do not add to 100 because "underweight" is not shown.
Source: National Center for Health Statistics, Health, United States, 2011, Internet site http://www.cdc.gov/nchs/hus.htm

Table 3.4 Leisure-Time Physical Activity Level by Sex and Age, 2010

(percent distribution of people aged 18 or older by leisure-time physical activity level, by sex and age, 2010)

	total	physically inactive	met at least one guideline	met aerobic and muscle-strengthening guidelines
Total people	**100.0%**	**49.5%**	**30.1%**	**20.4%**
Aged 18 to 24	100.0	39.4	31.0	29.6
Aged 25 to 44	100.0	44.4	31.3	24.3
Aged 45 to 54	100.0	48.9	31.9	19.2
Aged 55 to 64	100.0	53.7	30.4	15.9
Aged 65 or older	100.0	64.6	25.0	10.4
Total men	**100.0**	**43.8**	**31.1**	**25.1**
Aged 18 to 44	100.0	37.1	31.1	31.8
Aged 45 to 54	100.0	45.2	33.9	20.9
Aged 55 to 64	100.0	50.1	30.8	19.1
Aged 65 to 74	100.0	55.6	27.8	16.6
Aged 75 or older	100.0	62.8	28.1	9.1
Total women	**100.0**	**54.0**	**29.5**	**16.5**
Aged 18 to 44	100.0	49.0	31.4	19.6
Aged 45 to 54	100.0	52.4	30.1	17.5
Aged 55 to 64	100.0	57.0	29.9	13.1
Aged 65 to 74	100.0	63.6	25.4	11.0
Aged 75 or older	100.0	75.3	20.1	4.6

Note: The federal government recommends that adults perform at least 150 minutes (2 hours and 30 minutes) a week of moderate-intensity or 75 minutes (1 hour and 15 minutes) a week of vigorous-intensity aerobic physical activity, or an equivalent combination. Aerobic activity should be performed in episodes of at least 10 minutes, and preferably should be spread throughout the week. It also recommends that adults perform muscle-strengthening activities that are moderate or high intensity and involve all major muscle groups on two or more days a week.
Source: National Center for Health Statistics, Health, United States, 2011, Internet site http://www.cdc.gov/nchs/hus.htm

Nearly One in Five 45-to-54-Year-Olds Smokes Cigarettes

Fewer 55-to-64-year-olds are smokers.

The percentage of Americans who smoke cigarettes has declined sharply from what it was a few decades ago. Nevertheless, a substantial 17 percent of people aged 18 or older were current smokers in 2010. Among people aged 45 to 54, about 19 percent smoke cigarettes. The figure is a smaller 16 percent among 55-to-64-year-olds. A significant number of adults say they are former smokers, including 24 to 35 percent of 45-to-64-year-olds.

Drinking is much more popular than smoking. Overall, 55 percent of people aged 18 or older have had an alcoholic beverage in the past month. The proportion peaks at 61 percent in the 25-to-34 age group. Among 45-to-64-year-olds, 54 to 58 percent have had an alcoholic beverage in the past 30 days.

Although many Boomers have experience with illicit drugs, particularly marijuana, few continue to use them. Only 3 to 7 percent of people aged 45 to 64 have used illicit drugs in the past month. But most people between the ages of 19 and 59 have used illicit drugs at some point in their lives. Most 45-to-59-year-olds have used marijuana in the past, although only 3 to 5 percent have used it in the past month.

■ As Boomers age and health concerns become increasingly important, the proportion of smokers and drinkers will decline.

As Boomers fill the 65-or-older age group, lifetime marijuana use will rise sharply in the oldest age group

(percent of people aged 45 or older who have ever used marijuana, 2010)

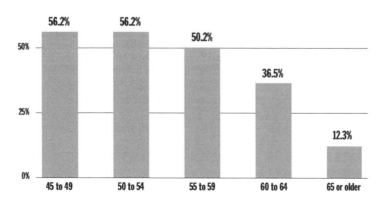

Table 3.5 Cigarette Smoking Status by Age, 2010

(percent distribution of people aged 18 or older by age and cigarette smoking status, 2010)

	total	current smokers			former smoker	never smoked
		total	smoke every day	smoke some days		
Total people	**100.0%**	**17.2%**	**12.4%**	**4.8%**	**25.1%**	**56.6%**
Aged 18 to 24	100.0	19.7	12.9	6.8	6.6	73.0
Aged 25 to 34	100.0	23.9	16.9	7.0	16.8	58.5
Aged 35 to 44	100.0	18.2	13.2	5.0	18.4	63.5
Aged 45 to 54	100.0	19.4	14.7	4.7	24.4	54.7
Aged 55 to 64	100.0	15.9	11.9	4.0	34.5	49.0
Aged 65 or older	100.0	8.5	6.3	2.2	43.6	47.9

Source: Centers for Disease Control and Prevention, Behavioral Risk Factor Surveillance System Prevalence Data, 2010, Internet site http://apps.nccd.cdc.gov/brfss/

Table 3.6 Alcohol Use by Age, 2010

(percent distribution of people aged 18 or older by whether they have had at least one drink of alcohol within the past 30 days, by age, 2010)

	total	yes	no
Total people	**100.0%**	**54.6%**	**45.4%**
Aged 18 to 24	100.0	48.3	51.7
Aged 25 to 34	100.0	61.0	39.0
Aged 35 to 44	100.0	60.2	39.8
Aged 45 to 54	100.0	57.7	42.3
Aged 55 to 64	100.0	53.6	46.4
Aged 65 or older	100.0	40.5	59.5

Source: Centers for Disease Control and Prevention, Behavioral Risk Factor Surveillance System Prevalence Data, 2010, Internet site http://apps.nccd.cdc.gov/brfss/

Table 3.7 Illicit Drug Use by People Aged 12 or Older, 2010

(percent of people aged 12 or older who ever used any illicit drug, who used an illicit drug in the past year, and who used an illicit drug in the past month, by age, 2010)

	ever used	used in past year	used in past month
Total people	**47.1%**	**15.3%**	**8.9%**
Aged 12	10.0	6.6	3.2
Aged 13	15.5	10.5	4.8
Aged 14	20.1	14.7	7.2
Aged 15	30.2	22.9	11.3
Aged 16	34.3	26.7	14.9
Aged 17	41.9	33.4	18.4
Aged 18	49.0	37.8	22.1
Aged 19	53.6	38.9	24.7
Aged 20	56.1	36.5	22.5
Aged 21	58.5	37.5	23.1
Aged 22	58.6	35.1	22.1
Aged 23	59.7	32.5	20.1
Aged 24	60.4	30.7	19.1
Aged 25	62.1	29.8	17.6
Aged 26 to 29	62.3	25.4	14.8
Aged 30 to 34	57.5	19.9	12.9
Aged 35 to 39	53.6	14.2	8.1
Aged 40 to 44	57.2	12.8	6.9
Aged 45 to 49	60.0	12.5	7.2
Aged 50 to 54	60.5	11.7	7.2
Aged 55 to 59	54.8	9.2	4.1
Aged 60 to 64	39.6	4.7	2.7
Aged 65 or older	16.0	1.7	1.1

Note: Illicit drugs include marijuana, hashish, cocaine (including crack), heroin, hallucinogens, inhalants, or any prescription-type psychotherapeutic used nonmedically.
Source: SAMHSA, Office of Applied Studies, 2010 National Survey on Drug Use and Health, Detailed Tables, Internet site http://www.samhsa.gov/data/NSDUH/2k10ResultsTables/Web/HTML/TOC.htm

Table 3.8 Marijuana Use by People Aged 12 or Older, 2010

(percent of people aged 12 or older who ever used marijuana, who used marijuana in the past year, and who used marijuana in the past month, by age, 2010)

	ever used	used in past year	used in past month
Total people	**41.9%**	**11.5%**	**6.9%**
Aged 12	1.0	0.9	0.2
Aged 13	4.7	4.0	1.5
Aged 14	10.6	9.1	4.2
Aged 15	20.2	17.0	8.6
Aged 16	27.0	21.8	12.4
Aged 17	36.2	29.2	16.2
Aged 18	42.6	32.9	19.3
Aged 19	47.4	33.7	21.6
Aged 20	49.6	31.7	20.0
Aged 21	53.3	31.8	19.3
Aged 22	53.1	30.1	19.3
Aged 23	55.0	27.9	17.1
Aged 24	54.3	25.5	16.4
Aged 25	55.7	23.6	14.0
Aged 26 to 29	56.6	20.0	11.4
Aged 30 to 34	51.6	15.5	9.8
Aged 35 to 39	46.9	9.8	5.8
Aged 40 to 44	51.8	8.3	4.9
Aged 45 to 49	56.2	8.4	5.0
Aged 50 to 54	56.2	7.3	4.9
Aged 55 to 59	50.2	6.5	3.1
Aged 60 to 64	36.5	3.3	1.9
Aged 65 or older	12.3	1.0	0.5

Source: SAMHSA, Office of Applied Studies, 2010 National Survey on Drug Use and Health, Detailed Tables, Internet site http://www.samhsa.gov/data/NSDUH/2k10ResultsTables/Web/HTML/TOC.htm

Many Middle-Aged Americans Lack Health Insurance

More than 13 million of the nation's uninsured are aged 45 to 64.

Among all Americans, nearly 50 million lacked health insurance in 2010—or 16 percent of the population. The figure ranges from 14 to 18 percent among 45-to-64-year-olds.

Fifty-five percent of the population has private, employment-based health insurance, but many of those with employment-based coverage get their insurance through a spouse rather than their own job. Slightly less than half of 45-to-64-year-olds have health insurance coverage through their own employment. Eight to 11 percent of 45-to-64-year-olds buy private health insurance on their own. Fourteen to 20 percent have government health insurance.

Not surprisingly, health care expenses rise with age. Median health care expenses for people aged 35 or older exceed $1,000 annually. Most health care expenses for people under age 65 are paid by private insurance. Median health care expenses for Baby Boomers surpassed $2,000 in 2009, and the generation accounted for one-third of the nation's health care spending.

■ Look for a renewed entrepreneurial spirit among Boomers as they sign up for Medicare and are free to pursue their dreams once health insurance is no longer an issue.

Many Americans under age 65 do not have health insurance coverage

(percent of people aged 18 or older without health insurance, by age, 2010)

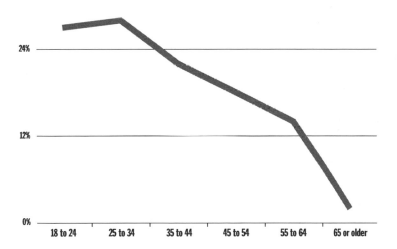

Table 3.9 Health Insurance Coverage by Age, 2010

(number and percent distribution of people by age and health insurance coverage status, 2010; numbers in thousands)

	total	with health insurance total	private	government	not covered
Total people	**306,110**	**256,206**	**195,874**	**95,003**	**49,904**
Under age 65	266,931	217,819	173,206	58,374	49,112
Under age 18	74,916	67,609	44,620	28,385	7,307
Aged 18 to 24	29,651	21,573	17,407	5,579	8,078
Aged 25 to 34	41,584	29,780	25,314	5,746	11,804
Aged 35 to 44	39,842	31,149	27,426	5,046	8,692
Aged 45 to 54	43,954	36,035	31,695	6,110	7,919
Aged 55 to 64	36,984	31,672	26,743	7,509	5,312
Aged 65 or older	39,179	38,387	22,668	36,629	792

PERCENT DISTRIBUTION BY COVERAGE STATUS

Total people	**100.0%**	**83.7%**	**64.0%**	**31.0%**	**16.3%**
Under age 65	100.0	81.6	64.9	21.9	18.4
Under age 18	100.0	90.2	59.6	37.9	9.8
Aged 18 to 24	100.0	72.8	58.7	18.8	27.2
Aged 25 to 34	100.0	71.6	60.9	13.8	28.4
Aged 35 to 44	100.0	78.2	68.8	12.7	21.8
Aged 45 to 54	100.0	82.0	72.1	13.9	18.0
Aged 55 to 64	100.0	85.6	72.3	20.3	14.4
Aged 65 or older	100.0	98.0	57.9	93.5	2.0

PERCENT DISTRIBUTION BY AGE

Total people	**100.0%**	**100.0%**	**100.0%**	**100.0%**	**100.0%**
Under age 65	87.2	85.0	88.4	61.4	98.4
Under age 18	24.5	26.4	22.8	29.9	14.6
Aged 18 to 24	9.7	8.4	8.9	5.9	16.2
Aged 25 to 34	13.6	11.6	12.9	6.0	23.7
Aged 35 to 44	13.0	12.2	14.0	5.3	17.4
Aged 45 to 54	14.4	14.1	16.2	6.4	15.9
Aged 55 to 64	12.1	12.4	13.7	7.9	10.6
Aged 65 or older	12.8	15.0	11.6	38.6	1.6

Note: Numbers may not add to total because some people have more than one type of health insurance coverage.
Source: Bureau of the Census, Health Insurance, Internet site http://www.census.gov/hhes/www/cpstables/032011/health/toc .htm; calculations by New Strategist

Table 3.10 Private Health Insurance Coverage by Age, 2010

(number and percent distribution of people by age and private health insurance coverage status, 2010; numbers in thousands)

	total	with private health insurance			
			employment based		
	total	**total**	**total**	**own**	**direct purchase**
Total people	**306,110**	**195,874**	**169,264**	**87,471**	**30,147**
Under age 65	266,931	173,206	156,536	77,875	18,880
Under age 18	74,916	44,620	41,083	179	4,291
Aged 18 to 24	29,651	17,407	13,612	3,671	1,987
Aged 25 to 34	41,584	25,314	23,221	17,341	2,478
Aged 35 to 44	39,842	27,426	25,573	18,080	2,604
Aged 45 to 54	43,954	31,695	29,201	21,014	3,600
Aged 55 to 64	36,984	26,743	23,846	17,591	3,922
Aged 65 or older	39,179	22,668	12,728	9,597	11,267

PERCENT DISTRIBUTION BY COVERAGE STATUS

Total people	**100.0%**	**64.0%**	**55.3%**	**28.6%**	**9.8%**
Under age 65	100.0	64.9	58.6	29.2	7.1
Under age 18	100.0	59.6	54.8	0.2	5.7
Aged 18 to 24	100.0	58.7	45.9	12.4	6.7
Aged 25 to 34	100.0	60.9	55.8	41.7	6.0
Aged 35 to 44	100.0	68.8	64.2	45.4	6.5
Aged 45 to 54	100.0	72.1	66.4	47.8	8.2
Aged 55 to 64	100.0	72.3	64.5	47.6	10.6
Aged 65 or older	100.0	57.9	32.5	24.5	28.8

PERCENT DISTRIBUTION BY AGE

Total people	**100.0%**	**100.0%**	**100.0%**	**100.0%**	**100.0%**
Under age 65	87.2	88.4	92.5	89.0	62.6
Under age 18	24.5	22.8	24.3	0.2	14.2
Aged 18 to 24	9.7	8.9	8.0	4.2	6.6
Aged 25 to 34	13.6	12.9	13.7	19.8	8.2
Aged 35 to 44	13.0	14.0	15.1	20.7	8.6
Aged 45 to 54	14.4	16.2	17.3	24.0	11.9
Aged 55 to 64	12.1	13.7	14.1	20.1	13.0
Aged 65 or older	12.8	11.6	7.5	11.0	37.4

Note: Numbers may not add to total because some people have more than one type of health insurance coverage.
Source: Bureau of the Census, Health Insurance, Internet site http://www.census.gov/hhes/www/cpstables/032011/health/toc
.htm; calculations by New Strategist

Table 3.11 Government Health Insurance Coverage by Age, 2010

(number and percent distribution of people by age and government health insurance coverage status, 2010; numbers in thousands)

	total	with government health insurance			
		total	Medicaid	Medicare	military
Total people	**306,110**	**95,003**	**48,580**	**44,327**	**12,848**
Under age 65	266,931	58,374	44,993	7,870	9,666
Under age 18	74,916	28,385	26,067	602	2,461
Aged 18 to 24	29,651	5,579	4,516	257	1,035
Aged 25 to 34	41,584	5,746	4,249	610	1,244
Aged 35 to 44	39,842	5,046	3,449	900	1,172
Aged 45 to 54	43,954	6,110	3,607	1,901	1,553
Aged 55 to 64	36,984	7,509	3,105	3,600	2,201
Aged 65 or older	39,179	36,629	3,587	36,457	3,182

PERCENT DISTRIBUTION BY COVERAGE STATUS

Total people	**100.0%**	**31.0%**	**15.9%**	**14.5%**	**4.2%**
Under age 65	100.0	21.9	16.9	2.9	3.6
Under age 18	100.0	37.9	34.8	0.8	3.3
Aged 18 to 24	100.0	18.8	15.2	0.9	3.5
Aged 25 to 34	100.0	13.8	10.2	1.5	3.0
Aged 35 to 44	100.0	12.7	8.7	2.3	2.9
Aged 45 to 54	100.0	13.9	8.2	4.3	3.5
Aged 55 to 64	100.0	20.3	8.4	9.7	6.0
Aged 65 or older	100.0	93.5	9.2	93.1	8.1

PERCENT DISTRIBUTION BY AGE

Total people	**100.0%**	**100.0%**	**100.0%**	**100.0%**	**100.0%**
Under age 65	87.2	61.4	92.6	17.8	75.2
Under age 18	24.5	29.9	53.7	1.4	19.2
Aged 18 to 24	9.7	5.9	9.3	0.6	8.1
Aged 25 to 34	13.6	6.0	8.7	1.4	9.7
Aged 35 to 44	13.0	5.3	7.1	2.0	9.1
Aged 45 to 54	14.4	6.4	7.4	4.3	12.1
Aged 55 to 64	12.1	7.9	6.4	8.1	17.1
Aged 65 or older	12.8	38.6	7.4	82.2	24.8

Note: Numbers may not add to total because some people have more than one type of health insurance coverage.
Source: Bureau of the Census, Health Insurance, Internet site http://www.census.gov/hhes/www/cpstables/032011/health/toc
.htm; calculations by New Strategist

Table 3.12 Spending on Health Care by Age, 2009

(percent of people with health care expense, median expense per person, total expenses, and percent distribution of total expenses by source of payment, by age, 2009)

	total (thousands)	percent with expense	median expense per person	total expenses amount (millions)	total expenses percent distribution
Total people	**306,661**	**84.6%**	**$1,301**	**$1,259,456**	**100.0%**
Under age 18	74,836	86.5	548	143,261	11.4
Aged 18 to 24	29,787	74.0	665	54,682	4.3
Aged 25 to 34	40,861	74.3	920	96,666	7.7
Aged 35 to 44	40,495	79.7	1,174	126,885	10.1
Aged 45 to 49	21,892	83.3	1,492	90,712	7.2
Aged 50 to 54	22,699	88.8	1,958	104,769	8.3
Aged 55 to 59	19,335	91.6	2,314	123,052	9.8
Aged 60 to 64	16,417	90.9	3,129	126,709	10.1
Aged 65 or older	40,338	96.6	4,542	392,721	31.2

	total	percent distribution by source of payment out of pocket	private insurance	Medicare	Medicaid	other
Total people	**100.0%**	**14.6%**	**42.6%**	**23.8%**	**9.7%**	**9.3%**
Under age 18	100.0	12.9	57.3	1.2	21.7	6.9
Aged 18 to 24	100.0	17.6	48.5	0.7	20.2	13.0
Aged 25 to 34	100.0	16.6	55.3	2.7	14.8	10.5
Aged 35 to 44	100.0	16.1	59.5	6.3	9.2	8.8
Aged 45 to 49	100.0	15.8	55.4	9.5	8.4	10.9
Aged 50 to 54	100.0	16.6	52.3	11.7	9.9	9.5
Aged 55 to 59	100.0	15.2	56.2	10.1	8.3	10.1
Aged 60 to 64	100.0	15.1	52.5	12.6	7.8	12.0
Aged 65 or older	100.0	12.5	14.8	60.6	4.2	7.8

Note: "Other" insurance includes Department of Veterans Affairs (except Tricare), American Indian Health Service, state and local clinics, worker's compensation, homeowner's and automobile insurance, etc.
Source: Agency for Healthcare Research and Quality, Medical Expenditure Panel Survey, 2009, Internet site http://meps.ahrq .gov/mepsweb/survey_comp/household.jsp; calculations by New Strategist

Table 3.13 Spending on Health Care by Generation, 2009

(percent of people with health care expense, median expense per person, total expenses, and percent distribution of total expenses by source of payment, by generation, 2009)

	total (thousands)	percent with expense	median expense per person	total expenses amount (millions)	total expenses percent distribution
Total people	**306,661**	**84.6%**	**$1,301**	**$1,259,456**	**100.0%**
iGeneration (under 15)	62,153	87.2	531	120,682	9.6
Millennials (15 to 32)	75,919	75.6	748	155,210	12.3
Generation X (33 to 44)	47,907	79.0	1,157	145,601	11.6
Baby Boomers (45 to 63)	77,800	88.3	2,108	426,592	33.9
Older Americans (64 or older)	42,882	96.3	4,477	411,371	32.7

	percent distribution by source of payment					
	total	out of pocket	private insurance	Medicare	Medicaid	other
Total people	**100.0%**	**14.6%**	**42.6%**	**23.8%**	**9.7%**	**9.3%**
iGeneration (under 15)	100.0	12.0	58.3	1.3	21.9	6.5
Millennials (15 to 32)	100.0	17.3	53.1	1.3	16.7	11.6
Generation X (33 to 44)	100.0	16.1	58.3	6.2	10.8	8.6
Baby Boomers (45 to 63)	100.0	15.7	54.5	10.6	8.6	10.7
Older Americans (64 or older)	100.0	12.6	16.2	58.9	4.4	8.0

Note: "Other" insurance includes Department of Veterans Affairs (except Tricare), American Indian Health Service, state and local clinics, worker's compensation, homeowner's and automobile insurance, etc.
Source: Agency for Healthcare Research and Quality, Medical Expenditure Panel Survey, 2009, Internet site http://meps.ahrq .gov/mepsweb/survey_comp/household.jsp; calculations by New Strategist

Health Problems Increase in the 45-to-64 Age Group

Chronic joint symptoms are the most common health condition among the middle aged.

Thirty-eight percent of Americans aged 45 to 64 have experienced joint pain lasting longer than three months, making it the most common health condition in the age group. Hypertension follows, with 34 percent of 45-to-64-year-olds experiencing this problem. Thirty-two percent had pain in their lower back that lasted at least one day.

The percentage of people experiencing health problems rises, sometimes steeply, in the 45-to-64 age group. Only 9 percent of 18-to-44-year-olds have hypertension, for example, versus 34 percent of those aged 45 to 64. The prevalence of arthritis rises from 7 percent among younger adults to 30 percent in the 45-to-64 age group. The prevalence of hearing problems rises from 7 percent among younger adults to 19 percent among 45-to-64-year-olds.

The percentage of people with hypertension reaches 50 percent in the 55-to-64 age group. The percentage with doctor-diagnosed diabetes climbs from 8 percent in the 45-to-54 age group to a substantial 15 percent among 55-to-64-year-olds.

■ As the Baby-Boom generation ages into its late sixties, the number of people with heart disease, arthritis, hearing problems, and diabetes will rise.

The percentage of people with diabetes rises with age

(percent of people diagnosed with diabetes, by age, 2010)

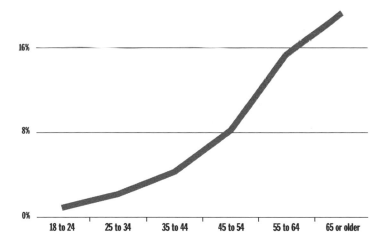

Table 3.14 Number of Adults with Health Conditions by Age, 2010

(number of people aged 18 or older with selected health conditions, by type of condition and age, 2010; numbers in thousands)

	total	18 to 44	45 to 64	aged 65 or older total	65 to 74	75 or older
Total people aged 18 or older	**229,505**	**110,615**	**80,198**	**38,692**	**21,291**	**17,401**
Selected circulatory diseases						
Heart disease, all types	27,066	4,897	10,568	11,601	5,173	6,428
Coronary	15,262	1,494	5,803	7,965	3,508	4,457
Hypertension	59,259	10,303	27,521	21,425	11,485	9,940
Stroke	6,226	664	2,403	3,158	1,302	1,856
Selected respiratory conditions						
Emphysema	4,314	361	1,703	2,250	1,153	1,097
Asthma, ever	29,057	15,020	9,723	4,314	2,492	1,822
Asthma, still	18,734	8,902	6,704	3,128	1,849	1,279
Hay fever	17,937	6,656	8,638	2,642	1,684	958
Sinusitis	29,821	11,584	13,025	5,213	3,240	1,973
Chronic bronchitis	9,882	3,265	4,247	2,371	1,279	1,092
Selected types of cancer						
Any cancer	19,441	2,427	7,939	9,075	4,343	4,732
Breast cancer	3,169	91	1,387	1,691	803	888
Cervical cancer	1,448	675	581	193	108	85
Prostate cancer	2,457	0	634	1,817	679	1,138
Other selected diseases and conditions						
Diabetes	20,974	3,022	9,676	8,276	4,563	3,713
Ulcers	14,992	4,591	6,418	3,983	2,241	1,742
Kidney disease	3,931	804	1,578	1,549	740	809
Liver disease	3,288	978	1,835	476	309	167
Arthritis	51,948	7,838	24,292	19,817	10,426	9,391
Chronic joint symptoms	67,024	18,794	30,801	17,429	9,572	7,857
Migraines or severe headaches	37,529	22,580	12,485	2,464	1,578	886
Pain in neck	36,177	14,459	16,002	5,717	3,292	2,425
Pain in lower back	66,106	27,811	26,007	12,288	6,923	5,365
Pain in face or jaw	11,460	5,460	4,779	1,221	725	496
Selected sensory problems						
Hearing	37,117	7,448	15,193	14,476	6,630	7,846
Vision	21,516	6,825	9,298	5,393	2,591	2,802
Absence of all natural teeth	17,539	2,322	5,817	9,400	4,096	5,304

Note: The conditions shown are those that have ever been diagnosed by a doctor, except as noted. Hay fever, sinusitis, and chronic bronchitis have been diagnosed in the past 12 months. Kidney and liver diseases have been diagnosed in the past 12 months and exclude kidney stones, bladder infections, and incontinence. Chronic joint symptoms are shown if respondent had pain, aching, or stiffness in or around a joint (excluding back and neck) and the condition began more than three months ago. Migraines and pain in neck, lower back, face, or jaw are shown only if pain lasted a whole day or more.
Source: National Center for Health Statistics, Summary Health Statistics for U.S. Adults: National Health Interview Survey, 2010, Vital and Health Statistics, Series 10, No. 252, 2012, Internet site http://www.cdc.gov/nchs/nhis.htm

Table 3.15 Distribution of Health Conditions among Adults by Age, 2010

(percent distribution of people aged 18 or older with selected health conditions, by type of condition and age, 2010)

				aged 65 or older		
	total	18 to 44	45 to 64	total	65 to 74	75 or older
Total people aged 18 or older	100.0%	48.2%	34.9%	16.9%	9.3%	7.6%
Selected circulatory diseases						
Heart disease, all types	100.0	18.1	39.0	42.9	19.1	23.7
Coronary	100.0	9.8	38.0	52.2	23.0	29.2
Hypertension	100.0	17.4	46.4	36.2	19.4	16.8
Stroke	100.0	10.7	38.6	50.7	20.9	29.8
Selected respiratory conditions						
Emphysema	100.0	8.4	39.5	52.2	26.7	25.4
Asthma, ever	100.0	51.7	33.5	14.8	8.6	6.3
Asthma, still	100.0	47.5	35.8	16.7	9.9	6.8
Hay fever	100.0	37.1	48.2	14.7	9.4	5.3
Sinusitis	100.0	38.8	43.7	17.5	10.9	6.6
Chronic bronchitis	100.0	33.0	43.0	24.0	12.9	11.1
Selected types of cancer						
Any cancer	100.0	12.5	40.8	46.7	22.3	24.3
Breast cancer	100.0	2.9	43.8	53.4	25.3	28.0
Cervical cancer	100.0	46.6	40.1	13.3	7.5	5.9
Prostate cancer	100.0	0.0	25.8	74.0	27.6	46.3
Other selected diseases and conditions						
Diabetes	100.0	14.4	46.1	39.5	21.8	17.7
Ulcers	100.0	30.6	42.8	26.6	14.9	11.6
Kidney disease	100.0	20.5	40.1	39.4	18.8	20.6
Liver disease	100.0	29.7	55.8	14.5	9.4	5.1
Arthritis	100.0	15.1	46.8	38.1	20.1	18.1
Chronic joint symptoms	100.0	28.0	46.0	26.0	14.3	11.7
Migraines or severe headaches	100.0	60.2	33.3	6.6	4.2	2.4
Pain in neck	100.0	40.0	44.2	15.8	9.1	6.7
Pain in lower back	100.0	42.1	39.3	18.6	10.5	8.1
Pain in face or jaw	100.0	47.6	41.7	10.7	6.3	4.3
Selected sensory problems						
Hearing	100.0	20.1	40.9	39.0	17.9	21.1
Vision	100.0	31.7	43.2	25.1	12.0	13.0
Absence of all natural teeth	100.0	13.2	33.2	53.6	23.4	30.2

Note: The conditions shown are those that have ever been diagnosed by a doctor, except as noted. Hay fever, sinusitis, and chronic bronchitis have been diagnosed in the past 12 months. Kidney and liver diseases have been diagnosed in the past 12 months and exclude kidney stones, bladder infections, and incontinence. Chronic joint symptoms are shown if respondent had pain, aching, or stiffness in or around a joint (excluding back and neck) and the condition began more than three months ago. Migraines and pain in neck, lower back, face, or jaw are shown only if pain lasted a whole day or more.
Source: National Center for Health Statistics, Summary Health Statistics for U.S. Adults: National Health Interview Survey, 2010, Vital and Health Statistics, Series 10, No. 252, 2012, Internet site http://www.cdc.gov/nchs/nhis.htm

Table 3.16 Percent of Adults with Health Conditions by Age, 2010

(percent of people aged 18 or older with selected health conditions, by type of condition and age, 2010)

	total	18 to 44	45 to 64	aged 65 or older total	65 to 74	75 or older
Total people aged 18 or older	100.0%	100.0%	100.0%	100.0%	100.0%	100.0%
Selected circulatory diseases						
Heart disease, all types	11.8	4.4	13.2	30.0	24.3	37.1
Coronary	6.7	1.4	7.2	20.6	16.5	25.8
Hypertension	25.9	9.3	34.4	55.4	54.2	57.3
Stroke	2.7	0.6	3.0	8.2	6.1	10.7
Selected respiratory conditions						
Emphysema	1.9	0.3	2.1	5.8	5.4	6.3
Asthma, ever	12.7	13.6	12.1	11.1	11.7	10.5
Asthma, still	8.2	8.1	8.4	8.1	8.7	7.4
Hay fever	7.8	6.0	10.8	6.8	7.9	5.5
Sinusitis	13.0	10.5	16.3	13.5	15.2	11.4
Chronic bronchitis	4.2	3.0	5.3	6.1	6.0	6.3
Selected types of cancer						
Any cancer	8.5	2.2	9.9	23.5	20.4	27.2
Breast cancer	1.4	0.1	1.7	4.4	3.8	5.1
Cervical cancer	1.2	0.6	1.4	0.5	0.9	0.8
Prostate cancer	2.2	0.0	1.6	4.7	6.9	16.4
Other selected diseases and conditions						
Diabetes	9.3	2.8	12.3	21.4	22.0	21.7
Ulcers	6.5	4.2	8.0	10.3	10.5	10.0
Kidney disease	1.7	0.7	2.0	4.0	3.5	4.7
Liver disease	1.4	0.9	2.3	1.2	1.5	1.0
Arthritis	22.7	7.1	30.3	51.2	49.0	54.1
Chronic joint symptoms	29.2	17.0	38.4	45.0	45.0	45.3
Migraines or severe headaches	16.4	20.4	15.6	6.4	7.4	5.1
Pain in neck	15.8	13.1	20.0	14.8	15.5	14.0
Pain in lower back	28.8	25.2	32.4	31.8	32.5	30.9
Pain in face or jaw	5.0	4.9	6.0	3.2	3.4	2.9
Selected sensory problems						
Hearing	16.2	6.7	18.9	37.4	31.2	45.1
Vision	9.4	6.2	11.6	13.9	12.2	16.1
Absence of all natural teeth	7.6	2.1	7.3	24.3	19.3	30.5

Note: The conditions shown are those that have ever been diagnosed by a doctor, except as noted. Hay fever, sinusitis, and chronic bronchitis have been diagnosed in the past 12 months. Kidney and liver diseases have been diagnosed in the past 12 months and exclude kidney stones, bladder infections, and incontinence. Chronic joint symptoms are shown if respondent had pain, aching, or stiffness in or around a joint (excluding back and neck) and the condition began more than three months ago. Migraines and pain in neck, lower back, face, or jaw are shown only if pain lasted a whole day or more.
Source: National Center for Health Statistics, Summary Health Statistics for U.S. Adults: National Health Interview Survey, 2010, Vital and Health Statistics, Series 10, No. 252, 2012, Internet site http://www.cdc.gov/nchs/nhis.htm

Table 3.17 Hypertension by Sex and Age, 1988–94 to 2007–10

(percent of people aged 20 or older with hypertension by sex and age, 1988–94 to 2007–10; and percentage point change, 1988–94 to 2007–10)

	2007–10	1988–94	percentage point change
Total aged 20 or older	**32.2%**	**24.1%**	**8.1**
Men aged 20 or older	**31.7**	**23.8**	**7.9**
Aged 20 to 34	6.8	7.1	-0.3
Aged 35 to 44	20.7	17.1	3.6
Aged 45 to 54	35.5	29.2	6.3
Aged 55 to 64	49.5	40.6	8.9
Aged 65 to 74	64.1	54.4	9.7
Aged 75 or older	71.7	60.4	11.3
Women aged 20 or older	**32.8**	**24.4**	**8.4**
Aged 20 to 34	3.8	2.9	0.9
Aged 35 to 44	14.2	11.2	3.0
Aged 45 to 54	31.2	23.9	7.3
Aged 55 to 64	50.4	42.6	7.8
Aged 65 to 74	69.3	56.2	13.1
Aged 75 or older	81.3	73.6	7.7

Note: Hypertension is defined as a systolic pressure of at least 140 mmHg or a diastolic pressure of at least 90 mmHg; in addition, anyone who takes antihypertensive medication is considered to have hypertension.
Source: National Center for Health Statistics, Health, United States, 2011, Internet site http://www.cdc.gov/nchs/hus.htm; calculations by New Strategist

Table 3.18 High Cholesterol by Sex and Age, 1988–94 to 2007–10

(percent of people aged 20 or older with high serum cholesterol by sex and age, 1988–94 to 2007–10; and percentage point change, 1988–94 to 2007–10)

	2007–10	1988–94	percentage point change
Total aged 20 or older	**28.7%**	**21.5%**	**7.2**
Men aged 20 or older	**28.7**	**19.6**	**9.1**
Aged 20 to 34	8.5	8.2	0.3
Aged 35 to 44	22.5	21.0	1.5
Aged 45 to 54	34.0	29.6	4.4
Aged 55 to 64	46.2	30.8	15.4
Aged 65 to 74	48.9	27.4	21.5
Aged 75 or older	45.2	24.4	20.8
Women aged 20 or older	**28.7**	**23.2**	**5.5**
Aged 20 to 34	6.8	7.3	-0.5
Aged 35 to 44	15.7	13.5	2.2
Aged 45 to 54	29.1	28.2	0.9
Aged 55 to 64	51.4	45.8	5.6
Aged 65 to 74	53.3	46.9	6.4
Aged 75 or older	52.5	41.2	11.3

Note: High cholesterol is defined as 240 mg/dL or more.
Source: National Center for Health Statistics, Health, United States, 2011, Internet site http://www.cdc.gov/nchs/hus.htm; calculations by New Strategist

Table 3.19 Diabetes Diagnosis by Age, 2010

(percent distribution of people aged 18 or older by age and diabetes diagnosis status, 2010)

	diagnosed with diabetes by a doctor		
	total	yes	no
Total people	**100.0%**	**8.7%**	**91.3%**
Aged 18 to 24	100.0	0.9	99.1
Aged 25 to 34	100.0	2.2	97.8
Aged 35 to 44	100.0	4.3	95.7
Aged 45 to 54	100.0	8.2	91.8
Aged 55 to 64	100.0	15.3	84.7
Aged 65 or older	100.0	19.3	80.7

Source: Centers for Disease Control and Prevention, Behavioral Risk Factor Surveillance System Prevalence Data, 2010, Internet site http://apps.nccd.cdc.gov/brfss/

Prescription Drug Use Is Increasing

More Americans use a growing number of prescriptions.

The use of prescription drugs to treat a variety of illnesses, particularly chronic conditions, increased substantially between 1988–94 and 2005–08. The percentage of people who took at least one drug in the past month rose from 38 to 48 percent during those years. The percentage using three or more prescription drugs in the past month climbed from 11 to 21 percent. Sixty-five percent of people aged 45 to 64 have taken at least one prescription drug in the past month, and 34 percent have taken three or more.

Most adults aged 30 or older have incurred a prescription drug expense during the past year, according to the federal government's Medical Expenditure Panel Survey. Expenses for prescription drugs rise with age, to nearly $1,300 for people aged 65 or older. Nearly three of four Baby Boomers had a prescription drug expense in 2009, spending a median of $557. Boomers paid 21 percent of that cost out-of-pocket.

■ Behind the increase in the use of prescriptions is the introduction and marketing of new drugs to treat chronic health problems.

Most Boomers have prescription drug expenses

(percent of people with prescription drug expenses, by generation, 2009)

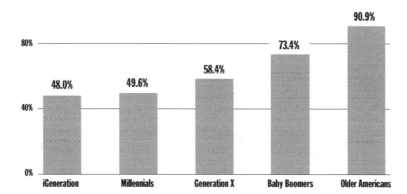

Table 3.20 Prescription Drug Use by Sex and Age, 1988—94 to 2005—08

(percent of people taking at least one or three or more prescription drugs in the past month, by sex and age, 1988–94 to 2005–08; percentage point change, 1988–94 to 2005–08)

	at least one			three or more		
	2005–08	1988–94	percentage point change	2005–08	1988–94	percentage point change
Total people	**47.9%**	**37.8%**	**10.1**	**21.4%**	**11.0%**	**10.4**
Under age 18	25.3	20.5	4.8	4.4	2.4	2.0
Aged 18 to 44	37.8	31.3	6.5	9.8	5.7	4.1
Aged 45 to 64	64.8	54.8	10.0	34.1	20.0	14.1
Aged 65 or older	90.1	73.6	16.5	65.0	35.3	29.7
Total females	**53.9**	**44.6**	**9.3**	**24.8**	**13.6**	**11.2**
Under age 18	25.2	20.6	4.6	3.8	2.3	1.5
Aged 18 to 44	47.9	40.7	7.2	13.3	7.6	5.7
Aged 45 to 64	70.2	62.0	8.2	39.4	24.7	14.7
Aged 65 or older	90.5	78.3	12.2	65.3	38.2	27.1
Total males	**41.7**	**30.6**	**11.1**	**17.8**	**8.3**	**9.5**
Under age 18	25.3	20.4	4.9	5.0	2.6	2.4
Aged 18 to 44	27.5	21.5	6.0	6.2	3.6	2.6
Aged 45 to 64	59.3	47.2	12.1	28.6	15.1	13.5
Aged 65 or older	89.7	67.2	22.5	64.6	31.3	33.3

Source: National Center for Health Statistics, Health, United States, 2011, Internet site http://www.cdc.gov/nchs/hus.htm; calculations by New Strategist

Table 3.21 Spending on Prescription Medications by Age, 2009

(percent of people with prescription medication expense, median expense per person, total expenses, and percent distribution of total expenses by source of payment, by age, 2009)

	total (thousands)	percent with expense	median expense per person	total expenses amount (millions)	total expenses percent distribution
Total people	**306,661**	**62.5%**	**$310**	**$257,593**	**100.0%**
Under age 18	74,836	48.2	65	17,806	6.9
Aged 18 to 29	51,023	49.6	111	14,116	5.5
Aged 30 to 39	39,195	54.2	154	18,577	7.2
Aged 40 to 44	20,924	61.5	274	15,877	6.2
Aged 45 to 49	21,892	65.3	314	21,197	8.2
Aged 50 to 54	22,699	72.5	511	26,166	10.2
Aged 55 to 59	19,335	77.3	729	28,747	11.2
Aged 60 to 64	16,417	83.1	892	28,106	10.9
Aged 65 or older	40,338	91.2	1,290	87,001	33.8

	percent distribution by source of payment total	out of pocket	private insurance	Medicare	Medicaid	other
Total people	**100.0%**	**21.7%**	**39.3%**	**24.0%**	**8.7%**	**6.3%**
Under age 18	100.0	12.3	47.2	3.7	33.3	3.5
Aged 18 to 29	100.0	26.8	48.7	3.1	15.7	5.8
Aged 30 to 39	100.0	20.6	51.8	10.2	13.3	4.1
Aged 40 to 44	100.0	23.4	46.6	10.8	13.2	6.0
Aged 45 to 49	100.0	19.3	47.1	18.9	7.9	6.9
Aged 50 to 54	100.0	22.5	46.5	13.8	10.2	6.9
Aged 55 to 59	100.0	21.5	53.9	12.8	7.1	4.7
Aged 60 to 64	100.0	21.4	52.2	11.7	6.7	8.0
Aged 65 or older	100.0	23.4	19.0	49.1	1.6	7.0

Note: "Other" insurance includes Department of Veterans Affairs (except Tricare), American Indian Health Service, state and local clinics, worker's compensation, homeowner's and automobile insurance, etc.
Source: Agency for Healthcare Research and Quality, Medical Expenditure Panel Survey, 2009, Internet site http://meps.ahrq .gov/mepsweb/survey_comp/household.jsp; calculations by New Strategist

Table 3.22 Spending on Prescription Medications by Generation, 2009

(percent of people with prescription medication expense, median expense per person, total expenses, and percent distribution of total expenses by source of payment, by generation, 2009)

	total (thousands)	percent with expense	median expense per person	total expenses amount (millions)	total expenses percent distribution
Total people	**306,661**	**62.5%**	**$310**	**$257,593**	**100.0%**
iGeneration (under age 15)	62,153	48.0	62	14,000	5.4
Millennials (15 to 32)	75,919	49.6	107	22,049	8.6
Generation X (33 to 44)	47,907	58.4	213	30,328	11.8
Baby Boomers (45 to 63)	77,800	73.4	557	99,132	38.5
Older Americans (64 or older)	42,882	90.9	1,281	92,085	35.7

	percent distribution by source of payment total	out of pocket	private insurance	Medicare	Medicaid	other
Total people	**100.0%**	**21.7%**	**39.3%**	**24.0%**	**8.7%**	**6.3%**
iGeneration (under age 15)	100.0	11.7	43.8	4.2	36.5	3.7
Millennials (15 to 32)	100.0	23.8	51.0	4.0	16.2	5.1
Generation X (33 to 44)	100.0	21.8	49.2	10.7	13.3	5.0
Baby Boomers (45 to 63)	100.0	21.3	50.8	13.6	7.8	6.6
Older Americans (64 or older)	100.0	23.3	20.0	47.5	2.1	7.0

Note: "Other" insurance includes Department of Veterans Affairs (except Tricare), American Indian Health Service, state and local clinics, worker's compensation, homeowner's and automobile insurance, etc.
Source: Agency for Healthcare Research and Quality, Medical Expenditure Panel Survey, 2009, Internet site http://meps.ahrq .gov/mepsweb/survey_comp/household.jsp; calculations by New Strategist

Millions of Middle-Aged Americans Are Disabled

Fifteen million 45-to-64-year-olds have physical difficulties.

Among Americans aged 18 or older in 2010, a substantial 36 million had one or more difficulties in physical functioning, according to a survey by the National Center for Health Statistics. The percentage of people with problems rises from a low of 5 percent among people aged 18 to 44 to a high of 46 percent among people aged 75 or older. In the 45-to-64-age group, 19 percent have physical difficulties. The most common problem is the inability to stoop, bend, or kneel, mentioned by 12 percent. More than 11 percent have difficulty standing for two hours, and 8 percent cannot walk a quarter mile.

People with AIDS sometimes count themselves among the nation's disabled. As of 2009, more than 1 million people had been diagnosed with AIDS. The largest share (21 percent) were diagnosed between the ages of 35 and 39.

■ Although Boomers are supposed to be more health-conscious than older generations of Americans, many are already experiencing disabilities. As they age, the percentage with disabilities will rise.

Disabilities rise in middle age

(percent of people with physical difficulties, by age, 2010)

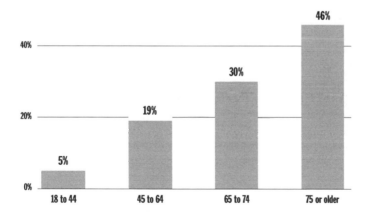

Table 3.23 Difficulties in Physical Functioning among Adults by Age, 2010

(number and percent distribution of people aged 18 or older with difficulties in physical functioning, by type of difficulty and age, 2010; numbers in thousands)

	total	18 to 44	45 to 64	65 or older total	65 to 74	75 or older
Total people aged 18 or older	229,505	110,615	80,198	38,692	21,291	17,401
Total with any physical difficulty	35,847	6,019	15,331	14,497	6,470	8,027
Walk quarter of a mile	16,747	1,984	6,581	8,182	3,318	4,864
Climb 10 steps without resting	11,855	1,270	4,757	5,828	2,413	3,415
Stand for two hours	21,319	3,189	9,027	9,103	3,951	5,152
Sit for two hours	7,350	1,697	3,930	1,723	898	825
Stoop, bend, or kneel	21,033	3,030	9,637	8,365	3,834	4,531
Reach over head	6,131	922	2,703	2,506	1,053	1,453
Grasp or handle small objects	3,965	595	1,824	1,546	703	843
Lift or carry 10 pounds	10,132	1,093	4,457	4,581	1,782	2,799
Push or pull large objects	14,532	1,918	6,551	6,063	2,670	3,393

PERCENT WITH PHYSICAL DIFFICULTY BY AGE

	total	18 to 44	45 to 64	65 or older total	65 to 74	75 or older
Total people aged 18 or older	100.0%	100.0%	100.0%	100.0%	100.0%	100.0%
Total with any physical difficulty	15.6	5.4	19.1	37.5	30.4	46.1
Walk quarter of a mile	7.3	1.8	8.2	21.1	15.6	28.0
Climb 10 steps without resting	5.2	1.1	5.9	15.1	11.3	19.6
Stand for two hours	9.3	2.9	11.3	23.5	18.6	29.6
Sit for two hours	3.2	1.5	4.9	4.5	4.2	4.7
Stoop, bend, or kneel	9.2	2.7	12.0	21.6	18.0	26.0
Reach over head	2.7	0.8	3.4	6.5	4.9	8.4
Grasp or handle small objects	1.7	0.5	2.3	4.0	3.3	4.8
Lift or carry 10 pounds	4.4	1.0	5.6	11.8	8.4	16.1
Push or pull large objects	6.3	1.7	8.2	15.7	12.5	19.5

PERCENT DISTRIBUTION OF THOSE WITH PHYSICAL DIFFICULTIES BY AGE

	total	18 to 44	45 to 64	65 or older total	65 to 74	75 or older
Total people aged 18 or older	100.0%	48.2%	34.9%	16.9%	9.3%	7.6%
Total with any physical difficulty	100.0	16.8	42.8	40.4	18.0	22.4
Walk quarter of a mile	100.0	11.8	39.3	48.9	19.8	29.0
Climb 10 steps without resting	100.0	10.7	40.1	49.2	20.4	28.8
Stand for two hours	100.0	15.0	42.3	42.7	18.5	24.2
Sit for two hours	100.0	23.1	53.5	23.4	12.2	11.2
Stoop, bend, or kneel	100.0	14.4	45.8	39.8	18.2	21.5
Reach over head	100.0	15.0	44.1	40.9	17.2	23.7
Grasp or handle small objects	100.0	15.0	46.0	39.0	17.7	21.3
Lift or carry 10 pounds	100.0	10.8	44.0	45.2	17.6	27.6
Push or pull large objects	100.0	13.2	45.1	41.7	18.4	23.3

Note: Respondents were classified as having difficulties if they responded "very difficult" or "can't do at all."
Source: National Center for Health Statistics, Summary Health Statistics for U.S. Adults: National Health Interview Survey, 2010, Vital and Health Statistics, Series 10, No. 252, 2012, Internet site http://www.cdc.gov/nchs/nhis.htm

Table 3.24 Cumulative Number of AIDS Cases by Sex and Age, through 2009

(cumulative number and percent distribution of AIDS cases by sex and age at diagnosis, through 2009)

	number	percent distribution
Total cases	**1,108,611**	**100.0%**
Sex		
Males 13 or older	878,366	79.2
Females 13 or older	220,795	19.9
Age		
Under age 13	9,448	0.9
Aged 13 to 14	1,321	0.1
Aged 15 to 19	7,214	0.7
Aged 20 to 24	42,920	3.9
Aged 25 to 29	129,639	11.7
Aged 30 to 34	214,149	19.3
Aged 35 to 39	234,575	21.2
Aged 40 to 44	193,237	17.4
Aged 45 to 49	126,380	11.4
Aged 50 to 54	72,327	6.5
Aged 55 to 59	39,025	3.5
Aged 60 to 64	20,633	1.9
Aged 65 or older	17,743	1.6

Source: Centers for Disease Control and Prevention, Cases of HIV/AIDS and AIDS in the United States and Dependent Areas, 2009, Internet site http://www.cdc.gov/hiv/surveillance/resources/reports/2009report/; calculations by New Strategist

Boomers Are Filling Physician Waiting Rooms

People aged 45 to 64 visit a doctor an average of four times a year.

In 2009, Americans visited a physician more than 1 billion times. Among the broad age groups examined by the National Center for Health Statistics, people aged 45 to 64 accounted for the largest share (30 percent) of physician visits.

The age group also accounts for 28 percent of visits to hospital outpatient departments and for a smaller 21 percent of visits to emergency departments. Only 8 percent of 45-to-64-year-olds spent a night in the hospital during the past year.

When adults who visited a doctor or health care clinic are asked to rate the care they received, only half give it the highest rating (a 9 or 10 on a scale of 0 to 10). The proportion that rates the experience a 9 or 10 is lowest among the Millennial generation (40 percent) and rises to a peak of 64 percent among older Americans, virtually all of whom are on Medicare.

■ As the Baby-Boom generation ages, older Americans will become the dominant health care consumers, boosting demand for physicians trained in geriatric medicine.

Doctor visits rise with advancing age

(average number of physician visits per person per year, by age, 2009)

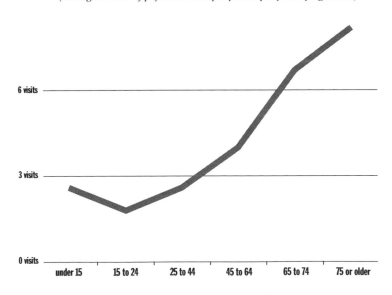

Table 3.25 Physician Office Visits by Sex and Age, 2009

(total number, percent distribution, and number of physician office visits per person per year, by sex and age, 2009; numbers in thousands)

	total	percent distribution	average visits per year
Total visits	**1,037,796**	**100.0%**	**3.4**
Under age 15	158,907	15.3	2.6
Aged 15 to 24	74,080	7.1	1.8
Aged 25 to 44	208,901	20.1	2.6
Aged 45 to 64	316,395	30.5	4.0
Aged 65 or older	279,514	26.9	7.4
Aged 65 to 74	137,452	13.2	6.7
Aged 75 or older	142,062	13.7	8.2
Visits by females	**611,064**	**58.9**	**4.0**
Under age 15	72,243	7.0	2.4
Aged 15 to 24	48,029	4.6	2.3
Aged 25 to 44	144,022	13.9	3.5
Aged 45 to 64	184,994	17.8	4.6
Aged 65 to 74	75,428	7.3	6.8
Aged 75 or older	86,348	8.3	8.2
Visits by males	**426,732**	**41.1**	**2.9**
Under age 15	86,664	8.4	2.7
Aged 15 to 24	26,052	2.5	1.2
Aged 25 to 44	64,879	6.3	1.6
Aged 45 to 64	131,400	12.7	3.4
Aged 65 to 74	62,023	6.0	6.5
Aged 75 or older	55,713	5.4	8.1

Source: National Center for Health Statistics, National Ambulatory Medical Care Survey: 2009 Summary Tables, Internet site http://www.cdc.gov/nchs/ahcd/web_tables.htm#2009

Table 3.26 Hospital Outpatient Department Visits by Age and Reason, 2008

(number and percent distribution of visits to hospital outpatient departments by age and major reason for visit, 2008; numbers in thousands)

| | total | | major reason for visit | | | | | | |
	number	percent distribution	total	new problem	chronic problem, routine	chronic problem, flare-up	pre- or post-surgery or injury follow-up	preventive care	unknown
Total visits	**109,889**	**100.0%**	**100.0%**	**38.1%**	**30.3%**	**6.1%**	**4.7%**	**19.2%**	**1.6%**
Under age 15	22,332	20.3	100.0	51.9	16.2	2.6	1.5	26.3	1.5
Aged 15 to 24	11,563	10.5	100.0	42.8	18.5	4.2	3.1	30.2	1.2
Aged 25 to 44	26,186	23.8	100.0	40.9	25.8	6.5	4.6	21.2	1.1
Aged 45 to 64	31,150	28.3	100.0	31.4	40.3	7.8	6.4	12.3	1.6
Aged 65 or older	18,658	17.0	100.0	26.1	43.8	8.3	6.7	12.5	2.5
Aged 65 to 74	10,273	9.3	100.0	26.8	42.3	8.1	7.3	13.5	2.0
Aged 75 or older	835	0.8	100.0	25.4	45.6	8.5	6.1	11.3	3.2

Source: National Center for Health Statistics, National Ambulatory Medical Care Survey: 2008 Outpatient Department Summary Tables, Internet site http://www.cdc.gov/nchs/ahcd/web_tables.htm#2009

Table 3.27 Emergency Department Visits by Age and Urgency of Problem, 2008

(number of visits to emergency rooms and percent distribution by urgency of problem, by age, 2008; numbers in thousands)

| | total | | percent distribution by urgency of problem | | | | | | |
	number	percent distribution	total	immediate	emergent	urgent	semiurgent	nonurgent	unknown
Total visits	**123,761**	**100.0%**	**100.0%**	**3.7%**	**11.9%**	**38.9%**	**21.2%**	**8.0%**	**16.3%**
Under age 15	23,157	18.7	100.0	1.9	8.3	36.0	25.1	8.8	20.0
Aged 15 to 24	19,823	16.0	100.0	2.6	9.2	37.0	24.9	9.8	16.5
Aged 25 to 44	35,185	28.4	100.0	3.1	10.1	39.0	23.0	9.1	15.7
Aged 45 to 64	26,335	21.3	100.0	5	14.0	40.2	18.4	7.1	15.3
Aged 65 or older	19,261	15.6	100.0	6.2	19.5	42.2	13.5	4.6	14.0
Aged 65 to 74	7,479	6.0	100.0	5.2	19.3	41.3	15.3	5.5	13.3
Aged 75 or older	11,781	9.5	100.0	6.9	19.7	42.8	12.4	4.0	14.4

Note: "Immediate" is a visit in which the patient should be seen immediately. "Emergent" is a visit in which the patient should be seen within 1 to 14 minutes; "urgent" is a visit in which the patient should be seen within 15 to 60 minutes; "semiurgent" is a visit in which the patient should be seen within 61 to 120 minutes; "nonurgent" is a visit in which the patient should be seen within 121 minutes to 24 hours; "unknown" is a visit with no mention of immediacy or triage or the patient was dead on arrival.
Source: National Center for Health Statistics, National Ambulatory Medical Care Survey: 2008 Emergency Department Summary Tables, Internet site http://www.cdc.gov/nchs/ahcd/web_tables.htm#2009

Table 3.28 Number of Overnight Hospital Stays by Age, 2010

(total number of people and percent distribution by experience of an overnight hospital stay in past 12 months, by age, 2010; numbers in thousands)

	total		number of stays	
	number	percent	none	one or more
Total people	**304,126**	**100.0%**	**92.1%**	**7.9%**
Under age 12	50,457	100.0	92.8	7.2
Aged 12 to 17	24,168	100.0	97.7	2.3
Aged 18 to 44	110,614	100.0	93.7	6.3
Aged 45 to 64	80,210	100.0	91.7	8.3
Aged 65 or older	38,678	100.0	84.1	15.9

Source: National Center for Health Statistics, Summary Health Statistics for the U.S. Population: National Health Interview Survey, 2010, Vital and Health Statistics, Series 10, No. 251, 2011, Internet site http://www.cdc.gov/nchs/nhis.htm; calculations by New Strategist

Table 3.29 Rating of Health Care Received from Doctor's Office or Clinic by Age, 2009

(number of people aged 18 or older visiting a doctor or health care clinic in past 12 months, and percent distribution by rating for health care received on a scale from 0 (worst) to 10 (best), by age, 2009; people in thousands)

	with health care visit		rating		
	number	percent	9 to 10	7 to 8	0 to 6
Total adults	**155,909**	**100.0%**	**50.1%**	**36.5%**	**12.2%**
Aged 18 to 29	26,931	100.0	40.2	42.3	16.4
Aged 30 to 39	24,107	100.0	41.0	44.0	13.8
Aged 40 to 44	13,415	100.0	44.6	42.1	12.0
Aged 45 to 49	14,379	100.0	48.9	36.4	14.1
Aged 50 to 54	15,980	100.0	48.2	35.9	14.9
Aged 55 to 59	15,259	100.0	52.7	34.8	11.5
Aged 60 to 64	12,989	100.0	58.7	31.7	7.8
Aged 65 or older	32,847	100.0	64.0	26.8	7.5

Source: Agency for Healthcare Research and Quality, Medical Expenditure Panel Survey, 2009, Internet site http://meps.ahrq.gov/mepsweb/survey_comp/household.jsp; calculations by New Strategist

Table 3.30 Rating of Health Care Received from Doctor's Office or Clinic by Generation, 2009

(number of people aged 18 or older visiting a doctor or health care clinic in past 12 months, and percent distribution by rating for health care received on a scale from 0 (worst) to 10 (best), by generation, 2009; people in thousands)

	with health care visit		rating		
	number	percent	9 to 10	7 to 8	0 to 6
Total adults	**155,909**	**100.0%**	**50.1%**	**36.5%**	**12.2%**
Millennials (18 to 32)	34,072	100.0	39.9	42.8	16.1
Generation X (33 to 44)	30,382	100.0	43.1	43.0	12.6
Baby Boomers (45 to 63)	56,573	100.0	51.5	35.0	12.5
Older Americans (64 or older)	34,883	100.0	63.9	27.0	7.3

*Source: Agency for Healthcare Research and Quality, Medical Expenditure Panel Survey, 2009, Internet site http://meps.ahrq
.gov/mepsweb/survey_comp/household.jsp; calculations by New Strategist*

Table 3.31 Adults Who Use Complementary and Alternative Medicine by Age, 2007

(percent of people aged 18 or older who used complementary or alternative medicine in the past 12 months, by age, 2007)

	any use	biologically based therapies	mind-body therapies	alternative medical systems	manipulative and body-based therapies
Total adults	**38.3%**	**19.9%**	**19.2%**	**3.4%**	**15.2%**
Aged 18 to 29	36.3	15.9	21.3	3.2	15.1
Aged 30 to 39	39.6	19.8	19.9	3.6	17.2
Aged 40 to 49	40.1	20.4	19.7	4.6	17.4
Aged 50 to 59	44.1	24.2	22.9	4.9	17.3
Aged 60 to 69	41.0	25.4	17.3	2.8	13.8
Aged 70 to 84	32.1	19.3	11.9	1.8	9.9
Aged 85 or older	24.2	13.7	9.8	1.9	7.0

Definitions: Biologically based therapies include chelation therapy, nonvitamin, nonmineral, natural products and diet-based therapies. Mind-body therapies include biofeedback meditation, guided imagery, progressive relaxation, deep breathing exercises, hypnosis, yoga, tai chi, and qi gong. Alternative medical systems include acupuncture, ayurveda, homeopathic treatment, naturopathy, and traditional healers. Manipulative body-based therapies include chiropractic or osteopathic manipulation, massage, and movement therapies.
Source: National Center for Health Statistics, Complementary and Alternative Medicine Use Among Adults and Children: United States, 2007, National Health Statistics Report, No. 12, 2008, Internet site http://www.cdc.gov/nchs/products/nhsr.htm

Boomers Account for One in Five Deaths

Cancer and heart disease are the leading causes of death among Boomers.

Heart disease and cancer are the two leading causes of death in the United States. Among 45-to-64-year-olds, however, the order is reversed—cancer kills more than heart disease. Accidents are the third leading cause of death among 45-to-64-year-olds. While the 45-to-64 age group accounts for 20 percent of all deaths, it accounts for the 58 percent majority of deaths due to chronic liver disease and cirrhosis. This condition ranks fifth as a cause of death among Boomers, but 12th overall.

If middle age is defined as the point when people have lived half their lives, then 40-year-olds are exactly middle-aged and 50-year-olds are definitely over the hill. Men aged 50 can expect to live 29.6 more years, on average. Women aged 50 can expect to live another 33.2 years.

■ As Boomers age, managing heart disease and cancer will become an increasingly important focus of their daily life.

Baby Boomers have lived more years than they have remaining

(years of life remaining for people at selected ages, 2010)

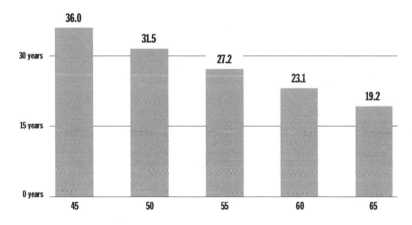

Table 3.32 Leading Causes of Death among People Aged 45 to 64, 2010

(total number of deaths, number and and percent distribution of deaths among people aged 45 to 64, and age group share of total, for the 10 leading causes of death among people aged 45 to 64, 2010)

			aged 45 to 64		
		total	number	percent distribution	share of total
	All causes	**2,465,932**	**493,376**	**100.0%**	**20.0%**
1.	Malignant neoplasms (cancer) (2)	573,855	159,379	32.3	27.8
2.	Diseases of heart (1)	595,444	103,812	21.0	17.4
3.	Accidents (unintentional injuries) (5)	118,043	32,667	6.6	27.7
4.	Chronic lower respiratory disease (3)	137,789	18,616	3.8	13.5
5.	Chronic liver disease and cirrhosis (12)	31,802	18,348	3.7	57.7
6.	Diabetes mellitus (7)	68,905	17,224	3.5	25.0
7.	Cerebrovascular diseases (4)	129,180	16,565	3.4	12.8
8.	Suicide (10)	37,793	14,912	3.0	39.5
9.	Nephritis, nephrotic syndrome, nephrosis (8)	50,472	7,306	1.5	14.5
10.	Septicemia (11)	34,843	6,957	1.4	20.0
	All other causes	687,806	97,590	19.8	14.2

Note: Number in parentheses shows cause of death rank for total population.
Source: National Center for Health Statistics, Deaths: Preliminary Data for 2010, National Vital Statistics Reports, Vol. 60, No. 4, 2012, Internet site http://www.cdc.gov/nchs/deaths.htm; calculations by New Strategist

Table 3.33 Life Expectancy by Age and Sex, 2010

(expected years of life remaining at selected ages, by sex, 2010)

	total	females	males
At birth	78.7	81.1	76.2
Aged 1	78.2	80.5	75.7
Aged 5	74.3	76.6	71.8
Aged 10	69.3	71.6	66.8
Aged 15	64.4	66.7	61.9
Aged 20	59.5	61.8	57.1
Aged 25	54.8	56.9	52.4
Aged 30	50.0	52.0	47.8
Aged 35	45.3	47.2	43.1
Aged 40	40.6	42.5	38.5
Aged 45	36.0	37.8	33.9
Aged 50	31.5	33.2	29.6
Aged 55	27.2	28.8	25.4
Aged 60	23.1	24.5	21.5
Aged 65	19.2	20.3	17.7
Aged 70	15.5	16.5	14.2
Aged 75	12.2	12.9	11.0
Aged 80	9.2	9.7	8.2
Aged 85	6.6	7.0	5.9
Aged 90	4.7	4.9	4.1
Aged 95	3.3	3.4	2.9
Aged 100	2.4	2.4	2.1

Source: National Center for Health Statistics, Deaths: Preliminary Data for 2010, National Vital Statistics Reports, Vol. 60, No. 4, 2012, Internet site http://www.cdc.gov/nchs/deaths.htm; calculations by New Strategist

4

Housing

■ The homeownership rate in the United States reached a peak of 69.0 percent in 2004. Since then, the rate has fallen by 2.9 percentage points. Among Boomers, those aged 45 to 49 have been hurt the most.

■ During the past decade the Baby Boom generation filled the 45-to-64 age group, when homeownership rates peak. Boomer demand for homes helped to fuel the housing bubble.

■ Although married couples are most likely to own a home, most householders aged 45 or older are homeowners regardless of household type.

■ Homeownership surpasses 50 percent among non-Hispanic whites in the 25-to-34 age group. Among Asians, the majority owns a home in the 35-to-44 age group. Among blacks and Hispanics, the percentage reaches at least 50 percent in the 45-to-54 age group.

■ The majority of American households (69 percent) live in single-family homes or duplexes (one unit detached or attached). Householders aged 35 to 64 are most likely to live in this type of home, at 74 percent.

■ Twelve percent of Americans aged 1 or older moved between March 2010 and March 2011, but the proportion was a smaller 7 percent among people aged 45 to 64.

Homeownership Rate Has Declined

Rate was lower in 2011 than in 2000 in most age groups.

The homeownership rate in the United States reached a peak of 69.0 percent in 2004. Since then, the rate has fallen by 2.9 percentage points, to 66.1 percent in 2011, because of the Great Recession and the collapse of the housing market. Among Baby Boomers, those aged 45 to 49 have been hurt the most. The homeownership rate of 45-to-49-year-olds fell by more than 5 percentage points between 2004 and 2011.

The overall homeownership rate of 2011 was 1.4 percentage points below the rate of 2000. For 45-to-54-year-olds, the homeownership rate was 4 percentage points lower in 2011 than in 2000. Among 55-to-64-year-olds, the 2011 homeownership rate was 1.8 percentage points lower. The homeownership rate of Boomers has fallen, in part, because some have lost their homes in the economic downturn.

■ The collapse of the housing market and the decline in housing prices is preventing many Boomers from selling their homes and downsizing as they retire.

After peaking in 2004, homeownership has fallen among householders aged 45 to 64

(homeownership rate of householders aged 45 to 64, by age, 2004 and 2011)

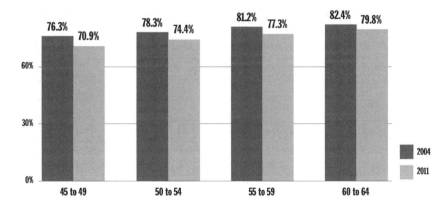

Table 4.1 Homeownership by Age of Householder, 2000 to 2011

(percentage of householders who own their home by age of householder, 2000 to 2011; percentage point change, 2004–11 and 2000–11)

					percentage point change	
	2011	2010	2004	2000	2004–11	2000–11
Total households	**66.1%**	**66.8%**	**69.0%**	**67.5%**	**–2.9**	**–1.4**
Under age 35	37.7	39.0	43.1	40.7	–5.4	–3.0
Aged 35 to 44	63.5	65.0	69.2	68.0	–5.8	–4.6
Aged 45 to 54	72.7	73.5	77.2	76.5	–4.5	–3.8
Aged 45 to 49	70.9	72.0	76.3	75.0	–5.4	–4.1
Aged 50 to 54	74.4	75.0	78.3	78.7	–3.9	–4.3
Aged 55 to 64	78.5	79.0	81.7	80.3	–3.2	–1.8
Aged 55 to 59	77.3	77.7	81.2	79.8	–3.9	–2.5
Aged 60 to 64	79.8	80.4	82.4	80.6	–2.6	–0.8
Aged 65 or older	80.9	80.5	81.1	80.5	–0.2	0.4

Source: Bureau of the Census, Housing Vacancies and Homeownership, Internet site http://www.census.gov/hhes/www/housing/hvs/hvs.html; calculations by New Strategist

Homeownership Rises with Age

At least seven out of 10 householders aged 45 or older own their home.

The housing bubble was not the only reason for the booming housing industry over the past decade. Another factor was the aging of the Baby Boom generation into the lifestage when homeownership peaks. The homeownership rate climbs steeply as people enter their thirties, forties, and fifties. During the past two decades, Boomers filled those age groups, fueling the real estate, construction, and home improvement industries. In fact, growing Boomer demand for homes helped to create the housing bubble.

Those least likely to own a home are young adults who have not yet accumulated the savings for a down payment and are not yet earning enough to qualify for a mortgage. Only 38 percent of householders under age 35 own a home. The homeownership rate peaks at more than 80 percent among Americans aged 65 or older.

■ Although homeownership rates have declined from their peak, the pattern of homeownership—with rates rising as people age—is unchanged.

Homeowners greatly outnumber renters among 45-to-64-year-olds

(percent distribution of householders aged 45 to 64 by homeownership status and age, 2011)

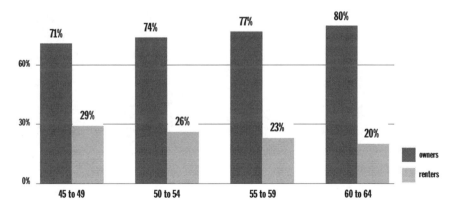

Table 4.2 Owners and Renters by Age of Householder, 2011

(number and percent distribution of householders by homeownership status, and owner and renter share of total, by age of householder, 2011; numbers in thousands)

	total	owners			renters		
		number	percent distribution	share of total	number	percent distribution	share of total
Total households	**113,534**	**75,091**	**100.0%**	**66.1%**	**38,443**	**100.0%**	**33.9%**
Under age 35	25,098	9,465	12.6	37.7	15,633	40.7	62.3
Aged 35 to 44	20,183	12,807	17.1	63.5	7,376	19.2	36.5
Aged 45 to 64	64,611	49,367	65.7	76.4	15,244	39.7	23.6
Aged 45 to 54	23,233	16,885	22.5	72.7	6,348	16.5	27.3
Aged 45 to 49	11,449	8,123	10.8	70.9	3,326	8.7	29.1
Aged 50 to 54	11,784	8,762	11.7	74.4	3,022	7.9	25.6
Aged 55 to 64	20,689	16,241	21.6	78.5	4,448	11.6	21.5
Aged 55 to 59	10,848	8,385	11.2	77.3	2,463	6.4	22.7
Aged 60 to 64	9,841	7,856	10.5	79.8	1,985	5.2	20.2
Aged 65 or older	24,330	19,693	26.2	80.9	4,637	12.1	19.1

Source: Bureau of the Census, Housing Vacancies and Homeownership, Internet site http://www.census.gov/hhes/www/housing/ hvs/hvs.html; calculations by New Strategist

Married Couples Are Most Likely to Be Homeowners

Homeownership rates are highest in the Midwest.

The homeownership rate among all married couples stood at 81.5 percent in 2011, much higher than the 66.1 percent for all households. Among Boomer couples, the homeownership rate ranges from 85 to 91 percent. Homeownership is much lower for other types of households and lowest for female-headed families, at 48.1 percent in 2011. Regardless of household type, however, most householders aged 45 or older are homeowners.

The homeownership rate is highest in the Midwest and lowest in the West. Among Boomers, the homeownership rate peaks at 83.2 percent among householders aged 60 to 64 in the Midwest. The homeownership rate is a smaller 75.1 percent among householders aged 60 to 64 in the West.

■ The lax lending standards of the housing bubble era did not eliminate differences in homeownership rates by household type.

Ninety percent of couples aged 55 or older own their home

(percent of married-couple householders who own their home, by age, 2011)

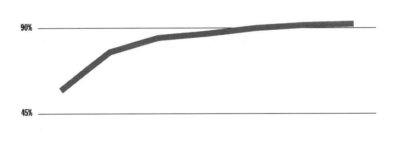

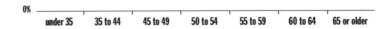

Table 4.3 Homeownership Rate by Age of Householder and Type of Household, 2011

(percent of households owning their home, by age of householder and type of household, 2011)

	total	married couples	female family householder, no spouse present	male family householder, no spouse present	people living alone	
					females	males
Total households	**66.1%**	**81.5%**	**48.1%**	**55.6%**	**58.5%**	**50.6%**
Under age 35	37.7	57.2	25.5	40.0	22.0	26.6
Aged 35 to 44	63.5	77.4	42.4	54.4	43.8	44.1
Aged 45 to 54	72.7	85.9	58.4	65.8	53.9	53.2
Aged 45 to 49	70.9	84.8	55.7	65.0	48.7	51.6
Aged 50 to 54	74.4	87.0	61.6	66.7	57.7	54.8
Aged 55 to 64	78.5	90.7	66.2	74.5	64.8	59.1
Aged 55 to 59	77.3	89.9	63.8	73.3	62.3	57.1
Aged 60 to 64	79.8	91.5	69.4	76.2	67.1	61.3
Aged 65 or older	80.9	92.1	80.5	80.4	70.9	68.9

Source: Bureau of the Census, Housing Vacancies and Homeownership, Internet site http://www.census.gov/hhes/www/housing/ hvs/hvs.html; calculations by New Strategist

Table 4.4 Homeownership Rate by Age of Householder and Region, 2011

(percent of households owning their home, by age of householder and region, 2011)

	total	Northeast	Midwest	South	West
Total households	**66.1%**	**63.6%**	**70.2%**	**68.3%**	**60.5%**
Under age 35	37.7	34.5	42.7	38.9	33.2
Aged 35 to 44	63.5	61.6	69.3	66.2	55.0
Aged 45 to 54	72.7	70.2	77.5	74.4	66.9
Aged 45 to 49	70.9	68.0	75.9	72.9	65.2
Aged 50 to 54	74.4	72.3	79.0	75.8	68.6
Aged 55 to 64	78.5	75.1	81.5	81.1	74.0
Aged 55 to 59	77.3	74.3	80.0	79.7	73.0
Aged 60 to 64	79.8	75.9	83.2	82.6	75.1
Aged 65 or older	80.9	73.7	82.0	85.3	78.9

Source: Bureau of the Census, Housing Vacancies and Homeownership, Internet site http://www.census.gov/hhes/www/housing/ hvs/hvs.html; calculations by New Strategist

Most Middle-Aged Blacks and Hispanics Are Homeowners

The homeownership rate exceeds 60 percent for blacks aged 65 or older.

The homeownership rate of Asians, blacks, and Hispanics is below average. According to the 2010 census, the homeownership rate was 65.1 percent for all households in 2010. Among Asians, the rate was 58.0 percent. Among blacks it was 44.3 percent, and the Hispanic homeownership rate was 47.3 percent. In contrast, an above-average 72.2 percent of non-Hispanic whites owned their home in 2010.

Homeownership surpasses the 50 percent threshold among non-Hispanic whites in the 25-to-34 age group. Among Asians, the majority owns a home in the 35-to-44 age group. Among blacks and Hispanics, the percentage reaches at least 50 percent in the 45-to-54 age group.

■ Although Hispanics outnumber blacks in the United States, black and Hispanic homeowners are nearly equal in number.

Most Boomers are homeowners, regardless of race or Hispanic origin

(homeownership rate of householders aged 45 to 64, by race and Hispanic origin, 2010)

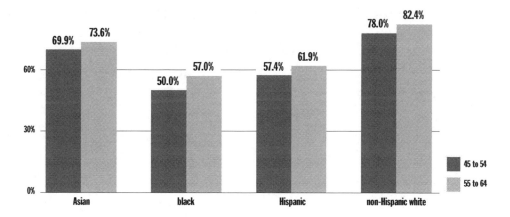

Table 4.5 Homeownership by Age, Race, and Hispanic Origin, 2010

(number and percent of households that own their home, by age, race, and Hispanic origin of householder, 2010; numbers in thousands)

	total	Asian	black	Hispanic	non-Hispanic white
Total households	**116,716**	**4,632**	**14,130**	**13,461**	**82,333**
Under age 25	5,401	217	802	885	3,333
Aged 25 to 34	17,957	924	2,466	3,122	11,003
Aged 35 to 44	21,291	1,145	2,890	3,457	13,362
Aged 45 to 54	24,907	1,002	3,190	2,808	17,438
Aged 55 to 64	21,340	720	2,450	1,693	16,129
Aged 65 or older	25,820	624	2,331	1,496	21,069
Aged 65 to 74	13,505	371	1,374	883	10,692
Aged 75 to 84	8,716	191	722	476	7,238
Aged 85 or older	3,599	62	235	136	3,139
HOMEOWNERS					
Total households	**75,986**	**2,689**	**6,261**	**6,368**	**59,484**
Under age 25	870	26	63	133	622
Aged 25 to 34	7,547	319	557	976	5,538
Aged 35 to 44	13,256	706	1,190	1,659	9,461
Aged 45 to 54	17,804	701	1,594	1,611	13,601
Aged 55 to 64	16,503	530	1,398	1,048	13,285
Aged 65 or older	20,007	407	1,460	941	16,977
Aged 65 to 74	10,834	260	851	558	9,028
Aged 75 to 84	6,789	114	463	303	5,844
Aged 85 or older	2,384	33	146	80	2,105
HOMEOWNERSHIP RATE					
Total households	**65.1%**	**58.0%**	**44.3%**	**47.3%**	**72.2%**
Under age 25	16.1	12.1	7.8	15.1	18.7
Aged 25 to 34	42.0	34.5	22.6	31.3	50.3
Aged 35 to 44	62.3	61.7	41.2	48.0	70.8
Aged 45 to 54	71.5	69.9	50.0	57.4	78.0
Aged 55 to 64	77.3	73.6	57.0	61.9	82.4
Aged 65 or older	77.5	65.2	62.6	62.9	80.6
Aged 65 to 74	80.2	70.2	61.9	63.2	84.4
Aged 75 to 84	77.9	59.4	64.2	63.5	80.7
Aged 85 or older	66.2	52.9	62.3	59.1	67.1

Note: Asians and blacks are those who identify themselves as being of the race alone. Hispanics may be of any race. Non-Hispanic whites are those who identify themselves as being white alone and not Hispanic.
Source: Bureau of the Census, 2010 Census, American Factfinder,Internet site http://factfinder2.census.gov/faces/nav/jsf/pages/index.xhtml; calculations by New Strategist"

The Middle Aged Are Most Likely to Live in Single-Family Homes

Only 20 percent of householders aged 35 to 64 live in multi-unit buildings.

The majority of American households (69 percent) live in single-family homes or duplexes (one unit detached or attached). Householders aged 35 to 64 are most likely to live in this type of home, at 74 percent. Not surprisingly, homeowners are much more likely than renters to live in a single-family home. Among householders aged 35 to 64, fully 89 percent of homeowners live in a single-family home versus 38 percent of renters.

Apartment living is most popular among younger adults. Forty-five percent of householders under age 35 live in a multi-unit building, while just under half live in a single-family home or duplex. Interestingly, however, adults aged 65 or older are more likely than middle-aged or younger adults to live in a building with 50 or more units. Behind this figure is the movement of older adults into multi-unit retirement complexes and assisted living facilities.

Six percent of households live in mobile homes, boats, RVs, and so on. This category is dominated by mobile homes. The proportion of householders who live in a mobile home does not vary much by age.

■ The demand for single-family homes helped to fuel the housing bubble.

Most of the middle aged are in single-family homes

(percent of households living in single-family homes, by age of householder, 2010)

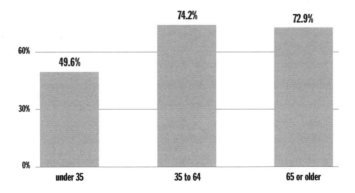

Table 4.6 Number of Units in Structure by Age of Householder and Homeownership Status, 2010

(number and percent distribution of households by age of householder, homeownership status, and number of units in structure, 2010; numbers in thousands)

| | total | one detached or attached | multi-unit building | | | | | mobile home, boat, RV, etc. |
			total	2 to 4	5 to 19	20 to 49	50 or more	
Total households	**114,567**	**79,080**	**28,507**	**9,032**	**10,094**	**3,906**	**5,475**	**6,979**
Under age 35	22,695	11,267	10,160	3,060	4,214	1,424	1,462	1,267
Aged 35 to 64	66,998	49,692	13,247	4,665	4,705	1,687	2,190	4,061
Aged 65 or older	24,874	18,121	5,100	1,307	1,175	795	1,823	1,651
Owner-occupied	**74,873**	**65,779**	**3,986**	**1,590**	**1,034**	**493**	**869**	**5,108**
Under age 35	8,062	6,837	602	191	208	77	126	622
Aged 35 to 64	47,265	42,140	2,100	906	536	234	424	3,026
Aged 65 or older	19,546	16,802	1,284	493	290	182	319	1,460
Renter-occupied	**39,694**	**13,301**	**24,521**	**7,442**	**9,060**	**3,413**	**4,606**	**1,871**
Under age 35	14,633	4,430	9,558	2,869	4,006	1,347	1,336	645
Aged 35 to 64	19,733	7,552	11,147	3,759	4,169	1,453	1,766	1,035
Aged 65 or older	5,328	1,319	3,816	814	885	613	1,504	191

PERCENT DISTRIBUTION BY UNITS IN STRUCTURE

| | total | one detached or attached | multi-unit building | | | | | mobile home, boat, RV, etc. |
			total	2 to 4	5 to 19	20 to 49	50 or more	
Total households	**100.0%**	**69.0%**	**24.9%**	**7.9%**	**8.8%**	**3.4%**	**4.8%**	**6.1%**
Under age 35	100.0	49.6	44.8	13.5	18.6	6.3	6.4	5.6
Aged 35 to 64	100.0	74.2	19.8	7.0	7.0	2.5	3.3	6.1
Aged 65 or older	100.0	72.9	20.5	5.3	4.7	3.2	7.3	6.6
Owner-occupied	**100.0**	**87.9**	**5.3**	**2.1**	**1.4**	**0.7**	**1.2**	**6.8**
Under age 35	100.0	84.8	7.5	2.4	2.6	1.0	1.6	7.7
Aged 35 to 64	100.0	89.2	4.4	1.9	1.1	0.5	0.9	6.4
Aged 65 or older	100.0	86.0	6.6	2.5	1.5	0.9	1.6	7.5
Renter-occupied	**100.0**	**33.5**	**61.8**	**18.7**	**22.8**	**8.6**	**11.6**	**4.7**
Under age 35	100.0	30.3	65.3	19.6	27.4	9.2	9.1	4.4
Aged 35 to 64	100.0	38.3	56.5	19.0	21.1	7.4	8.9	5.2
Aged 65 or older	100.0	24.8	71.6	15.3	16.6	11.5	28.2	3.6

Source: Bureau of the Census, 2010 American Community Survey, Internet site http://factfinder2.census.gov/faces/nav/jsf/pages/index.xhtml; calculations by New Strategist

Mobility Rates Are Low in Middle Age

The largest share of the middle aged move for housing-related reasons.

Twelve percent of Americans aged 1 or older moved between March 2010 and March 2011, but the proportion was a smaller 7 percent among people aged 45 to 64. Within the age group, the mobility rate falls from 8.5 percent among 45-to-49-year-olds to just 4 percent among 62-to-64-year-olds. Most movers stay within the same county. Only 14 percent of people who moved between 2010 and 2011 went to a different state.

Regardless of age, housing is the primary motivation for moving. The 47 percent plurality of movers aged 45 to 64 say housing was the main reason for the move. Family reasons ranked second as a motivation for moving, and employment ranks third. Among those who moved between 2010 and 2011 because of retirement, 40 percent were aged 45 to 64.

■ Mobility has been declining in the United States for decades, and the Great Recession lowered mobility rates even further.

Few of the middle aged move

(percent of people who moved between March 2010 and March 2011, by age)

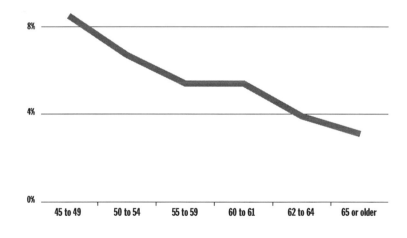

Table 4.7 Geographic Mobility by Age and Type of Move, 2010–11

(total number of people aged 1 or older, and number and percent who moved between March 2010 and March 2011, by age and type of move; numbers in thousands)

	total	total movers	same county	different county, same state	different state total	same region	different region	movers from abroad
Total, aged 1 or older	**302,005**	**35,075**	**23,325**	**5,912**	**4,779**	**2,323**	**2,456**	**1,058**
Under age 18	70,811	9,465	6,591	1,494	1,162	554	608	216
Aged 18 to 34	71,234	14,796	9,777	2,564	1,956	975	981	499
Aged 35 to 44	39,842	4,387	2,917	696	617	291	326	157
Aged 45 to 64	80,939	5,513	3,311	950	796	409	387	134
Aged 45 to 49	21,989	1,878	1,274	301	255	137	118	47
Aged 50 to 54	21,965	1,471	979	266	198	112	86	29
Aged 55 to 59	19,554	1,057	620	205	190	88	102	41
Aged 60 to 61	7,276	393	238	69	80	31	49	6
Aged 62 to 64	10,155	393	200	109	73	41	32	11
Aged 65 or older	39,178	1,233	729	209	246	92	154	51

PERCENT DISTRIBUTION BY MOBILITY STATUS

Total, aged 1 or older	**100.0%**	**11.6%**	**7.7%**	**2.0%**	**1.6%**	**0.8%**	**0.8%**	**0.4%**
Under age 18	100.0	13.4	9.3	2.1	1.6	0.8	0.9	0.3
Aged 18 to 34	100.0	20.8	13.7	3.6	2.7	1.4	1.4	0.7
Aged 35 to 44	100.0	11.0	7.3	1.7	1.5	0.7	0.8	0.4
Aged 45 to 64	100.0	6.8	4.1	1.2	1.0	0.5	0.5	0.2
Aged 45 to 49	100.0	8.5	5.8	1.4	1.2	0.6	0.5	0.2
Aged 50 to 54	100.0	6.7	4.5	1.2	0.9	0.5	0.4	0.1
Aged 55 to 59	100.0	5.4	3.2	1.0	1.0	0.5	0.5	0.2
Aged 60 to 61	100.0	5.4	3.3	0.9	1.1	0.4	0.7	0.1
Aged 62 to 64	100.0	3.9	2.0	1.1	0.7	0.4	0.3	0.1
Aged 65 or older	100.0	3.1	1.9	0.5	0.6	0.2	0.4	0.1

PERCENT DISTRIBUTION OF MOVERS BY TYPE OF MOVE

Total, aged 1 or older	–	**100.0%**	**66.5%**	**16.9%**	**13.6%**	**6.6%**	**7.0%**	**3.0%**
Under age 18	–	100.0	69.6	15.8	12.3	5.9	6.4	2.3
Aged 18 to 34	–	100.0	66.1	17.3	13.2	6.6	6.6	3.4
Aged 35 to 44	–	100.0	66.5	15.9	14.1	6.6	7.4	3.6
Aged 45 to 64	–	100.0	60.1	17.2	14.4	7.4	7.0	2.4
Aged 45 to 49	–	100.0	67.8	16.0	13.6	7.3	6.3	2.5
Aged 50 to 54	–	100.0	66.6	18.1	13.5	7.6	5.8	2.0
Aged 55 to 59	–	100.0	58.7	19.4	18.0	8.3	9.6	3.9
Aged 60 to 61	–	100.0	60.6	17.6	20.4	7.9	12.5	1.5
Aged 62 to 64	–	100.0	50.9	27.7	18.6	10.4	8.1	2.8
Aged 65 or older	–	100.0	59.1	17.0	20.0	7.5	12.5	4.1

Note: "–" means not applicable.
Source: Bureau of the Census, Geographic Mobility: 2010 to 2011, Detailed Tables, Internet site http://www.census.gov/hhes/ migration/data/cps/cps2011.html; calculations by New Strategist

Table 4.8 Reason for Moving among People Aged 45 to 64, 2010–11

(number and percent distribution of movers aged 45 to 64 by primary reason for move and share of total movers between March 2010 and March 2011; numbers in thousands)

	total movers	movers aged 45 to 64		
		number	percent distribution	share of total
Total movers	**35,075**	**5,192**	**100.0%**	**14.8%**
Family reasons	**9,784**	**1,375**	**26.5**	**14.1**
Change in marital status	1,949	322	6.2	16.5
To establish own household	3,334	322	6.2	9.7
Other familiy reasons	4,501	731	14.1	16.2
Employment reasons	**6,481**	**934**	**18.0**	**14.4**
New job or job transfer	2,829	372	7.2	13.1
To look for work or lost job	924	116	2.2	12.6
To be closer to work/easier commute	2,081	309	6.0	14.8
Retired	108	43	0.8	39.8
Other job-related reason	539	94	1.8	17.4
Housing reasons	**15,736**	**2,435**	**46.9**	**15.5**
Wanted own home, not rent	1,530	230	4.4	15.0
Wanted better home/apartment	5,665	817	15.7	14.4
Wanted better neighborhood/less crime	1,360	174	3.4	12.8
Wanted cheaper housing	3,684	604	11.6	16.4
Foreclosure/eviction	412	82	1.6	19.9
Other housing reasons	3,085	528	10.2	17.1
Other reasons	**3,073**	**450**	**8.7**	**14.6**
To attend or leave college	890	20	0.4	2.2
Change of climate	149	21	0.4	14.1
Health reasons	564	162	3.1	28.7
Natural disaster	31	9	0.2	29.0
Other reasons	1,439	238	4.6	16.5

Source: Bureau of the Census, Geographic Mobility: 2010 to 2011, Detailed Tables, Internet site http://www.census.gov/hhes/ migration/data/cps/cps2011.html; calculations by New Strategist

Income

■ Householders aged 45 to 54 saw their median income decline by a substantial 14 percent between 2000 and 2010, after adjusting for inflation. Among householders aged 55 to 64, median income was stable over the decade, but fell 6 percent between 2007 and 2010.

■ Between 2000 and 2010, the median income of men aged 45 to 54 fell by a substantial 13 percent, after adjusting for inflation. The median income of men aged 55 to 64 fell 5 percent.

■ The median income of women aged 45 to 54 fell 8 percent between 2000 and 2010 as the Great Recession led to widespread unemployment. In contrast, women aged 55 to 64 saw their median income rise by 19 percent during the decade.

■ A college degree has been well worth the cost for the Baby-Boom generation. The higher their educational level, the greater their earnings. Among men aged 55 to 64, those with professional degrees had median earnings of $150,317.

■ While 15.1 percent of all Americans were poor in 2010, the poverty rate among the Baby-Boom generation was a smaller 10.4 percent. Boomers account for only 18 percent of the nation's poor.

Median Income Is Declining for Households Headed by the Middle Aged

Householders aged 55 to 64 have made gains since 1990, however.

Between 2000 and 2010, median household income fell by a substantial 7 percent, after adjusting for inflation. Householders aged 45 to 54 saw an even larger decline in their median income. In fact, the 45-to-54 age group was one of the ones hurt the most by the Great Recession, suffering a 14 percent decline in median household income during the decade and a 9 percent decline since 2007.

In contrast, the median income of householders aged 55 to 64 was relatively stable between 2000 and 2010. Since 2007, however, their median has fallen by 6 percent, after adjusting for inflation.

Overall, median household income in 2010 was higher than in 1990—despite the Great Recession. But this is not the case for householders aged 45 to 54. In 2010, the median income of households headed by 45-to-54-year-olds was 8 percent below the median of their counterparts in 1990. Householders aged 55 to 64 saw their median income climb 8 percent during the two decades.

■ Twenty years ago, the median income of householders aged 45 to 54 exceeded the overall median by 40 percent. By 2010, the margin had fallen to 26 percent.

Households headed by Boomers lost ground during the past decade

(percent change in median income of households headed by people aged 45 to 64, by age, 2000–10; in 2010 dollars)

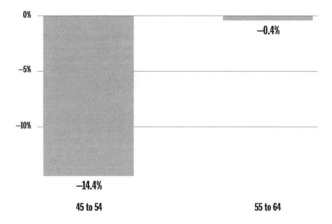

Table 5.1 Median Income of Households Headed by People Aged 45 to 64, 1990 to 2010

(median income of total households and households headed by people aged 45 to 64, and index of age group to total, 1990 to 2010; percent change for selected years; in 2010 dollars)

	total households	45 to 54	index, 45–54 to total	55 to 64	index, 55–64 to total
2010	$49,445	$62,485	126	$56,575	114
2009	50,599	65,295	129	57,914	114
2008	50,939	65,163	128	57,989	114
2007	52,823	68,852	130	60,345	114
2006	52,124	70,154	135	59,035	113
2005	51,739	69,718	135	58,366	113
2004	51,174	70,443	138	58,167	114
2003	51,353	71,416	139	58,344	114
2002	51,398	71,531	139	57,208	111
2001	52,005	71,485	137	56,483	109
2000	53,164	72,981	137	56,789	107
1999	53,252	74,457	140	58,445	110
1998	51,944	72,333	139	57,664	111
1997	50,123	70,264	140	56,016	112
1996	49,112	69,841	142	55,094	112
1995	48,408	68,271	141	54,092	112
1994	46,937	68,755	146	51,255	109
1993	46,419	68,657	148	49,737	107
1992	46,646	67,658	145	51,757	111
1991	47,032	68,304	145	51,994	111
1990	48,423	67,795	140	52,340	108
Percent change					
2007 to 2010	−6.4%	−9.2%	–	−6.2%	–
2000 to 2010	7.0	−14.4	–	−0.4	–
1990 to 2010	2.1	−7.8	–	8.1	–

Note: The index is calculated by dividing the median income of the age group by the national median and multiplying by 100. "–" means not applicable.
Source: Bureau of the Census, Historical Income Statistics—Households, Internet site http://www.census.gov/hhes/www/income/data/historical/household/; calculations by New Strategist

Household Income Peaks in Late Forties

Householders aged 45 to 49 have the highest incomes.

Household income peaks in middle age because many middle-aged householders are dual-income married couples at the height of their careers. Median household income tops out at $63,233 among householders aged 45 to 49, well above the $49,445 national median.

Among the nation's most affluent households—those with incomes of $100,000 or more in 2010—the 45-to-64 age group accounts for the 51 percent majority. (Boomers were aged 46 to 64 in that year.) At least 28 percent of households headed by people ranging in age from 45 to 59 have incomes of $100,000 or more.

■ Although the middle aged continue to be the nation's most affluent householders, their incomes have fallen sharply because of the Great Recession.

The middle aged have the highest incomes

(median income of households by age of householder, 2010)

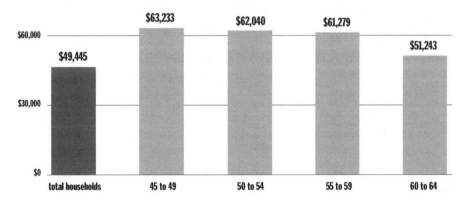

Table 5.2 Income of Households Headed by People Aged 45 to 64, 2010: Total Households

(number and percent distribution of total households and households headed by people aged 45 to 64, by income, 2010; households in thousands as of 2011)

| | | aged 45 to 64 | | | |
	total	total	45 to 49	50 to 54	55 to 59	60 to 64
Total households	**118,682**	**46,358**	**12,220**	**12,310**	**11,445**	**10,383**
Under $10,000	9,231	3,374	855	838	882	799
$10,000 to $19,999	14,321	4,133	891	1,046	1,031	1,165
$20,000 to $29,999	13,667	4,115	1,074	1,061	916	1,064
$30,000 to $39,999	12,055	4,035	1,017	1,027	971	1,020
$40,000 to $49,999	10,557	3,804	981	933	875	1,015
$50,000 to $59,999	9,291	3,635	931	1,007	899	798
$60,000 to $69,999	7,991	3,174	879	857	769	669
$70,000 to $79,999	6,887	3,006	828	802	728	648
$80,000 to $89,999	5,823	2,527	692	701	606	528
$90,000 to $99,999	4,626	2,085	587	590	518	390
$100,000 or more	24,234	12,464	3,483	3,448	3,247	2,286
$100,000 to $124,999	9,008	4,247	1,209	1,210	1,018	810
$125,000 to $149,999	5,294	2,661	691	758	718	494
$150,000 to $174,999	3,386	1,918	592	481	523	322
$175,000 to $199,999	1,919	1,018	261	259	314	184
$200,000 or more	4,627	2,620	730	740	674	476
Median income	$49,445	$60,261	$63,233	$62,040	$61,279	$51,243
Total households	**100.0%**	**100.0%**	**100.0%**	**100.0%**	**100.0%**	**100.0%**
Under $10,000	7.8	7.3	7.0	6.8	7.7	7.7
$10,000 to $19,999	12.1	8.9	7.3	8.5	9.0	11.2
$20,000 to $29,999	11.5	8.9	8.8	8.6	8.0	10.2
$30,000 to $39,999	10.2	8.7	8.3	8.3	8.5	9.8
$40,000 to $49,999	8.9	8.2	8.0	7.6	7.6	9.8
$50,000 to $59,999	7.8	7.8	7.6	8.2	7.9	7.7
$60,000 to $69,999	6.7	6.8	7.2	7.0	6.7	6.4
$70,000 to $79,999	5.8	6.5	6.8	6.5	6.4	6.2
$80,000 to $89,999	4.9	5.5	5.7	5.7	5.3	5.1
$90,000 to $99,999	3.9	4.5	4.8	4.8	4.5	3.8
$100,000 or more	20.4	26.9	28.5	28.0	28.4	22.0
$100,000 to $124,999	7.6	9.2	9.9	9.8	8.9	7.8
$125,000 to $149,999	4.5	5.7	5.7	6.2	6.3	4.8
$150,000 to $174,999	2.9	4.1	4.8	3.9	4.6	3.1
$175,000 to $199,999	1.6	2.2	2.1	2.1	2.7	1.8
$200,000 or more	3.9	5.7	6.0	6.0	5.9	4.6

Source: Bureau of the Census, 2011 Current Population Survey, Internet site http://www.census.gov/hhes/www/ cpstables/032011/hhinc/toc.htm; calculations by New Strategist

Among Boomers, Asians and Non-Hispanic Whites Have the Highest Incomes

Blacks and Hispanics have lower household incomes.

Although the Baby-Boom generation in every race and Hispanic origin group has been hurt by the Great Recession, income patterns remain the same. Asian and non-Hispanic whites have the highest household incomes, while blacks and Hispanics have lower household incomes. The median income of households headed by Asians in the 45-to-64 age group was close to $75,000 in 2010, while that of non-Hispanic whites in the age group was just over $67,000. In contrast, the median household income of their black counterparts was less than $37,000, and the Hispanic median was about $44,000.

More than 30 percent of Asian and non-Hispanic white householders in the 45-to-64 age group have a household income of $100,000 or more. Among Asians, a lofty 36 percent have incomes that high. The figure is a smaller but still substantial 31 percent among non-Hispanic whites. In contrast, only 12 percent of black householders aged 45 to 64 have incomes of $100,000 or more. The figure is 16 percent for Hispanics.

■ Black household incomes are below those of Asians and non-Hispanic whites because married couples—the most affluent household type—make up a much smaller share of black households. For Hispanics, incomes are lower because they are much less educated and, consequently, have little earning power.

Median household income varies by race and Hispanic origin

(median income of households headed by people aged 45 to 64, by race and Hispanic origin, 2010)

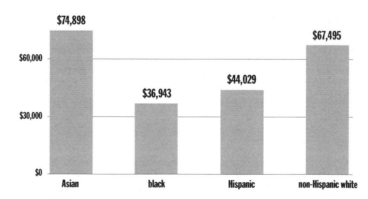

Table 5.3 Income of Households Headed by People Aged 45 to 64, 2010: Asian Households

(number and percent distribution of total Asian households and Asian households headed by people aged 45 to 64, by income, 2010; households in thousands as of 2011)

	total	aged 45 to 64				
		total	45 to 49	50 to 54	55 to 59	60 to 64
Total Asian households	**5,040**	**1,814**	**581**	**470**	**410**	**353**
Under $10,000	353	90	23	23	22	22
$10,000 to $19,999	406	110	34	25	21	30
$20,000 to $29,999	460	148	42	34	36	36
$30,000 to $39,999	358	123	31	33	27	32
$40,000 to $49,999	382	118	35	34	28	21
$50,000 to $59,999	376	127	51	32	22	22
$60,000 to $69,999	387	143	50	32	40	21
$70,000 to $79,999	265	98	31	31	22	14
$80,000 to $89,999	243	100	28	28	21	23
$90,000 to $99,999	213	96	21	33	16	26
$100,000 or more	1,594	659	235	163	156	105
$100,000 to $124,999	508	194	67	51	53	23
$125,000 to $149,999	335	151	45	40	32	34
$150,000 to $174,999	258	115	44	25	26	20
$175,000 to $199,999	135	39	11	10	14	4
$200,000 or more	358	160	68	37	31	24
Median income	$63,726	$74,898	$78,166	$76,084	$75,008	$66,010
Total Asian households	**100.0%**	**100.0%**	**100.0%**	**100.0%**	**100.0%**	**100.0%**
Under $10,000	7.0	5.0	4.0	4.9	5.4	6.2
$10,000 to $19,999	8.1	6.1	5.9	5.3	5.1	8.5
$20,000 to $29,999	9.1	8.2	7.2	7.2	8.8	10.2
$30,000 to $39,999	7.1	6.8	5.3	7.0	6.6	9.1
$40,000 to $49,999	7.6	6.5	6.0	7.2	6.8	5.9
$50,000 to $59,999	7.5	7.0	8.8	6.8	5.4	6.2
$60,000 to $69,999	7.7	7.9	8.6	6.8	9.8	5.9
$70,000 to $79,999	5.3	5.4	5.3	6.6	5.4	4.0
$80,000 to $89,999	4.8	5.5	4.8	6.0	5.1	6.5
$90,000 to $99,999	4.2	5.3	3.6	7.0	3.9	7.4
$100,000 or more	31.6	36.3	40.4	34.7	38.0	29.7
$100,000 to $124,999	10.1	10.7	11.5	10.9	12.9	6.5
$125,000 to $149,999	6.6	8.3	7.7	8.5	7.8	9.6
$150,000 to $174,999	5.1	6.3	7.6	5.3	6.3	5.7
$175,000 to $199,999	2.7	2.1	1.9	2.1	3.4	1.1
$200,000 or more	7.1	8.8	11.7	7.9	7.6	6.8

Note: Asians are those who identify themselves as being of the race alone and those who identify themselves as being of the race in combination with other races.
Source: Bureau of the Census, 2011 Current Population Survey, Internet site http://www.census.gov/hhes/www/ cpstables/032011/hhinc/toc.htm; calculations by New Strategist

Table 5.4 Income of Households Headed by People Aged 45 to 64, 2010: Black Households

(number and percent distribution of total black households and black households headed by people aged 45 to 64, by income, 2010; households in thousands as of 2011)

	total	aged 45 to 64				
		total	45 to 49	50 to 54	55 to 59	60 to 64
Total black households	**15,613**	**5,993**	**1,650**	**1,661**	**1,429**	**1,253**
Under $10,000	2,564	926	237	233	250	206
$10,000 to $19,999	2,573	857	199	234	204	220
$20,000 to $29,999	2,208	762	215	214	155	178
$30,000 to $39,999	1,770	651	191	170	162	128
$40,000 to $49,999	1,454	548	134	168	137	109
$50,000 to $59,999	1,063	440	138	129	77	96
$60,000 to $69,999	836	349	112	93	82	62
$70,000 to $79,999	777	323	87	84	88	64
$80,000 to $89,999	507	224	66	72	43	43
$90,000 to $99,999	354	166	44	58	41	23
$100,000 or more	1,509	747	227	204	190	126
$100,000 to $124,999	675	306	94	74	82	56
$125,000 to $149,999	345	168	42	56	44	26
$150,000 to $174,999	213	128	46	39	27	16
$175,000 to $199,999	84	44	11	7	18	8
$200,000 or more	192	101	34	28	19	20
Median income	$32,106	$36,943	$38,950	$38,365	$36,147	$31,329
Total black households	**100.0%**	**100.0%**	**100.0%**	**100.0%**	**100.0%**	**100.0%**
Under $10,000	16.4	15.5	14.4	14.0	17.5	16.4
$10,000 to $19,999	16.5	14.3	12.1	14.1	14.3	17.6
$20,000 to $29,999	14.1	12.7	13.0	12.9	10.8	14.2
$30,000 to $39,999	11.3	10.9	11.6	10.2	11.3	10.2
$40,000 to $49,999	9.3	9.1	8.1	10.1	9.6	8.7
$50,000 to $59,999	6.8	7.3	8.4	7.8	5.4	7.7
$60,000 to $69,999	5.4	5.8	6.8	5.6	5.7	4.9
$70,000 to $79,999	5.0	5.4	5.3	5.1	6.2	5.1
$80,000 to $89,999	3.2	3.7	4.0	4.3	3.0	3.4
$90,000 to $99,999	2.3	2.8	2.7	3.5	2.9	1.8
$100,000 or more	9.7	12.5	13.8	12.3	13.3	10.1
$100,000 to $124,999	4.3	5.1	5.7	4.5	5.7	4.5
$125,000 to $149,999	2.2	2.8	2.5	3.4	3.1	2.1
$150,000 to $174,999	1.4	2.1	2.8	2.3	1.9	1.3
$175,000 to $199,999	0.5	0.7	0.7	0.4	1.3	0.6
$200,000 or more	1.2	1.7	2.1	1.7	1.3	1.6

Note: Blacks are those who identify themselves as being of the race alone and those who identify themselves as being of the race in combination with other races.
Source: Bureau of the Census, 2011 Current Population Survey, Internet site http://www.census.gov/hhes/www/ cpstables/032011/hhinc/toc.htm; calculations by New Strategist

Table 5.5 Income of Households Headed by People Aged 45 to 64, 2010: Hispanic Households

(number and percent distribution of total Hispanic households and Hispanic households headed by people aged 45 to 64, by income, 2010; households in thousands as of 2011)

	total	aged 45 to 64				
		total	45 to 49	50 to 54	55 to 59	60 to 64
Total Hispanic households	**13,665**	**4,458**	**1,484**	**1,245**	**925**	**804**
Under $10,000	1,363	386	110	95	72	109
$10,000 to $19,999	1,967	556	171	162	118	105
$20,000 to $29,999	2,100	592	209	155	122	106
$30,000 to $39,999	1,678	529	180	152	114	83
$40,000 to $49,999	1,329	412	152	88	80	92
$50,000 to $59,999	1,132	406	124	136	82	64
$60,000 to $69,999	895	292	94	79	71	48
$70,000 to $79,999	679	235	83	69	45	38
$80,000 to $89,999	564	194	75	52	37	30
$90,000 to $99,999	391	161	58	43	40	20
$100,000 or more	1,563	694	226	214	143	111
$100,000 to $124,999	665	269	84	88	49	48
$125,000 to $149,999	390	168	64	48	28	28
$150,000 to $174,999	211	102	37	23	28	14
$175,000 to $199,999	97	49	14	19	9	7
$200,000 or more	200	106	27	36	29	14
Median income	$37,759	$44,029	$45,136	$46,979	$43,964	$39,827
Total Hispanic households	**100.0%**	**100.0%**	**100.0%**	**100.0%**	**100.0%**	**100.0%**
Under $10,000	10.0	8.7	7.4	7.6	7.8	13.6
$10,000 to $19,999	14.4	12.5	11.5	13.0	12.8	13.1
$20,000 to $29,999	15.4	13.3	14.1	12.4	13.2	13.2
$30,000 to $39,999	12.3	11.9	12.1	12.2	12.3	10.3
$40,000 to $49,999	9.7	9.2	10.2	7.1	8.6	11.4
$50,000 to $59,999	8.3	9.1	8.4	10.9	8.9	8.0
$60,000 to $69,999	6.5	6.6	6.3	6.3	7.7	6.0
$70,000 to $79,999	5.0	5.3	5.6	5.5	4.9	4.7
$80,000 to $89,999	4.1	4.4	5.1	4.2	4.0	3.7
$90,000 to $99,999	2.9	3.6	3.9	3.5	4.3	2.5
$100,000 or more	11.4	15.6	15.2	17.2	15.5	13.8
$100,000 to $124,999	4.9	6.0	5.7	7.1	5.3	6.0
$125,000 to $149,999	2.9	3.8	4.3	3.9	3.0	3.5
$150,000 to $174,999	1.5	2.3	2.5	1.8	3.0	1.7
$175,000 to $199,999	0.7	1.1	0.9	1.5	1.0	0.9
$200,000 or more	1.5	2.4	1.8	2.9	3.1	1.7

Source: Bureau of the Census, 2011 Current Population Survey, Internet site http://www.census.gov/hhes/www/cpstables/032011/hhinc/toc.htm; calculations by New Strategist

Table 5.6 Income of Households Headed by People Aged 45 to 64, 2010: Non-Hispanic White Households

(number and percent distribution of total non-Hispanic white households and non-Hispanic white households headed by people aged 45 to 64, by income, 2010; households in thousands as of 2011)

		aged 45 to 64				
	total	total	45 to 49	50 to 54	55 to 59	60 to 64
Total non-Hispanic white households	**83,471**	**33,674**	**8,394**	**8,842**	**8,553**	**7,885**
Under $10,000	4,859	1,935	484	470	528	453
$10,000 to $19,999	9,247	2,544	469	620	665	790
$20,000 to $29,999	8,796	2,579	603	643	587	746
$30,000 to $39,999	8,157	2,696	601	672	651	772
$40,000 to $49,999	7,312	2,682	651	640	619	772
$50,000 to $59,999	6,650	2,630	609	701	712	608
$60,000 to $69,999	5,813	2,363	614	645	565	539
$70,000 to $79,999	5,116	2,326	620	611	570	525
$80,000 to $89,999	4,455	1,974	510	542	498	424
$90,000 to $99,999	3,641	1,646	457	451	420	318
$100,000 or more	19,425	10,297	2,774	2,849	2,739	1,935
$100,000 to $124,999	7,093	3,453	952	988	828	685
$125,000 to $149,999	4,187	2,146	533	611	600	402
$150,000 to $174,999	2,686	1,569	464	392	443	270
$175,000 to $199,999	1,596	884	226	221	273	164
$200,000 or more	3,863	2,245	599	637	595	414
Median income	$54,620	$67,495	$72,327	$70,391	$68,848	$56,352
Total non-Hispanic white households	**100.0%**	**100.0%**	**100.0%**	**100.0%**	**100.0%**	**100.0%**
Under $10,000	5.8	5.7	5.8	5.3	6.2	5.7
$10,000 to $19,999	11.1	7.6	5.6	7.0	7.8	10.0
$20,000 to $29,999	10.5	7.7	7.2	7.3	6.9	9.5
$30,000 to $39,999	9.8	8.0	7.2	7.6	7.6	9.8
$40,000 to $49,999	8.8	8.0	7.8	7.2	7.2	9.8
$50,000 to $59,999	8.0	7.8	7.3	7.9	8.3	7.7
$60,000 to $69,999	7.0	7.0	7.3	7.3	6.6	6.8
$70,000 to $79,999	6.1	6.9	7.4	6.9	6.7	6.7
$80,000 to $89,999	5.3	5.9	6.1	6.1	5.8	5.4
$90,000 to $99,999	4.4	4.9	5.4	5.1	4.9	4.0
$100,000 or more	23.3	30.6	33.0	32.2	32.0	24.5
$100,000 to $124,999	8.5	10.3	11.3	11.2	9.7	8.7
$125,000 to $149,999	5.0	6.4	6.3	6.9	7.0	5.1
$150,000 to $174,999	3.2	4.7	5.5	4.4	5.2	3.4
$175,000 to $199,999	1.9	2.6	2.7	2.5	3.2	2.1
$200,000 or more	4.6	6.7	7.1	7.2	7.0	5.3

Note: Non-Hispanic whites are those who identify themselves as being white alone and not Hispanic.
Source: Bureau of the Census, 2011 Current Population Survey, Internet site http://www.census.gov/hhes/www/cpstables/032011/hhinc/toc.htm; calculations by New Strategist

Married Couples Have the Highest Incomes

No other household type comes close to the affluence of married couples.

Among households headed by people aged 45 to 64 (Boomers were aged 46 to 64 in 2010), the median household income of married couples is far above the median of other household types. Married-couples aged 45 to 54 had a median income of $88,442 in 2010. Fully 42 percent had an income of $100,000 or more. Among Boomer households, women aged 60 to 64 who live alone have the lowest incomes, a median of just $25,950.

Dual earners explain the higher incomes of married couples. The more earners in a household, the higher the income. Female-headed families have low incomes because they typically have only one earner in the home. Similarly, men and women who live alone also have relatively low incomes because there is at best one earner in the household.

■ Thirty-eight percent of married couples aged 55 to 64 have incomes of $100,000 or more.

Incomes peak among married couples aged 45 to 54

(median income of married couples aged 45 to 64 by age of householder, 2010)

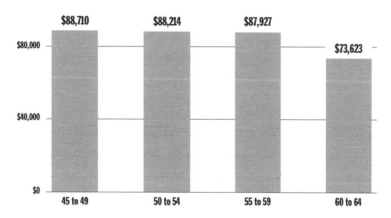

Table 5.7 Income of Households by Household Type, 2010: Aged 45 to 54

(number and percent distribution of households headed by people aged 45 to 54, by income and household type, 2010; households in thousands as of 2011)

| | | family households | | | nonfamily households | | | |
| | | | female householder, no spouse present | male householder, no spouse present | female householder | | male householder | |
	total	married couples			total	living alone	total	living alone
Total households headed by 45-to-54-year-olds	**24,530**	**13,506**	**3,134**	**1,150**	**3,079**	**2,538**	**3,661**	**3,034**
Under $10,000	1,693	250	380	67	514	487	483	457
$10,000 to $19,999	1,937	454	404	101	454	396	524	473
$20,000 to $29,999	2,135	648	440	135	465	398	446	397
$30,000 to $39,999	2,044	791	399	120	347	295	386	329
$40,000 to $49,999	1,914	825	277	130	332	295	349	299
$50,000 to $59,999	1,937	938	284	120	246	190	350	275
$60,000 to $69,999	1,736	997	226	108	161	121	246	205
$70,000 to $79,999	1,630	1,037	176	67	133	99	216	164
$80,000 to $89,999	1,392	960	124	81	88	68	141	106
$90,000 to $99,999	1,177	877	101	43	63	45	95	66
$100,000 or more	6,933	5,729	323	176	277	142	423	265
$100,000 to $124,999	2,420	1,895	148	81	137	84	156	104
$125,000 to $149,999	1,449	1,248	48	37	47	17	68	42
$150,000 to $174,999	1,073	900	42	22	38	17	70	30
$175,000 to $199,999	522	459	17	13	9	0	23	16
$200,000 or more	1,469	1,227	68	23	46	24	106	73
Median income	$62,485	$88,442	$38,563	$51,091	$32,135	$29,592	$39,606	$34,978
Total households headed by 45-to-54-year-olds	**100.0%**	**100.0%**	**100.0%**	**100.0%**	**100.0%**	**100.0%**	**100.0%**	**100.0%**
Under $10,000	6.9	1.9	12.1	5.8	16.7	19.2	13.2	15.1
$10,000 to $19,999	7.9	3.4	12.9	8.8	14.7	15.6	14.3	15.6
$20,000 to $29,999	8.7	4.8	14.0	11.7	15.1	15.7	12.2	13.1
$30,000 to $39,999	8.3	5.9	12.7	10.4	11.3	11.6	10.5	10.8
$40,000 to $49,999	7.8	6.1	8.8	11.3	10.8	11.6	9.5	9.9
$50,000 to $59,999	7.9	6.9	9.1	10.4	8.0	7.5	9.6	9.1
$60,000 to $69,999	7.1	7.4	7.2	9.4	5.2	4.8	6.7	6.8
$70,000 to $79,999	6.6	7.7	5.6	5.8	4.3	3.9	5.9	5.4
$80,000 to $89,999	5.7	7.1	4.0	7.0	2.9	2.7	3.9	3.5
$90,000 to $99,999	4.8	6.5	3.2	3.7	2.0	1.8	2.6	2.2
$100,000 or more	28.3	42.4	10.3	15.3	9.0	5.6	11.6	8.7
$100,000 to $124,999	9.9	14.0	4.7	7.0	4.4	3.3	4.3	3.4
$125,000 to $149,999	5.9	9.2	1.5	3.2	1.5	0.7	1.9	1.4
$150,000 to $174,999	4.4	6.7	1.3	1.9	1.2	0.7	1.9	1.0
$175,000 to $199,999	2.1	3.4	0.5	1.1	0.3	0.0	0.6	0.5
$200,000 or more	6.0	9.1	2.2	2.0	1.5	0.9	2.9	2.4

Source: Bureau of the Census, 2011 Current Population Survey, Internet site http://www.census.gov/hhes/www/cpstables/032011/hhinc/toc.htm; calculations by New Strategist

Table 5.8 Income of Households by Household Type, 2010: Aged 45 to 49

(number and percent distribution of households headed by people aged 45 to 49, by income and household type, 2010; households in thousands as of 2011)

| | | family households | | | nonfamily households | | | |
| | | | female householder, no spouse present | male householder, no spouse present | female householder | | male householder | |
	total	married couples			total	living alone	total	living alone
Total households headed by 45-to-49-year-olds	12,220	6,721	1,741	585	1,320	1,072	1,853	1,524
Under $10,000	855	124	231	35	222	212	243	231
$10,000 to $19,999	891	212	224	51	175	153	229	200
$20,000 to $29,999	1,074	330	235	80	201	176	228	196
$30,000 to $39,999	1,017	394	258	50	155	129	161	144
$40,000 to $49,999	981	396	140	76	150	130	218	189
$50,000 to $59,999	931	438	134	68	104	77	187	150
$60,000 to $69,999	879	490	124	40	84	64	142	115
$70,000 to $79,999	828	536	97	32	60	41	103	68
$80,000 to $89,999	692	498	60	40	28	20	68	58
$90,000 to $99,999	587	438	61	16	28	21	46	31
$100,000 or more	3,483	2,870	177	96	112	49	230	142
$100,000 to $124,999	1,209	968	80	42	47	28	74	49
$125,000 to $149,999	691	578	24	25	27	9	37	19
$150,000 to $174,999	592	488	29	11	22	8	42	21
$175,000 to $199,999	261	234	6	8	3	0	11	8
$200,000 or more	730	602	38	10	13	4	66	45
Median income	$63,233	$88,710	$37,017	$49,950	$32,133	$29,567	$41,789	$38,694
Total households headed by 45-to-49-year-olds	100.0%	100.0%	100.0%	100.0%	100.0%	100.0%	100.0%	100.0%
Under $10,000	7.0	1.8	13.3	6.0	16.8	19.8	13.1	15.2
$10,000 to $19,999	7.3	3.2	12.9	8.7	13.3	14.3	12.4	13.1
$20,000 to $29,999	8.8	4.9	13.5	13.7	15.2	16.4	12.3	12.9
$30,000 to $39,999	8.3	5.9	14.8	8.5	11.7	12.0	8.7	9.4
$40,000 to $49,999	8.0	5.9	8.0	13.0	11.4	12.1	11.8	12.4
$50,000 to $59,999	7.6	6.5	7.7	11.6	7.9	7.2	10.1	9.8
$60,000 to $69,999	7.2	7.3	7.1	6.8	6.4	6.0	7.7	7.5
$70,000 to $79,999	6.8	8.0	5.6	5.5	4.5	3.8	5.6	4.5
$80,000 to $89,999	5.7	7.4	3.4	6.8	2.1	1.9	3.7	3.8
$90,000 to $99,999	4.8	6.5	3.5	2.7	2.1	2.0	2.5	2.0
$100,000 or more	28.5	42.7	10.2	16.4	8.5	4.6	12.4	9.3
$100,000 to $124,999	9.9	14.4	4.6	7.2	3.6	2.6	4.0	3.2
$125,000 to $149,999	5.7	8.6	1.4	4.3	2.0	0.8	2.0	1.2
$150,000 to $174,999	4.8	7.3	1.7	1.9	1.7	0.7	2.3	1.4
$175,000 to $199,999	2.1	3.5	0.3	1.4	0.2	0.0	0.6	0.5
$200,000 or more	6.0	9.0	2.2	1.7	1.0	0.4	3.6	3.0

Source: Bureau of the Census, 2011 Current Population Survey, Internet site http://www.census.gov/hhes/www/cpstables/032011/hhinc/toc.htm; calculations by New Strategist

Table 5.9 Income of Households by Household Type, 2010: Aged 50 to 54

(number and percent distribution of households headed by people aged 50 to 54, by income and household type, 2010; households in thousands as of 2011)

| | | family households | | | nonfamily households | | | |
| | | | female householder, no spouse present | male householder, no spouse present | female householder | | male householder | |
	total	married couples			total	living alone	total	living alone
Total households headed by 50-to-54-year-olds	**12,310**	**6,785**	**1,393**	**565**	**1,759**	**1,466**	**1,807**	**1,510**
Under $10,000	838	126	149	33	291	275	240	226
$10,000 to $19,999	1,046	242	179	51	277	242	295	274
$20,000 to $29,999	1,061	318	205	54	265	223	219	201
$30,000 to $39,999	1,027	398	142	71	191	166	226	184
$40,000 to $49,999	933	429	137	53	182	166	131	110
$50,000 to $59,999	1,007	501	149	52	142	113	164	125
$60,000 to $69,999	857	507	101	68	77	58	104	89
$70,000 to $79,999	802	502	79	36	73	59	113	97
$80,000 to $89,999	701	461	64	41	61	48	74	48
$90,000 to $99,999	590	440	40	27	34	24	49	35
$100,000 or more	3,448	2,862	149	79	164	92	193	120
$100,000 to $124,999	1,210	928	71	38	90	56	82	53
$125,000 to $149,999	758	670	23	12	21	7	33	21
$150,000 to $174,999	481	414	14	11	16	9	27	10
$175,000 to $199,999	259	225	11	5	5	0	12	8
$200,000 or more	740	625	30	13	32	20	39	28
Median income	$62,040	$88,214	$41,253	$53,234	$32,137	$29,611	$35,929	$31,840
Total households headed by 50-to-54-year-olds	**100.0%**	**100.0%**	**100.0%**	**100.0%**	**100.0%**	**100.0%**	**100.0%**	**100.0%**
Under $10,000	6.8	1.9	10.7	5.8	16.5	18.8	13.3	15.0
$10,000 to $19,999	8.5	3.6	12.8	9.0	15.7	16.5	16.3	18.1
$20,000 to $29,999	8.6	4.7	14.7	9.6	15.1	15.2	12.1	13.3
$30,000 to $39,999	8.3	5.9	10.2	12.6	10.9	11.3	12.5	12.2
$40,000 to $49,999	7.6	6.3	9.8	9.4	10.3	11.3	7.2	7.3
$50,000 to $59,999	8.2	7.4	10.7	9.2	8.1	7.7	9.1	8.3
$60,000 to $69,999	7.0	7.5	7.3	12.0	4.4	4.0	5.8	5.9
$70,000 to $79,999	6.5	7.4	5.7	6.4	4.2	4.0	6.3	6.4
$80,000 to $89,999	5.7	6.8	4.6	7.3	3.5	3.3	4.1	3.2
$90,000 to $99,999	4.8	6.5	2.9	4.8	1.9	1.6	2.7	2.3
$100,000 or more	28.0	42.2	10.7	14.0	9.3	6.3	10.7	7.9
$100,000 to $124,999	9.8	13.7	5.1	6.7	5.1	3.8	4.5	3.5
$125,000 to $149,999	6.2	9.9	1.7	2.1	1.2	0.5	1.8	1.4
$150,000 to $174,999	3.9	6.1	1.0	1.9	0.9	0.6	1.5	0.7
$175,000 to $199,999	2.1	3.3	0.8	0.9	0.3	0.0	0.7	0.5
$200,000 or more	6.0	9.2	2.2	2.3	1.8	1.4	2.2	1.9

Source: Bureau of the Census, 2011 Current Population Survey, Internet site http://www.census.gov/hhes/www/cpstables/032011/hhinc/toc.htm; calculations by New Strategist

Table 5.10 Income of Households by Household Type, 2010: Aged 55 to 64

(number and percent distribution of households headed by people aged 55 to 64, by income and household type, 2010; households in thousands as of 2011)

| | | family households | | | nonfamily households | | | |
| | | | female householder, no spouse present | male householder, no spouse present | female householder | | male householder | |
	total	married couples			total	living alone	total	living alone
Total households headed by 55-to-64-year-olds	**21,828**	**11,851**	**1,745**	**672**	**4,035**	**3,613**	**3,524**	**3,081**
Under $10,000	1,681	241	157	24	694	675	563	541
$10,000 to $19,999	2,196	458	234	55	837	794	613	567
$20,000 to $29,999	1,980	640	248	79	534	499	479	421
$30,000 to $39,999	1,991	828	234	74	473	417	382	344
$40,000 to $49,999	1,890	949	201	71	371	325	298	253
$50,000 to $59,999	1,697	941	146	78	279	244	253	227
$60,000 to $69,999	1,439	898	112	54	219	190	156	129
$70,000 to $79,999	1,378	906	102	65	178	159	126	107
$80,000 to $89,999	1,134	822	73	45	92	61	103	82
$90,000 to $99,999	908	651	75	30	67	48	86	62
$100,000 or more	5,535	4,518	162	97	290	198	465	347
$100,000 to $124,999	1,828	1,396	91	40	127	95	174	148
$125,000 to $149,999	1,211	995	32	14	65	48	105	71
$150,000 to $174,999	847	697	13	24	45	24	69	46
$175,000 to $199,999	499	412	13	3	17	7	51	30
$200,000 or more	1,150	1,018	13	16	36	24	66	52
Median income	$56,575	$80,570	$39,989	$53,323	$29,157	$26,980	$32,199	$30,269
Total households headed by 55-to-64-year-olds	**100.0%**	**100.0%**	**100.0%**	**100.0%**	**100.0%**	**100.0%**	**100.0%**	**100.0%**
Under $10,000	7.7	2.0	9.0	3.6	17.2	18.7	16.0	17.6
$10,000 to $19,999	10.1	3.9	13.4	8.2	20.7	22.0	17.4	18.4
$20,000 to $29,999	9.1	5.4	14.2	11.8	13.2	13.8	13.6	13.7
$30,000 to $39,999	9.1	7.0	13.4	11.0	11.7	11.5	10.8	11.2
$40,000 to $49,999	8.7	8.0	11.5	10.6	9.2	9.0	8.5	8.2
$50,000 to $59,999	7.8	7.9	8.4	11.6	6.9	6.8	7.2	7.4
$60,000 to $69,999	6.6	7.6	6.4	8.0	5.4	5.3	4.4	4.2
$70,000 to $79,999	6.3	7.6	5.8	9.7	4.4	4.4	3.6	3.5
$80,000 to $89,999	5.2	6.9	4.2	6.7	2.3	1.7	2.9	2.7
$90,000 to $99,999	4.2	5.5	4.3	4.5	1.7	1.3	2.4	2.0
$100,000 or more	25.4	38.1	9.3	14.4	7.2	5.5	13.2	11.3
$100,000 to $124,999	8.4	11.8	5.2	6.0	3.1	2.6	4.9	4.8
$125,000 to $149,999	5.5	8.4	1.8	2.1	1.6	1.3	3.0	2.3
$150,000 to $174,999	3.9	5.9	0.7	3.6	1.1	0.7	2.0	1.5
$175,000 to $199,999	2.3	3.5	0.7	0.4	0.4	0.2	1.4	1.0
$200,000 or more	5.3	8.6	0.7	2.4	0.9	0.7	1.9	1.7

Source: Bureau of the Census, 2011 Current Population Survey, Internet site http://www.census.gov/hhes/www/ cpstables/032011/hhinc/toc.htm; calculations by New Strategist

Table 5.11 Income of Households by Household Type, 2010: Aged 55 to 59

(number and percent distribution of households headed by people aged 55 to 59, by income and household type, 2010; households in thousands as of 2011)

| | | family households | | | nonfamily households | | | |
| | | | female householder, no spouse present | male householder, no spouse present | female householder | | male householder | |
	total	married couples			total	living alone	total	living alone
Total households headed by 55-to-59-year-olds	**11,445**	**6,228**	**972**	**373**	**1,911**	**1,680**	**1,961**	**1,678**
Under $10,000	882	112	72	9	352	338	336	323
$10,000 to $19,999	1,031	184	143	24	348	327	331	300
$20,000 to $29,999	916	274	138	42	213	204	250	210
$30,000 to $39,999	971	398	126	33	198	175	216	195
$40,000 to $49,999	875	399	107	36	195	164	138	114
$50,000 to $59,999	899	490	83	53	148	126	127	117
$60,000 to $69,999	769	465	66	28	119	103	91	76
$70,000 to $79,999	728	457	65	43	89	80	76	61
$80,000 to $89,999	606	415	34	34	48	32	75	62
$90,000 to $99,999	518	381	38	21	31	25	47	29
$100,000 or more	3,247	2,655	101	49	166	108	277	192
$100,000 to $124,999	1,018	760	59	17	76	55	105	82
$125,000 to $149,999	718	606	22	8	26	21	56	32
$150,000 to $174,999	523	438	7	9	26	8	45	30
$175,000 to $199,999	314	259	9	3	14	5	29	15
$200,000 or more	674	592	4	12	24	19	42	33
Median income	$61,279	$87,927	$40,428	$56,652	$32,122	$28,486	$32,203	$30,209
Total households headed by 55-to-59-year-olds	**100.0%**	**100.0%**	**100.0%**	**100.0%**	**100.0%**	**100.0%**	**100.0%**	**100.0%**
Under $10,000	7.7	1.8	7.4	2.4	18.4	20.1	17.1	19.2
$10,000 to $19,999	9.0	3.0	14.7	6.4	18.2	19.5	16.9	17.9
$20,000 to $29,999	8.0	4.4	14.2	11.3	11.1	12.1	12.7	12.5
$30,000 to $39,999	8.5	6.4	13.0	8.8	10.4	10.4	11.0	11.6
$40,000 to $49,999	7.6	6.4	11.0	9.7	10.2	9.8	7.0	6.8
$50,000 to $59,999	7.9	7.9	8.5	14.2	7.7	7.5	6.5	7.0
$60,000 to $69,999	6.7	7.5	6.8	7.5	6.2	6.1	4.6	4.5
$70,000 to $79,999	6.4	7.3	6.7	11.5	4.7	4.8	3.9	3.6
$80,000 to $89,999	5.3	6.7	3.5	9.1	2.5	1.9	3.8	3.7
$90,000 to $99,999	4.5	6.1	3.9	5.6	1.6	1.5	2.4	1.7
$100,000 or more	28.4	42.6	10.4	13.1	8.7	6.4	14.1	11.4
$100,000 to $124,999	8.9	12.2	6.1	4.6	4.0	3.3	5.4	4.9
$125,000 to $149,999	6.3	9.7	2.3	2.1	1.4	1.3	2.9	1.9
$150,000 to $174,999	4.6	7.0	0.7	2.4	1.4	0.5	2.3	1.8
$175,000 to $199,999	2.7	4.2	0.9	0.8	0.7	0.3	1.5	0.9
$200,000 or more	5.9	9.5	0.4	3.2	1.3	1.1	2.1	2.0

Source: Bureau of the Census, 2011 Current Population Survey, Internet site http://www.census.gov/hhes/www/cpstables/032011/hhinc/toc.htm; calculations by New Strategist

Table 5.12 Income of Households by Household Type, 2010: Aged 60 to 64

(number and percent distribution of households headed by people aged 60 to 64, by income and household type, 2010; households in thousands as of 2011)

| | total | family households | | | nonfamily households | | | |
| | | | female householder, no spouse present | male householder, no spouse present | female householder | | male householder | |
		married couples			total	living alone	total	living alone
Total households headed by 60-to-64-year-olds	**10,383**	**5,623**	**773**	**299**	**2,124**	**1,933**	**1,563**	**1,402**
Under $10,000	799	129	86	15	342	337	228	218
$10,000 to $19,999	1,165	274	89	30	488	467	283	266
$20,000 to $29,999	1,064	367	110	37	320	296	230	210
$30,000 to $39,999	1,020	432	107	40	275	242	166	151
$40,000 to $49,999	1,015	550	93	35	176	161	160	139
$50,000 to $59,999	798	451	65	24	131	119	127	110
$60,000 to $69,999	669	433	46	25	100	87	64	53
$70,000 to $79,999	648	449	37	23	89	78	50	46
$80,000 to $89,999	528	408	39	10	44	30	28	20
$90,000 to $99,999	390	270	36	8	36	24	38	34
$100,000 or more	2,286	1,860	62	52	121	90	189	158
$100,000 to $124,999	810	636	32	24	50	41	69	68
$125,000 to $149,999	494	389	10	7	39	27	48	39
$150,000 to $174,999	322	257	6	16	18	15	24	17
$175,000 to $199,999	184	152	5	0	3	2	24	15
$200,000 or more	476	426	9	5	11	5	24	19
Median income	$51,243	$73,623	$39,063	$48,345	$27,599	$25,950	$32,193	$30,357
Total households headed by 60-to-64-year-olds	**100.0%**	**100.0%**	**100.0%**	**100.0%**	**100.0%**	**100.0%**	**100.0%**	**100.0%**
Under $10,000	7.7	2.3	11.1	5.0	16.1	17.4	14.6	15.5
$10,000 to $19,999	11.2	4.9	11.5	10.0	23.0	24.2	18.1	19.0
$20,000 to $29,999	10.2	6.5	14.2	12.4	15.1	15.3	14.7	15.0
$30,000 to $39,999	9.8	7.7	13.8	13.4	12.9	12.5	10.6	10.8
$40,000 to $49,999	9.8	9.8	12.0	11.7	8.3	8.3	10.2	9.9
$50,000 to $59,999	7.7	8.0	8.4	8.0	6.2	6.2	8.1	7.8
$60,000 to $69,999	6.4	7.7	6.0	8.4	4.7	4.5	4.1	3.8
$70,000 to $79,999	6.2	8.0	4.8	7.7	4.2	4.0	3.2	3.3
$80,000 to $89,999	5.1	7.3	5.0	3.3	2.1	1.6	1.8	1.4
$90,000 to $99,999	3.8	4.8	4.7	2.7	1.7	1.2	2.4	2.4
$100,000 or more	22.0	33.1	8.0	17.4	5.7	4.7	12.1	11.3
$100,000 to $124,999	7.8	11.3	4.1	8.0	2.4	2.1	4.4	4.9
$125,000 to $149,999	4.8	6.9	1.3	2.3	1.8	1.4	3.1	2.8
$150,000 to $174,999	3.1	4.6	0.8	5.4	0.8	0.8	1.5	1.2
$175,000 to $199,999	1.8	2.7	0.6	0.0	0.1	0.1	1.5	1.1
$200,000 or more	4.6	7.6	1.2	1.7	0.5	0.3	1.5	1.4

Source: Bureau of the Census, 2011 Current Population Survey, Internet site http://www.census.gov/hhes/www/ cpstables/032011/hhinc/toc.htm; calculations by New Strategist

The Median Income of Middle-Aged Men Has Declined

The incomes of women aged 55 to 64 have grown.

Between 2000 and 2010, the median income of men aged 45 to 54 fell by a substantial 13 percent, after adjusting for inflation. The median income of men aged 55 to 64 fell 5 percent. (Boomers were aged 46 to 64 in 2010.) The Great Recession is not the only reason for the decline in men's income, because men aged 45 to 54 have been struggling to stay even for decades. The decline in the median income of men aged 55 to 64 between 2000 and 2010 occurred despite their increased labor force participation.

The median income of women aged 45 to 54 fell 8 percent between 2000 and 2010 as the Great Recession led to widespread unemployment. In contrast, women aged 55 to 64 saw their median income rise by 19 percent during the decade. Behind the increase was the entry of career-oriented Baby-Boom women into the age group.

■ As men's incomes have declined over the past several decades, women's incomes have become increasingly important to the financial well-being of the nation's families.

Boomer men and women aged 45 to 54 saw their incomes fall

(percent change in median income of people aged 45 to 64 by age and sex, 2000–10; in 2010 dollars)

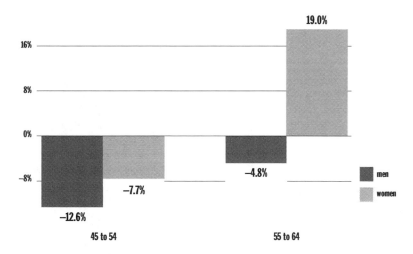

Table 5.13 Median Income of Men Aged 45 to 64, 1990 to 2010

(median income of men aged 15 or older and aged 45 to 64, and index of age group to total, 1990 to 2010; percent change for selected years; in 2010 dollars)

	total men	45 to 54	index, 45–54 to total	55 to 64	index, 55–64 to total
2010	$32,137	$45,420	141	$41,197	128
2009	32,715	45,469	139	41,978	128
2008	33,580	46,116	137	42,285	126
2007	34,908	48,213	138	44,301	127
2006	34,891	49,412	142	44,853	129
2005	34,929	48,725	139	45,404	130
2004	35,224	48,324	137	45,350	129
2003	35,483	49,884	141	46,133	130
2002	35,435	49,653	140	43,966	124
2001	35,839	50,621	141	43,888	122
2000	35,885	51,960	145	43,287	121
1999	35,714	53,394	150	43,816	123
1998	35,389	51,993	147	43,783	124
1997	34,149	50,961	149	42,202	124
1996	32,980	50,136	152	40,857	124
1995	32,051	50,553	158	41,169	128
1994	31,598	50,820	161	39,389	125
1993	31,354	49,262	157	37,353	119
1992	31,145	48,998	157	39,001	125
1991	31,956	49,613	155	39,748	124
1990	32,817	50,144	153	40,112	122
Percent change					
2000 to 2010	–10.4%	–12.6%	–	–4.8%	–
1990 to 2010	–2.1	–9.4	–	2.7	–

Note: The index is calculated by dividing the median income of the age group by the national median and multiplying by 100. "–" means not applicable.
Source: Bureau of the Census, Historical Income Statistics—People, Internet site http://www.census.gov/hhes/www/income/ data/historical/people/; calculations by New Strategist

Table 5.14 Median Income of Women Aged 45 to 64, 1990 to 2010

(median income of women aged 15 or older and aged 45 to 64, and index of age group to total, 1990 to 2010; percent change for selected years; in 2010 dollars)

	total women	45 to 54	index, 45–54 to total	55 to 64	index, 55–64 to total
2010	$20,831	$27,748	133	$25,502	122
2009	21,303	29,089	137	25,527	120
2008	21,131	28,593	135	25,838	122
2007	22,001	30,972	141	26,565	121
2006	21,643	30,110	139	26,155	121
2005	20,747	29,570	143	24,707	119
2004	20,393	30,279	148	24,012	118
2003	20,460	30,664	150	24,146	118
2002	20,375	30,499	150	23,227	114
2001	20,461	29,723	145	21,950	107
2000	20,338	30,047	148	21,423	105
1999	20,026	29,531	147	20,861	104
1998	19,276	28,838	150	19,603	102
1997	18,560	27,813	150	19,472	105
1996	17,733	26,355	149	18,426	104
1995	17,232	25,177	146	17,588	102
1994	16,681	24,806	149	15,809	95
1993	16,413	24,255	148	16,090	98
1992	16,313	24,136	148	15,428	95
1991	16,355	22,987	141	15,459	95
1990	16,285	23,012	141	15,201	93
Percent change					
2000 to 2010	2.4%	–7.7%	–	19.0%	–
1990 to 2010	27.9	20.6	–	67.8	–

Note: The index is calculated by dividing the median income of the age group by the national median and multiplying by 100. "–" means not applicable.
Source: Bureau of the Census, Historical Income Statistics—People, Internet site http://www.census.gov/hhes/www/income/ data/historical/people/; calculations by New Strategist

Men Aged 45 to 54 Have the Highest Incomes

The incomes of non-Hispanic white men in the age group are higher than those of Asians.

Income grows through middle age as men rise through the ranks in their career. Median income peaks among men aged 45 to 54, at $45,420 in 2010. Median income is lower for men aged 55 to 64, but only because fewer are in the labor force. Men aged 55 to 64 who work full-time have higher incomes than full-time workers aged 45 to 54.

Among men aged 45 to 54 who work full-time, non-Hispanic whites have the highest incomes, a median of $61,212 in 2010. Asian men in the age group who work full time have a median income of $52,895. The median income of black men aged 45 to 64 who work full-time is $42,219, and the Hispanic median is just $36,474. The percentage of men aged 45 to 64 who work full-time ranges from 54 percent among blacks to 74 percent among Asians.

■ Among non-Hispanic white men aged 45 to 54, nearly 30 percent have an income of $75,000 or more.

Median income tops $60,000 for men aged 60 to 64 who work full-time

(median income of men aged 45 to 64 who work full-time, by age, 2010)

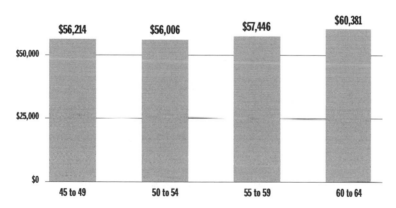

Table 5.15 Income of Men Aged 45 to 64, 2010: Total Men

(number and percent distribution of men aged 15 or older and men aged 45 to 64 by income and age, 2010; median income of men with income and of men working full-time, year-round; percent working full-time, year-round; men in thousands as of 2011)

	total	aged 45 to 54 total	45 to 49	50 to 54	aged 55 to 64 total	55 to 59	60 to 64
Total men	**118,871**	**21,495**	**10,800**	**10,695**	**17,946**	**9,499**	**8,447**
Without income	13,520	1,096	594	502	806	431	375
With income	105,351	20,399	10,206	10,193	17,140	9,068	8,072
Under $5,000	7,350	720	353	367	607	324	284
$5,000 to $9,999	7,741	962	514	448	869	451	417
$10,000 to $14,999	8,933	1,307	615	693	1,162	518	646
$15,000 to $19,999	8,914	1,180	571	609	1,203	568	634
$20,000 to $24,999	8,525	1,316	625	692	1,179	578	601
$25,000 to $29,999	7,133	1,157	601	556	1,119	564	555
$30,000 to $34,999	6,846	1,217	605	612	1,129	613	516
$35,000 to $39,999	5,840	1,047	516	532	968	482	486
$40,000 to $44,999	5,714	1,193	654	539	975	535	440
$45,000 to $49,999	4,325	943	476	468	690	359	331
$50,000 to $54,999	4,978	1,225	611	614	929	530	399
$55,000 to $59,999	3,091	815	435	380	615	343	272
$60,000 to $64,999	3,416	868	459	409	621	323	298
$65,000 to $69,999	2,335	530	258	272	460	263	197
$70,000 to $74,999	2,371	596	296	300	452	229	223
$75,000 to $79,999	2,040	584	274	310	399	212	186
$80,000 to $84,999	1,979	564	280	284	431	263	168
$85,000 to $89,999	1,211	336	161	175	251	132	119
$90,000 to $94,999	1,362	398	215	183	300	177	123
$95,000 to $99,999	860	234	116	118	235	138	96
$100,000 or more	10,386	3,207	1,573	1,635	2,546	1,465	1,081
Median income							
Men with income	$32,137	$45,420	$45,405	$45,436	$41,197	$43,287	$38,562
Working full-time	50,063	56,122	56,214	56,006	58,650	57,446	60,381
Percent full-time	47.5%	67.3%	67.8%	66.9%	53.2%	61.5%	44.0%
PERCENT DISTRIBUTION							
Total men	**100.0%**	**100.0%**	**100.0%**	**100.0%**	**100.0%**	**100.0%**	**100.0%**
Without income	11.4	5.1	5.5	4.7	4.5	4.5	4.4
With income	88.6	94.9	94.5	95.3	95.5	95.5	95.6
Under $15,000	20.2	13.9	13.7	14.1	14.7	13.6	15.9
$15,000 to $24,999	14.7	11.6	11.1	12.2	13.3	12.1	14.6
$25,000 to $34,999	11.8	11.0	11.2	10.9	12.5	12.4	12.7
$35,000 to $49,999	13.4	14.8	15.2	14.4	14.7	14.5	14.9
$50,000 to $74,999	13.6	18.8	19.1	18.5	17.1	17.8	16.4
$75,000 or more	15.0	24.8	24.3	25.3	23.2	25.1	21.0

Source: Bureau of the Census, 2011 Current Population Survey Annual Social and Economic Supplement, Internet site http://www.census.gov/hhes/www/cpstables/032011/perinc/toc.htm; calculations by New Strategist

Table 5.16 Income of Men Aged 45 to 64, 2010: Asian Men

(number and percent distribution of Asian men aged 15 or older and aged 45 to 64 by income and age, 2010; median income of men with income and of men working full-time, year-round; percent working full-time, year-round; men in thousands as of 2011)

| | total | aged 45 to 54 | | | aged 55 to 64 | | |
		total	45 to 49	50 to 54	total	55 to 59	60 to 64
Asian men	**5,787**	**987**	**530**	**458**	**708**	**389**	**319**
Without income	865	69	36	34	56	28	28
With income	4,922	918	494	424	652	361	291
Under $5,000	356	26	18	9	20	12	8
$5,000 to $9,999	304	26	15	11	30	17	13
$10,000 to $14,999	401	54	24	28	50	28	20
$15,000 to $19,999	334	57	29	28	28	14	14
$20,000 to $24,999	395	64	29	36	50	26	24
$25,000 to $29,999	318	56	33	24	57	31	26
$30,000 to $34,999	314	65	29	37	50	18	31
$35,000 to $39,999	227	52	25	26	31	19	13
$40,000 to $44,999	210	41	17	26	32	20	12
$45,000 to $49,999	186	42	18	23	26	13	13
$50,000 to $54,999	202	48	24	24	37	20	17
$55,000 to $59,999	111	27	17	9	18	9	8
$60,000 to $64,999	195	35	18	17	19	9	11
$65,000 to $69,999	100	12	8	4	15	6	8
$70,000 to $74,999	135	34	23	11	17	10	7
$75,000 to $79,999	108	21	15	7	12	6	6
$80,000 to $84,999	100	17	7	10	26	13	13
$85,000 to $89,999	91	10	6	4	18	16	2
$90,000 to $94,999	78	12	8	4	14	9	5
$95,000 to $99,999	40	8	2	6	11	8	4
$100,000 or more	716	211	128	83	92	57	35
Median income							
Men with income	$35,622	$46,199	$51,084	$41,875	$41,385	$43,275	$38,996
Working full-time	52,444	52,895	62,034	46,713	52,332	51,724	54,341
Percent full-time	53.0%	74.2%	74.7%	73.4%	60.9%	65.8%	54.9%
PERCENT DISTRIBUTION							
Asian men	**100.0%**	**100.0%**	**100.0%**	**100.0%**	**100.0%**	**100.0%**	**100.0%**
Without income	14.9	7.0	6.8	7.4	7.9	7.2	8.8
With income	85.1	93.0	93.2	92.6	92.1	92.8	91.2
Under $15,000	18.3	10.7	10.8	10.5	14.1	14.7	12.9
$15,000 to $24,999	12.6	12.3	10.9	14.0	11.0	10.3	11.9
$25,000 to $34,999	10.9	12.3	11.7	13.3	15.1	12.6	17.9
$35,000 to $49,999	10.8	13.7	11.3	16.4	12.6	13.4	11.9
$50,000 to $74,999	12.8	15.8	17.0	14.2	15.0	13.9	16.0
$75,000 or more	19.6	28.3	31.3	24.9	24.4	28.0	20.4

Note: Asians are those who identify themselves as being of the race alone and those who identify themselves as being of the race in combination with other races.
Source: Bureau of the Census, 2011 Current Population Survey Annual Social and Economic Supplement, Internet site http://www.census.gov/hhes/www/cpstables/032011/perinc/toc.htm; calculations by New Strategist

Table 5.17 Income of Men Aged 45 to 64, 2010: Black Men

(number and percent distribution of black men aged 15 or older and aged 45 to 64 by income and age, 2010; median income of men with income and of men working full-time, year-round; percent working full-time, year-round; men in thousands as of 2011)

| | total | aged 45 to 54 | | | aged 55 to 64 | | |
		total	45 to 49	50 to 54	total	55 to 59	60 to 64
Black men	**14,101**	**2,461**	**1,269**	**1,192**	**1,813**	**1,014**	**799**
Without income	2,843	255	140	115	173	100	73
With income	11,258	2,206	1,129	1,077	1,640	914	726
Under $5,000	1,052	117	59	57	66	40	27
$5,000 to $9,999	1,471	197	117	80	212	115	97
$10,000 to $14,999	1,270	222	110	112	158	71	87
$15,000 to $19,999	1,035	177	101	77	158	82	75
$20,000 to $24,999	1,067	156	67	89	151	87	65
$25,000 to $29,999	831	191	98	94	123	65	57
$30,000 to $34,999	795	157	68	88	123	78	44
$35,000 to $39,999	617	151	79	72	109	52	58
$40,000 to $44,999	568	137	78	59	67	44	23
$45,000 to $49,999	432	94	41	53	64	36	27
$50,000 to $54,999	367	96	45	52	52	35	17
$55,000 to $59,999	252	80	45	35	58	29	29
$60,000 to $64,999	244	60	34	25	34	20	12
$65,000 to $69,999	195	44	15	30	45	34	12
$70,000 to $74,999	217	63	27	35	37	21	15
$75,000 to $79,999	122	32	12	20	23	10	13
$80,000 to $84,999	132	47	21	26	26	19	8
$85,000 to $89,999	55	19	12	6	10	5	5
$90,000 to $94,999	66	20	6	13	16	15	1
$95,000 to $99,999	51	19	13	6	10	5	6
$100,000 or more	418	127	82	45	98	51	48
Median income							
Men with income	$23,061	$30,915	$30,718	$31,049	$27,548	$29,584	$26,049
Working full-time	37,805	42,219	43,198	41,570	44,279	43,421	45,307
Percent full-time	38.0%	53.9%	51.5%	56.5%	40.7%	45.8%	34.3%
PERCENT DISTRIBUTION							
Black men	**100.0%**	**100.0%**	**100.0%**	**100.0%**	**100.0%**	**100.0%**	**100.0%**
Without income	20.2	10.4	11.0	9.6	9.5	9.9	9.1
With income	79.8	89.6	89.0	90.4	90.5	90.1	90.9
Under $15,000	26.9	21.8	22.5	20.9	24.0	22.3	26.4
$15,000 to $24,999	14.9	13.5	13.2	13.9	17.0	16.7	17.5
$25,000 to $34,999	11.5	14.1	13.1	15.3	13.6	14.1	12.6
$35,000 to $49,999	11.5	15.5	15.6	15.4	13.2	13.0	13.5
$50,000 to $74,999	9.0	13.9	13.1	14.8	12.5	13.7	10.6
$75,000 or more	6.0	10.7	11.5	9.7	10.1	10.4	10.1

Note: Blacks are those who identify themselves as being of the race alone and those who identify themselves as being of the race in combination with other races.
Source: Bureau of the Census, 2011 Current Population Survey Annual Social and Economic Supplement, Internet site http:// www.census.gov/hhes/www/cpstables/032011/perinc/toc.htm; calculations by New Strategist

Table 5.18 Income of Men Aged 45 to 64, 2010: Hispanic Men

(number and percent distribution of Hispanic men aged 15 or older and aged 45 to 64 by income and age, 2010; median income of men with income and of men working full-time, year-round; percent working full-time, year-round; men in thousands as of 2011)

	total	aged 45 to 54			aged 55 to 64		
		total	45 to 49	50 to 54	total	55 to 59	60 to 64
Hispanic men	**18,105**	**2,693**	**1,507**	**1,186**	**1,573**	**889**	**684**
Without income	3,140	197	113	84	133	81	52
With income	14,965	2,496	1,394	1,102	1,440	808	632
Under $5,000	1,094	102	61	41	67	33	34
$5,000 to $9,999	1,573	165	82	83	135	72	64
$10,000 to $14,999	1,918	280	151	129	179	87	92
$15,000 to $19,999	1,902	256	138	117	170	98	72
$20,000 to $24,999	1,669	280	159	121	136	82	54
$25,000 to $29,999	1,305	220	132	89	117	77	40
$30,000 to $34,999	1,041	218	127	91	123	73	50
$35,000 to $39,999	780	137	80	58	53	32	21
$40,000 to $44,999	711	133	78	55	97	52	45
$45,000 to $49,999	503	98	63	35	40	18	22
$50,000 to $54,999	516	113	60	54	58	35	23
$55,000 to $59,999	275	79	48	30	32	20	12
$60,000 to $64,999	328	69	36	31	48	25	22
$65,000 to $69,999	171	27	16	11	23	11	12
$70,000 to $74,999	168	40	26	14	21	13	8
$75,000 to $79,999	149	37	14	23	18	10	9
$80,000 to $84,999	147	30	14	16	18	9	9
$85,000 to $89,999	91	27	11	15	13	7	7
$90,000 to $94,999	71	27	15	12	6	2	3
$95,000 to $99,999	42	15	7	7	4	2	2
$100,000 or more	511	144	76	68	84	52	32
Median income							
Men with income	$22,233	$28,302	$28,800	$27,448	$26,070	$26,506	$25,090
Working full-time	31,671	36,474	37,134	35,737	36,513	35,576	40,254
Percent full-time	46.3%	60.9%	59.9%	62.1%	49.3%	55.2%	41.7%
PERCENT DISTRIBUTION							
Hispanic men	**100.0%**	**100.0%**	**100.0%**	**100.0%**	**100.0%**	**100.0%**	**100.0%**
Without income	17.3	7.3	7.5	7.1	8.5	9.1	7.6
With income	82.7	92.7	92.5	92.9	91.5	90.9	92.4
Under $15,000	25.3	20.3	19.5	21.3	24.2	21.6	27.8
$15,000 to $24,999	19.7	19.9	19.7	20.1	19.5	20.2	18.4
$25,000 to $34,999	13.0	16.3	17.2	15.2	15.3	16.9	13.2
$35,000 to $49,999	11.0	13.7	14.7	12.5	12.1	11.5	12.9
$50,000 to $74,999	8.1	12.2	12.3	11.8	11.6	11.7	11.3
$75,000 or more	5.6	10.4	9.1	11.9	9.1	9.2	9.1

Source: Bureau of the Census, 2011 Current Population Survey Annual Social and Economic Supplement, Internet site http://www.census.gov/hhes/www/cpstables/032011/perinc/toc.htm; calculations by New Strategist

Table 5.19 Income of Men Aged 45 to 64, 2010: Non-Hispanic White Men

(number and percent distribution of non-Hispanic white men aged 15 or older and aged 45 to 54 by income and age, 2010; median income of men with income and of men working full-time, year-round; percent working full-time, year-round; men in thousands as of 2011)

	total	aged 45 to 54			aged 55 to 64		
		total	45 to 49	50 to 54	total	55 to 59	60 to 64
Non-Hispanic white men	**80,108**	**15,165**	**7,395**	**7,770**	**13,666**	**7,106**	**6,560**
Without income	6,617	562	298	264	431	218	214
With income	73,491	14,603	7,097	7,506	13,235	6,888	6,346
Under $5,000	4,754	465	211	253	443	234	209
$5,000 to $9,999	4,356	548	290	259	480	237	243
$10,000 to $14,999	5,318	740	326	415	766	326	440
$15,000 to $19,999	5,542	672	296	377	833	366	468
$20,000 to $24,999	5,388	806	365	440	825	369	454
$25,000 to $29,999	4,633	686	335	351	816	392	424
$30,000 to $34,999	4,634	766	371	395	815	434	382
$35,000 to $39,999	4,169	699	332	367	771	377	393
$40,000 to $44,999	4,193	878	477	401	772	417	355
$45,000 to $49,999	3,165	697	342	354	546	287	259
$50,000 to $54,999	3,860	964	481	482	773	435	339
$55,000 to $59,999	2,412	612	315	297	499	279	221
$60,000 to $64,999	2,615	695	366	329	510	260	250
$65,000 to $69,999	1,868	444	220	224	377	210	166
$70,000 to $74,999	1,840	459	215	243	373	184	189
$75,000 to $79,999	1,650	492	232	261	343	188	155
$80,000 to $84,999	1,586	468	236	231	353	216	135
$85,000 to $89,999	968	278	130	148	210	106	103
$90,000 to $94,999	1,133	334	181	153	263	149	114
$95,000 to $99,999	718	193	93	100	208	123	85
$100,000 or more	8,691	2,707	1,281	1,426	2,260	1,298	962
Median income							
Men with income	$37,037	$51,126	$51,324	$50,928	$45,784	$50,048	$41,603
Working full-time	54,192	61,212	61,141	61,296	62,165	61,669	63,366
Percent full-time	49.1%	70.5%	71.8%	69.3%	55.1%	64.6%	44.9%
PERCENT DISTRIBUTION							
Non-Hispanic white men	**100.0%**	**100.0%**	**100.0%**	**100.0%**	**100.0%**	**100.0%**	**100.0%**
Without income	8.3	3.7	4.0	3.4	3.2	3.1	3.3
With income	91.7	96.3	96.0	96.6	96.8	96.9	96.7
Under $15,000	18.0	11.6	11.2	11.9	12.4	11.2	13.6
$15,000 to $24,999	13.6	9.7	8.9	10.5	12.1	10.3	14.1
$25,000 to $34,999	11.6	9.6	9.5	9.6	11.9	11.6	12.3
$35,000 to $49,999	14.4	15.0	15.6	14.4	15.3	15.2	15.4
$50,000 to $74,999	15.7	20.9	21.6	20.3	18.5	19.3	17.8
$75,000 or more	18.4	29.5	29.1	29.8	26.6	29.3	23.7

Note: Non-Hispanic whites are those who identify themselves as being white alone and not Hispanic.
Source: Bureau of the Census, 2011 Current Population Survey Annual Social and Economic Supplement, Internet site http:// www.census.gov/hhes/www/cpstables/032011/perinc/toc.htm; calculations by New Strategist

Women's Incomes Are Flat through Middle Age

Non-Hispanic white women have the highest incomes.

The median income of women in the broad 45-to-64 age group is below $30,000. Among women in the age group who work full-time, median income is higher, exceeding $40,000 in every five-year bracket. Among women aged 45 to 54, the 51 percent majority works full-time. In the 55-to-64 age group, only 40 percent of women have full-time jobs.

Compared with men, women's incomes vary less by race and Hispanic origin. The median income of non-Hispanic white women aged 45 to 54 who work full-time stood at $42,334 in 2010. For their Asian counterparts, the figure was a slightly lower $41,557. Among blacks, the median income of full-time workers aged 45 to 54 was $36,490. Hispanic women in the age group have the lowest incomes. Among those working full-time, median income was just $29,769 in 2010.

■ Women's incomes do not rise to a peak in middle age because many choose lower-paying jobs that allow them to spend more time with their family.

Among women who work full-time, median income tops $40,000

(median income of women aged 45 to 64 who work full-time, by age, 2010)

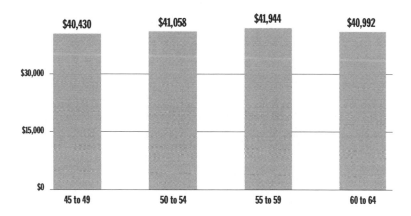

Table 5.20 Income of Women Aged 45 to 64, 2010: Total Women

(number and percent distribution of women aged 15 or older and women aged 45 to 64 by income and age, 2010; median income of women with income and of women working full-time, year-round; percent working full-time, year-round; women in thousands as of 2011)

| | total | aged 45 to 54 | | | aged 55 to 64 | | |
		total	45 to 49	50 to 54	total	55 to 59	60 to 64
Total women	**125,084**	**22,459**	**11,189**	**11,270**	**19,038**	**10,055**	**8,983**
Without income	18,942	2,359	1,163	1,196	1,775	998	777
With income	106,142	20,100	10,026	10,074	17,263	9,057	8,206
Under $5,000	12,538	1,969	1,028	942	1,717	897	821
$5,000 to $9,999	14,061	1,649	834	815	1,887	832	1,055
$10,000 to $14,999	13,672	1,864	917	947	1,962	894	1,068
$15,000 to $19,999	10,971	1,766	905	861	1,612	804	807
$20,000 to $24,999	8,842	1,788	879	909	1,296	671	625
$25,000 to $29,999	7,228	1,513	723	790	1,285	689	595
$30,000 to $34,999	6,582	1,373	725	649	1,132	597	535
$35,000 to $39,999	5,443	1,196	592	604	924	506	418
$40,000 to $44,999	4,778	1,175	597	578	860	473	387
$45,000 to $49,999	3,701	872	428	444	698	410	288
$50,000 to $54,999	3,527	850	430	420	748	415	331
$55,000 to $59,999	2,239	581	266	315	447	280	167
$60,000 to $64,999	2,276	567	286	281	477	282	196
$65,000 to $69,999	1,464	374	176	198	274	155	119
$70,000 to $74,999	1,492	351	169	182	323	198	126
$75,000 to $79,999	1,060	291	158	133	249	141	108
$80,000 to $84,999	971	271	116	155	201	121	80
$85,000 to $89,999	669	197	94	103	175	103	72
$90,000 to $94,999	619	178	79	98	145	82	63
$95,000 to $99,999	425	141	68	73	114	73	41
$100,000 or more	3,584	1,134	557	577	737	432	306
Median income							
Women with income	$20,831	$27,748	$27,523	$27,969	$25,502	$27,525	$22,485
Working full-time	38,531	40,726	40,430	41,058	41,578	41,944	40,992
Percent full-time	34.2%	51.3%	51.6%	51.1%	40.3%	46.4%	33.5%
PERCENT DISTRIBUTION							
Total women	**100.0%**	**100.0%**	**100.0%**	**100.0%**	**100.0%**	**100.0%**	**100.0%**
Without income	15.1	10.5	10.4	10.6	9.3	9.9	8.6
With income	84.9	89.5	89.6	89.4	90.7	90.1	91.4
Under $15,000	32.2	24.4	24.8	24.0	29.2	26.1	32.8
$15,000 to $24,999	15.8	15.8	15.9	15.7	15.3	14.7	15.9
$25,000 to $34,999	11.0	12.9	12.9	12.8	12.7	12.8	12.6
$35,000 to $49,999	11.1	14.4	14.5	14.4	13.0	13.8	12.2
$50,000 to $74,999	8.8	12.1	11.9	12.4	11.9	13.2	10.5
$75,000 or more	5.9	9.8	9.6	10.1	8.5	9.5	7.5

Source: Bureau of the Census, 2011 Current Population Survey Annual Social and Economic Supplement, Internet site http://www.census.gov/hhes/www/cpstables/032011/perinc/toc.htm; calculations by New Strategist

Table 5.21 Income of Women Aged 45 to 64, 2010: Asian Women

(number and percent distribution of Asian women aged 15 or older and aged 45 to 64 by income and age, 2010; median income of women with income and of women working full-time, year-round; percent working full-time, year-round; women in thousands as of 2011)

	total	aged 45 to 54			aged 55 to 64		
		total	45 to 49	50 to 54	total	55 to 59	60 to 64
Asian women	**6,460**	**1,099**	**586**	**513**	**862**	**479**	**383**
Without income	1,413	138	74	64	147	79	68
With income	5,047	961	512	449	715	400	315
Under $5,000	694	92	48	43	75	45	31
$5,000 to $9,999	617	67	38	29	63	33	30
$10,000 to $14,999	518	89	46	43	76	36	42
$15,000 to $19,999	397	92	47	45	66	42	24
$20,000 to $24,999	380	81	49	31	53	28	25
$25,000 to $29,999	293	61	29	33	55	36	19
$30,000 to $34,999	333	78	44	34	53	29	23
$35,000 to $39,999	229	44	25	19	34	19	16
$40,000 to $44,999	250	53	27	27	33	15	17
$45,000 to $49,999	144	27	16	12	22	13	10
$50,000 to $54,999	188	33	18	15	40	25	15
$55,000 to $59,999	113	25	14	12	23	14	8
$60,000 to $64,999	146	33	22	11	22	13	7
$65,000 to $69,999	89	15	11	4	13	7	6
$70,000 to $74,999	92	23	10	12	9	4	5
$75,000 to $79,999	68	14	8	7	9	6	4
$80,000 to $84,999	76	23	8	15	8	3	6
$85,000 to $89,999	42	11	2	9	4	3	1
$90,000 to $94,999	58	15	4	12	7	5	2
$95,000 to $99,999	20	5	4	1	4	2	2
$100,000 or more	297	82	43	39	46	24	22
Median income							
Women with income	$23,664	$29,922	$29,688	$30,135	$26,625	$26,567	$26,776
Working full-time	41,821	41,557	41,176	41,798	40,115	38,832	40,852
Percent full-time	36.6%	53.5%	50.2%	57.3%	43.7%	50.1%	36.0%
PERCENT DISTRIBUTION							
Asian women	**100.0%**	**100.0%**	**100.0%**	**100.0%**	**100.0%**	**100.0%**	**100.0%**
Without income	21.9	12.6	12.6	12.5	17.1	16.5	17.8
With income	78.1	87.4	87.4	87.5	82.9	83.5	82.2
Under $15,000	28.3	22.6	22.5	22.4	24.8	23.8	26.9
$15,000 to $24,999	12.0	15.7	16.4	14.8	13.8	14.6	12.8
$25,000 to $34,999	9.7	12.6	12.5	13.1	12.5	13.6	11.0
$35,000 to $49,999	9.6	11.3	11.6	11.3	10.3	9.8	11.2
$50,000 to $74,999	9.7	11.7	12.8	10.5	12.4	13.2	10.7
$75,000 or more	8.7	13.6	11.8	16.2	9.0	9.0	9.7

Note: Asians are those who identify themselves as being of the race alone and those who identify themselves as being of the race in combination with other races.
Source: Bureau of the Census, 2011 Current Population Survey Annual Social and Economic Supplement, Internet site http://www.census.gov/hhes/www/cpstables/032011/perinc/toc.htm; calculations by New Strategist

Table 5.22 Income of Women Aged 45 to 64, 2010: Black Women

(number and percent distribution of black women aged 15 or older and aged 45 to 64 by income and age, 2010; median income of women with income and of women working full-time, year-round; percent working full-time, year-round; women in thousands as of 2011)

	total	aged 45 to 54			aged 55 to 64		
		total	45 to 49	50 to 54	total	55 to 59	60 to 64
Black women	**16,879**	**3,001**	**1,527**	**1,474**	**2,219**	**1,160**	**1,059**
Without income	2,948	307	153	154	235	124	111
With income	13,931	2,694	1,374	1,320	1,984	1,036	948
Under $5,000	1,507	210	112	98	137	59	79
$5,000 to $9,999	2,173	302	141	160	321	168	154
$10,000 to $14,999	1,965	295	142	152	257	110	146
$15,000 to $19,999	1,402	258	134	124	217	122	95
$20,000 to $24,999	1,274	280	148	133	157	78	80
$25,000 to $29,999	1,086	243	120	122	196	99	97
$30,000 to $34,999	925	174	102	71	130	73	56
$35,000 to $39,999	730	165	85	80	98	54	44
$40,000 to $44,999	612	158	82	76	97	60	38
$45,000 to $49,999	452	120	67	54	67	30	36
$50,000 to $54,999	416	115	58	56	66	35	30
$55,000 to $59,999	242	60	29	33	29	16	13
$60,000 to $64,999	248	67	40	27	37	23	14
$65,000 to $69,999	128	40	24	15	17	11	7
$70,000 to $74,999	144	46	18	28	23	16	6
$75,000 to $79,999	108	15	6	9	23	15	8
$80,000 to $84,999	111	40	17	23	17	11	6
$85,000 to $89,999	60	15	11	5	13	10	3
$90,000 to $94,999	65	18	11	7	13	8	5
$95,000 to $99,999	36	11	5	6	10	5	5
$100,000 or more	247	63	21	42	60	35	25
Median income							
Women with income	$19,634	$25,036	$25,273	$24,738	$21,439	$23,121	$19,990
Working full-time	33,918	36,490	35,641	37,536	35,216	35,861	33,614
Percent full-time	35.7%	51.8%	54.5%	49.0%	40.6%	46.6%	34.0%
PERCENT DISTRIBUTION							
Black women	**100.0%**	**100.0%**	**100.0%**	**100.0%**	**100.0%**	**100.0%**	**100.0%**
Without income	17.5	10.2	10.0	10.4	10.6	10.7	10.5
With income	82.5	89.8	90.0	89.6	89.4	89.3	89.5
Under $15,000	33.4	26.9	25.9	27.8	32.2	29.1	35.8
$15,000 to $24,999	15.9	17.9	18.5	17.4	16.9	17.2	16.5
$25,000 to $34,999	11.9	13.9	14.5	13.1	14.7	14.8	14.4
$35,000 to $49,999	10.6	14.8	15.3	14.2	11.8	12.4	11.1
$50,000 to $74,999	7.0	10.9	11.1	10.8	7.8	8.7	6.6
$75,000 or more	3.7	5.4	4.6	6.2	6.1	7.2	4.9

Note: Blacks are those who identify themselves as being of the race alone and those who identify themselves as being of the race in combination with other races.
Source: Bureau of the Census, 2011 Current Population Survey Annual Social and Economic Supplement, Internet site http:// www.census.gov/hhes/www/cpstables/032011/perinc/toc.htm; calculations by New Strategist

Table 5.23 Income of Women Aged 45 to 64, 2010: Hispanic Women

(number and percent distribution of Hispanic women aged 15 or older and aged 45 to 64 by income and age, 2010; median income of women with income and of women working full-time, year-round; percent working full-time, year-round; women in thousands as of 2011)

	total	aged 45 to 54			aged 55 to 64		
		total	45 to 49	50 to 54	total	55 to 59	60 to 64
Hispanic women	**16,964**	**2,668**	**1,455**	**1,213**	**1,681**	**912**	**769**
Without income	4,842	523	263	259	349	199	150
With income	12,122	2,145	1,192	954	1,332	713	619
Under $5,000	1,654	190	114	76	155	75	81
$5,000 to $9,999	2,058	249	137	111	239	100	139
$10,000 to $14,999	1,901	314	157	157	221	115	106
$15,000 to $19,999	1,442	273	159	115	152	84	68
$20,000 to $24,999	1,165	246	147	98	118	66	51
$25,000 to $29,999	829	178	92	86	93	58	36
$30,000 to $34,999	713	148	86	62	63	37	26
$35,000 to $39,999	570	104	69	36	69	40	29
$40,000 to $44,999	410	81	38	43	41	22	19
$45,000 to $49,999	257	57	34	22	29	19	9
$50,000 to $54,999	270	71	38	33	29	17	12
$55,000 to $59,999	133	35	15	19	17	10	6
$60,000 to $64,999	154	45	19	25	18	8	10
$65,000 to $69,999	100	28	18	9	6	6	0
$70,000 to $74,999	68	13	8	6	16	9	7
$75,000 to $79,999	56	17	9	8	13	11	3
$80,000 to $84,999	59	12	4	7	10	9	2
$85,000 to $89,999	45	12	4	9	11	11	0
$90,000 to $94,999	33	10	6	5	3	3	0
$95,000 to $99,999	16	6	3	3	3	0	3
$100,000 or more	187	57	33	24	27	13	14
Median income							
Women with income	$16,269	$20,744	$20,715	$20,796	$16,319	$18,519	$14,024
Working full-time	28,944	29,769	28,925	30,463	29,298	28,872	29,508
Percent full-time	30.5%	45.5%	47.4%	43.3%	32.7%	37.7%	26.7%
PERCENT DISTRIBUTION							
Hispanic women	**100.0%**	**100.0%**	**100.0%**	**100.0%**	**100.0%**	**100.0%**	**100.0%**
Without income	28.5	19.6	18.1	21.4	20.8	21.8	19.5
With income	71.5	80.4	81.9	78.6	79.2	78.2	80.5
Under $15,000	33.1	28.2	28.0	28.4	36.6	31.8	42.4
$15,000 to $24,999	15.4	19.5	21.0	17.6	16.1	16.4	15.5
$25,000 to $34,999	9.1	12.2	12.2	12.2	9.3	10.4	8.1
$35,000 to $49,999	7.3	9.1	9.7	8.3	8.3	8.9	7.4
$50,000 to $74,999	4.3	7.2	6.7	7.6	5.1	5.5	4.6
$75,000 or more	2.3	4.3	4.1	4.6	4.0	5.2	2.9

Source: Bureau of the Census, 2011 Current Population Survey Annual Social and Economic Supplement, Internet site http:// www.census.gov/hhes/www/cpstables/032011/perinc/toc.htm; calculations by New Strategist

Table 5.24 Income of Women Aged 45 to 64, 2010: Non-Hispanic White Women

(number and percent distribution of non-Hispanic white women aged 15 or older and aged 45 to 64 by income and age, 2010; median income of women with income and of women working full-time, year-round; percent working full-time, year-round; women in thousands as of 2011)

	total	aged 45 to 54			aged 55 to 64		
		total	45 to 49	50 to 54	total	55 to 59	60 to 64
Non-Hispanic white women	**84,028**	**15,529**	**7,551**	**7,978**	**14,088**	**7,390**	**6,698**
Without income	9,663	1,387	671	716	1,018	584	434
With income	74,365	14,142	6,880	7,262	13,070	6,806	6,264
Under $5,000	8,605	1,454	747	707	1,336	709	627
$5,000 to $9,999	9,108	1,008	509	499	1,242	524	718
$10,000 to $14,999	9,217	1,158	569	589	1,386	620	766
$15,000 to $19,999	7,665	1,128	562	566	1,154	539	615
$20,000 to $24,999	5,946	1,174	533	641	953	490	463
$25,000 to $29,999	4,964	1,029	477	552	926	487	439
$30,000 to $34,999	4,551	956	480	475	873	448	424
$35,000 to $39,999	3,868	875	410	465	712	387	325
$40,000 to $44,999	3,505	874	438	435	685	373	311
$45,000 to $49,999	2,820	663	309	354	574	346	229
$50,000 to $54,999	2,638	631	315	316	607	333	274
$55,000 to $59,999	1,738	454	208	246	377	240	136
$60,000 to $64,999	1,728	418	201	217	401	235	165
$65,000 to $69,999	1,129	288	123	165	233	129	105
$70,000 to $74,999	1,172	264	131	132	270	164	107
$75,000 to $79,999	826	244	136	109	203	111	91
$80,000 to $84,999	717	194	86	108	161	98	62
$85,000 to $89,999	518	155	74	82	148	81	67
$90,000 to $94,999	462	134	60	75	123	67	57
$95,000 to $99,999	344	117	56	62	95	63	31
$100,000 or more	2,844	925	458	467	607	358	249
Median income							
Women with income	$21,754	$30,450	$30,308	$30,612	$27,067	$30,302	$24,304
Working full-time	41,307	42,334	42,263	42,419	44,968	45,561	43,491
Percent full-time	34.6%	52.2%	51.8%	52.5%	41.1%	47.3%	34.2%
PERCENT DISTRIBUTION							
Non-Hispanic white women	**100.0%**	**100.0%**	**100.0%**	**100.0%**	**100.0%**	**100.0%**	**100.0%**
Without income	11.5	8.9	8.9	9.0	7.2	7.9	6.5
With income	88.5	91.1	91.1	91.0	92.8	92.1	93.5
Under $15,000	32.0	23.3	24.2	22.5	28.1	25.1	31.5
$15,000 to $24,999	16.2	14.8	14.5	15.1	15.0	13.9	16.1
$25,000 to $34,999	11.3	12.8	12.7	12.9	12.8	12.7	12.9
$35,000 to $49,999	12.1	15.5	15.3	15.7	14.0	15.0	12.9
$50,000 to $74,999	10.0	13.2	13.0	13.5	13.4	14.9	11.7
$75,000 or more	6.8	11.4	11.5	11.3	9.5	10.5	8.3

Note: Non-Hispanic whites are those who identify themselves as being white alone and not Hispanic.
Source: Bureau of the Census, 2011 Current Population Survey Annual Social and Economic Supplement, Internet site http://www.census.gov/hhes/www/cpstables/032011/perinc/toc.htm; calculations by New Strategist

Earnings Rise with Education

The highest earners are men with professional degrees.

A college degree has been well worth the cost for Baby Boomers. The higher their educational level, the greater their earnings. Among men aged 55 to 64 who work full-time, those with professional degrees (such as physicians and lawyers) had median earnings of $150,317. Among women as well, median earnings are highest for those with a professional degree, peaking at $100,539 in the 55-to-64 age group.

Among men aged 45 to 64 who did not finish high school, the median earnings of those who work full-time ranged from just $25,820 to $32,288 in 2010. For male full-time workers with at least a bachelor's degree, median earnings are above $81,000. The pattern is the same for women. Among women aged 45 to 64 who did not finish high school, median annual earnings of those who work full-time range from $18,797 to $24,744. Among college graduates, median earnings are above $56,000.

■ The steeply rising cost of a college degree may reduce the financial return of a college education in the years ahead.

College bonus is big for Boomers

(median earnings of men aged 45 to 54 who work full-time, by education, 2010)

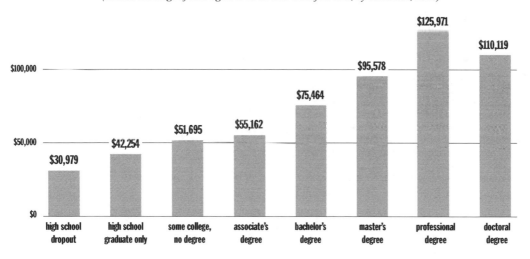

Table 5.25 Earnings of Men by Education, 2010: Aged 45 to 54

(number and percent distribution of men aged 45 to 54 who work full-time, year-round, by earnings and educational attainment, 2010; median earnings of men with earnings; men in thousands as of 2011)

| | total | less than 9th grade | 9th to 12th grade, no degree | high school graduate | some college | associate's degree | bachelor's degree or more | | | | |
							total	bachelor's degree	master's degree	professional degree	doctoral degree
Men aged 45 to 54 who work full-time	**14,471**	**411**	**685**	**4,507**	**2,207**	**1,470**	**5,191**	**3,264**	**1,271**	**363**	**293**
Under $5,000	91	5	4	26	20	12	23	18	6	0	0
$5,000 to $9,999	95	10	29	31	12	5	8	3	2	0	3
$10,000 to $14,999	294	32	59	118	30	16	40	25	6	7	1
$15,000 to $19,999	463	62	88	176	68	20	50	37	9	4	0
$20,000 to $24,999	770	85	67	374	103	48	91	80	10	0	1
$25,000 to $29,999	814	52	63	406	120	75	98	70	22	1	5
$30,000 to $34,999	993	44	97	459	161	94	138	106	24	4	4
$35,000 to $39,999	847	31	53	385	142	95	142	109	26	4	3
$40,000 to $44,999	998	24	47	393	196	124	214	152	47	10	4
$45,000 to $49,999	791	21	26	347	133	73	190	142	41	6	2
$50,000 to $54,999	1,141	12	47	419	203	170	290	224	43	9	14
$55,000 to $59,999	684	7	16	225	122	69	244	184	41	3	16
$60,000 to $64,999	819	11	27	247	150	115	271	179	69	8	15
$65,000 to $69,999	462	1	3	134	69	81	176	125	38	6	6
$70,000 to $74,999	538	2	8	137	102	72	217	153	43	13	8
$75,000 to $79,999	548	2	13	121	96	85	230	135	73	10	13
$80,000 to $84,999	514	0	5	104	107	46	251	169	66	13	3
$85,000 to $89,999	296	0	2	35	72	49	136	88	33	11	4
$90,000 to $94,999	362	2	5	71	41	50	194	143	34	10	7
$95,000 to $99,999	159	1	3	25	18	13	100	63	23	5	8
$100,000 or more	2,792	7	22	272	242	159	2,089	1,056	617	238	179
Median earnings	$54,084	$25,820	$30,979	$42,254	$51,695	$55,162	$81,900	$75,464	$95,578	$125,971	$110,119

PERCENT DISTRIBUTION

| | total | less than 9th grade | 9th to 12th grade, no degree | high school graduate | some college | associate's degree | bachelor's degree or more | | | | |
							total	bachelor's degree	master's degree	professional degree	doctoral degree
Men aged 45 to 54 who work full-time	**100.0%**	**100.0%**	**100.0%**	**100.0%**	**100.0%**	**100.0%**	**100.0%**	**100.0%**	**100.0%**	**100.0%**	**100.0%**
Under $15,000	3.3	11.4	13.4	3.9	2.8	2.2	1.4	1.4	1.1	1.9	1.4
$15,000 to $24,999	8.5	35.8	22.6	12.2	7.7	4.6	2.7	3.6	1.5	1.1	0.3
$25,000 to $34,999	12.5	23.4	23.4	19.2	12.7	11.5	4.5	5.4	3.6	1.4	3.1
$35,000 to $49,999	18.2	18.5	18.4	25.0	21.3	19.9	10.5	12.3	9.0	5.5	3.1
$50,000 to $74,999	25.2	8.0	14.7	25.8	29.3	34.5	23.1	26.5	18.4	10.7	20.1
$75,000 to $99,999	13.0	1.2	4.1	7.9	15.1	16.5	17.5	18.3	18.0	13.5	11.9
$100,000 or more	19.3	1.7	3.2	6.0	11.0	10.8	40.2	32.4	48.5	65.6	61.1

Note: Earnings include wages and salary only.
Source: Bureau of the Census, 2011 Current Population Survey Annual Social and Economic Supplement, Internet site http://www.census.gov/hhes/www/cpstables/032011/perinc/toc.htm; calculations by New Strategist

Table 5.26 Earnings of Men by Education, 2010: Aged 55 to 64

(number and percent distribution of men aged 55 to 64 who work full-time, year-round, by earnings and educational attainment, 2010; median earnings of men with earnings; men in thousands as of 2011)

	total	less than 9th grade	9th to 12th grade, no degree	high school graduate	some college	associate's degree	bachelor's degree or more total	bachelor's degree	master's degree	professional degree	doctoral degree
Men aged 55 to 64 who work full-time	**9,555**	**250**	**402**	**2,514**	**1,633**	**821**	**3,935**	**2,221**	**1,091**	**305**	**317**
Under $5,000	80	0	6	16	20	9	29	23	7	0	0
$5,000 to $9,999	66	3	10	18	11	3	20	14	4	2	1
$10,000 to $14,999	181	29	22	63	30	11	24	20	4	0	0
$15,000 to $19,999	265	36	34	85	41	14	55	42	4	5	3
$20,000 to $24,999	430	42	52	171	80	22	65	41	23	0	0
$25,000 to $29,999	539	33	31	210	90	57	118	86	29	0	4
$30,000 to $34,999	710	35	54	263	125	78	154	107	38	5	4
$35,000 to $39,999	560	14	23	226	121	48	128	109	15	3	1
$40,000 to $44,999	678	12	45	253	132	90	144	90	40	3	12
$45,000 to $49,999	448	9	19	145	95	48	132	79	47	5	1
$50,000 to $54,999	793	6	25	279	149	69	265	164	79	9	12
$55,000 to $59,999	443	3	20	100	111	49	161	103	46	4	9
$60,000 to $64,999	508	11	10	137	119	57	174	96	58	6	13
$65,000 to $69,999	298	6	11	77	57	19	128	79	44	0	5
$70,000 to $74,999	355	2	7	96	58	36	155	73	57	12	13
$75,000 to $79,999	306	1	5	74	53	33	141	87	37	3	15
$80,000 to $84,999	343	4	9	64	66	30	170	115	35	10	10
$85,000 to $89,999	206	0	2	30	37	27	110	62	30	2	17
$90,000 to $94,999	243	0	0	50	38	25	130	60	45	16	10
$95,000 to $99,999	155	3	0	12	17	11	112	78	24	0	9
$100,000 or more	1,951	1	16	144	186	81	1,521	695	428	222	176
Median earnings	$55,221	$26,610	$32,288	$42,407	$51,404	$51,157	$81,316	$72,229	$81,276	$150,317	$101,845

PERCENT DISTRIBUTION

Men aged 55 to 64 who work full-time	100.0%	100.0%	100.0%	100.0%	100.0%	100.0%	100.0%	100.0%	100.0%	100.0%	100.0%
Under $15,000	3.4	12.8	9.5	3.9	3.7	2.8	1.9	2.6	1.4	0.7	0.3
$15,000 to $24,999	7.3	31.2	21.4	10.2	7.4	4.4	3.0	3.7	2.5	1.6	0.9
$25,000 to $34,999	13.1	27.2	21.1	18.8	13.2	16.4	6.9	8.7	6.1	1.6	2.5
$35,000 to $49,999	17.6	14.0	21.6	24.8	21.3	22.7	10.3	12.5	9.3	3.6	4.4
$50,000 to $74,999	25.1	11.2	18.2	27.4	30.3	28.0	22.4	23.2	26.0	10.2	16.4
$75,000 to $99,999	13.1	3.2	4.0	9.1	12.9	15.3	16.8	18.1	15.7	10.2	19.2
$100,000 or more	20.4	0.4	4.0	5.7	11.4	9.9	38.7	31.3	39.2	72.8	55.5

Note: Earnings include wages and salary only.
Source: Bureau of the Census, 2011 Current Population Survey Annual Social and Economic Supplement, Internet site http://www.census.gov/hhes/www/cpstables/032011/perinc/toc.htm; calculations by New Strategist

Table 5.27 Earnings of Women by Education, 2010: Aged 45 to 54

(number and percent distribution of women aged 45 to 54 who work full-time, year-round, by earnings and educational attainment, 2010; median earnings of women with earnings; women in thousands as of 2011)

	total	less than 9th grade	9th to 12th grade, no degree	high school graduate	some college	associate's degree	bachelor's degree or more				
							total	bachelor's degree	master's degree	professional degree	doctoral degree
Women aged 45 to 54 who work full-time	**11,524**	**231**	**388**	**3,245**	**2,066**	**1,578**	**4,017**	**2,504**	**1,201**	**134**	**179**
Under $5,000	74	1	3	21	12	7	30	21	0	7	1
$5,000 to $9,999	108	15	5	33	20	8	28	19	9	0	0
$10,000 to $14,999	418	48	55	141	66	45	64	53	5	3	4
$15,000 to $19,999	845	60	111	356	162	74	81	65	13	1	2
$20,000 to $24,999	1,156	53	75	548	225	133	122	97	19	2	4
$25,000 to $29,999	1,087	29	40	455	251	143	168	140	18	4	6
$30,000 to $34,999	1,111	7	41	441	243	182	196	143	51	0	3
$35,000 to $39,999	956	8	23	289	206	138	293	213	72	5	3
$40,000 to $44,999	962	1	4	302	200	143	312	249	54	2	6
$45,000 to $49,999	754	3	14	167	143	148	279	174	93	7	5
$50,000 to $54,999	769	3	6	183	133	119	324	199	106	5	14
$55,000 to $59,999	459	0	2	48	90	69	251	165	82	2	2
$60,000 to $64,999	463	3	4	71	60	83	241	131	85	6	20
$65,000 to $69,999	288	0	0	35	35	43	174	88	68	6	13
$70,000 to $74,999	307	0	0	27	61	77	142	72	56	1	12
$75,000 to $79,999	272	0	3	17	25	38	189	101	81	5	2
$80,000 to $84,999	250	0	0	28	38	28	157	80	56	8	13
$85,000 to $89,999	143	0	0	14	25	15	89	48	34	5	1
$90,000 to $94,999	146	0	1	12	8	15	110	51	45	4	10
$95,000 to $99,999	110	0	0	1	10	11	87	33	43	5	6
$100,000 or more	845	0	1	54	50	59	680	360	211	55	53
Median earnings	$40,025	$18,797	$21,172	$30,473	$35,891	$41,285	$56,671	$51,172	$63,636	$86,484	$71,775

PERCENT DISTRIBUTION

Women aged 45 to 54 who work full-time	100.0%	100.0%	100.0%	100.0%	100.0%	100.0%	100.0%	100.0%	100.0%	100.0%	100.0%
Under $15,000	5.2	27.7	16.2	6.0	4.7	3.8	3.0	3.7	1.2	7.5	2.8
$15,000 to $24,999	17.4	48.9	47.9	27.9	18.7	13.1	5.1	6.5	2.7	2.2	3.4
$25,000 to $34,999	19.1	15.6	20.9	27.6	23.9	20.6	9.1	11.3	5.7	3.0	5.0
$35,000 to $49,999	23.2	5.2	10.6	23.4	26.6	27.2	22.0	25.4	18.2	10.4	7.8
$50,000 to $74,999	19.8	2.6	3.1	11.2	18.3	24.8	28.2	26.2	33.1	14.9	34.1
$75,000 to $99,999	8.0	0.0	1.0	2.2	5.1	6.8	15.7	12.5	21.6	20.1	17.9
$100,000 or more	7.3	0.0	0.3	1.7	2.4	3.7	16.9	14.4	17.6	41.0	29.6

Note: Earnings include wages and salary only.
Source: Bureau of the Census, 2011 Current Population Survey Annual Social and Economic Supplement, Internet site http://www.census.gov/hhes/www/cpstables/032011/perinc/toc.htm; calculations by New Strategist

Table 5.28 Earnings of Women by Education, 2010: Aged 55 to 64

(number and percent distribution of women aged 55 to 64 who work full-time, year-round, by earnings and educational attainment, 2010; median earnings of women with earnings; women in thousands as of 2011)

	total	less than 9th grade	9th to 12th grade, no degree	high school graduate	some college	associate's degree	bachelor's degree or more total	bachelor's degree	master's degree	professional degree	doctoral degree
Women aged 55 to 64 who work full-time	**7,673**	**144**	**276**	**2,218**	**1,409**	**873**	**2,752**	**1,549**	**933**	**116**	**153**
Under $5,000	69	2	3	6	18	10	29	22	8	0	0
$5,000 to $9,999	75	2	2	29	21	4	14	14	0	0	0
$10,000 to $14,999	269	23	30	103	46	27	41	37	1	0	3
$15,000 to $19,999	501	43	62	198	75	58	65	55	8	0	2
$20,000 to $24,999	657	29	41	305	112	81	89	66	21	1	0
$25,000 to $29,999	763	20	31	344	189	67	111	86	21	1	3
$30,000 to $34,999	777	12	30	287	200	108	138	98	33	0	8
$35,000 to $39,999	637	4	26	245	119	91	153	109	36	5	2
$40,000 to $44,999	651	2	19	190	152	91	197	150	36	7	4
$45,000 to $49,999	449	4	6	87	109	63	179	131	38	1	9
$50,000 to $54,999	576	1	0	121	105	86	264	136	109	4	13
$55,000 to $59,999	328	1	8	81	67	35	136	56	71	1	9
$60,000 to $64,999	341	2	5	69	35	32	198	98	80	10	9
$65,000 to $69,999	211	0	1	25	33	29	124	65	49	4	5
$70,000 to $74,999	227	0	0	30	20	16	162	89	65	4	5
$75,000 to $79,999	176	0	3	28	11	14	121	40	71	10	0
$80,000 to $84,999	162	0	2	18	28	15	99	47	47	2	3
$85,000 to $89,999	98	0	0	13	14	9	63	35	24	2	2
$90,000 to $94,999	117	0	0	13	9	5	90	41	38	5	6
$95,000 to $99,999	73	0	0	8	9	5	52	28	23	0	2
$100,000 or more	514	0	4	21	37	28	424	145	153	60	66
Median earnings	$40,425	$20,352	$24,744	$31,416	$36,171	$39,421	$57,845	$50,152	$65,221	$100,539	$84,923

PERCENT DISTRIBUTION

Women aged 55 to 64 who work full-time	**100.0%**	**100.0%**	**100.0%**	**100.0%**	**100.0%**	**100.0%**	**100.0%**	**100.0%**	**100.0%**	**100.0%**	**100.0%**
Under $15,000	5.4	18.8	12.7	6.2	6.0	4.7	3.1	4.7	1.0	0.0	2.0
$15,000 to $24,999	15.1	50.0	37.3	22.7	13.3	15.9	5.6	7.8	3.1	0.9	1.3
$25,000 to $34,999	20.1	22.2	22.1	28.4	27.6	20.0	9.0	11.9	5.8	0.9	7.2
$35,000 to $49,999	22.6	6.9	18.5	23.5	27.0	28.1	19.2	25.2	11.8	11.2	9.8
$50,000 to $74,999	21.9	2.8	5.1	14.7	18.5	22.7	32.1	28.7	40.1	19.8	26.8
$75,000 to $99,999	8.2	0.0	1.8	3.6	5.0	5.5	15.4	12.3	21.8	16.4	8.5
$100,000 or more	6.7	0.0	1.4	0.9	2.6	3.2	15.4	9.4	16.4	51.7	43.1

Note: Earnings include wages and salary only.
Source: Bureau of the Census, 2011 Current Population Survey Annual Social and Economic Supplement, Internet site http://www.census.gov/hhes/www/cpstables/032011/perinc/toc.htm; calculations by New Strategist

Poverty Rate among Boomers Is below Average

Among black and Hispanic boomers, the poverty rate is in the double digits.

While 15.1 percent of all Americans were poor in 2010, the poverty rate among the Baby-Boom generation, aged 46 to 64, was a smaller 10.4 percent. Boomers account for only 18 percent of the nation's poor, much smaller than their share of the population.

The poverty rate for non-Hispanic white Boomers was just 7.8 percent in 2010, less than half the rate among their black and Hispanic counterparts. A larger 17.8 percent of Hispanics and 19.8 percent of blacks aged 45 to 64 are poor. Although higher than the rate for non-Hispanic whites, these figures are well below the 26.6 percent poverty rate for all Hispanics and the 27.4 percent rate for all blacks. Among Asians, 11.9 percent are poor, including 8.9 percent of Asians aged 45 to 64. Non-Hispanic whites account for the 54 percent majority of poor Boomers, while blacks account for 22 percent, Hispanics for 18 percent, and Asians for 4 percent.

■ The poverty rate bottoms out in the 65-plus age group, now filling with the Baby-Boom generation.

Black Boomers are most likely to be poor

(percent of people aged 45 to 64 below poverty level, by race and Hispanic origin, 2010)

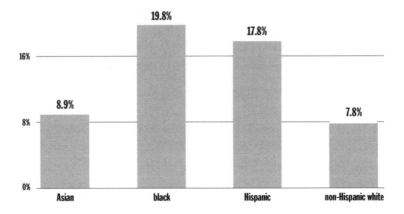

Table 5.29 People below Poverty Level by Age, Race, and Hispanic Origin, 2010

(number, percent, and percent distribution of people below poverty level by age, race, and Hispanic origin, 2010; people in thousands as of 2011)

NUMBER IN POVERTY	total	Asian	black	Hispanic	non-Hispanic white
Total people	**46,180**	**1,859**	**11,361**	**13,243**	**19,599**
Under age 18	16,401	547	4,817	6,110	5,002
Aged 18 to 24	6,507	296	1,514	1,547	3,132
Aged 25 to 34	6,333	255	1,485	1,917	2,682
Aged 35 to 44	5,028	223	1,032	1,618	2,129
Aged 45 to 64	8,389	326	1,877	1,537	4,540
Aged 45 to 54	4,662	181	1,039	968	2,421
Aged 55 to 59	1,972	89	445	308	1,095
Aged 60 to 64	1,755	56	393	261	1,024
Aged 65 or older	3,520	213	636	514	2,116
PERCENT IN POVERTY					
Total people	**15.1%**	**11.9%**	**27.4%**	**26.6%**	**9.9%**
Under age 18	22.0	13.6	38.2	35.0	12.4
Aged 18 to 24	21.9	19.8	31.9	26.8	17.8
Aged 25 to 34	15.2	10.2	25.1	23.6	10.8
Aged 35 to 44	12.6	8.8	19.8	22.9	8.6
Aged 45 to 64	10.4	8.9	19.8	17.8	7.8
Aged 45 to 54	10.6	8.7	19.0	18.1	7.9
Aged 55 to 59	10.1	10.2	20.5	17.1	7.6
Aged 60 to 64	10.1	8.0	21.2	18.0	7.7
Aged 65 or older	9.0	14.4	18.2	18.0	6.8
PERCENT DISTRIBUTION OF POOR BY AGE					
Total people	**100.0%**	**100.0%**	**100.0%**	**100.0%**	**100.0%**
Under age 18	35.5	29.4	42.4	46.1	25.5
Aged 18 to 24	14.1	15.9	13.3	11.7	16.0
Aged 25 to 34	13.7	13.7	13.1	14.5	13.7
Aged 35 to 44	10.9	12.0	9.1	12.2	10.9
Aged 45 to 64	18.2	17.5	16.5	11.6	23.2
Aged 45 to 54	10.1	9.7	9.1	7.3	12.4
Aged 55 to 59	4.3	4.8	3.9	2.3	5.6
Aged 60 to 64	3.8	3.0	3.5	2.0	5.2
Aged 65 or older	7.6	11.5	5.6	3.9	10.8
PERCENT DISTRIBUTION OF POOR BY RACE AND HISPANIC ORIGIN					
Total people	**100.0%**	**4.0%**	**24.6%**	**28.7%**	**42.4%**
Under age 18	100.0	3.3	29.4	37.3	30.5
Aged 18 to 24	100.0	4.5	23.3	23.8	48.1
Aged 25 to 34	100.0	4.0	23.4	30.3	42.3
Aged 35 to 44	100.0	4.4	20.5	32.2	42.3
Aged 45 to 64	100.0	3.9	22.4	18.3	54.1
Aged 45 to 54	100.0	3.9	22.3	20.8	51.9
Aged 55 to 59	100.0	4.5	22.6	15.6	55.5
Aged 60 to 64	100.0	3.2	22.4	14.9	58.3
Aged 65 or older	100.0	6.1	18.1	14.6	60.1

Note: Numbers do not add to total because Asians and blacks are those who identify themselves as being of the race alone and those who identify themselves as being of the race in combination with other races, because Hispanics may be of any race, and because not all races are shown. Non-Hispanic whites are those who identify themselves as being white alone and not Hispanic. Source: Bureau of the Census, 2011 Current Population Survey Annual Social and Economic Supplement, Internet site http://www.census.gov/hhes/www/cpstables/032011/pov/toc.htm; calculations by New Strategist

6

Labor Force

■ Among men aged 45 to 54, the labor force participation rate fell by more than 2 percentage points between 2000 and 2011, in part because of an increase in discouraged workers.

■ Among men aged 55 to 64, the labor force participation rate increased between 2000 and 2011 as early retirement became less common.

■ Among the nation's 154 million workers in 2011, fully 59 million were aged 45 to 64, accounting for 38 percent of the labor force.

■ Sixty-nine percent of couples aged 45 to 54 are dual earners. The dual-earner lifestyle accounts for a smaller 50 percent of couples aged 55 to 64.

■ Boomers account for 64 percent of mail carriers, 63 percent of chief executives, and 60 percent of aircraft pilots. Only 13 percent of waiters and waitresses are in the 45-to-64 age group.

■ Between 2000 and 2010, long-term employment fell for men ranging in age from 30 to 59. But it increased among men aged 60 to 64 as early retirement became less common.

■ As Boomers enter their late sixties and early seventies during the next decade, the number of workers aged 65 or older will expand by 80 percent.

Labor Force Participation Rose among Older Boomers

Men and women aged 55 to 64 are more likely to work.

Trends in the labor force participation rates of middle-aged men and women are complicated by job losses, the entry of career-oriented Baby-Boom women into the older age groups, and the end of early retirement.

Among men aged 45 to 54 (the Baby-Boom generation was aged 47 to 65 in 2011), the labor force participation rate fell by more than 2 percentage points between 2000 and 2011. (Note: Labor force participation rates include both the employed and the unemployed.) This decline is partly due to the increase in discouraged workers—the unemployed who have given up looking for a job and are no longer counted in the labor force. Among men aged 55 to 64, the labor force participation rate rose by 1 to 4 percentage points between 2000 and 2011. Behind the rise is the end of early retirement. Among men aged 65 or older, the labor force participation rate increased 5 percentage points.

Among women aged 45 to 49, the labor force participation rate fell by nearly 3 percentage points between 2000 and 2011 because of the weak economy and the increase in discouraged workers. Among women aged 55 to 64, rates were up by 6 to 10 percentage points as Boomers filled the age group. Women aged 65 or older are also more likely to work, their labor force participation rate increasing by nearly 5 percentage points during those years.

■ Since many Boomers have experienced losses in their retirement accounts, expect labor force participation rates in the older age groups to continue to climb.

A growing share of 60-to-64-year-olds is in the labor force

(percent of people aged 60 to 64 in the labor force, by sex, 2000 and 2011)

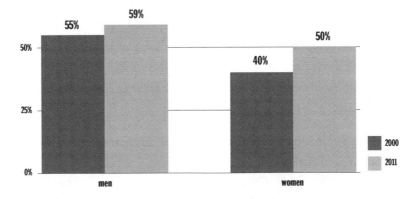

Table 6.1 Labor Force Participation Rate by Sex and Age, 2000 to 2011

(civilian labor force participation rate of people aged 16 or older, by sex and age, 2000 to 2011; percentage point change, 2000–11)

	2011	2010	2000	percentage point change 2000–11
Men aged 16 or older	**70.5%**	**71.2%**	**74.8%**	**–4.3**
Aged 16 to 17	20.4	21.8	40.9	–20.5
Aged 18 to 19	48.3	49.6	65.0	–16.7
Aged 20 to 24	74.7	74.5	82.6	–7.9
Aged 25 to 29	87.8	88.4	92.5	–4.7
Aged 30 to 34	90.6	91.1	94.2	–3.6
Aged 35 to 39	91.5	92.2	93.2	–1.7
Aged 40 to 44	90.4	90.7	92.1	–1.7
Aged 45 to 49	88.1	88.5	90.2	–2.1
Aged 50 to 54	84.2	85.1	86.8	–2.6
Aged 55 to 59	78.2	78.5	77.0	1.2
Aged 60 to 64	59.1	60.0	54.9	4.2
Aged 65 or older	22.8	22.1	17.7	5.1
Women aged 16 or older	**58.1**	**58.6**	**59.9**	**–1.8**
Aged 16 to 17	22.6	23.0	40.8	–18.2
Aged 18 to 19	47.4	48.6	61.3	–13.9
Aged 20 to 24	67.8	68.3	73.1	–5.3
Aged 25 to 29	74.4	75.6	76.7	–2.3
Aged 30 to 34	73.4	73.8	75.5	–2.1
Aged 35 to 39	73.7	74.1	75.7	–2.0
Aged 40 to 44	75.6	76.2	78.7	–3.1
Aged 45 to 49	76.5	76.8	79.1	–2.6
Aged 50 to 54	74.3	74.6	74.1	0.2
Aged 55 to 59	67.7	68.4	61.4	6.3
Aged 60 to 64	50.3	50.7	40.2	10.1
Aged 65 or older	14.0	13.8	9.4	4.6

Source: Bureau of Labor Statistics, Labor Force Statistics from the Current Population Survey, Internet site http://www.bls .gov/cps/tables.htm#empstat; calculations by New Strategist

Boomers Are a Large Share of Workers

Nearly half of Boomer workers are women.

Among the 154 million Americans in the labor force in 2011, fully 59 million were aged 45 to 64 (Boomers were aged 47 to 65 in that year), accounting for 38 percent of the labor force. Among workers in the 45-to-64 age group, 28 million—or 48 percent—are women.

Boomers are now in the age groups in which many workers retire. Among men aged 45 to 49, fully 88 percent are in the labor force. The participation rate declines with advancing age to 59 percent among men aged 60 to 64. A similar pattern occurs among women, their labor force participation rate falling from 76 percent in the 45-to-49 age group to 50 percent in the 60-to-64 age group.

Because unemployment is less common among the middle aged than young adults, people aged 45 to 64 account for a smaller share of the unemployed (30 percent) than they do of the labor force as a whole. In 2011, Boomer women were slightly less likely to be unemployed than their male counterparts—6.4 versus 7.3 percent.

■ Few Boomers will retire before reaching the age of eligibility for Social Security and Medicare benefits, and many will continue to work long after.

Labor force participation rate falls with age among Boomer men

(percent of men aged 45 to 64 in the labor force, by age, 2011)

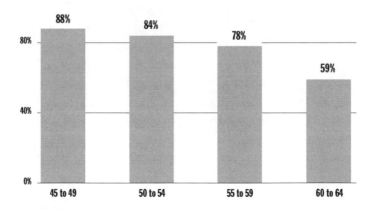

Table 6.2 Employment Status by Sex and Age, 2011

(number and percent of people aged 16 or older in the civilian labor force by sex and age, 2011; numbers in thousands)

	civilian noninstitutional population	civilian labor force			unemployed	
		total	percent of population	employed	number	percent of labor force
Total aged 16 or older	**239,618**	**153,617**	**64.1%**	**139,869**	**13,747**	**8.9%**
Aged 16 to 44	119,060	87,380	73.4	78,169	9,210	10.5
Aged 45 to 64	80,829	59,125	73.1	55,053	4,072	6.9
Aged 45 to 54	43,842	35,360	80.7	32,867	2,493	7.1
Aged 45 to 49	21,788	17,901	82.2	16,594	1,307	7.3
Aged 50 to 54	22,054	17,458	79.2	16,272	1,186	6.8
Aged 55 to 64	36,987	23,765	64.3	22,186	1,579	6.6
Aged 55 to 59	19,670	14,324	72.8	13,389	935	6.5
Aged 60 to 64	17,317	9,440	54.5	8,796	644	6.8
Aged 65 and over	39,729	7,112	17.9	6,647	465	6.5
Men aged 16 or older	**116,317**	**81,975**	**70.5**	**74,290**	**7,684**	**9.4**
Aged 16 to 44	59,582	47,152	79.1	41,978	5,171	11.0
Aged 45 to 64	39,261	30,833	78.5	28,582	2,252	7.3
Aged 45 to 54	21,451	18,483	86.2	17,113	1,370	7.4
Aged 45 to 49	10,682	9,410	88.1	8,695	715	7.6
Aged 50 to 54	10,770	9,073	84.2	8,418	655	7.2
Aged 55 to 64	17,810	12,350	69.3	11,469	882	7.1
Aged 55 to 59	9,524	7,450	78.2	6,932	518	7.0
Aged 60 to 64	8,286	4,900	59.1	4,536	364	7.4
Aged 65 and over	17,474	3,990	22.8	3,730	261	6.5
Women aged 16 or older	**123,300**	**71,642**	**58.1**	**65,579**	**6,063**	**8.5**
Aged 16 to 44	59,477	40,231	67.6	36,192	4,039	10.0
Aged 45 to 64	41,568	28,290	68.1	26,470	1,820	6.4
Aged 45 to 54	22,391	16,876	75.4	15,753	1,123	6.7
Aged 45 to 49	11,106	8,491	76.5	7,899	592	7.0
Aged 50 to 54	11,284	8,386	74.3	7,854	531	6.3
Aged 55 to 64	19,177	11,414	59.5	10,717	697	6.1
Aged 55 to 59	10,146	6,874	67.7	6,457	417	6.1
Aged 60 to 64	9,031	4,540	50.3	4,260	280	6.2
Aged 65 and over	22,255	3,121	14.0	2,917	204	6.5

Source: Bureau of Labor Statistics, Labor Force Statistics from the Current Population Survey, Internet site http://www.bls.gov/cps/tables.htm#empstat; calculations by New Strategist

Among Boomer Men, Hispanics Have the Highest Labor Force Rate

Blacks have the highest unemployment rate.

Among men aged 45 to 64, from 80 to 84 percent of Asians, Hispanics, and whites were in the labor force in 2011 (when Boomers were aged 47 to 65). The labor force includes both the employed and the unemployed. Among black men, 68 percent of those aged 45 to 64 were in the labor force in 2011.

The unemployment rates were significantly higher in 2011 for black and Hispanic men than for Asian or white men. White men aged 45 to 64 had the lowest unemployment rate in 2011, at 6.6 percent. Among Asian men in the age group, unemployment was 7.3 percent. Hispanic men aged 45 to 64 had a 9.9 percent unemployment rate, and for black men the rate was 12.6 percent.

■ Among men aged 65 or older, the labor force participation rate ranges much more narrowly by race and Hispanic origin.

Labor force participation rate varies by race and Hispanic origin

(percent of men aged 45 to 64 in the labor force by race and Hispanic origin, 2011)

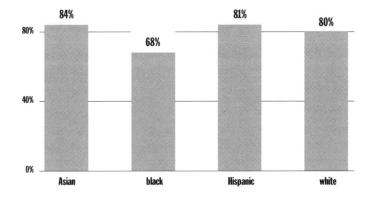

Table 6.3 Employment Status of Men by Race, Hispanic Origin, and Age, 2011

(number and percent of men aged 16 or older in the civilian labor force by race, Hispanic origin, and age, 2011; numbers in thousands)

	civilian noninstitutional population	civilian labor force			unemployed	
		total	percent of population	employed	number	percent of labor force
ASIAN MEN						
Total aged 16 or older	**5,429**	**3,972**	**73.2%**	**3,703**	**269**	**6.8%**
Aged 16 to 44	3,103	2,398	77.3	2,243	156	6.5
Aged 45 to 64	1,663	1,405	84.5	1,302	102	7.3
Aged 45 to 54	956	874	91.4	810	63	7.2
Aged 45 to 49	504	468	92.7	437	31	6.6
Aged 50 to 54	451	406	89.9	374	32	7.9
Aged 55 to 64	707	531	75.0	492	39	7.3
Aged 55 to 59	387	325	84.0	302	24	7.3
Aged 60 to 64	320	205	64.2	191	15	7.2
Aged 65 or older	663	169	25.5	158	11	6.4
BLACK MEN						
Total aged 16 or older	**13,164**	**8,454**	**64.2**	**6,953**	**1,502**	**17.8**
Aged 16 to 44	7,626	5,360	70.3	4,238	1,123	21.0
Aged 45 to 64	4,194	2,837	67.6	2,479	358	12.6
Aged 45 to 54	2,435	1,854	76.1	1,621	233	12.5
Aged 45 to 49	1,233	965	78.2	840	125	12.9
Aged 50 to 54	1,202	889	73.9	781	108	12.1
Aged 55 to 64	1,759	983	55.9	858	125	12.7
Aged 55 to 59	972	612	63.0	535	77	12.6
Aged 60 to 64	787	371	47.2	323	48	12.9
Aged 65 or older	1,344	257	19.1	236	21	8.2
HISPANIC MEN						
Total aged 16 or older	**17,753**	**13,576**	**76.5**	**12,049**	**1,527**	**11.2**
Aged 16 to 44	12,172	9,789	80.4	8,636	1,152	11.8
Aged 45 to 64	4,321	3,494	80.9	3,147	347	9.9
Aged 45 to 54	2,717	2,372	87.3	2,141	231	9.8
Aged 45 to 49	1,502	1,325	88.2	1,197	128	9.6
Aged 50 to 54	1,216	1,047	86.1	943	104	9.9
Aged 55 to 64	1,604	1,122	69.9	1,006	116	10.4
Aged 55 to 59	913	714	78.2	644	70	9.8
Aged 60 to 64	692	408	59.0	362	46	11.3
Aged 65 or older	1,260	293	23.3	266	28	9.5

	civilian noninstitutional population	civilian labor force			unemployed	
		total	percent of population	employed	number	percent of labor force
WHITE MEN						
Total aged 16 or older	**94,801**	**67,551**	**71.3%**	**61,920**	**5,631**	**8.3%**
Aged 16 to 44	46,968	38,028	81.0	34,347	3,681	9.7
Aged 45 to 64	32,620	26,029	79.8	24,302	1,727	6.6
Aged 45 to 54	17,602	15,400	87.5	14,370	1,030	6.7
Aged 45 to 49	8,705	7,786	89.5	7,251	536	6.9
Aged 50 to 54	8,897	7,614	85.6	7,120	494	6.5
Aged 55 to 64	15,018	10,629	70.8	9,932	697	6.6
Aged 55 to 59	7,981	6,387	80.0	5,982	405	6.3
Aged 60 to 64	7,037	4,242	60.3	3,950	292	6.9
Aged 65 or older	15,213	3,494	23.0	3,271	223	6.4

Note: People who selected more than one race are not included. Hispanics may be of any race.
Source: Bureau of Labor Statistics, Labor Force Statistics from the Current Population Survey, Internet site http://www.bls
.gov/cps/tables.htm#empstat; calculations by New Strategist

Most Boomer Women Are in the Labor Force

Among Boomer women, Hispanics have the highest unemployment rate.

Among women aged 45 to 64, the labor force participation rate by race and Hispanic origin ranges narrowly from 63 to 69 percent. Most women aged 45 to 59 are in the labor force. In the 60-to-64 age group, participation drops below 50 percent for Asians, blacks, and Hispanics, but remains slightly above the 50 percent mark among non-Hispanic whites.

Among 45-to-64-year-olds, Hispanic women are most likely to be unemployed, at 9.7 percent in 2011. The figure was 9.1 percent among blacks, 6.7 percent among Asians, and 6.0 percent among whites.

■ Among women aged 65 or older, only 12 to 14 percent are in the labor force regardless of race or Hispanic origin.

Labor force participation rates are similar among women by race and Hispanic origin

(percent of women aged 45 to 64 in the labor force by race and Hispanic origin, 2011)

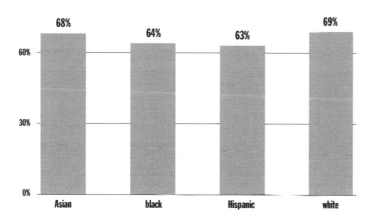

Table 6.4 Employment Status of Women by Race, Hispanic Origin, and Age, 2011

(number and percent of women aged 16 or older in the civilian labor force by race, Hispanic origin, and age, 2011; numbers in thousands)

	civilian noninstitutional population	civilian labor force			unemployed	
		total	percent of population	employed	number	percent of labor force
ASIAN WOMEN						
Total aged 16 or older	**6,011**	**3,414**	**56.8%**	**3,165**	**250**	**7.3%**
Aged 16 to 44	3,264	2,019	61.9	1,862	158	7.8
Aged 45 to 64	1,906	1,298	68.1	1,211	87	6.7
Aged 45 to 54	1,058	797	75.3	750	47	5.9
Aged 45 to 49	564	417	73.9	391	26	6.3
Aged 50 to 54	494	380	77.0	360	20	5.4
Aged 55 to 64	848	501	59.1	461	40	7.9
Aged 55 to 59	465	311	67.0	289	22	7.1
Aged 60 to 64	383	189	49.5	172	18	9.3
Aged 65 or older	841	97	11.6	92	5	5.3
BLACK WOMEN						
Total aged 16 or older	**15,950**	**9,427**	**59.1**	**8,098**	**1,329**	**14.1**
Aged 16 to 44	8,736	5,853	67.0	4,848	1,007	17.2
Aged 45 to 64	5,118	3,276	64.0	2,978	297	9.1
Aged 45 to 54	2,922	2,104	72.0	1,892	211	10.0
Aged 45 to 49	1,485	1,098	73.9	977	121	11.0
Aged 50 to 54	1,436	1,006	70.0	916	90	9.0
Aged 55 to 64	2,196	1,172	53.4	1,086	86	7.4
Aged 55 to 59	1,184	739	62.4	684	55	7.4
Aged 60 to 64	1,012	433	42.8	402	31	7.2
Aged 65 or older	2,096	298	14.2	272	25	8.5
HISPANIC WOMEN						
Total aged 16 or older	**16,685**	**9,322**	**55.9**	**8,220**	**1,102**	**11.8**
Aged 16 to 44	10,639	6,313	59.3	5,499	815	12.9
Aged 45 to 64	4,403	2,792	63.4	2,521	270	9.7
Aged 45 to 54	2,696	1,899	70.4	1,707	192	10.1
Aged 45 to 49	1,469	1,061	72.2	949	112	10.5
Aged 50 to 54	1,227	839	68.3	758	81	9.6
Aged 55 to 64	1,707	893	52.3	814	78	8.8
Aged 55 to 59	934	546	58.5	493	53	9.7
Aged 60 to 64	773	347	44.9	321	25	7.3
Aged 65 or older	1,643	217	13.2	200	17	8.0

	civilian noninstitutional population	civilian labor force			unemployed	
		total	percent of population	employed	number	percent of labor force
WHITE WOMEN						
Total aged 16 or older	**98,276**	**57,028**	**58.0%**	**52,770**	**4,257**	**7.5%**
Aged 16 to 44	45,578	31,152	68.3	28,450	2,703	8.7
Aged 45 to 64	33,706	23,195	68.8	21,811	1,383	6.0
Aged 45 to 54	17,925	13,636	76.1	12,806	829	6.1
Aged 45 to 49	8,819	6,800	77.1	6,377	423	6.2
Aged 50 to 54	9,106	6,836	75.1	6,429	406	5.9
Aged 55 to 64	15,781	9,559	60.6	9,005	554	5.8
Aged 55 to 59	8,313	5,707	68.6	5,378	329	5.8
Aged 60 to 64	7,468	3,853	51.6	3,627	226	5.9
Aged 65 or older	18,992	2,681	14.1	2,509	171	6.4

Note: People who selected more than one race are not included. Hispanics may be of any race.
Source: Bureau of Labor Statistics, Labor Force Statistics from the Current Population Survey, Internet site http://www.bls
.gov/cps/tables.htm#empstat; calculations by New Strategist

Most Couples under Age 55 Are Dual Earners

In only 22 percent of couples is the husband alone in the labor force.

Dual incomes are by far the norm among married couples. Both husband and wife are in the labor force in 53 percent of all married couples. In another 22 percent, the husband is the only worker. Not far behind are the 17 percent of couples in which neither spouse is in the labor force. The wife is the sole worker in 7 percent of couples.

Sixty-nine percent of couples aged 45 to 54 are dual earners, while the husband is the only spouse in the labor force in another 21 percent. The dual-earner lifestyle accounts for a much smaller 50 percent of couples aged 55 to 64. The wife is the only one employed in a substantial 13 percent of couples in this age group. In these homes, typically, the older husband is retired while the younger wife is still at work. For 71 percent of couples aged 65 or older, neither husband nor wife is working.

■ Only 11 percent of couples aged 65 or older are dual-income. Expect this share to rise as aging Boomers postpone retirement.

Dual earners are the norm among Boomers aged 45 to 54

(percent of married couples in which both husband and wife are in the labor force, by age, 2011)

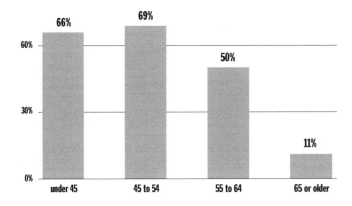

Table 6.5 Labor Force Status of Married-Couple Family Groups by Age, 2011

(number and percent distribution of married-couple family groups by age of reference person and labor force status of husband and wife, 2011; numbers in thousands)

	total	husband and wife in labor force	husband only in labor force	wife only in labor force	neither husband nor wife in labor force
Total married-couple family groups	**60,155**	**31,994**	**13,241**	**4,455**	**10,464**
Under age 45	22,732	15,103	6,268	853	506
Aged 45 to 54	14,017	9,609	2,963	869	577
Aged 55 to 64	12,158	6,035	2,601	1,615	1,906
Aged 65 or older	11,248	1,247	1,409	1,118	7,475

PERCENT DISTRIBUTION BY LABOR FORCE STATUS

	total	husband and wife in labor force	husband only in labor force	wife only in labor force	neither husband nor wife in labor force
Total married-couple family groups	**100.0%**	**53.2%**	**22.0%**	**7.4%**	**17.4%**
Under age 45	100.0	66.4	27.6	3.8	2.2
Aged 45 to 54	100.0	68.6	21.1	6.2	4.1
Aged 55 to 64	100.0	49.6	21.4	13.3	15.7
Aged 65 or older	100.0	11.1	12.5	9.9	66.5

PERCENT DISTRIBUTION BY AGE

	total	husband and wife in labor force	husband only in labor force	wife only in labor force	neither husband nor wife in labor force
Total married-couple family groups	**100.0%**	**100.0%**	**100.0%**	**100.0%**	**100.0%**
Under age 45	37.8	47.2	47.3	19.1	4.8
Aged 45 to 54	23.3	30.0	22.4	19.5	5.5
Aged 55 to 64	20.2	18.9	19.6	36.3	18.2
Aged 65 or older	18.7	3.9	10.6	25.1	71.4

Source: Bureau of the Census, America's Families and Living Arrangements: 2011, Internet site http://www.census.gov/population/www/socdemo/hh-fam/cps2011.html; calculations by New Strategist

Boomers Are Almost Half of Nation's Managers

They account for only 20 percent of food prep workers.

Among the 140 million employed Americans in 2011, more than 55 million (or 39 percent) were in the broad 45-to-64 age group (Boomers were aged 47 to 65 in that year). In some occupations, more than 50 percent of workers are aged 45 to 64. Boomers account for 73 percent of postal service clerks, 64 percent of mail carriers, and 63 percent of chief executives. They are also 60 percent of aircraft pilots, 57 percent of bus drivers, and 57 percent of clergy.

At the other extreme, only 13 percent of waiters and waitresses are aged 45 to 64. Not surprisingly, aging boomers account for only 15 percent of lifeguards. They are also underrepresented in many computer occupations. People aged 45 to 64 account for only 30 percent of software developers.

■ The median age of workers ranges widely depending on the occupation. Farmers and ranchers have a median age of 56. Waiters and waitresses have a median age of 26.

People aged 45 to 64 account for more than half of workers in some occupations

(percent of workers in the 45-to-64 age group, by selected occupation, 2011)

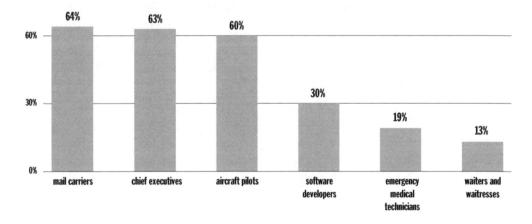

Table 6.6 Occupations of Workers Aged 45 to 64, 2011

(number of employed workers aged 16 or older, median age of workers, and number of workers aged 45 to 64, by occupation, 2011; numbers in thousands)

	total	median age	aged 45 to 64		
			total	45 to 54	55 to 64
TOTAL WORKERS	**139,869**	**42.1**	**55,053**	**32,867**	**22,186**
Management and professional occupations	**52,547**	**44.2**	**22,660**	**13,277**	**9,383**
Management, business and financial operations	21,589	45.7	10,062	6,014	4,048
Management	15,250	46.7	7,440	4,437	3,003
Business and financial operations	6,339	43.3	2,622	1,578	1,044
Professional and related occupations	30,957	43.1	12,597	7,262	5,335
Computer and mathematical	3,608	40.5	1,253	845	408
Architecture and engineering	2,785	43.9	1,242	755	487
Life, physical, and social sciences	1,303	42.3	490	261	229
Community and social services	2,352	44.8	1,016	527	489
Legal	1,770	46.1	803	425	378
Education, training, and library	8,619	43.6	3,598	2,013	1,585
Arts, design, entertainment, sports, and media	2,779	40.9	982	563	419
Health care practitioner and technician	7,740	43.3	3,214	1,873	1,341
Service occupations	**24,787**	**37.6**	**7,866**	**4,794**	**3,072**
Health care support	3,359	38.8	1,146	698	448
Protective service	3,210	40.4	1,082	675	407
Food preparation and serving	7,747	29.3	1,585	1,028	557
Building and grounds cleaning and maintenance	5,492	43.8	2,379	1,412	967
Personal care and service	4,979	39.5	1,675	981	694
Sales and office occupations	**33,066**	**41.5**	**12,651**	**7,346**	**5,305**
Sales and related occupations	15,330	39.9	5,372	3,166	2,206
Office and administrative support	17,736	42.7	7,369	4,270	3,099
Natural resources, construction, and maintenance occupations	**13,009**	**41.0**	**4,910**	**3,144**	**1,766**
Farming, fishing, and forestry	1,001	37.0	300	183	117
Construction and extraction	7,125	40.4	2,562	1,679	883
Installation, maintenance, and repair	4,883	42.6	2,049	1,283	766
Production, transportation, and material-moving occupations	**16,461**	**42.8**	**6,874**	**4,215**	**2,659**
Production	8,142	43.1	3,531	2,185	1,346
Transportation and material moving	8,318	42.6	3,343	2,030	1,313

Source: Bureau of Labor Statistics, unpublished data from the 2011 Current Population Survey; calculations by New Strategist

Table 6.7 Share of Workers Aged 45 to 64 by Occupation, 2011

(percent distribution of employed people aged 16 or older and aged 45 to 64 by occupation, 2011)

	total	aged 45 to 64		
		total	45 to 54	55 to 64
TOTAL WORKERS	**100.0%**	**39.4%**	**23.5%**	**15.9%**
Management and professional occupations	**100.0**	**43.1**	**25.3**	**17.9**
Management, business and financial operations	100.0	46.6	27.9	18.8
Management	100.0	48.8	29.1	19.7
Business and financial operations	100.0	41.4	24.9	16.5
Professional and related occupations	100.0	40.7	23.5	17.2
Computer and mathematical	100.0	34.7	23.4	11.3
Architecture and engineering	100.0	44.6	27.1	17.5
Life, physical, and social sciences	100.0	37.6	20.0	17.6
Community and social services	100.0	43.2	22.4	20.8
Legal	100.0	45.4	24.0	21.4
Education, training, and library	100.0	41.7	23.4	18.4
Arts, design, entertainment, sports, and media	100.0	35.3	20.3	15.1
Health care practitioner and technician	100.0	41.5	24.2	17.3
Service occupations	**100.0**	**31.7**	**19.3**	**12.4**
Health care support	100.0	34.1	20.8	13.3
Protective service	100.0	33.7	21.0	12.7
Food preparation and serving	100.0	20.5	13.3	7.2
Building and grounds cleaning and maintenance	100.0	43.3	25.7	17.6
Personal care and service	100.0	33.6	19.7	13.9
Sales and office occupations	**100.0**	**38.3**	**22.2**	**16.0**
Sales and related occupations	100.0	35.0	20.7	14.4
Office and administrative support	100.0	41.5	24.1	17.5
Natural resources, construction, and maintenance occupations	**100.0**	**37.7**	**24.2**	**13.6**
Farming, fishing, and forestry	100.0	30.0	18.3	11.7
Construction and extraction	100.0	36.0	23.6	12.4
Installation, maintenance, and repair	100.0	42.0	26.3	15.7
Production, transportation, and material-moving occupations	**100.0**	**41.8**	**25.6**	**16.2**
Production	100.0	43.4	26.8	16.5
Transportation and material moving	100.0	40.2	24.4	15.8

Source: Bureau of Labor Statistics, unpublished data from the 2011 Current Population Survey; calculations by New Strategist

Table 6.8 Distribution of Workers Aged 45 to 64 by Occupation, 2011

(percent distribution of total employed and employed aged 45 to 64, by occupation, 2011)

	total	aged 45 to 64		
		total	45 to 54	55 to 64
TOTAL WORKERS	100.0%	100.0%	100.0%	100.0%
Management and professional occupations	37.6	41.2	40.4	42.3
Management, business and financial operations	15.4	18.3	18.3	18.2
Management	10.9	13.5	13.5	13.5
Business and financial operations	4.5	4.8	4.8	4.7
Professional and related occupations	22.1	22.9	22.1	24.0
Computer and mathematical	2.6	2.3	2.6	1.8
Architecture and engineering	2.0	2.3	2.3	2.2
Life, physical, and social sciences	0.9	0.9	0.8	1.0
Community and social services	1.7	1.8	1.6	2.2
Legal	1.3	1.5	1.3	1.7
Education, training, and library	6.2	6.5	6.1	7.1
Arts, design, entertainment, sports, and media	2.0	1.8	1.7	1.9
Health care practitioner and technician	5.5	5.8	5.7	6.0
Service occupations	17.7	14.3	14.6	13.8
Health care support	2.4	2.1	2.1	2.0
Protective service	2.3	2.0	2.1	1.8
Food preparation and serving	5.5	2.9	3.1	2.5
Building and grounds cleaning and maintenance	3.9	4.3	4.3	4.4
Personal care and service	3.6	3.0	3.0	3.1
Sales and office occupations	23.6	23.0	22.4	23.9
Sales and related occupations	11.0	9.8	9.6	9.9
Office and administrative support	12.7	13.4	13.0	14.0
Natural resources, construction, and maintenance occupations	9.3	8.9	9.6	8.0
Farming, fishing, and forestry	0.7	0.5	0.6	0.5
Construction and extraction	5.1	4.7	5.1	4.0
Installation, maintenance, and repair	3.5	3.7	3.9	3.5
Production, transportation, and material-moving occupations	11.8	12.5	12.8	12.0
Production	5.8	6.4	6.6	6.1
Transportation and material moving	5.9	6.1	6.2	5.9

Source: Bureau of Labor Statistics, unpublished data from the 2011 Current Population Survey; calculations by New Strategist

Table 6.9 Workers Aged 45 to 64 by Detailed Occupation, 2011

(number of employed workers aged 16 or older, median age, and number and percent aged 45 to 64, for detailed occupations with at least 100,000 workers, 2011; numbers in thousands)

	total workers	median age	aged 45 to 54 number	aged 45 to 54 percent of total	aged 55 to 64 number	aged 55 to 64 percent of total
TOTAL WORKERS	**139,869**	**42.1**	**32,867**	**23.5%**	**22,186**	**15.9%**
Chief executives	1,515	52.0	556	36.7	392	25.9
General and operations managers	978	45.4	324	33.1	182	18.6
Marketing and sales managers	1,009	42.1	262	26.0	125	12.4
Administrative services managers	128	48.9	45	35.2	28	21.9
Computer and information systems managers	553	43.1	162	29.3	74	13.4
Financial managers	1,107	43.6	300	27.1	176	15.9
Human resources managers	243	45.1	71	29.2	44	18.1
Industrial production managers	259	46.3	81	31.3	55	21.2
Purchasing managers	204	48.7	73	35.8	41	20.1
Transportation, storage, and distribution managers	254	43.8	68	26.8	42	16.5
Farmers, ranchers, and other agricultural managers	978	55.9	214	21.9	253	25.9
Construction managers	926	46.9	294	31.7	182	19.7
Education administrators	853	46.9	220	25.8	202	23.7
Architectural and engineering managers	106	47.6	39	36.8	20	18.9
Food service managers	1,051	39.7	255	24.3	126	12.0
Lodging managers	148	46.7	31	20.9	32	21.6
Medical and health services managers	529	49.6	178	33.6	134	25.3
Property, real estate, community association managers	587	49.5	146	24.9	126	21.5
Social and community service managers	329	48.2	97	29.5	71	21.6
Managers, all other	3,173	46.6	931	29.3	638	20.1
Wholesale and retail buyers, except farm products	170	40.7	33	19.4	28	16.5
Purchasing agents, except wholesale, retail, farm products	259	43.5	70	27.0	51	19.7
Claims adjusters, appraisers, examiners, investigators	296	42.6	74	25.0	44	14.9
Compliance officers	198	45.9	59	29.8	42	21.2
Cost estimators	119	44.7	28	23.5	22	18.5
Human resources workers	595	42.4	146	24.5	89	15.0
Training and development specialists	130	45.0	35	26.9	25	19.2
Management analysts	707	46.6	192	27.2	138	19.5
Meeting, convention, and event planners	109	37.4	18	16.5	13	11.9
Market research analysts and marketing specialists	205	36.4	42	20.5	14	6.8
Business operations specialists, all other	281	43.6	65	23.1	52	18.5
Accountants and auditors	1,653	43.1	410	24.8	262	15.8
Personal financial advisors	371	43.9	86	23.2	57	15.4
Insurance underwriters	117	44.0	33	28.2	19	16.2
Credit counselors and loan officers	326	42.0	82	25.2	44	13.5
Tax preparers	110	50.2	23	20.9	25	22.7
Computer systems analysts	447	43.1	133	29.8	64	14.3
Computer programmers	459	41.8	105	22.9	66	14.4
Software developers, applications and systems software	1,044	39.4	230	22.0	87	8.3
Web developers	182	37.0	28	15.4	12	6.6
Computer support specialists	461	39.1	90	19.5	60	13.0
Database administrators	134	42.5	40	29.9	21	15.7
Network and computer systems administrators	233	40.6	52	22.3	22	9.4
Computer occupations, all other	306	40.8	81	26.5	37	12.1
Operations research analysts	116	41.3	28	24.1	15	12.9
Architects, except naval	181	46.7	49	27.1	41	22.7

	total workers	median age	aged 45 to 54		aged 55 to 64	
			number	percent of total	number	percent of total
Aerospace engineers	144	43.9	37	25.7%	27	18.8%
Civil engineers	383	42.5	97	25.3	62	16.2
Electrical and electronics engineers	309	45.0	96	31.1	47	15.2
Industrial engineers, including health and safety	174	43.4	53	30.5	24	13.8
Mechanical engineers	322	42.5	92	28.6	43	13.4
Engineers, all other	337	43.3	83	24.6	59	17.5
Drafters	147	44.0	32	21.8	31	21.1
Engineering technicians, except drafters	376	46.5	113	30.1	83	22.1
Biological scientists	114	42.6	23	20.2	24	21.1
Medical scientists	156	39.5	29	18.6	18	11.5
Physical scientists, all other	152	40.4	29	19.1	19	12.5
Psychologists	197	48.3	35	17.8	46	23.4
Counselors	732	43.0	141	19.3	152	20.8
Social workers	769	42.6	174	22.6	132	17.2
Social and human service assistants	131	44.1	32	24.4	27	20.6
Clergy	414	52.5	106	25.6	128	30.9
Lawyers	1,085	47.2	255	23.5	238	21.9
Paralegals and legal assistants	404	42.8	99	24.5	73	18.1
Miscellaneous legal support workers	209	44.8	52	24.9	45	21.5
Postsecondary teachers	1,355	45.7	281	20.7	279	20.6
Preschool and kindergarten teachers	707	39.2	142	20.1	85	12.0
Elementary and middle school teachers	2,848	43.0	676	23.7	507	17.8
Secondary school teachers	1,136	43.2	271	23.9	205	18.0
Special education teachers	388	43.3	104	26.8	65	16.8
Other teachers and instructors	812	43.7	169	20.8	146	18.0
Librarians	198	52.0	46	23.2	64	32.3
Teacher assistants	950	44.9	276	29.1	178	18.7
Other education, training, and library workers	140	46.3	30	21.4	34	24.3
Artists and related workers	180	45.3	35	19.4	36	20.0
Designers	766	41.8	187	24.4	109	14.2
Producers and directors	149	40.3	31	20.8	20	13.4
Athletes, coaches, umpires, and related workers	272	30.8	40	14.7	29	10.7
Musicians, singers, and related workers	191	43.2	31	16.2	38	19.9
Public relations specialists	158	39.2	29	18.4	21	13.3
Editors	166	41.4	31	18.7	27	16.3
Writers and authors	218	46.1	52	23.9	40	18.3
Broadcast, sound engineering technicians, radio operators	106	39.7	18	17.0	14	13.2
Photographers	148	40.6	25	16.9	25	16.9
Dentists	181	51.0	44	24.3	46	25.4
Dietitians and nutritionists	102	47.7	32	31.4	20	19.6
Pharmacists	274	41.1	49	17.9	38	13.9
Physicians and surgeons	822	46.3	206	25.1	157	19.1
Occupational therapists	112	41.7	27	24.1	12	10.7
Physical therapists	222	40.5	57	25.7	19	8.6
Respiratory therapists	134	44.5	37	27.6	24	17.9
Speech-language pathologists	125	40.5	18	14.4	20	16.0
Therapists, all other	138	40.7	28	20.3	20	14.5
Registered nurses	2,706	44.7	679	25.1	552	20.4
Nurse practitioners	100	46.9	33	33.0	21	21.0
Clinical laboratory technologists and technicians	321	43.2	87	27.1	56	17.4
Dental hygienists	148	42.2	33	22.3	25	16.9
Diagnostic related technologists and technicians	342	42.1	97	28.4	48	14.0
Emergency medical technicians and paramedics	185	31.8	27	14.6	8	4.3
Health practitioner support technologists and technicians	511	34.8	96	18.8	44	8.6

	total workers	median age	aged 45 to 54		aged 55 to 64	
			number	percent of total	number	percent of total
Licensed practical and licensed vocational nurses	560	43.2	135	24.1%	95	17.0%
Medical records and health information technicians	116	42.7	22	19.0	23	19.8
Nursing, psychiatric, and home health aides	1,981	40.3	441	22.3	284	14.3
Massage therapists	146	40.5	29	19.9	24	16.4
Dental assistants	307	36.3	54	17.6	33	10.7
Medical assistants	395	34.6	67	17.0	36	9.1
Phlebotomists	119	38.3	25	21.0	14	11.8
First-line supervisors of police and detectives	107	46.0	37	34.6	20	18.7
First-line supervisors of protective service workers, all other	111	47.2	34	30.6	25	22.5
Firefighters	305	37.3	55	18.0	11	3.6
Bailiffs, correctional officers, and jailers	446	39.7	99	22.2	49	11.0
Detectives and criminal investigators	151	42.3	41	27.2	17	11.3
Police and sheriff's patrol officers	668	39.3	126	18.9	59	8.8
Security guards and gaming surveillance officers	963	41.9	181	18.8	165	17.1
Lifeguards and other recreational, and all other protective service workers	146	21.8	10	6.8	12	8.2
Chefs and head cooks	347	38.8	60	17.3	35	10.1
First-line supervisors of food preparation and serving workers	505	36.8	93	18.4	56	11.1
Cooks	1,990	33.8	359	18.0	174	8.7
Food preparation workers	784	28.0	110	14.0	57	7.3
Bartenders	392	31.8	50	12.8	28	7.1
Combined food preparation and serving workers, including fast food	326	28.1	47	14.4	24	7.4
Counter attendants, cafeteria, food concession, and coffee shop	255	21.4	13	5.1	9	3.5
Waiters and waitresses	2,059	26.1	180	8.7	88	4.3
Food servers, nonrestaurant	181	32.3	30	16.6	23	12.7
Dining room, cafeteria attendants and bartender helpers	347	25.4	42	12.1	28	8.1
Dishwashers	273	28.3	33	12.1	23	8.4
Hosts and hostesses, restaurant, lounge, and coffee shop	286	21.4	12	4.2	9	3.1
First-line supervisors of housekeeping, janitorial workers	292	48.9	98	33.6	72	24.7
First-line supervisors of landscaping, lawn service, and groundskeeping workers	274	43.5	74	27.0	44	16.1
Janitors and building cleaners	2,186	46.4	586	26.8	459	21.0
Maids and housekeeping cleaners	1,419	45.2	408	28.8	245	17.3
Grounds maintenance workers	1,247	37.1	231	18.5	136	10.9
First-line supervisors of gaming workers	120	40.6	25	20.8	14	11.7
First-line supervisors of personal service workers	192	43.1	49	25.5	30	15.6
Nonfarm animal caretakers	179	37.2	40	22.3	20	11.2
Gaming services workers	113	40.5	26	23.0	15	13.3
Misc. entertainment attendants and related workers	182	26.4	17	9.3	17	9.3
Hairdressers, hairstylists, and cosmetologists	758	39.8	144	19.0	104	13.7
Miscellaneous personal appearance workers	251	40.8	50	19.9	32	12.7
Childcare workers	1,231	37.2	229	18.6	156	12.7
Personal care aides	1,057	43.9	252	23.8	189	17.9
Recreation and fitness workers	390	36.6	65	16.7	49	12.6
Personal care and service workers, all other	105	33.2	14	13.3	9	8.6
First-line supervisors of retail sales workers	3,217	42.6	817	25.4	489	15.2
First-line supervisors of nonretail sales workers	1,088	46.3	319	29.3	201	18.5
Cashiers	3,158	27.2	363	11.5	265	8.4
Counter and rental clerks	139	38.2	26	18.7	20	14.4
Parts salespersons	131	40.9	28	21.4	23	17.6

	total workers	median age	aged 45 to 54		aged 55 to 64	
			number	percent of total	number	percent of total
Retail salespersons	3,224	35.9	535	16.6%	457	14.2%
Advertising sales agents	254	39.6	61	24.0	24	9.4
Insurance sales agents	531	45.8	137	25.8	99	18.6
Securities, commodities, financial services sales agents	267	41.7	54	20.2	41	15.4
Sales representatives, services, all other	503	40.7	109	21.7	75	14.9
Sales representatives, wholesale and manufacturing	1,297	44.6	361	27.8	212	16.3
Real estate brokers and sales agents	811	50.3	203	25.0	192	23.7
Telemarketers	108	30.5	14	13.0	11	10.2
Door-to-door sales workers, news and street vendors, and related workers	201	43.8	47	23.4	33	16.4
Sales and related workers, all other	226	44.2	51	22.6	36	15.9
First-line supervisors of office and administrative support workers	1,423	45.7	391	27.5	296	20.8
Bill and account collectors	211	38.9	42	19.9	25	11.8
Billing and posting clerks	471	42.2	134	28.5	69	14.6
Bookkeeping, accounting, and auditing clerks	1,300	48.5	362	27.8	283	21.8
Payroll and timekeeping clerks	168	46.1	58	34.5	32	19.0
Tellers	413	31.8	59	14.3	50	12.1
Customer service representatives	1,916	37.0	369	19.3	229	12.0
File Clerks	334	40.8	77	23.1	49	14.7
Hotel, motel, and resort desk clerks	135	30.1	13	9.6	12	8.9
Interviewers, except eligibility and loan	153	40.8	36	23.5	26	17.0
Library assistants, clerical	113	44.8	15	13.3	29	25.7
Loan interviewers and clerks	117	40.4	26	22.2	12	10.3
Order clerks	113	41.7	25	22.1	23	20.4
Receptionists and information clerks	1,259	38.3	227	18.0	192	15.3
Information and record clerks, all other	118	45.7	30	25.4	25	21.2
Couriers and messengers	249	46.5	78	31.3	35	14.1
Dispatchers	239	41.5	54	22.6	38	15.9
Postal service clerks	146	53.1	46	31.5	60	41.1
Postal service mail carriers	348	49.9	151	43.4	71	20.4
Production, planning, and expediting clerks	236	44.1	63	26.7	45	19.1
Shipping, receiving, and traffic clerks	559	40.0	133	23.8	70	12.5
Stock clerks and order fillers	1,503	34.2	262	17.4	187	12.4
Secretaries and administrative assistants	2,871	47.9	803	28.0	670	23.3
Computer operators	126	48.9	41	32.5	34	27.0
Data entry keyers	334	40.0	80	24.0	40	12.0
Word processors and typists	136	46.5	37	27.2	29	21.3
Insurance claims and policy processing clerks	246	41.7	62	25.2	42	17.1
Office clerks, general	1,061	42.2	255	24.0	168	15.8
Office and administrative support workers, all other	513	42.4	118	23.0	91	17.7
Miscellaneous agricultural workers	708	33.8	112	15.8	66	9.3
First-line supervisors of construction trades and extraction workers	634	45.2	195	30.8	117	18.5
Brickmasons, blockmasons, and stonemasons	146	41.8	37	25.3	19	13.0
Carpenters	1,330	41.4	338	25.4	170	12.8
Carpet, floor, and tile installers and finishers	189	37.0	35	18.5	14	7.4
Construction laborers	1,253	36.9	254	20.3	114	9.1
Operating engineers and other construction equipment operators	369	43.0	93	25.2	62	16.8
Drywall installers, ceiling tile installers, and tapers	150	37.6	20	13.3	14	9.3
Electricians	682	41.5	177	26.0	86	12.6
Painters, construction and maintenance	528	40.9	114	21.6	70	13.3
Pipelayers, plumbers, pipefitters, and steamfitters	519	41.4	134	25.8	66	12.7

	total workers	median age	aged 45 to 54		aged 55 to 64	
			number	percent of total	number	percent of total
Roofers	222	34.2	39	17.6%	14	6.3%
Sheet metal workers	126	40.0	34	27.0	14	11.1
Highway maintenance workers	105	45.3	37	35.2	18	17.1
First-line supervisors of mechanics, installers, repairers	313	49.7	102	32.6	87	27.8
Computer, automated teller, and office machine repairers	305	40.6	69	22.6	40	13.1
Radio and telecommunications equipment installers and repairers	150	41.9	35	23.3	24	16.0
Aircraft mechanics and service technicians	164	44.0	56	34.1	20	12.2
Automotive body and related repairers	140	41.1	34	24.3	17	12.1
Automotive service technicians and mechanics	855	39.1	198	23.2	108	12.6
Bus and truck mechanics and diesel engine specialists	312	42.4	82	26.3	53	17.0
Heavy vehicle and mobile equipment service technicians and mechanics	199	43.4	56	28.1	29	14.6
Heating, air conditioning, and refrigeration mechanics and installers	338	39.4	83	24.6	40	11.8
Industrial and refractory machinery mechanics	433	45.7	135	31.2	86	19.9
Maintenance and repair workers, general	422	48.4	131	31.0	93	22.0
Electrical power-line installers and repairers	124	40.6	31	25.0	17	13.7
Telecommunications line installers and repairers	201	39.8	47	23.4	16	8.0
Other installation, maintenance, and repair workers	215	41.8	53	24.7	25	11.6
First-line supervisors of production, operating workers	727	47.1	251	34.5	146	20.1
Electrical, electronics, and electromechanical assemblers	156	45.9	46	29.5	30	19.2
Miscellaneous assemblers and fabricators	860	41.5	222	25.8	124	14.4
Bakers	207	40.3	49	23.7	30	14.5
Butchers and other meat, poultry, fish processing workers	342	39.0	74	21.6	42	12.3
Food processing workers, all other	115	41.0	34	29.6	8	7.0
Cutting, punching, and press machine setters, operators, and tenders, metal and plastic	100	40.0	24	24.0	16	16.0
Machinists	419	45.6	116	27.7	85	20.3
Welding, soldering, and brazing workers	505	40.9	118	23.4	69	13.7
Metal workers and plastic workers, all other	368	41.7	90	24.5	55	14.9
Printing press operators	217	43.6	69	31.8	33	15.2
Laundry and dry-cleaning workers	174	44.6	39	22.4	37	21.3
Sewing machine operators	169	48.0	48	28.4	36	21.3
Inspectors, testers, sorters, samplers, and weighers	647	43.6	176	27.2	116	17.9
Packaging and filling machine operators and tenders	288	39.1	70	24.3	37	12.8
Painting workers	120	40.8	30	25.0	13	10.8
Production workers, all other	777	42.2	205	26.4	115	14.8
Supervisors of transportation, material-moving workers	228	44.3	72	31.6	35	15.4
Aircraft pilots and flight engineers	121	49.0	45	37.2	28	23.1
Bus drivers	573	52.6	171	29.8	158	27.6
Driver/sales workers and truck drivers	3,059	45.4	858	28.0	547	17.9
Taxi drivers and chauffeurs	342	48.8	92	26.9	67	19.6
Industrial truck and tractor operators	528	39.8	124	23.5	57	10.8
Cleaners of vehicles and equipment	331	32.7	42	12.7	32	9.7
Laborers and freight, stock, and material movers, hand	1,787	35.0	322	18.0	188	10.5
Packers and packagers, hand	393	37.9	78	19.8	50	12.7

Source: Bureau of Labor Statistics, unpublished tables from the 2011 Current Population Survey; calculations by New Strategist

Many Workers Have Part-Time Jobs

One in five workers aged 25 to 54 works part-time.

Among workers ranging in age from 25 to 54, a substantial 20 percent had part-time jobs in 2011. Among those with part-time jobs, many would prefer full-time employment. Among working men in the age group, 14 percent work part-time. Of those who do, more than one in three (39 percent) work part-time for economic reasons—meaning they want a full-time job. Among working women in the age group, 27 percent work part-time and 23 percent of the part-timers want a full-time position.

Among workers aged 55 or older, part-time work becomes more common—and more desired—for both men and women. Twenty-three percent of employed men and 35 percent of employed women aged 55 or older have part-time jobs. Only 19 percent of the men and 14 percent of the women work part-time because they cannot find full-time work.

■ The percentage of workers who have part-time jobs because they cannot find full-time employment has been rising because of the Great Recession.

Many part-time workers want full-time jobs

(percent of employed men who work part time but would prefer a full-time job, by age, 2011)

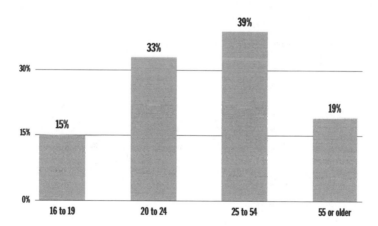

Table 6.10 Full-Time and Part-Time Workers by Age and Sex, 2011

(number and percent distribution of people aged 16 or older at work in nonagricultural industries by age, employment status, and sex, 2011; numbers in thousands)

	total			men			women		
	total	full-time	part-time	total	full-time	part-time	total	full-time	part-time
Total at work	132,717	98,446	34,271	70,440	56,598	13,841	62,278	41,848	20,430
Aged 16 to 19	4,065	888	3,178	1,951	534	1,417	2,114	353	1,761
Aged 20 to 24	12,515	7,226	5,289	6,543	4,097	2,446	5,972	3,129	2,843
Aged 25 to 54	89,430	71,366	18,064	47,964	41,213	6,751	41,466	30,153	11,313
Aged 55 or older	26,707	18,967	7,741	13,982	10,754	3,228	12,726	8,213	4,513

PERCENT DISTRIBUTION BY EMPLOYMENT STATUS

	total			men			women		
Total at work	100.0%	74.2%	25.8%	100.0%	80.3%	19.6%	100.0%	67.2%	32.8%
Aged 16 to 19	100.0	21.8	78.2	100.0	27.4	72.6	100.0	16.7	83.3
Aged 20 to 24	100.0	57.7	42.3	100.0	62.6	37.4	100.0	52.4	47.6
Aged 25 to 54	100.0	79.8	20.2	100.0	85.9	14.1	100.0	72.7	27.3
Aged 55 or older	100.0	71.0	29.0	100.0	76.9	23.1	100.0	64.5	35.5

PERCENT DISTRIBUTION BY AGE

	total			men			women		
Total at work	100.0%	100.0%	100.0%	100.0%	100.0%	100.0%	100.0%	100.0%	100.0%
Aged 16 to 19	3.1	0.9	9.3	2.8	0.9	10.2	3.4	0.8	8.6
Aged 20 to 24	9.4	7.3	15.4	9.3	7.2	17.7	9.6	7.5	13.9
Aged 25 to 54	67.4	72.5	52.7	68.1	72.8	48.8	66.6	72.1	55.4
Aged 55 or older	20.1	19.3	22.6	19.8	19.0	23.3	20.4	19.6	22.1

Note: "Part-time" work is less than 35 hours per week. Part-time workers exclude those who worked less than 35 hours in the previous week because of vacation, holidays, child care problems, weather issues, and other temporary, noneconomic reasons.
Source: Bureau of Labor Statistics, Labor Force Statistics from the Current Population Survey, Internet site http://www.bls .gov/cps/tables.htm#empstat; calculations by New Strategist

Table 6.11 Part-Time Workers by Sex, Age, and Reason, 2011

(total number of people aged 16 or older who work in nonagricultural industries part-time, and number and percent working part-time for economic reasons, by sex and age, 2011; numbers in thousands)

	total	working part-time for economic reasons	
		number	share of total
Men working part-time	**13,841**	**4,285**	**31.0%**
Aged 16 to 19	1,417	217	15.3
Aged 20 to 24	2,446	816	33.4
Aged 25 to 54	6,751	2,627	38.9
Aged 55 or older	3,228	625	19.4
Women working part-time	**20,430**	**4,138**	**20.3**
Aged 16 to 19	1,761	226	12.8
Aged 20 to 24	2,843	703	24.7
Aged 25 to 54	11,313	2,556	22.6
Aged 55 or older	4,513	653	14.5

Note: "Part-time" work is less than 35 hours per week. Part-time workers exclude those who worked less than 35 hours in the previous week because of vacation, holidays, child care problems, weather issues, and other temporary, noneconomic reasons. "Economic reasons" means a worker's hours have been reduced or worker cannot find full-time employment.
Source: Bureau of Labor Statistics, Labor Force Statistics from the Current Population Survey, Internet site http://www.bls .gov/cps/tables.htm#empstat; calculations by New Strategist

Few Boomers Are Self-Employed

Workers aged 65 or older are most likely to be self-employed.

Despite plenty of media hype about America's entrepreneurial spirit, few Americans are self-employed. Only 6.8 percent of the nation's workers were self-employed in 2011. Men are more likely than women to be self-employed, 7.9 versus 5.4 percent. For both men and women, the percentage who are self-employed rises with age.

The oldest workers are most likely to be self-employed. Twelve percent of working men and 7.5 percent of working women aged 55 to 64 work for themselves. The figure rises to 20.5 percent among working men and 13.8 percent among working women in the 65-or-older age group.

■ Many more workers would opt for self-employment if health insurance were not an obstacle.

Self-employment rises with age

(percent of workers who are self-employed, by age, 2011)

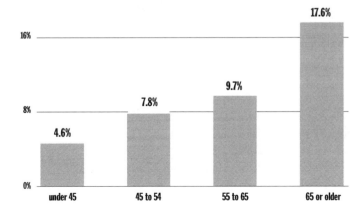

Table 6.12 Self-Employed Workers by Sex and Age, 2011

(number of employed workers aged 16 or older, number and percent who are self-employed, and percent distribution of self-employed, by age, 2011; numbers in thousands)

	total	self-employed		percent distribution of self-employed by age
		number	percent	
Total aged 16 or older	**139,869**	**9,449**	**6.8%**	**100.0%**
Aged 16 to 44	78,172	3,573	4.6	37.8
Aged 45 to 64	55,053	4,708	8.6	49.8
Aged 45 to 54	32,867	2,567	7.8	27.2
Aged 55 to 64	22,186	2,141	9.7	22.7
Aged 65 or older	6,647	1,168	17.6	12.4
Total men	**74,290**	**5,894**	**7.9**	**100.0**
Aged 16 to 44	41,978	2,204	5.3	37.4
Aged 45 to 64	28,582	2,925	10.2	49.6
Aged 45 to 54	17,113	1,588	9.3	26.9
Aged 55 to 64	11,469	1,337	11.7	22.7
Aged 65 or older	3,729	764	20.5	13.0
Total women	**65,579**	**3,555**	**5.4**	**100.0**
Aged 16 to 44	36,193	1,369	3.8	38.5
Aged 45 to 64	26,470	1,783	6.7	50.2
Aged 45 to 54	15,753	980	6.2	27.6
Aged 55 to 64	10,717	803	7.5	22.6
Aged 65 or older	2,917	404	13.8	11.4

Source: Bureau of Labor Statistics, Labor Force Statistics from the Current Population Survey, Internet site http://www.bls .gov/cps/tables.htm#empstat; calculations by New Strategist

Job Tenure among Younger Boomers Has Decreased

Long-term employment is less common for most of the middle aged.

Overall job tenure (the median number of years a worker has been with the current employer) has increased since 2000 because of the aging of the labor force. But among workers aged 45 to 64, median job tenure has declined. The decline has been particularly severe among men aged 45 to 54, the median number of years that men in the age group have been on the job falling from 9.5 years in 2000 to 8.5 years in 2010.

As job tenure declines, so does long-term employment. Between 2000 and 2010, long-term employment (defined as having been with one's current employer for at least 10 years) fell for men ranging in age from 30 to 59. But long-term employment increased among men aged 60 to 64 during the decade as early retirement became less common. Among women between the ages of 45 and 64, long-term employment fell in all but one five-year age group.

■ As fewer workers opt for early retirement, long-term employment among older workers may rise.

Older Boomer men are staying on the job longer

(percent of men aged 45 to 64 who have worked for their current employer for 10 or more years, 2000 and 2010)

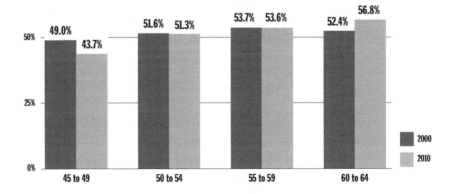

Table 6.13 Job Tenure by Sex and Age, 2000 and 2010

(median number of years workers aged 16 or older have been with their current employer by sex and age, 2000 and 2010; change in years, 2000–10)

	2010	2000	change in years 2000–10
Total employed men	**4.6**	**3.8**	**0.8**
Aged 16 to 17	0.7	0.6	0.1
Aged 18 to 19	1.0	0.7	0.3
Aged 20 to 24	1.6	1.2	0.4
Aged 25 to 34	3.2	2.7	0.5
Aged 35 to 44	5.3	5.3	0.0
Aged 45 to 54	8.5	9.5	−1.0
Aged 55 to 64	10.4	10.2	0.2
Aged 65 or older	9.7	9.0	0.7
Total employed women	**4.2**	**3.3**	**0.9**
Aged 16 to 17	0.7	0.6	0.1
Aged 18 to 19	1.0	0.7	0.3
Aged 20 to 24	1.5	1.0	0.5
Aged 25 to 34	3.0	2.5	0.5
Aged 35 to 44	4.9	4.3	0.6
Aged 45 to 54	7.1	7.3	−0.2
Aged 55 to 64	9.7	9.9	−0.2
Aged 65 or older	10.1	9.7	0.4

Source: Bureau of Labor Statistics, Employee Tenure, Internet site http://www.bls.gov/news.release/tenure.toc.htm; calculations by New Strategist

Table 6.14 Long-Term Employment by Sex and Age, 2000 and 2010

(percent of employed wage and salary workers aged 25 or older who have been with their current employer for 10 or more years, by sex and age, 2000 and 2010; percentage point change in share, 2000–10)

	2010	2000	percentage point change 2000–10
Total employed men	**34.3%**	**33.4%**	**0.9**
Aged 25 to 29	3.1	3.0	0.1
Aged 30 to 34	14.3	15.1	−0.8
Aged 35 to 39	27.2	29.4	−2.2
Aged 40 to 44	37.5	40.2	−2.7
Aged 45 to 49	43.7	49.0	−5.3
Aged 50 to 54	51.3	51.6	−0.3
Aged 55 to 59	53.6	53.7	−0.1
Aged 60 to 64	56.8	52.4	4.4
Aged 65 or older	51.9	48.6	3.3
Total employed women	**31.9**	**29.5**	**2.4**
Aged 25 to 29	1.6	1.9	−0.3
Aged 30 to 34	11.1	12.5	−1.4
Aged 35 to 39	24.0	22.3	1.7
Aged 40 to 44	32.9	31.2	1.7
Aged 45 to 49	38.0	41.4	−3.4
Aged 50 to 54	46.5	45.8	0.7
Aged 55 to 59	51.2	52.5	−1.3
Aged 60 to 64	52.2	53.6	−1.4
Aged 65 or older	54.3	51.0	3.3

Source: Bureau of Labor Statistics, Employee Tenure, Internet site http://www.bls.gov/news.release/tenure.toc.htm; calculations by New Strategist

Most Minimum-Wage Workers Are Young Adults

Only 16 percent are Boomers.

Among the nation's 74 million workers who are paid hourly rates, nearly 4 million (5 percent) made minimum wage or less in 2011, according to the Bureau of Labor Statistics. Fully 81 percent of minimum-wage workers are under age 45. Only 16 percent are between the ages of 45 and 64 (Boomers were aged 47 to 65 in 2011). Among hourly workers in the 45-to-64 age group, only 2 percent make minimum wage or less.

The percentage of workers who make minimum wage or less rises to 4 percent in the 65-or-older age group. Many of these are retirees working part-time jobs to supplement their retirement income.

■ Younger workers are most likely to earn minimum wage or less because many are in entry-level jobs or are part-time workers.

Boomers account for few minimum-wage workers

(percent distribution of workers who make minimum wage or less, by age, 2011)

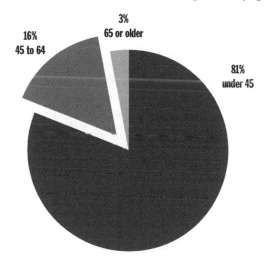

3%
65 or older

16%
45 to 64

81%
under 45

Table 6.15 Workers Earning Minimum Wage by Age, 2011

(number, percent, and percent distribution of workers paid hourly rates at or below minimum wage, by age, 2011; numbers in thousands)

	total paid hourly rates	at or below minimum wage		
		number	share of total	percent distribution
Total aged 16 or older	**73,926**	**3,829**	**5.2%**	**100.0%**
Aged 16 to 44	45,760	3,102	6.8	81.0
Aged 45 to 64	25,376	604	2.4	15.8
Aged 45 to 49	7,793	208	2.7	5.4
Aged 50 to 54	7,537	175	2.3	4.6
Aged 55 to 59	6,135	123	2.0	3.2
Aged 60 to 64	3,911	98	2.5	2.6
Aged 65 or older	2,790	123	4.4	3.2

Source: Bureau of Labor Statistics, Characteristics of Minimum Wage Workers, 2011, Internet site http://www.bls.gov/cps/minwage2011.htm; calculations by New Strategist

Union Representation Peaks among Workers Aged 55 to 64

Men and women are almost equally likely to be represented by a union.

Union representation has fallen sharply over the past few decades. In 2011, only 13 percent of wage and salary workers were represented by a union.

The percentage of workers who are represented by a union peaks in the 55-to-64 age group at 17 percent. Union representation is almost the same for men and women, a departure from the past when men were far more likely than women to be represented by a union. The difference in union representation by sex occurred because men were more likely to work in manufacturing—the traditional stronghold of labor unions. The decline of labor unions is partly the result of the shift in jobs from manufacturing to services.

■ Union representation could rise along with workers' concerns about job security and the cost of health care coverage.

Few workers are represented by a union

(percent of employed wage and salary workers who are represented by unions, by age, 2011)

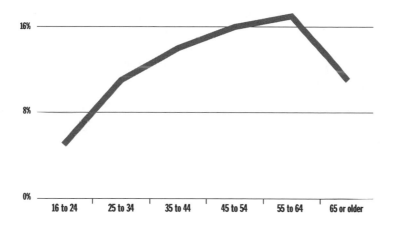

Table 6.16 Union Representation by Sex and Age, 2011

(number and percent of employed wage and salary workers aged 16 or older by union representation status, sex, and age, 2011; numbers in thousands)

	total employed	represented by unions	
		number	percent
Total aged 16 or older	**125,187**	**16,290**	**13.0%**
Aged 16 to 24	16,910	845	5.0
Aged 25 to 34	28,682	3,155	11.0
Aged 35 to 44	27,231	3,804	14.0
Aged 45 to 54	28,693	4,707	16.4
Aged 55 to 64	18,751	3,219	17.2
Aged 65 or older	4,920	559	11.4
Men aged 16 or older	**64,686**	**8,731**	**13.5**
Aged 16 to 24	8,636	486	5.6
Aged 25 to 34	15,465	1,706	11.0
Aged 35 to 44	14,412	2,114	14.7
Aged 45 to 54	14,415	2,513	17.4
Aged 55 to 64	9,212	1,623	17.6
Aged 65 or older	2,547	290	11.4
Women aged 16 or older	**60,502**	**7,558**	**12.5**
Aged 16 to 24	8,274	360	4.8
Aged 25 to 34	13,218	1,449	11.0
Aged 35 to 44	12,819	1,690	13.2
Aged 45 to 54	14,278	2,195	15.4
Aged 55 to 64	9,540	1,596	16.7
Aged 65 or older	2,373	269	10.7

Note: Workers represented by unions are either members of a labor union or similar employee association or workers who report no union affiliation but whose jobs are covered by a union or an employee association contract.
Source: Bureau of Labor Statistics, Labor Force Statistics from the Current Population Survey, Internet site http://www.bls .gov/cps/tables.htm#empstat; calculations by New Strategist

Number of Workers Aged 65 or Older Will Soar during the Decade

The labor force participation rate of older workers is projected to rise.

During the next decade, the oldest members of the Baby-Boom generation will enter their late sixties and early seventies. Because early retirement will be increasingly uncommon among Boomers, the labor force participation rate of people aged 65 or older is projected to increase.

Among men aged 65 or older, labor force participation will rise by 4.6 percentage points between 2010 and 2020, to 26.7 percent. Women aged 65 or older will see their labor force participation rate climb by 5.4 percentage points during those years, to 19.2 percent. The number of workers aged 65 or older will expand by 80 percent as Boomers move into the age group.

■ Millions of Baby Boomers will work well into their late sixties and early seventies because of inadequate retirement savings.

Expect more older workers in the labor force

(number of people aged 65 or older in the labor force, 2010 and 2020)

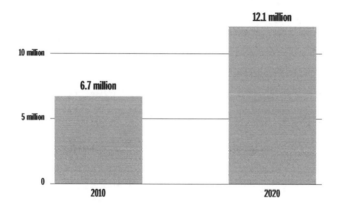

Table 6.17 Projections of the Labor Force by Sex and Age, 2010 and 2020

(number of people aged 16 or older in the civilian labor force by sex and age, 2010 and 2020; percent change, 2010–20; numbers in thousands)

	2010	2020	percent change
Total labor force	**153,889**	**164,360**	**6.8%**
Aged 16 to 24	20,934	18,331	−12.4
Aged 25 to 34	33,615	36,421	8.3
Aged 35 to 44	33,366	35,147	5.3
Aged 45 to 54	35,960	33,050	−8.1
Aged 55 to 64	23,297	29,299	25.8
Aged 65 or older	6,717	12,112	80.3
Aged 65 to 74	5,424	9,945	83.4
Aged 75 or older	1,293	2,167	67.6
Total men in labor force	**81,985**	**87,128**	**6.3**
Aged 16 to 24	10,855	9,690	−10.7
Aged 25 to 34	18,352	19,667	7.2
Aged 35 to 44	18,119	19,303	6.5
Aged 45 to 54	18,856	17,415	−7.6
Aged 55 to 64	12,103	14,662	21.1
Aged 65 or older	3,700	6,391	72.7
Aged 65 to 74	2,971	5,236	76.2
Aged 75 or older	729	1,155	58.4
Total women in labor force	**71,904**	**77,232**	**7.4**
Aged 16 to 24	10,079	8,641	−14.3
Aged 25 to 34	15,263	16,754	9.8
Aged 35 to 44	15,247	15,844	3.9
Aged 45 to 54	17,104	15,635	−8.6
Aged 55 to 64	11,194	14,637	30.8
Aged 65 or older	3,017	5,721	89.6
Aged 65 to 74	2,453	4,709	92.0
Aged 75 or older	564	1,012	79.4

Source: Bureau of Labor Statistics, Employment Projections, Internet site http://www.bls.gov/emp/; calculations by New Strategist

Table 6.18 Projections of Labor Force Participation by Sex and Age, 2010 and 2020

(percent of people aged 16 or older in the civilian labor force by sex and age, 2010 and 2020; percentage point change, 2010–20)

	2010	2020	percentage point change
Total labor force participation rate	**64.7%**	**62.5%**	**−2.2**
Men in labor force	**71.2**	**68.2**	**−3.0**
Aged 16 to 19	34.9	27.9	−7.0
Aged 20 to 24	74.5	69.4	−5.1
Aged 25 to 34	90.3	86.9	−3.4
Aged 35 to 44	91.5	91.3	−0.2
Aged 45 to 54	86.8	86.0	−0.8
Aged 55 to 64	70.0	71.1	1.1
Aged 55 to 59	78.5	78.6	0.1
Aged 60 to 64	60.0	63.2	3.2
Aged 60 to 61	67.4	62.9	−4.5
Aged 62 to 64	54.6	63.4	8.8
Aged 65 or older	22.1	26.7	4.6
Aged 65 to 69	36.5	41.4	4.9
Aged 70 to 74	22.0	27.0	5.0
Aged 75 or older	10.4	12.8	2.4
Women in labor force	**58.6**	**57.1**	**−1.5**
Aged 16 to 19	35.0	25.2	−9.8
Aged 20 to 24	68.3	62.3	−6.0
Aged 25 to 34	74.7	74.2	−0.5
Aged 35 to 44	75.2	74.0	−1.2
Aged 45 to 54	75.7	75.7	0.0
Aged 55 to 64	60.2	66.6	6.4
Aged 55 to 59	68.4	74.1	5.7
Aged 60 to 64	50.7	58.8	8.1
Aged 60 to 61	58.0	65.4	7.4
Aged 62 to 64	45.3	54.1	8.8
Aged 65 or older	13.8	19.2	5.4
Aged 65 to 69	27.0	34.5	7.5
Aged 70 to 74	14.7	19.2	4.5
Aged 75 or older	5.3	8.0	2.7

Source: Bureau of Labor Statistics, Employment Projections, Internet site http://www.bls.gov/emp/; calculations by New Strategist

7

Living Arrangements

■ Married couples account for 55 percent of households headed by people aged 45 to 64 (Boomers were aged 47 to 65 in 2011).

■ Household size peaks among householders aged 35 to 39. As householders age into their forties and fifties, the nest empties.

■ Many Boomer households include children. The 58 percent majority of householders aged 45 to 49 have children in their home, as do 45 percent of householders aged 50 to 54 and a still substantial 25 percent of those aged 55 to 64.

■ Only 15 percent of Boomer women live alone, but as they age the figure will more than double.

■ Most Boomers are currently married, but many have experienced divorce. Among men and women in their fifties, more than one-third has been through a divorce.

Most Boomer Households Are Headed by Married Couples

Households vary little by type among the middle aged.

In middle age, the lifestyles of the Baby-Boom generation are similar–despite the nearly 20-year span between the youngest and oldest boomers. Married couples account for 54 to 55 percent of households headed by people ranging in age from their late forties to their early sixties (Boomers were aged 47 to 65 in 2011).

There is much more variation in the proportion of Boomer households that are headed by women who live alone. The figure ranges from 9 percent in the 45-to-49 age group to 19 percent in the 60-to-64 age group as some Boomer wives become widows. Only 12 percent of Boomer households are headed by men who live alone, a figure that varies little by age.

■ Among people who live alone, women begin to significantly outnumber men in the 60-to-64 age group.

In middle age, a growing share of households are headed by women who live alone

(single-person households headed by women as a share of total households, by age of householder, 2011)

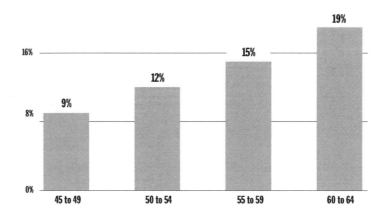

Table 7.1 Households Headed by People Aged 45 to 64 by Household Type, 2011: Total Households

(number and percent distribution of total households and households headed by people aged 45 to 64, by household type, 2011; numbers in thousands)

| | total | aged 45 to 64 | | | | | | |
| | | total | aged 45 to 54 | | | aged 55 to 64 | | |
			total	45 to 49	50 to 54	total	55 to 59	60 to 64
TOTAL HOUSEHOLDS	118,682	46,358	24,530	12,220	12,310	21,828	11,445	10,383
Family households	78,613	32,058	17,790	9,047	8,743	14,269	7,573	6,695
Married couples	58,036	25,357	13,506	6,721	6,785	11,851	6,228	5,623
Female householder, no spouse present	15,019	4,879	3,134	1,741	1,393	1,745	972	773
Male householder, no spouse present	5,559	1,822	1,150	585	565	672	373	299
Nonfamily households	40,069	14,299	6,740	3,173	3,567	7,559	3,872	3,687
Female householder	21,234	7,114	3,079	1,320	1,759	4,035	1,911	2,124
Living alone	18,184	6,151	2,538	1,072	1,466	3,613	1,680	1,933
Male householder	18,835	7,184	3,660	1,853	1,807	3,524	1,961	1,563
Living alone	14,539	6,114	3,034	1,524	1,510	3,081	1,678	1,402
Percent distribution by type								
TOTAL HOUSEHOLDS	100.0%	100.0%	100.0%	100.0%	100.0%	100.0%	100.0%	100.0%
Family households	66.2	69.2	72.5	74.0	71.0	65.4	66.2	64.5
Married couples	48.9	54.7	55.1	55.0	55.1	54.3	54.4	54.2
Female householder, no spouse present	12.7	10.5	12.8	14.2	11.3	8.0	8.5	7.4
Male householder, no spouse present	4.7	3.9	4.7	4.8	4.6	3.1	3.3	2.9
Nonfamily households	33.8	30.8	27.5	26.0	29.0	34.6	33.8	35.5
Female householder	17.9	15.3	12.6	10.8	14.3	18.5	16.7	20.5
Living alone	15.3	13.3	10.3	8.8	11.9	16.6	14.7	18.6
Male householder	15.9	15.5	14.9	15.2	14.7	16.1	17.1	15.1
Living alone	12.3	13.2	12.4	12.5	12.3	14.1	14.7	13.5
Percent distribution by age								
TOTAL HOUSEHOLDS	100.0%	39.1%	20.7%	10.3%	10.4%	18.4%	9.6%	8.7%
Family households	100.0	40.8	22.6	11.5	11.1	18.2	9.6	8.5
Married couples	100.0	43.7	23.3	11.6	11.7	20.4	10.7	9.7
Female householder, no spouse present	100.0	32.5	20.9	11.6	9.3	11.6	6.5	5.1
Male householder, no spouse present	100.0	32.8	20.7	10.5	10.2	12.1	6.7	5.4
Nonfamily households	100.0	35.7	16.8	7.9	8.9	18.9	9.7	9.2
Female householder	100.0	33.5	14.5	6.2	8.3	19.0	9.0	10.0
Living alone	100.0	33.8	14.0	5.9	8.1	19.9	9.2	10.6
Male householder	100.0	38.1	19.4	9.8	9.6	18.7	10.4	8.3
Living alone	100.0	42.1	20.9	10.5	10.4	21.2	11.5	9.6

Source: Bureau of the Census, America's Families and Living Arrangements: 2011, Internet site http://www.census.gov/ population/www/socdemo/hh-fam/cps2011.html; calculations by New Strategist

Few Black Households Are Headed by Married Couples

Couples dominate Asian, Hispanic, and non-Hispanic white households.

In 2011, married couples accounted for the majority of Asian, Hispanic, and non-Hispanic white households headed by people aged 45 to 64 (the Baby-Boom generation was aged 47 to 65 in 2011). The married-couple share of households ranges from 54 percent among Hispanics to 68 percent among Asians. In contrast, married couples head only 33 percent of black households in the 45-to-64 age group. Female-headed families are a large share (22 percent) of black households headed by the middle aged. In contrast, among non-Hispanic whites, female-headed families account for just 8 percent of households in the 45-to-64 age group.

In the 45-to-64 age group, only 9 percent of Hispanic and Asian households are headed by women living alone. The figures are a larger 13 percent for non-Hispanic whites and 19 percent for blacks.

■ The household incomes of blacks are lower than those of non-Hispanic whites in large part because married couples—the most affluent household type—are a much smaller share of households.

Married couples head a minority of households among blacks

(married couples as a percent of households headed by people aged 45 to 64, by race and Hispanic origin, 2011)

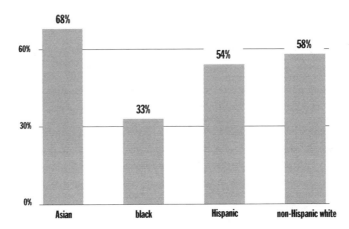

Table 7.2 Households Headed by People Aged 45 to 64 by Household Type, 2011: Asian Households

(number and percent distribution of total households headed by Asians and households headed by Asians aged 45 to 64, by household type, 2011; numbers in thousands)

		aged 45 to 64						
			aged 45 to 54				aged 55 to 64	
	total	total	total	45 to 49	50 to 54	total	55 to 59	60 to 64
TOTAL ASIAN HOUSEHOLDS	**5,040**	**1,814**	**1,051**	**581**	**470**	**763**	**410**	**353**
Family households	3,722	1,484	892	488	404	592	323	268
Married couples	2,939	1,241	739	407	332	502	265	237
Female householder, no spouse present	492	173	109	52	57	64	39	25
Male householder, no spouse present	291	70	44	29	15	26	19	6
Nonfamily households	1,318	332	160	94	66	172	88	84
Female householder	702	189	88	52	36	101	46	55
Living alone	558	161	77	45	32	84	37	47
Male householder	616	143	72	42	30	71	42	29
Living alone	437	111	57	37	20	54	25	29

Percent distribution by type

TOTAL ASIAN HOUSEHOLDS	**100.0%**	**100.0%**	**100.0%**	**100.0%**	**100.0%**	**100.0%**	**100.0%**	**100.0%**
Family households	**73.8**	**81.8**	**84.9**	**84.0**	**86.0**	**77.6**	**78.8**	**75.9**
Married couples	58.3	68.4	70.3	70.1	70.6	65.8	64.6	67.1
Female householder, no spouse present	9.8	9.5	10.4	9.0	12.1	8.4	9.5	7.1
Male householder no spouse present	5.8	3.9	4.2	5.0	3.2	3.4	4.6	1.7
Nonfamily households	26.2	18.3	15.2	16.2	14.0	22.5	21.5	23.8
Female householder	13.9	10.4	8.4	9.0	7.7	13.2	11.2	15.6
Living alone	11.1	8.9	7.3	7.7	6.8	11.0	9.0	13.3
Male householder	12.2	7.9	6.9	7.2	6.4	9.3	10.2	8.2
Living alone	8.7	6.1	5.4	6.4	4.3	7.1	6.1	8.2

Percent distribution by age

TOTAL ASIAN HOUSEHOLDS	**100.0%**	**36.0%**	**20.9%**	**11.5%**	**9.3%**	**15.%1**	**8.1%**	**7.0%**
Family households	**100.0**	**39.9**	**24.0**	**13.1**	**10.9**	**15.9**	**8.7**	**7.2**
Married couples	100.0	42.2	25.1	13.8	11.3	17.1	9.0	8.1
Female householder no spouse present	100.0	35.2	22.2	10.6	11.6	13.0	7.9	5.1
Male householder no spouse present	100.0	24.1	15.1	10.0	5.2	8.9	6.5	2.1
Nonfamily households	**100.0**	**25.2**	**12.1**	**7.1**	**5.0**	**13.1**	**6.7**	**6.4**
Female householder	100.0	26.9	12.5	7.4	5.1	14.4	6.6	7.8
Living alone	100.0	28.9	13.8	8.1	5.7	15.1	6.6	8.4
Male householder	100.0	23.2	11.7	6.8	4.9	11.5	6.8	4.7
Living alone	100.0	25.4	13.0	8.5	4.6	12.4	5.7	6.6

Note: Asians are those who identify themselves as being of the race alone and those who identify themselves as being of the race in combination with other races.

Source: Bureau of the Census, America's Families and Living Arrangements: 2011, Internet site http://www.census.gov/ population/www/socdemo/hh-fam/cps2011.html; calculations by New Strategist

Table 7.3 Households Headed by People Aged 45 to 64 by Household Type, 2011: Black Households

(number and percent distribution of total households headed by blacks and households headed by blacks aged 45 to 64, by household type, 2011; numbers in thousands)

	total	aged 45 to 64 total	aged 45 to 54 total	45 to 49	50 to 54	aged 55 to 64 total	55 to 59	60 to 64
TOTAL BLACK HOUSEHOLDS	**15,613**	**5,993**	**3,311**	**1,650**	**1,661**	**2,682**	**1,429**	**1,253**
Family households	**9,766**	**3,599**	**2,117**	**1,072**	**1,045**	**1,482**	**812**	**669**
Married couples	4,353	1,980	1,088	532	556	892	471	421
Female householder, no spouse present	4,459	1,332	857	451	406	475	281	194
Male householder, no spouse present	954	286	172	89	83	114	60	54
Nonfamily households	**5,847**	**2,394**	**1,194**	**578**	**616**	**1,200**	**616**	**584**
Female householder	3,238	1,264	624	285	339	640	303	337
Living alone	2,933	1,165	558	264	294	607	292	316
Male householder	2,609	1,131	571	294	277	560	313	247
Living alone	2,189	1,004	505	267	238	499	278	221
Percent distribution by type								
TOTAL BLACK HOUSEHOLDS	**100.0%**	**100.0%**	**100.0%**	**100.0%**	**100.0%**	**100.0%**	**100.0%**	**100.0%**
Family households	**62.6**	**60.1**	**63.9**	**65.0**	**62.9**	**55.3**	**56.8**	**53.4**
Married couples	27.9	33.0	32.9	32.2	33.5	33.3	33.0	33.6
Female householder, no spouse present	28.6	22.2	25.9	27.3	24.4	17.7	19.7	15.5
Male householder, no spouse present	6.1	4.8	5.2	5.4	5.0	4.3	4.2	4.3
Nonfamily households	**37.4**	**39.9**	**36.1**	**35.0**	**37.1**	**44.7**	**43.1**	**46.6**
Female householder	20.7	21.1	18.8	17.3	20.4	23.9	21.2	26.9
Living alone	18.8	19.4	16.9	16.0	17.7	22.6	20.4	25.2
Male householder	16.7	18.9	17.2	17.8	16.7	20.9	21.9	19.7
Living alone	14.0	16.8	15.3	16.2	14.3	18.6	19.5	17.6
Percent distribution by age								
TOTAL BLACK HOUSEHOLDS	**100.0%**	**38.4%**	**21.2%**	**10.6%**	**10.6%**	**17.2%**	**9.2%**	**8.0%**
Family households	**100.0**	**36.9**	**21.7**	**11.0**	**10.7**	**15.2**	**8.3**	**6.9**
Married couples	100.0	45.5	25.0	12.2	12.8	20.5	10.8	9.7
Female householder, no spouse present	100.0	29.9	19.2	10.1	9.1	10.7	6.3	4.4
Male householder, no spouse present	100.0	30.0	18.0	9.3	8.7	11.9	6.3	5.7
Nonfamily households	**100.0**	**40.9**	**20.4**	**9.9**	**10.5**	**20.5**	**10.5**	**10.0**
Female householder	100.0	39.0	19.3	8.8	10.5	19.8	9.4	10.4
Living alone	100.0	39.7	19.0	9.0	10.0	20.7	10.0	10.8
Male householder	100.0	43.3	21.9	11.3	10.6	21.5	12.0	9.5
Living alone	100.0	45.9	23.1	12.2	10.9	22.8	12.7	10.1

Note: Blacks are those who identify themselves as being of the race alone and those who identify themselves as being of the race in combination with other races.
Source: Bureau of the Census, America's Families and Living Arrangements: 2011, Internet site http://www.census.gov/population/www/socdemo/hh-fam/cps2011.html; calculations by New Strategist

Table 7.4 Households Headed by People Aged 45 to 64 by Household Type, 2011: Hispanic Households

(number and percent distribution of total households headed by Hispanics and households headed by Hispanics aged 45 to 64, by household type, 2011; numbers in thousands)

| | total | aged 45 to 64 | | | | | | |
| | | total | aged 45 to 54 | | | aged 55 to 64 | | |
			total	45 to 49	50 to 54	total	55 to 59	60 to 64
TOTAL HISPANIC HOUSEHOLDS	13,665	4,458	2,729	1,484	1,245	1,729	925	804
Family households	10,659	3,459	2,226	1,225	1,001	1,233	678	555
Married couples	6,725	2,398	1,520	843	677	878	478	400
Female householder, no spouse present	2,754	782	516	281	235	266	143	123
Male householder, no spouse present	1,180	280	191	101	90	89	57	32
Nonfamily households	3,006	998	503	259	244	495	247	249
Female householder	1,371	473	217	92	125	256	112	145
Living alone	1,098	396	171	67	104	225	98	127
Male householder	1,635	525	286	167	119	239	135	104
Living alone	1,100	400	202	120	82	198	107	91

Percent distribution by type

	total	total	total	45 to 49	50 to 54	total	55 to 59	60 to 64
TOTAL HISPANIC HOUSEHOLDS	100.0%	100.0%	100.0%	100.0%	100.0%	100.0%	100.0%	100.0%
Family households	78.0	77.6	81.6	82.5	80.4	71.3	73.3	69.0
Married couples	49.2	53.8	55.7	56.8	54.4	50.8	51.7	49.8
Female householder, no spouse present	20.2	17.5	18.9	18.9	18.9	15.4	15.5	15.3
Male householder, no spouse present	8.6	6.3	7.0	6.8	7.2	5.1	6.2	4.0
Nonfamily households	22.0	22.4	18.4	17.5	19.6	28.6	26.7	31.0
Female householder	10.0	10.6	8.0	6.2	10.0	14.8	12.1	18.0
Living alone	8.0	8.9	6.3	4.5	8.4	13.0	10.6	15.8
Male householder	12.0	11.8	10.5	11.3	9.6	13.8	14.6	12.9
Living alone	8.0	9.0	7.4	8.1	6.6	11.5	11.6	11.3

Percent distribution by age

	total	total	total	45 to 49	50 to 54	total	55 to 59	60 to 64
TOTAL HISPANIC HOUSEHOLDS	100.0%	32.6%	20.0%	10.9%	9.1%	12.7%	6.8%	5.9%
Family households	100.0	32.5	20.9	11.5	9.4	11.6	6.4	5.2
Married couples	100.0	35.7	22.6	12.5	10.1	13.1	7.1	5.9
Female householder, no spouse present	100.0	28.4	18.7	10.2	8.5	9.7	5.2	4.5
Male householder, no spouse present	100.0	23.7	16.2	8.6	7.6	7.5	4.8	2.7
Nonfamily households	100.0	33.2	16.7	8.6	8.1	16.5	8.2	8.3
Female householder	100.0	34.5	15.8	6.7	9.1	18.7	8.2	10.6
Living alone	100.0	36.1	15.6	6.1	9.5	20.5	8.9	11.6
Male householder	100.0	32.1	17.5	10.2	7.3	14.6	8.3	6.4
Living alone	100.0	36.4	18.4	10.9	7.5	18.0	9.7	8.3

Source: Bureau of the Census, America's Families and Living Arrangements: 2011, Internet site http://www.census.gov/ population/www/socdemo/hh-fam/cps2011.html; calculations by New Strategist

Table 7.5 Households Headed by People Aged 45 to 64 by Household Type, 2011: Non-Hispanic White Households

(number and percent distribution of total households headed by non-Hispanic whites and households headed by non-Hispanic whites aged 45 to 64, by household type, 2011; numbers in thousands)

		aged 45 to 64						
		total	aged 45 to 54			aged 55 to 64		
	total	total	total	45 to 49	50 to 54	total	55 to 59	60 to 64
TOTAL NON-HISPANIC WHITE HOUSEHOLDS	**83,471**	**33,674**	**17,236**	**8,394**	**8,842**	**16,438**	**8,553**	**7,885**
Family households	**53,859**	**23,255**	**12,436**	**6,198**	**6,238**	**10,819**	**5,679**	**5,138**
Married couples	43,554	19,516	10,049	4,878	5,171	9,467	4,949	4,517
Female householder, no spouse present	7,277	2,570	1,653	952	701	917	496	420
Male householder, no spouse present	3,078	1,169	734	368	366	435	234	201
Nonfamily households	**29,562**	**10,419**	**4,800**	**2,196**	**2,604**	**5,619**	**2,874**	**2,746**
Female householder	15,749	5,120	2,116	873	1,243	3,004	1,426	1,579
Living alone	13,456	4,376	1,707	685	1,022	2,669	1,232	1,437
Male householder	13,813	5,300	2,685	1,324	1,361	2,615	1,448	1,167
Living alone	10,675	4,521	2,223	1,077	1,146	2,298	1,251	1,048
Percent distribution by type								
TOTAL NON-HISPANIC WHITE HOUSEHOLDS	**100.0%**	**100.0%**	**100.0%**	**100.0%**	**100.0%**	**100.0%**	**100.0%**	**100.0%**
Family households	**64.5**	**69.1**	**72.2**	**73.8**	**70.5**	**65.8**	**66.4**	**65.2**
Married couples	52.2	58.0	58.3	58.1	58.5	57.6	57.9	57.3
Female householder, no spouse present	8.7	7.6	9.6	11.3	7.9	5.6	5.8	5.3
Male householder, no spouse present	3.7	3.5	4.3	4.4	4.1	2.6	2.7	2.5
Nonfamily households	**35.4**	**30.9**	**27.8**	**26.2**	**29.5**	**34.2**	**33.6**	**34.8**
Female householder	18.9	15.2	12.3	10.4	14.1	18.3	16.7	20.0
Living alone	16.1	13.0	9.9	8.2	11.6	16.2	14.4	18.2
Male householder	16.5	15.7	15.6	15.8	15.4	15.9	16.9	14.8
Living alone	12.8	13.4	12.9	12.8	13.0	14.0	14.6	13.3
Percent distribution by age								
TOTAL NON-HISPANIC WHITE HOUSEHOLDS	**100.0%**	**40.3%**	**20.6%**	**10.1%**	**10.6%**	**19.7%**	**10.2%**	**9.4%**
Family households	**100.0**	**43.2**	**23.1**	**11.5**	**11.6**	**20.1**	**10.5**	**9.5**
Married couples	100.0	44.8	23.1	11.2	11.9	–21.7	11.4	10.4
Female householder, no spouse present	100.0	35.3	22.7	13.1	9.6	12.6	6.8	5.8
Male householder, no spouse present	100.0	38.0	23.8	12.0	11.9	14.1	7.6	6.5
Nonfamily households	**100.0**	**35.2**	**16.2**	**7.4**	**8.8**	**19.0**	**9.7**	**9.3**
Female householder	100.0	32.5	13.4	5.5	7.9	19.1	9.1	10.0
Living alone	100.0	32.5	12.7	5.1	7.6	19.8	9.2	10.7
Male householder	100.0	38.4	19.4	9.6	9.9	18.9	10.5	8.4
Living alone	100.0	42.4	20.8	10.1	10.7	21.5	11.7	9.8

Note: Non-Hispanic whites are those who identify themselves as being white alone and not Hispanic.
Source: Bureau of the Census, America's Families and Living Arrangements: 2011, Internet site http://www.census.gov/population/www/socdemo/hh-fam/cps2011.html; calculations by New Strategist

Boomer Households Are Shrinking

Household size peaks in the 35-to-39 age group.

The average American household was home to 2.58 people in 2011. Household size peaks among householders aged 35 to 39, who are most likely to have more than one child at home. As householders age into their forties and fifties, the nest empties. The average number of children per household falls below one in the 45-to-49 age group.

Boomer households are shrinking as a growing proportion become empty-nesters. The youngest Boomers are exiting the crowded-nest stage, with an average of 3.00 people per household in the 45-to-49 age group. The oldest Boomer age group (60 to 64) has only 2.09 people, on average, in their homes.

■ Some Boomers have seen their household size rise over the past few years because of the economic downturn.

The nest is emptying for householders in their forties and fifties

(average household size by age of householder, 2011)

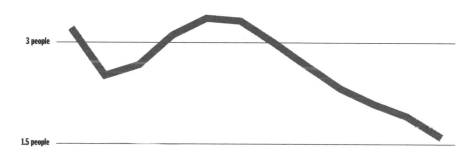

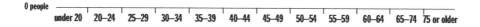

Table 7.6 Average Size of Household by Age of Householder, 2011

(number of households, average number of people per household, and average number of people under age 18 per household, by age of householder, 2011; number of households in thousands)

	number	average number of people	average number of people under age 18
TOTAL HOUSEHOLDS	**118,682**	**2.58**	**0.63**
Under age 20	771	3.21	1.01
Aged 20 to 24	5,369	2.51	0.54
Aged 25 to 29	9,331	2.67	0.83
Aged 30 to 34	10,241	3.11	1.28
Aged 35 to 39	10,334	3.36	1.45
Aged 40 to 44	10,917	3.32	1.27
Aged 45 to 49	12,220	3.00	0.83
Aged 50 to 54	12,310	2.65	0.45
Aged 55 to 59	11,445	2.32	0.22
Aged 60 to 64	10,383	2.09	0.15
Aged 65 to 74	13,348	1.91	0.09
Aged 75 or older	12,015	1.60	0.04

Source: Bureau of the Census, America's Families and Living Arrangements: 2011, Internet site http://www.census.gov/population/www/socdemo/hh-fam/cps2011.html; calculations by New Strategist

Most Boomers Are Empty-Nesters

But many have adult children in their home.

Most households headed by people aged 30 to 44 include children under age 18. The proportion falls to 43 percent in the 45-to-49 age group and declines with age. But the majority of householders in the 45-to-49 age group have children of any age in their home—meaning many have adult children living with them. The percentage of Boomer households with children of any age in the home ranges from 58 percent among householders aged 45 to 49 to a still substantial 25 percent among householders aged 55 to 64.

By race and Hispanic origin, Asian and Hispanic Boomers are most likely to have children of any age at home. Among Asian and Hispanic households headed by 55-to-64-year-olds, 42 to 43 percent include children. This compares with 28 percent of black and 22 percent of non-Hispanic white households in the age group.

■ The percentage of Boomer households that include adult children has grown in recent years because of the Great Recession.

Many Boomer households include children of any age

(percent of households with children of any age in the home, by age of householder, 2011)

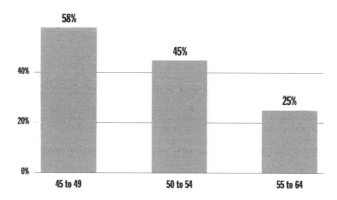

Table 7.7 Households by Type, Age of Householder, and Presence of Children, 2011: Total Households

(total number of households and number and percent with own children under age 18 or of any age at home, by household type and age of householder, 2011; numbers in thousands)

	total	with own children under 18		with own children, any age	
		number	percent	number	percent
TOTAL HOUSEHOLDS	**118,682**	**34,760**	**29.3%**	**47,150**	**39.7%**
Under age 25	6,140	1,738	28.3	1,779	29.0
Aged 25 to 29	9,331	3,883	41.6	3,902	41.8
Aged 30 to 34	10,241	5,971	58.3	6,033	58.9
Aged 35 to 39	10,334	6,824	66.0	6,997	67.7
Aged 40 to 44	10,917	6,576	60.2	7,251	66.4
Aged 45 to 49	12,220	5,251	43.0	7,070	57.9
Aged 50 to 54	12,310	2,957	24.0	5,483	44.5
Aged 55 to 64	21,828	1,371	6.3	5,442	24.9
Aged 65 to 74	13,348	127	1.0	1,830	13.7
Aged 75 or older	12,015	62	0.5	1,361	11.3
MARRIED COUPLES	**58,036**	**23,938**	**41.2**	**30,928**	**53.3**
Under age 25	1,077	580	53.9	587	54.5
Aged 25 to 29	3,348	2,207	65.9	2,219	66.3
Aged 30 to 34	5,203	4,070	78.2	4,106	78.9
Aged 35 to 39	5,820	4,811	82.7	4,887	84.0
Aged 40 to 44	6,267	4,901	78.2	5,245	83.7
Aged 45 to 49	6,721	3,927	58.4	5,054	75.2
Aged 50 to 54	6,785	2,226	32.8	3,888	57.3
Aged 55 to 64	11,851	1,087	9.2	3,663	30.9
Aged 65 to 74	6,871	91	1.3	926	13.5
Aged 75 or older	4,092	38	0.9	354	8.7
FEMALE-HEADED FAMILIES	**15,019**	**8,597**	**57.2**	**12,794**	**85.2**
Under age 25	1,414	962	68.0	975	69.0
Aged 25 to 29	1,585	1,359	85.7	1,365	86.1
Aged 30 to 34	1,696	1,547	91.2	1,570	92.6
Aged 35 to 39	1,780	1,614	90.7	1,697	95.3
Aged 40 to 44	1,700	1,313	77.2	1,577	92.8
Aged 45 to 49	1,741	1,046	60.1	1,602	92.0
Aged 50 to 54	1,393	536	38.5	1,209	86.8
Aged 55 to 64	1,745	177	10.1	1,301	74.6
Aged 65 to 74	976	19	1.9	680	69.7
Aged 75 or older	988	24	2.4	818	82.8
MALE-HEADED FAMILIES	**5,559**	**2,225**	**40.0**	**3,428**	**61.7**
Under age 25	825	196	23.8	217	26.3
Aged 25 to 29	623	316	50.7	317	50.9
Aged 30 to 34	610	354	58.0	357	58.5
Aged 35 to 39	572	399	69.8	414	72.4
Aged 40 to 44	569	362	63.6	430	75.6
Aged 45 to 49	585	277	47.4	414	70.8
Aged 50 to 54	565	195	34.5	386	68.3
Aged 55 to 64	672	108	16.1	478	71.1
Aged 65 to 74	300	18	6.0	225	75.0
Aged 75 or older	237	0	0.0	189	79.7

Source: Bureau of the Census, America's Families and Living Arrangements: 2011, Internet site http://www.census.gov/ population/www/socdemo/hh-fam/cps2011.html; calculations by New Strategist

Table 7.8 Households by Type, Age of Householder, and Presence of Children, 2011: Asian Households

(total number of Asian households and number and percent with own children under age 18 and of any age at home, by household type and age of householder, 2011; numbers in thousands)

	total	with own children under 18		with own children, any age	
		number	percent	number	percent
TOTAL ASIAN HOUSEHOLDS	**5,040**	**1,774**	**35.2%**	**2,417**	**48.0%**
Under age 25	295	37	12.5	38	12.9
Aged 25 to 29	495	113	22.8	113	22.8
Aged 30 to 34	576	260	45.1	263	45.7
Aged 35 to 39	649	417	64.3	426	65.6
Aged 40 to 44	513	358	69.8	367	71.5
Aged 45 to 49	581	344	59.2	415	71.4
Aged 50 to 54	470	160	34.0	304	64.7
Aged 55 to 64	763	77	10.1	323	42.3
Aged 65 to 74	428	6	1.4	122	28.5
Aged 75 or older	270	3	1.1	46	17.0
MARRIED COUPLES	**2,939**	**1,513**	**51.5**	**1,993**	**67.8**
Under age 25	27	18	66.7	18	66.7
Aged 25 to 29	162	79	48.8	79	48.8
Aged 30 to 34	343	224	65.3	226	65.9
Aged 35 to 39	439	365	83.1	369	84.1
Aged 40 to 44	357	301	84.3	310	86.8
Aged 45 to 49	407	309	75.9	360	88.5
Aged 50 to 54	332	140	42.2	256	77.1
Aged 55 to 64	502	68	13.5	258	51.4
Aged 65 to 74	256	5	2.0	96	37.5
Aged 75 or older	115	3	2.6	20	17.4
FEMALE-HEADED FAMILIES	**492**	**214**	**43.5**	**343**	**69.7**
Under age 25	50	18	36.0	18	36.0
Aged 25 to 29	57	27	47.4	27	47.4
Aged 30 to 34	55	34	61.8	34	61.8
Aged 35 to 39	52	45	86.5	48	92.3
Aged 40 to 44	49	43	87.8	44	89.8
Aged 45 to 49	52	24	46.2	43	82.7
Aged 50 to 54	57	16	28.1	41	71.9
Aged 55 to 64	64	6	9.4	47	73.4
Aged 65 to 74	33	0	0.0	23	69.7
Aged 75 or older	24	0	0.0	18	75.0
MALE-HEADED FAMILIES	**291**	**47**	**16.2**	**81**	**27.8**
Under age 25	67	1	1.5	2	3.0
Aged 25 to 29	42	6	14.3	6	14.3
Aged 30 to 34	38	2	5.3	2	5.3
Aged 35 to 39	30	6	20.0	9	30.0
Aged 40 to 44	27	14	51.9	14	51.9
Aged 45 to 49	29	10	34.5	12	41.4
Aged 50 to 54	15	4	26.7	7	46.7
Aged 55 to 64	26	3	11.5	18	69.2
Aged 65 to 74	7	0	0.0	3	42.9
Aged 75 or older	10	0	0.0	8	80.0

Note: Asians are those who identify themselves as being of the race alone and those who identify themselves as being of the race in combination with other races.
Source: Bureau of the Census, America's Families and Living Arrangements: 2011, Internet site http://www.census.gov/ population/www/socdemo/hh-fam/cps2011.html; calculations by New Strategist

Table 7.9 Households by Type, Age of Householder, and Presence of Children, 2011: Black Households

(total number of black households and number and percent with own children under age 18 or of any age at home, by household type and age of householder, 2011; numbers in thousands)

	total	with own children under 18		with own children, any age	
		number	percent	number	percent
TOTAL BLACK HOUSEHOLDS	**15,613**	**4,966**	**31.8%**	**6,916**	**44.3%**
Under age 25	1,201	410	34.1	416	34.6
Aged 25 to 29	1,471	786	53.4	793	53.9
Aged 30 to 34	1,526	919	60.2	936	61.3
Aged 35 to 39	1,514	980	64.7	1,035	68.4
Aged 40 to 44	1,494	808	54.1	940	62.9
Aged 45 to 49	1,650	553	33.5	843	51.1
Aged 50 to 54	1,661	307	18.5	670	40.3
Aged 55 to 64	2,682	161	6.0	761	28.4
Aged 65 to 74	1,423	28	2.0	299	21.0
Aged 75 or older	990	13	1.3	222	22.4
MARRIED COUPLES	**4,353**	**1,898**	**43.6**	**2,578**	**59.2**
Under age 25	82	60	73.2	60	73.2
Aged 25 to 29	270	211	78.1	217	80.4
Aged 30 to 34	372	299	80.4	307	82.5
Aged 35 to 39	480	401	83.5	413	86.0
Aged 40 to 44	508	389	76.6	423	83.3
Aged 45 to 49	532	270	50.8	374	70.3
Aged 50 to 54	556	154	27.7	288	51.8
Aged 55 to 64	892	94	10.5	358	40.1
Aged 65 to 74	462	16	3.5	100	21.6
Aged 75 or older	200	4	2.0	36	18.0
FEMALE-HEADED FAMILIES	**4,459**	**2,673**	**59.9**	**3,782**	**84.8**
Under age 25	460	319	69.3	325	70.7
Aged 25 to 29	559	496	88.7	497	88.9
Aged 30 to 34	614	563	91.7	572	93.2
Aged 35 to 39	560	503	89.8	543	97.0
Aged 40 to 44	479	362	75.6	445	92.9
Aged 45 to 49	451	239	53.0	412	91.4
Aged 50 to 54	406	130	32.0	341	84.0
Aged 55 to 64	475	45	9.5	321	67.6
Aged 65 to 74	239	6	2.5	166	69.5
Aged 75 or older	216	9	4.2	160	74.1
MALE-HEADED FAMILIES	**954**	**396**	**41.5**	**556**	**58.3**
Under age 25	150	30	20.0	31	20.7
Aged 25 to 29	141	79	56.0	79	56.0
Aged 30 to 34	91	58	63.7	58	63.7
Aged 35 to 39	103	77	74.8	79	76.7
Aged 40 to 44	96	57	59.4	72	75.0
Aged 45 to 49	89	45	50.6	57	64.0
Aged 50 to 54	83	23	27.7	41	49.4
Aged 55 to 64	114	22	19.3	82	71.9
Aged 65 to 74	55	6	10.9	33	60.0
Aged 75 or older	32	0	0.0	25	78.1

Note: Blacks are those who identify themselves as being of the race alone and those who identify themselves as being of the race in combination with other races.
Source: Bureau of the Census, America's Families and Living Arrangements: 2011, Internet site http://www.census.gov/population/www/socdemo/hh-fam/cps2011.html; calculations by New Strategist

Table 7.10 Households by Type, Age of Householder, and Presence of Children, 2011: Hispanic Households

(total number of Hispanic households and number and percent with own children under age 18 or of any age at home, by household type and age of householder, 2011; numbers in thousands)

	total	with own children under 18		with own children, any age	
		number	percent	number	percent
TOTAL HISPANIC HOUSEHOLDS	**13,665**	**6,373**	**46.6%**	**7,992**	**58.5%**
Under age 25	1,135	468	41.2	471	41.5
Aged 25 to 29	1,476	874	59.2	877	59.4
Aged 30 to 34	1,737	1,231	70.9	1,237	71.2
Aged 35 to 39	1,739	1,276	73.4	1,307	75.2
Aged 40 to 44	1,628	1,124	69.0	1,227	75.4
Aged 45 to 49	1,484	775	52.2	1,036	69.8
Aged 50 to 54	1,245	404	32.4	748	60.1
Aged 55 to 64	1,729	177	10.2	735	42.5
Aged 65 to 74	917	33	3.6	236	25.7
Aged 75 or older	574	11	1.9	118	20.6
MARRIED COUPLES	**6,725**	**4,106**	**61.1**	**5,034**	**74.9**
Under age 25	269	187	69.5	187	69.5
Aged 25 to 29	600	473	78.8	473	78.8
Aged 30 to 34	926	829	89.5	830	89.6
Aged 35 to 39	981	840	85.6	854	87.1
Aged 40 to 44	938	794	84.6	840	89.6
Aged 45 to 49	843	547	64.9	707	83.9
Aged 50 to 54	677	268	39.6	493	72.8
Aged 55 to 64	878	135	15.4	477	54.3
Aged 65 to 74	416	25	6.0	122	29.3
Aged 75 or older	196	8	4.1	51	26.0
FEMALE-HEADED FAMILIES	**2,754**	**1,803**	**65.5**	**2,345**	**85.1**
Under age 25	335	221	66.0	223	66.6
Aged 25 to 29	370	318	85.9	319	86.2
Aged 30 to 34	350	324	92.6	328	93.7
Aged 35 to 39	372	345	92.7	357	96.0
Aged 40 to 44	338	278	82.2	319	94.4
Aged 45 to 49	281	179	63.7	255	90.7
Aged 50 to 54	235	110	46.8	199	84.7
Aged 55 to 64	266	22	8.3	200	75.2
Aged 65 to 74	135	5	3.7	91	67.4
Aged 75 or older	73	3	4.1	55	75.3
MALE-HEADED FAMILIES	**1,180**	**465**	**39.4**	**613**	**51.9**
Under age 25	266	61	22.9	62	23.3
Aged 25 to 29	169	84	49.7	85	50.3
Aged 30 to 34	153	79	51.6	79	51.6
Aged 35 to 39	150	91	60.7	95	63.3
Aged 40 to 44	113	52	46.0	68	60.2
Aged 45 to 49	101	49	48.5	74	73.3
Aged 50 to 54	90	26	28.9	57	63.3
Aged 55 to 64	89	20	22.5	58	65.2
Aged 65 to 74	28	3	10.7	24	85.7
Aged 75 or older	19	0	0.0	12	63.2

Source: Bureau of the Census, America's Families and Living Arrangements: 2011, Internet site http://www.census.gov/ population/www/socdemo/hh-fam/cps2011.html; calculations by New Strategist

Table 7.11 Households by Type, Age of Householder, and Presence of Children, 2011: Non-Hispanic White Households

(total number of non-Hispanic white households and number and percent with own children under age 18 or of any age at home, by household type and age of householder, 2011; numbers in thousands)

	total	with own children under 18		with own children, any age	
		number	percent	number	percent
TOTAL NON-HISPANIC WHITE HOUSEHOLDS	**83,471**	**21,457**	**25.7%**	**29,529**	**35.4%**
Under age 25	3,481	830	23.8	859	24.7
Aged 25 to 29	5,845	2,103	36.0	2,113	36.2
Aged 30 to 34	6,344	3,531	55.7	3,568	56.2
Aged 35 to 39	6,340	4,085	64.4	4,162	65.6
Aged 40 to 44	7,220	4,262	59.0	4,684	64.9
Aged 45 to 49	8,394	3,532	42.1	4,732	56.4
Aged 50 to 54	8,842	2,068	23.4	3,731	42.2
Aged 55 to 64	16,439	949	5.8	3,573	21.7
Aged 65 to 74	10,473	62	0.6	1,145	10.9
Aged 75 or older	10,093	33	0.3	961	9.5
MARRIED COUPLES	**43,554**	**16,267**	**37.3**	**21,110**	**48.5**
Under age 25	694	323	46.5	332	47.8
Aged 25 to 29	2,303	1,436	62.4	1,443	62.7
Aged 30 to 34	3,544	2,709	76.4	2,732	77.1
Aged 35 to 39	3,845	3,139	81.6	3,181	82.7
Aged 40 to 44	4,424	3,391	76.7	3,642	82.3
Aged 45 to 49	4,878	2,763	56.6	3,569	73.2
Aged 50 to 54	5,171	1,654	32.0	2,830	54.7
Aged 55 to 64	9,467	785	8.3	2,541	26.8
Aged 65 to 74	5,672	45	0.8	595	10.5
Aged 75 or older	3,557	23	0.6	246	6.9
FEMALE-HEADED FAMILIES	**7,277**	**3,903**	**53.6**	**6,292**	**86.5**
Under age 25	574	406	70.7	412	71.8
Aged 25 to 29	604	524	86.8	527	87.3
Aged 30 to 34	666	614	92.2	624	93.7
Aged 35 to 39	803	727	90.5	757	94.3
Aged 40 to 44	838	639	76.3	774	92.4
Aged 45 to 49	952	593	62.3	887	93.2
Aged 50 to 54	701	280	39.9	629	89.7
Aged 55 to 64	917	104	11.3	717	78.2
Aged 65 to 74	556	8	1.4	388	69.8
Aged 75 or older	665	10	1.5	576	86.6
MALE-HEADED FAMILIES	**3,078**	**1,286**	**41.8**	**2,127**	**69.1**
Under age 25	338	101	29.9	116	34.3
Aged 25 to 29	269	144	53.5	144	53.5
Aged 30 to 34	317	209	65.9	212	66.9
Aged 35 to 39	283	220	77.7	224	79.2
Aged 40 to 44	323	233	72.1	268	83.0
Aged 45 to 49	368	176	47.8	276	75.0
Aged 50 to 54	366	135	36.9	271	74.0
Aged 55 to 64	435	60	13.8	315	72.4
Aged 65 to 74	206	9	4.4	162	78.6
Aged 75 or older	172	0	0.0	139	80.8

Note: Non-Hispanic whites are those who identify themselves as being white alone and not Hispanic.
Source: Bureau of the Census, America's Families and Living Arrangements: 2011, Internet site http://www.census.gov/ population/www/socdemo/hh-fam/cps2011.html; calculations by New Strategist

Table 7.12 Households by Presence and Age of Children and Age of Householder, 2011

(number and percent distribution of households by presence of own children at home, by age of children and age of householder, 2011; numbers in thousands)

	total	under 35	35 to 44	aged 45 to 64 total	45 to 49	50 to 54	55 to 64	65 or older
Total households	**118,682**	**25,712**	**21,251**	**46,358**	**12,220**	**12,310**	**21,828**	**25,363**
With children of any age	47,150	11,714	14,248	17,995	7,070	5,483	5,442	3,191
Under age 25	41,108	11,683	14,204	14,836	6,807	4,845	3,184	385
Under age 18	34,760	11,592	13,400	9,579	5,251	2,957	1,371	189
Under age 12	25,392	11,172	10,242	3,880	2,517	948	415	98
Under age 6	15,314	9,044	5,213	1,009	674	229	106	49
Under age 1	2,942	2,124	726	82	55	23	4	10
Aged 12 to 17	16,247	1,796	6,945	7,395	3,910	2,384	1,101	111

PERCENT DISTRIBUTION BY AGE OF CHILD

	total	under 35	35 to 44	aged 45 to 64 total	45 to 49	50 to 54	55 to 64	65 or older
Total households	**100.0%**	**100.0%**	**100.0%**	**100.0%**	**100.0%**	**100.0%**	**100.0%**	**100.0%**
With children of any age	39.7	45.6	67.0	38.8	57.9	44.5	24.9	12.6
Under age 25	34.6	45.4	66.8	32.0	55.7	39.4	14.6	1.5
Under age 18	29.3	45.1	63.1	20.7	43.0	24.0	6.3	0.7
Under age 12	21.4	43.5	48.2	8.4	20.6	7.7	1.9	0.4
Under age 6	12.9	35.2	24.5	2.2	5.5	1.9	0.5	0.2
Under age 1	2.5	8.3	3.4	0.2	0.5	0.2	0.0	0.0
Aged 12 to 17	13.7	7.0	32.7	16.0	32.0	19.4	5.0	0.4

PERCENT DISTRIBUTION BY AGE OF HOUSEHOLDER

	total	under 35	35 to 44	aged 45 to 64 total	45 to 49	50 to 54	55 to 64	65 or older
Total households	**100.0%**	**21.7%**	**17.9%**	**39.1%**	**10.3%**	**10.4%**	**18.4%**	**21.4%**
With children of any age	100.0	24.8	30.2	38.2	15.0	11.6	11.5	6.8
Under age 25	100.0	28.4	34.6	36.1	16.6	11.8	7.7	0.9
Under age 18	100.0	33.3	38.6	27.6	15.1	8.5	3.9	0.5
Under age 12	100.0	44.0	40.3	15.3	9.9	3.7	1.6	0.4
Under age 6	100.0	59.1	34.0	6.6	4.4	1.5	0.7	0.3
Under age 1	100.0	72.2	24.7	2.8	1.9	0.8	0.1	0.3
Aged 12 to 17	100.0	11.1	42.7	45.5	24.1	14.7	6.8	0.7

Source: Bureau of the Census, America's Families and Living Arrangements: 2011, Internet site http://www.census.gov/population/www/socdemo/hh-fam/cps2011.html; calculations by New Strategist

Boomers Account for More than One-Third of People Who Live Alone

The percentage of women who live alone rises steadily with age.

Boomers account for a substantial 37 percent of the 33 million Americans who live alone. In 2011, 15 percent of 45-to-64-year-olds (Boomers were aged 47 to 65 in that year) lived by themselves, about double the percentage among people under age 45.

Boomer women in their late forties and fifties are slightly less likely than Boomer men to live alone, but the opposite is the case among Boomers aged 60 to 64. In that age group, 17 percent of men and a larger 22 percent of women head single-person households.

■ Because of the higher mortality rate of men, a growing share of Boomer women will become widows and live by themselves in the years ahead.

Women are increasingly likely to live alone as they age

(percent of women aged 45 to 64 who live alone, by age, 2011)

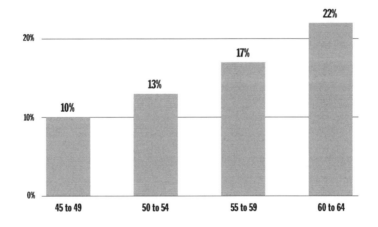

Table 7.13 People Who Live Alone by Age, 2011

(number of people aged 15 or older and number, percent, and percent distribution of people who live alone by sex and age, 2011; numbers in thousands)

	total	living alone		
		number	percent	percent distribution
Total people	**243,955**	**32,723**	**13.4%**	**100.0%**
Under age 45	123,838	9,154	7.4	28.0
Aged 45 to 64	80,938	12,266	15.2	37.5
Aged 45 to 49	21,989	2,596	11.8	7.9
Aged 50 to 54	21,965	2,976	13.5	9.1
Aged 55 to 59	19,554	3,358	17.2	10.3
Aged 60 to 64	17,430	3,335	19 1	10.2
Aged 65 or older	39,179	11,304	28.9	34.5
Total men	**118,871**	**14,539**	**12.2**	**100.0**
Under age 45	62,350	5,214	8.4	35.9
Aged 45 to 64	39,441	6,115	15.5	42.1
Aged 45 to 49	10,800	1,524	14.1	10.5
Aged 50 to 54	10,695	1,510	14.1	10.4
Aged 55 to 59	9,499	1,678	17.7	11.5
Aged 60 to 64	8,447	1,402	16.6	9.6
Aged 65 or older	17,081	3,210	18.8	22.1
Total women	**125,084**	**18,184**	**14.5**	**100.0**
Under age 45	61,488	3,940	6.4	21.7
Aged 45 to 64	41,497	6,151	14.8	33.8
Aged 45 to 49	11,189	1,072	9.6	5.9
Aged 50 to 54	11,270	1,466	13.0	8.1
Aged 55 to 59	10,055	1,680	16.7	9.2
Aged 60 to 64	8,983	1,933	21.5	10.6
Aged 65 or older	22,098	8,094	36.6	44.5

Source: Bureau of the Census, 2011 Current Population Survey, Internet site http://www.census.gov/hhes/www/income/data/incpovhlth/2010/dtables.html; calculations by New Strategist

Divorced Population Peaks in Middle Age

Most of the divorced eventually remarry.

The proportion of people who are currently divorced peaks among Baby Boomers. From 15 to 18 percent of men and women aged 45 to 64 are currently divorced. The percentage of Boomers who have ever divorced is much higher than these figures, since many of the divorced have remarried. Despite high rates of divorce, from 62 to 70 percent of men and women aged 45 to 64 are currently married and living with their spouse.

Older Americans are less likely than the middle aged to be currently divorced, but they are far more likely to be widowed. Among women age 65 or older, 39 percent are widows.

■ The lifestyles of Baby-Boom men and women will diverge as they enter their late sixties and a growing proportion of women become widows and live alone.

Most Boomers are married

(percent of people aged 45 to 64 who are currently married and living with their spouse, by sex and age, 2011)

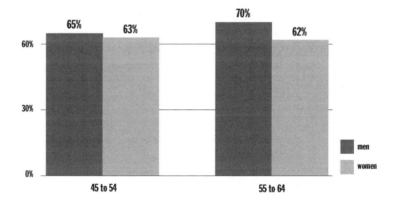

Table 7.14 Marital Status by Sex and Age, 2011: Total People

(number and percent distribution of people aged 15 or older by sex, age, and current marital status, 2011; numbers in thousands)

	total	never married	married spouse present	married spouse absent	separated	divorced	widowed
NUMBER							
Total men	**118,828**	**38,685**	**60,129**	**1,944**	**2,144**	**9,782**	**2,916**
Under age 45	62,329	33,215	21,539	1,040	997	2,191	118
Aged 45 to 54	21,486	3,105	14,070	379	556	3,150	227
Aged 45 to 49	10,791	1,722	6,932	195	320	1,542	81
Aged 50 to 54	10,695	1,383	7,138	184	236	1,608	146
Aged 55 to 64	17,937	1,605	12,476	267	363	2,804	422
Aged 65 or older	17,076	760	12,044	258	228	1,637	2,149
Total women	**125,030**	**34,963**	**60,155**	**1,754**	**3,091**	**13,762**	**11,306**
Under age 45	61,473	29,877	24,559	873	1,705	4,137	320
Aged 45 to 54	22,450	2,594	14,188	360	761	3,733	815
Aged 45 to 49	11,186	1,416	7,075	188	401	1,787	320
Aged 50 to 54	11,264	1,178	7,113	172	360	1,946	495
Aged 55 to 64	19,032	1,544	11,760	286	413	3,384	1,645
Aged 65 or older	22,075	948	9,648	235	212	2,508	8,526
PERCENT DISTRIBUTION							
Total men	**100.0%**	**32.6%**	**50.6%**	**1.6%**	**1.8%**	**8.2%**	**2.5%**
Under age 45	100.0	53.3	34.6	1.7	1.6	3.5	0.2
Aged 45 to 54	100.0	14.5	65.5	1.8	2.6	14.7	1.1
Aged 45 to 49	100.0	16.0	64.2	1.8	3.0	14.3	0.8
Aged 50 to 54	100.0	12.9	66.7	1.7	2.2	15.0	1.4
Aged 55 to 64	100.0	8.9	69.6	1.5	2.0	15.6	2.4
Aged 65 or older	100.0	4.5	70.5	1.5	1.3	9.6	12.6
Total women	**100.0**	**28.0**	**48.1**	**1.4**	**2.5**	**11.0**	**9.0**
Under age 45	100.0	48.6	40.0	1.4	2.8	6.7	0.5
Aged 45 to 54	100.0	11.6	63.2	1.6	3.4	16.6	3.6
Aged 45 to 49	100.0	12.7	63.2	1.7	3.6	16.0	2.9
Aged 50 to 54	100.0	10.5	63.1	1.5	3.2	17.3	4.4
Aged 55 to 64	100.0	8.1	61.8	1.5	2.2	17.8	8.6
Aged 65 or older	100.0	4.3	43.7	1.1	1.0	11.4	38.6

Source: Bureau of the Census, America's Families and Living Arrangements: 2011, Internet site http://www.census.gov/population/www/socdemo/hh-fam/cps2011.html; calculations by New Strategist

Regardless of Race, the Middle Aged Are Most Likely to Be Married

At every age, blacks are least likely to be married.

In the first half of the 20th century, blacks and whites were about equally likely to be married. But as the marriage rate fell, it dropped faster for blacks. Consequently, blacks today are far less likely to be married than Asians, Hispanics, or non-Hispanic whites.

Among black women ranging in age from 45 to 64, only 36 to 37 percent are currently married and living with their spouse. The figure is a higher 55 to 61 percent among Hispanic women in the age group. Among non-Hispanic whites, the figures are 66 to 68 percent. The percentage of women in the age group who are currently married peaks at 68 to 72 percent among Asians.

Among men in the 45-to-64 age group, blacks and Hispanics are least likely to be married and living with their spouse. Many Hispanic men are married and living apart from their spouse—possibly because they are immigrants who are separated from their wives. Asian men aged 45 to 64 are most likely to be married and living with their wife, the figure peaking at 83 percent among Asian men aged 50 to 54.

■ The differences in marital status by age, race, and Hispanic origin are a major reason for the diversity of incomes and lifestyles in America today.

Among the middle aged, men are much more likely than women to be married

(percent of people aged 55 to 64 who are currently married and living with their spouse, by race, Hispanic origin, and sex, 2011)

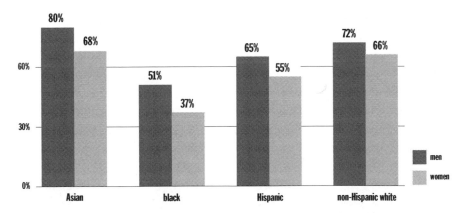

Table 7.15 Marital Status by Sex and Age, 2011: Asians

(number and percent distribution of Asians aged 15 or older by sex, age, and current marital status, 2011; numbers in thousands)

	total	never married	married spouse present	married spouse absent	separated	divorced	widowed
NUMBER							
Total Asian men	**5,786**	**2,031**	**3,234**	**168**	**55**	**208**	**89**
Under age 45	3,458	1,869	1,373	86	36	94	2
Aged 45 to 54	988	93	797	38	8	41	9
Aged 45 to 49	530	56	418	17	5	27	6
Aged 50 to 54	458	37	379	21	3	14	3
Aged 55 to 64	708	47	567	25	8	48	13
Aged 65 or older	632	23	498	19	4	25	64
Total Asian women	**6,460**	**1,742**	**3,600**	**177**	**112**	**365**	**464**
Under age 45	3,647	1,541	1,810	81	62	141	15
Aged 45 to 54	1,099	113	786	41	19	105	35
Aged 45 to 49	586	64	425	22	7	48	20
Aged 50 to 54	513	49	361	19	12	57	15
Aged 55 to 64	862	56	589	33	15	75	94
Aged 65 or older	850	33	416	23	16	43	319
PERCENT DISTRIBUTION							
Total Asian men	**100.0%**	**35.1%**	**55.9%**	**2.9%**	**1.0%**	**3.6%**	**1.5%**
Under age 45	100.0	54.0	39.7	2.5	1.0	2.7	0.1
Aged 45 to 54	100.0	9.4	80.7	3.8	0.8	4.1	0.9
Aged 45 to 49	100.0	10.6	78.9	3.2	0.9	5.1	1.1
Aged 50 to 54	100.0	8.1	82.8	4.6	0.7	3.1	0.7
Aged 55 to 64	100.0	6.6	80.1	3.5	1.1	6.8	1.8
Aged 65 or older	100.0	3.6	78.8	3.0	0.6	4.0	10.1
Total Asian women	**100.0**	**27.0**	**55.7**	**2.7**	**1.7**	**5.7**	**7.2**
Under age 45	100.0	42.3	49.6	2.2	1.7	3.9	0.4
Aged 45 to 54	100.0	10.3	71.5	3.7	1.7	9.6	3.2
Aged 45 to 49	100.0	10.9	72.5	3.8	1.2	8.2	3.4
Aged 50 to 54	100.0	9.6	70.4	3.7	2.3	11.1	2.9
Aged 55 to 64	100.0	6.5	68.3	3.8	1.7	8.7	10.9
Aged 65 or older	100.0	3.9	48.9	2.7	1.9	5.1	37.5

Note: Asians are those who identify themselves as being of the race alone and those who identify themselves as being of the race in combination with other races.
Source: Bureau of the Census, America's Families and Living Arrangements: 2011, Internet site http://www.census.gov/population/www/socdemo/hh-fam/cps2011.html; calculations by New Strategist

Table 7.16 Marital Status by Sex and Age, 2011: Blacks

(number and percent distribution of blacks aged 15 or older by sex, age, and current marital status, 2011; numbers in thousands)

	total	never married	married spouse present	married spouse absent	separated	divorced	widowed
NUMBER							
Total black men	**14,096**	**6,970**	**4,627**	**273**	**540**	**1,352**	**334**
Under age 45	8,455	5,874	1,764	130	274	396	18
Aged 45 to 54	2,459	666	1,161	65	114	422	29
Aged 45 to 49	1,267	410	543	35	67	199	12
Aged 50 to 54	1,192	256	618	30	47	223	17
Aged 55 to 64	1,812	340	918	43	91	337	82
Aged 65 or older	1,369	89	784	35	60	196	205
Total black women	**16,875**	**7,803**	**4,383**	**375**	**802**	**2,105**	**1,406**
Under age 45	9,528	6,331	1,916	182	369	655	72
Aged 45 to 54	3,001	861	1,093	89	251	568	137
Aged 45 to 49	1,527	475	546	62	126	260	57
Aged 50 to 54	1,474	386	547	27	125	308	80
Aged 55 to 64	2,218	431	829	71	117	541	229
Aged 65 or older	2,128	180	544	33	64	340	967
PERCENT DISTRIBUTION							
Total black men	**100.0%**	**49.4%**	**32.8%**	**1.9%**	**3.8%**	**9.6%**	**2.4%**
Under age 45	100.0	69.5	20.9	1.5	3.2	4.7	0.2
Aged 45 to 54	100.0	27.1	47.2	2.6	4.6	17.2	1.2
Aged 45 to 49	100.0	32.4	42.9	2.8	5.3	15.7	0.9
Aged 50 to 54	100.0	21.5	51.8	2.5	3.9	18.7	1.4
Aged 55 to 64	100.0	18.8	50.7	2.4	5.0	18.6	4.5
Aged 65 or older	100.0	6.5	57.3	2.6	4.4	14.3	15.0
Total black women	**100.0**	**46.2**	**26.0**	**2.2**	**4.8**	**12.5**	**8.3**
Under age 45	100.0	66.4	20.1	1.9	3.9	6.9	0.8
Aged 45 to 54	100.0	28.7	36.4	3.0	8.4	18.9	4.6
Aged 45 to 49	100.0	31.1	35.8	4.1	8.3	17.0	3.7
Aged 50 to 54	100.0	26.2	37.1	1.8	8.5	20.9	5.4
Aged 55 to 64	100.0	19.4	37.4	3.2	5.3	24.4	10.3
Aged 65 or older	100.0	8.5	25.6	1.6	3.0	16.0	45.4

Note: Blacks are those who identify themselves as being of the race alone and those who identify themselves as being of the race in combination with other races.
Source: Bureau of the Census, America's Families and Living Arrangements: 2011, Internet site http://www.census.gov/population/www/socdemo/hh-fam/cps2011.html; calculations by New Strategist

Table 7.17 Marital Status by Sex and Age, 2011: Hispanics

(number and percent distribution of Hispanics aged 15 or older by sex, age, and current marital status, 2011; numbers in thousands)

	total	never married	married spouse present	married spouse absent	separated	divorced	widowed
NUMBER							
Total Hispanic men	**18,097**	**8,118**	**7,382**	**652**	**1,090**	**553**	**302**
Under age 45	12,602	7,415	3,937	394	459	361	34
Aged 45 to 54	2,693	436	1,691	157	288	96	27
Aged 45 to 49	1,507	249	944	88	157	64	6
Aged 50 to 54	1,186	187	747	69	131	32	21
Aged 55 to 64	1,572	154	1,020	55	241	57	44
Aged 65 or older	1,230	114	735	46	103	39	195
Total Hispanic women	**16,954**	**5,909**	**7,491**	**374**	**1,495**	**742**	**942**
Under age 45	10,982	5,263	4,370	229	611	450	60
Aged 45 to 54	2,668	353	1,585	64	398	164	106
Aged 45 to 49	1,455	215	893	27	189	84	48
Aged 50 to 54	1,213	138	692	37	209	80	58
Aged 55 to 64	1,679	166	917	47	279	85	185
Aged 65 or older	1,624	126	621	34	208	44	591
PERCENT DISTRIBUTION							
Total Hispanic men	**100.0%**	**44.9%**	**40.8%**	**3.6%**	**6.0%**	**3.1%**	**1.7%**
Under age 45	100.0	58.8	31.2	3.1	3.6	2.9	0.3
Aged 45 to 54	100.0	16.2	62.8	5.8	10.7	3.6	1.0
Aged 45 to 49	100.0	16.5	62.6	5.8	10.4	4.2	0.4
Aged 50 to 54	100.0	15.8	63.0	5.8	11.0	2.7	1.8
Aged 55 to 64	100.0	9.8	64.9	3.5	15.3	3.6	2.8
Aged 65 or older	100.0	9.3	59.8	3.7	8.4	3.2	15.9
Total Hispanic women	**100.0**	**34.9**	**44.2**	**2.2**	**8.8**	**4.4**	**5.6**
Under age 45	100.0	47.9	39.8	2.1	5.6	4.1	0.5
Aged 45 to 54	100.0	13.2	59.4	2.4	14.9	6.1	4.0
Aged 45 to 49	100.0	14.8	61.4	1.9	13.0	5.8	3.3
Aged 50 to 54	100.0	11.4	57.0	3.1	17.2	6.6	4.8
Aged 55 to 64	100.0	9.9	54.6	2.8	16.6	5.1	11.0
Aged 65 or older	100.0	7.8	38.2	2.1	12.8	2.7	36.4

Source: Bureau of the Census, America's Families and Living Arrangements: 2011, Internet site http://www.census.gov/population/www/socdemo/hh-fam/cps2011.html; calculations by New Strategist

Table 7.18 Marital Status by Sex and Age, 2011: Non-Hispanic Whites

(number and percent distribution of non-Hispanic whites aged 15 or older by sex, age, and current marital status, 2011; numbers in thousands)

	total	never married	married spouse present	married spouse absent	separated	divorced	widowed
NUMBER							
Total non-Hispanic white men	**80,079**	**23,589**	**44,413**	**731**	**1,266**	**7,921**	**2,160**
Under age 45	37,554	20,111	14,344	307	608	2,119	65
Aged 45 to 54	15,158	1,880	10,308	125	333	2,357	154
Aged 45 to 49	7,388	991	4,958	58	180	1,145	55
Aged 50 to 54	7,770	889	5,350	67	153	1,212	99
Aged 55 to 64	13,659	1,063	9,841	140	203	2,139	273
Aged 65 or older	13,708	534	9,919	158	124	1,305	1,668
Total non-Hispanic white women	**83,992**	**19,435**	**44,265**	**812**	**1,429**	**9,662**	**8,389**
Under age 45	37,067	16,683	16,330	373	820	2,686	170
Aged 45 to 54	15,520	1,257	10,608	165	335	2,623	531
Aged 45 to 49	7,548	651	5,168	76	185	1,274	193
Aged 50 to 54	7,972	606	5,440	89	150	1,349	338
Aged 55 to 64	14,083	881	9,316	134	187	2,451	1,113
Aged 65 or older	17,322	611	8,009	139	87	1,902	6,574
PERCENT DISTRIBUTION							
Total non-Hispanic white men	**100.0%**	**29.5%**	**55.5%**	**0.9%**	**1.6%**	**9.9%**	**2.7%**
Under age 45	100.0	53.6	38.2	0.8	1.6	5.6	0.2
Aged 45 to 54	100.0	12.4	68.0	0.8	2.2	15.5	1.0
Aged 45 to 49	100.0	13.4	67.1	0.8	2.4	15.5	0.7
Aged 50 to 54	100.0	11.4	68.9	0.9	2.0	15.6	1.3
Aged 55 to 64	100.0	7.8	72.0	1.0	1.5	15.7	2.0
Aged 65 or older	100.0	3.9	72.4	1.2	0.9	9.5	12.2
Total non-Hispanic white women	**100.0**	**23.1**	**52.7**	**1.0**	**1.7**	**11.5**	**10.0**
Under age 45	100.0	45.0	44.1	1.0	2.2	7.2	0.5
Aged 45 to 54	100.0	8.1	68.4	1.1	2.2	16.9	3.4
Aged 45 to 49	100.0	8.6	68.5	1.0	2.5	16.9	2.6
Aged 50 to 54	100.0	7.6	68.2	1.1	1.9	16.9	4.2
Aged 55 to 64	100.0	6.3	66.2	1.0	1.3	17.4	7.9
Aged 65 or older	100.0	3.5	46.2	0.8	0.5	11.0	38.0

Note: Non-Hispanic whites are those who identify themselves as being white alone and not Hispanic.
Source: Bureau of the Census, America's Families and Living Arrangements: 2011, Internet site http://www.census.gov/population/www/socdemo/hh-fam/cps2011.html; calculations by New Strategist

Divorce Is Highest among Men and Women in Their Fifties

The oldest Boomers are most likely to have gone through a divorce.

The experience of divorce is most common among men aged 50 to 69 and women aged 50 to 59. Among men in their fifties and sixties, about 36 percent have ever divorced, according to a Census Bureau study of marriage and divorce. Among women in their fifties, 37 percent have experienced divorce.

Among all Americans aged 15 or older, 40.6 percent of women and 42.5 percent of men had married once and were still married. The figure topped 50 percent for men aged 30 or older and for women aged 30 to 49.

■ Government studies have suggested that the Vietnam War and women's changing roles were factors in the higher divorce rate of Boomers.

More than one in five adults have experienced divorce

(percent of people aged 15 or older by selected marital history and sex, 2009)

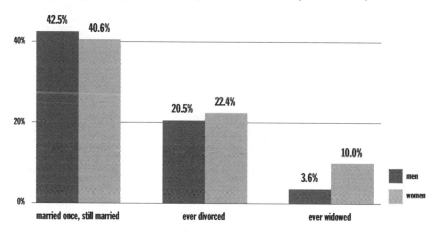

Table 7.19 Marital History of Men by Age, 2009

(number of men aged 15 or older and percent distribution by marital history and age, 2009; numbers in thousands)

	total	15–19	20–24	25–29	30–34	35–39	40–49	50–59	60–69	70+
TOTAL MEN, NUMBER	115,797	10,870	10,152	10,567	9,518	9,995	21,504	19,568	12,774	10,849
TOTAL MEN, PERCENT	100.0%	100.0%	100.0%	100.0%	100.0%	100.0%	100.0%	100.0%	100.0%	100.0%
Never married	33.0	98.0	87.5	59.7	35.6	23.5	16.4	10.8	4.6	3.4
Ever married	67.0	2.0	12.5	40.3	64.4	76.5	83.6	89.2	95.4	96.6
Married once	52.3	1.9	12.5	38.8	59.4	66.9	65.8	63.4	64.8	72.3
Still married	42.5	1.3	11.2	34.2	52.2	56.1	52.2	50.4	53.5	54.0
Married twice	11.6	0.1	0.0	1.5	4.8	8.7	14.8	20.0	22.1	18.9
Still married	9.0	0.1	0.0	1.3	4.0	7.4	11.3	15.5	17.5	13.2
Married three or more times	3.1	0.0	0.0	0.1	0.2	1.0	3.0	5.8	8.5	5.4
Still married	2.3	0.0	0.0	0.1	0.2	0.8	2.2	4.3	6.5	3.8
Ever divorced	20.5	0.3	0.8	5.0	10.5	17.9	28.5	35.7	36.5	23.4
Currently divorced	9.1	0.2	0.7	3.7	6.2	9.5	14.2	15.5	12.4	7.2
Ever widowed	3.6	0.4	0.1	0.3	0.2	0.5	1.3	2.5	6.4	22.6
Currently widowed	2.6	0.3	0.1	0.3	0.1	0.3	0.9	1.6	3.9	17.4

Source: Bureau of the Census, Number, Timing, and Duration of Marriages and Divorces: 2009, Current Population Reports P70-125, 2011, Internet site http://www.census.gov/hhes/socdemo/marriage/data/sipp/index.html; calculations by New Strategist

Table 7.20 Marital History of Women by Age, 2009

(number of women aged 15 or older and percent distribution by marital history and age, 2009; numbers in thousands)

	total	15–19	20–24	25–29	30–34	35–39	40–49	50–59	60–69	70+
TOTAL WOMEN, NUMBER	123,272	10,478	10,158	10,408	9,645	10,267	22,119	20,702	14,288	15,207
TOTAL WOMEN, PERCENT	100.0%	100.0%	100.0%	100.0%	100.0%	100.0%	100.0%	100.0%	100.0%	100.0%
Never married	27.2	97.5	77.3	46.8	26.7	17.3	13.0	9.1	6.0	4.3
Ever married	72.8	2.5	22.7	53.2	73.3	82.7	87.0	90.9	94.0	95.7
Married once	57.5	2.5	22.4	50.8	64.5	69.3	67.4	65.5	67.7	76.1
Still married	40.6	1.9	19.7	43.2	54.5	55.8	51.6	47.5	45.7	30.1
Married twice	12.1	0.1	0.3	2.3	8.0	11.6	15.8	19.5	20.1	15.2
Still married	7.9	0.6	0.2	2.0	6.9	9.1	11.3	13.4	13.2	5.2
Married three or more times	3.2	0.0	0.0	0.0	0.8	1.9	3.8	5.9	6.2	4.4
Still married	1.9	0.0	0.0	0.0	0.7	1.4	2.5	4.1	3.6	1.4
Ever divorced	22.4	0.2	1.8	7.3	15.6	22.7	31.0	37.3	34.5	21.4
Currently divorced	11.3	0.1	1.5	5.3	8.1	11.8	16.4	18.6	16.0	9.9
Ever widowed	10.0	0.3	0.1	0.2	0.6	1.4	2.6	6.5	17.0	51.2
Currently widowed	8.9	0.3	0.1	0.1	0.4	0.8	1.8	4.9	13.9	48.3

Source: Bureau of the Census, Number, Timing, and Duration of Marriages and Divorces: 2009, Current Population Reports P70-125, 2011, Internet site http://www.census.gov/hhes/socdemo/marriage/data/sipp/index.html; calculations by New Strategist

8

Population

■ The nation's 77 million Baby Boomers (born between 1946 and 1964) account for 25 percent of the U.S. population. They are the largest generation of Americans.

■ Seventy-two percent of the Baby-Boom generation is non-Hispanic white, greater than the 64 percent share among the population as a whole. But Boomers are much less diverse than younger Americans.

■ Half of Boomers were born in their state of residence. Fifteen percent were born in another country.

■ Nearly one in five legal immigrants admitted to the United States in 2011 was in the 45-to-64 age group.

■ Millennials outnumber Boomers in a number of states, many of them with large Hispanic populations such as Arizona, California, and Texas.

Boomers Are Still the Largest Generation

But Millennials are not far behind.

The Baby-Boom generation numbers 77 million, a figure that includes everyone born between 1946 and 1964 (aged 46 to 64 in 2010). Boomers account for 25 percent of the total population, making them the largest generation—but not by much. Millennials, most of them children of Boomers, are in second place. They numbered just over 76 million in 2010 and accounted for slightly less than 25 percent of the population.

Between 2000 and 2010, the oldest Boomers entirely filled the 55-to-64 age group. During those years, the number of 55-to-59-year-olds grew by 46 percent and the number of 60-to-64-year-olds grew by 56 percent—making them the two fastest-growing age groups. In contrast, as Boomers exited the 40-to-44 age group, it shrank by 7 percent.

■ Although the oldest Boomers are eligible for Social Security and Medicare, many will postpone retirement because of the economic downturn.

Boomers slightly outnumber Millennials

(number of people by generation, 2010)

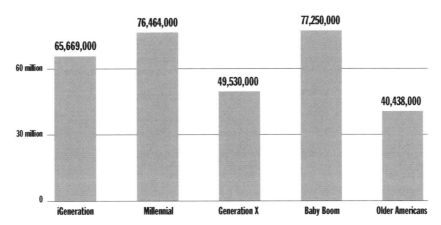

Table 8.1 Population by Age and Generation, 2010

(number and percent distribution of people by age and generation, 2010; numbers in thousands)

	number	percent distribution
Total people	**309,350**	**100.0%**
Under age 5	20,201	6.5
Aged 5 to 9	20,382	6.6
Aged 10 to 14	20,694	6.7
Aged 15 to 19	21,959	7.1
Aged 20 to 24	21,668	7.0
Aged 25 to 29	21,153	6.8
Aged 30 to 34	20,094	6.5
Aged 35 to 39	20,082	6.5
Aged 40 to 44	20,899	6.8
Aged 45 to 64	81,780	26.4
Aged 45 to 49	22,648	7.3
Aged 50 to 54	22,365	7.2
Aged 55 to 59	19,779	6.4
Aged 60 to 64	16,987	5.5
Aged 65 to 69	12,515	4.0
Aged 70 to 74	9,326	3.0
Aged 75 to 79	7,313	2.4
Aged 80 to 84	5,750	1.9
Aged 85 or older	5,533	1.8
Total people	**309,350**	**100.0**
iGeneration (under 16)	65,669	21.2
Millennial (16 to 33)	76,464	24.7
Generation X (34 to 45)	49,530	16.0
Baby Boom (46 to 64)	77,250	25.0
Older Americans (65 or older)	40,438	13.1

Source: Bureau of the Census, Population Estimates, Internet site http://www.census.gov/popest/data/intercensal/national/ nat2010.html; calculations by New Strategist

Table 8.2 Population by Age and Sex, 2010

(number of people by age and sex, and sex ratio by age, 2010; numbers in thousands)

	total	female	male	sex ratio
Total people	**309,350**	**157,242**	**152,108**	**97**
Under age 5	20,201	9,883	10,318	104
Aged 5 to 9	20,382	9,975	10,407	104
Aged 10 to 14	20,694	10,107	10,587	105
Aged 15 to 19	21,959	10,696	11,263	105
Aged 20 to 24	21,668	10,612	11,056	104
Aged 25 to 29	21,153	10,477	10,676	102
Aged 30 to 34	20,094	10,030	10,063	100
Aged 35 to 39	20,082	10,086	9,997	99
Aged 40 to 44	20,899	10,500	10,399	99
Aged 45 to 64	81,780	41,892	39,888	95
Aged 45 to 49	22,648	11,465	11,183	98
Aged 50 to 54	22,365	11,399	10,966	96
Aged 55 to 59	19,779	10,199	9,580	94
Aged 60 to 64	16,987	8,829	8,159	92
Aged 65 to 69	12,515	6,623	5,892	89
Aged 70 to 74	9,326	5,057	4,269	84
Aged 75 to 79	7,313	4,130	3,184	77
Aged 80 to 84	5,750	3,448	2,302	67
Aged 85 or older	5,533	3,726	1,807	49

Note: The sex ratio is the number of males per 100 females.
Source: Bureau of the Census, Population Estimates, Internet site http://www.census.gov/popest/data/intercensal/national/nat2010.html; calculations by New Strategist

Table 8.3 Population by Age, 2000 and 2010

(number of people by age, 2000 and 2010; percent change, 2000–10; numbers in thousands)

	2010	2000	percent change 2000–10
Total people	**309,350**	**282,162**	**9.6%**
Under age 5	20,201	19,178	5.3
Aged 5 to 9	20,382	20,464	–0.4
Aged 10 to 14	20,694	20,638	0.3
Aged 15 to 19	21,959	20,295	8.2
Aged 20 to 24	21,668	19,117	13.3
Aged 25 to 29	21,153	19,280	9.7
Aged 30 to 34	20,094	20,524	–2.1
Aged 35 to 39	20,082	22,651	–11.3
Aged 40 to 44	20,899	22,518	–7.2
Aged 45 to 49	22,648	20,220	12.0
Aged 50 to 54	22,365	17,779	25.8
Aged 55 to 59	19,779	13,566	45.8
Aged 60 to 64	16,987	10,863	56.4
Aged 65 to 69	12,515	9,524	31.4
Aged 70 to 74	9,326	8,860	5.3
Aged 75 to 79	7,313	7,439	–1.7
Aged 80 to 84	5,750	4,985	15.4
Aged 85 or older	5,533	4,262	29.8
Aged 18 to 24	30,708	27,315	12.4
Aged 18 or older	235,154	209,786	12.1
Aged 65 or older	40,438	35,070	15.3

Source: Bureau of the Census, Population Estimates, Internet site http://www.census.gov/popest/data/intercensal/national/nat2010.html; calculations by New Strategist

Boomers Are Less Diverse than Younger Americans

They are more diverse than older generations, however.

Seventy-two percent of the Baby-Boom generation is non-Hispanic white, according to the Census Bureau. This figure is greater than the 64 percent for the population as a whole and far surpasses the share among the youngest Americans—only 51 percent of children under age 5 are non-Hispanic white. The Baby-Boom generation is more diverse than older Americans, however. Among people aged 85 or older in 2010, fully 85 percent were non-Hispanic white.

Boomers are the largest generation only among non-Hispanic whites, accounting for 28 percent of the non-Hispanic white total. Among Asians, blacks, and Hispanics, the iGeneration and Millennials outnumber Boomers. Among Hispanics, even Generation X outnumbers Boomers.

■ The differing racial and ethnic makeup of Boomers versus younger generations of Americans may create political problems in the years ahead.

Nearly three of four Baby Boomers are non-Hispanic white

(non-Hispanic white share of population by generation, 2010)

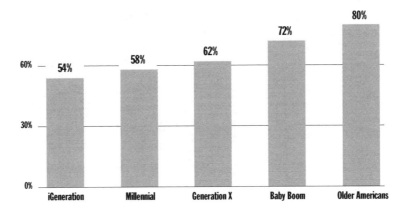

Table 8.4 Number of People by Age, Race Alone, and Hispanic Origin, 2010

(number of people by age, race alone, and Hispanic origin, 2010; numbers in thousands)

	total	Asian	black	Hispanic	non-Hispanic white	two or more races
Total people	**308,746**	**15,160**	**40,251**	**50,478**	**197,319**	**7,026**
Under age 5	20,201	948	3,055	5,114	10,307	1,123
Aged 5 to 9	20,349	972	3,013	4,791	10,885	948
Aged 10 to 14	20,677	922	3,154	4,525	11,449	836
Aged 15 to 19	22,040	999	3,573	4,532	12,387	726
Aged 20 to 24	21,586	1,149	3,240	4,322	12,467	571
Aged 25 to 29	21,102	1,279	2,911	4,310	12,268	491
Aged 30 to 34	19,962	1,284	2,743	4,124	11,534	424
Aged 35 to 39	20,180	1,334	2,706	3,856	12,018	357
Aged 40 to 44	20,891	1,188	2,752	3,442	13,250	315
Aged 45 to 64	81,489	3,675	9,616	8,677	58,514	937
Aged 45 to 49	22,709	1,105	2,901	3,022	15,387	302
Aged 50 to 54	22,298	1,004	2,753	2,441	15,813	269
Aged 55 to 59	19,665	863	2,246	1,841	14,476	209
Aged 60 to 64	16,818	703	1,715	1,372	12,839	157
Aged 65 to 69	12,435	483	1,181	949	9,693	106
Aged 70 to 74	9,278	361	865	700	7,265	73
Aged 75 to 79	7,318	255	625	511	5,867	51
Aged 80 to 84	5,743	171	430	351	4,751	35
Aged 85 or older	5,493	140	386	271	4,664	30
PERCENT DISTRIBUTION						
Total people	**100.0%**	**4.9%**	**13.0%**	**16.3%**	**63.9%**	**2.3%**
Under age 5	100.0	4.7	15.1	25.3	51.0	5.6
Aged 5 to 9	100.0	4.8	14.8	23.5	53.5	4.7
Aged 10 to 14	100.0	4.5	15.3	21.9	55.4	4.0
Aged 15 to 19	100.0	4.5	16.2	20.6	56.2	3.3
Aged 20 to 24	100.0	5.3	15.0	20.0	57.8	2.6
Aged 25 to 29	100.0	6.1	13.8	20.4	58.1	2.3
Aged 30 to 34	100.0	6.4	13.7	20.7	57.8	2.1
Aged 35 to 39	100.0	6.6	13.4	19.1	59.6	1.8
Aged 40 to 44	100.0	5.7	13.2	16.5	63.4	1.5
Aged 45 to 64	100.0	4.5	11.8	10.6	71.8	1.2
Aged 45 to 49	100.0	4.9	12.8	13.3	67.8	1.3
Aged 50 to 54	100.0	4.5	12.3	10.9	70.9	1.2
Aged 55 to 59	100.0	4.4	11.4	9.4	73.6	1.1
Aged 60 to 64	100.0	4.2	10.2	8.2	76.3	0.9
Aged 65 to 69	100.0	3.9	9.5	7.6	78.0	0.9
Aged 70 to 74	100.0	3.9	9.3	7.5	78.3	0.8
Aged 75 to 79	100.0	3.5	8.5	7.0	80.2	0.7
Aged 80 to 84	100.0	3.0	7.5	6.1	82.7	0.6
Aged 85 or older	100.0	2.5	7.0	4.9	84.9	0.6

Note: Asians and blacks are those who identify themselves as being of the race alone. Numbers do not add to total because not all races are shown and Hispanics may be of any race. Non-Hispanic whites are those who identify themselves as being white alone and not Hispanic.
Source: Bureau of the Census, 2010 Census, American Factfinder, Population Estimates, Internet site http://factfinder2.census.gov/faces/nav/jsf/pages/index.xhtml; calculations by New Strategist

Table 8.5 Number of People by Age, Race Alone or in Combination, and Hispanic Origin, 2010

(number of people by age, race alone or in combination, and Hispanic origin, 2010; numbers in thousands)

	total	Asian	black	Hispanic	non-Hispanic white
Total people	**308,746**	**17,321**	**42,021**	**50,478**	**197,319**
Under age 5	20,201	1,317	3,538	5,114	10,307
Aged 5 to 9	20,349	1,285	3,389	4,791	10,885
Aged 10 to 14	20,677	1,184	3,468	4,525	11,449
Aged 15 to 19	22,040	1,229	3,796	4,532	12,387
Aged 20 to 24	21,586	1,333	3,350	4,322	12,467
Aged 25 to 29	21,102	1,433	2,971	4,310	12,268
Aged 30 to 34	19,962	1,412	2,780	4,124	11,534
Aged 35 to 39	20,180	1,445	2,738	3,856	12,018
Aged 40 to 44	20,891	1,279	2,773	3,442	13,250
Aged 45 to 64	81,489	3,921	9,696	8,677	58,514
Aged 45 to 49	22,709	1,188	2,922	3,022	15,387
Aged 50 to 54	22,298	1,076	2,775	2,441	15,813
Aged 55 to 59	19,665	916	2,267	1,841	14,476
Aged 60 to 64	16,818	740	1,732	1,372	12,839
Aged 65 to 69	12,435	508	1,192	949	9,693
Aged 70 to 74	9,278	379	873	700	7,265
Aged 75 to 79	7,318	269	631	511	5,867
Aged 80 to 84	5,743	180	435	351	4,751
Aged 85 or older	5,493	147	392	271	4,664
PERCENT DISTRIBUTION					
Total people	**100.0%**	**5.6%**	**13.6%**	**16.3%**	**63.9%**
Under age 5	100.0	6.5	17.5	25.3	51.0
Aged 5 to 9	100.0	6.3	16.7	23.5	53.5
Aged 10 to 14	100.0	5.7	16.8	21.9	55.4
Aged 15 to 19	100.0	5.6	17.2	20.6	56.2
Aged 20 to 24	100.0	6.2	15.5	20.0	57.8
Aged 25 to 29	100.0	6.8	14.1	20.4	58.1
Aged 30 to 34	100.0	7.1	13.9	20.7	57.8
Aged 35 to 39	100.0	7.2	13.6	19.1	59.6
Aged 40 to 44	100.0	6.1	13.3	16.5	63.4
Aged 45 to 64	100.0	4.8	11.9	10.6	71.8
Aged 45 to 49	100.0	5.2	12.9	13.3	67.8
Aged 50 to 54	100.0	4.8	12.4	10.9	70.9
Aged 55 to 59	100.0	4.7	11.5	9.4	73.6
Aged 60 to 64	100.0	4.4	10.3	8.2	76.3
Aged 65 to 69	100.0	4.1	9.6	7.6	78.0
Aged 70 to 74	100.0	4.1	9.4	7.5	78.3
Aged 75 to 79	100.0	3.7	8.6	7.0	80.2
Aged 80 to 84	100.0	3.1	7.6	6.1	82.7
Aged 85 or older	100.0	2.7	7.1	4.9	84.9

Note: Asians and blacks are those who identify themselves as being of the race alone and those who identify themselves as being of the race in combination with other races. Numbers do not add to total because not all races are shown, some mixed-race individuals are counted more than once, and Hispanics may be of any race. Non-Hispanic whites are those who identify themselves as being white alone and not Hispanic.
Source: Bureau of the Census, 2010 Census, American Factfinder, Population Estimates, Internet site http://factfinder2.census .gov/faces/nav/jsf/pages/index.xhtml; calculations by New Strategist

Table 8.6 Population by Generation, Race Alone or in Combination, and Hispanic Origin, 2010

(number and percent distribution of people by generation, race alone or in combination, and Hispanic origin, 2010; numbers in thousands)

	total	Asian	black	Hispanic	non-Hispanic white
Total people	**308,746**	**17,321**	**42,021**	**50,478**	**197,319**
iGeneration (under age 16)	65,635	4,031	11,154	15,337	35,119
Millennial (16 to 33)	76,290	4,879	11,582	15,558	43,871
Generation X (34 to 45)	49,605	3,244	6,651	8,728	30,651
Baby Boom (46 to 64)	76,948	3,683	9,111	8,073	55,437
Older Americans (65 or older)	40,268	1,483	3,522	2,782	32,241

PERCENT DISTRIBUTION BY RACE AND HISPANIC ORIGIN

	total	Asian	black	Hispanic	non-Hispanic white
Total people	**100.0%**	**5.6%**	**13.6%**	**16.3%**	**63.9%**
iGeneration (under age 16)	100.0	6.1	17.0	23.4	53.5
Millennial (16 to 33)	100.0	6.4	15.2	20.4	57.5
Generation X (34 to 45)	100.0	6.5	13.4	17.6	61.8
Baby Boom (46 to 64)	100.0	4.8	11.8	10.5	72.0
Older Americans (65 or older)	100.0	3.7	8.7	6.9	80.1

PERCENT DISTRIBUTION BY GENERATION

	total	Asian	black	Hispanic	non-Hispanic white
Total people	**100.0%**	**100.0%**	**100.0%**	**100.0%**	**100.0%**
iGeneration (under age 16)	21.3	23.3	26.5	30.4	17.8
Millennial (16 to 33)	24.7	28.2	27.6	30.8	22.2
Generation X (34 to 45)	16.1	18.7	15.8	17.3	15.5
Baby Boom (46 to 64)	24.9	21.3	21.7	16.0	28.1
Older Americans (65 or older)	13.0	8.6	8.4	5.5	16.3

Note: Asians and blacks are those who identify themselves as being of the race alone and those who identify themselves as being of the race in combination with other races. Numbers do not add to total because not all races are shown, some mixed-race individuals are counted more than once, and Hispanics may be of any race. Non-Hispanic whites are those who identify themselves as being white alone and not Hispanic.
Source: Bureau of the Census, 2010 Census, American Factfinder, Population Estimates, Internet site http://factfinder2.census .gov/faces/nav/jsf/pages/index.xhtml; calculations by New Strategist

Many Boomers Live in Their State of Birth

One in seven is foreign-born.

According to the 2010 American Community Survey, 50 percent of people aged 45 to 64 (Boomers were aged 46 to 64 in that year) were born in the state of their current residence—a figure that is nearly identical to the one among U.S. residents aged 65 or older. Thirty-four percent of Boomers were born in the United States, but in a different state. Fifteen percent were born in another country—a slightly greater share than the 13 percent of all U.S. residents who are foreign-born.

Among the foreign-born, the 45-to-64 age group accounts for 30 percent of the total. The figure is smallest among the foreign-born from Mexico, where the 45-to-64 age group accounts for only 25 percent. The younger age distribution of the foreign-born from Mexico is reflected in their median age of just 37. Among the foreign-born from Europe, the median age is 52.

■ The foreign-born population adds to the multicultural mix, which is now a significant factor in American business and politics.

Among the foreign-born, those from Mexico are the youngest

(median age of the foreign-born by world region of birth, 2010)

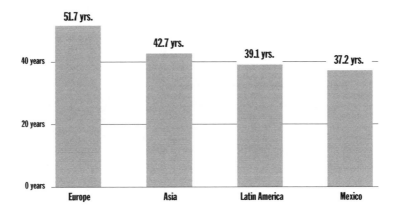

Table 8.7 Population by Age and Place of Birth, 2010

(number and percent distribution of people by age and place of birth, 2010; numbers in thousands)

| | | born in the United States | | | |
	total	in state of current residence	outside state of current residence	citizen born outside U.S.	foreign-born
Total people	**309,350**	**181,748**	**83,418**	**4,228**	**39,956**
Under age 5	20,134	17,981	1,768	121	263
Aged 5 to 17	54,031	42,287	8,580	597	2,568
Aged 18 to 24	30,895	19,665	7,263	468	3,499
Aged 25 to 34	40,972	21,661	10,755	662	7,894
Aged 35 to 44	41,192	19,842	11,949	701	8,701
Aged 45 to 64	81,691	40,800	27,587	1,236	12,068
Aged 45 to 54	44,929	22,521	14,474	738	7,196
Aged 55 to 59	19,683	9,944	6,803	270	2,666
Aged 60 to 61	7,222	3,583	2,595	94	951
Aged 62 to 64	9,857	4,752	3,714	135	1,256
Aged 65 to 74	21,854	10,324	8,430	255	2,845
Aged 75 or older	18,579	9,187	7,087	188	2,118
PERCENT DISTRIBUTION BY PLACE OF BIRTH					
Total people	**100.0%**	**58.8%**	**27.0%**	**1.4%**	**12.9%**
Under age 5	100.0	89.3	8.8	0.6	1.3
Aged 5 to 17	100.0	78.3	15.9	1.1	4.8
Aged 18 to 24	100.0	63.7	23.5	1.5	11.3
Aged 25 to 34	100.0	52.9	26.2	1.6	19.3
Aged 35 to 44	100.0	48.2	29.0	1.7	21.1
Aged 45 to 64	100.0	49.9	33.8	1.5	14.8
Aged 45 to 54	100.0	50.1	32.2	1.6	16.0
Aged 55 to 59	100.0	50.5	34.6	1.4	13.5
Aged 60 to 61	100.0	49.6	35.9	1.3	13.2
Aged 62 to 64	100.0	48.2	37.7	1.4	12.7
Aged 65 to 74	100.0	47.2	38.6	1.2	13.0
Aged 75 or older	100.0	49.4	38.1	1.0	11.4
PERCENT DISTRIBUTION BY AGE					
Total people	**100.0%**	**100.0%**	**100.0%**	**100.0%**	**100.0%**
Under age 5	6.5	9.9	2.1	2.9	0.7
Aged 5 to 17	17.5	23.3	10.3	14.1	6.4
Aged 18 to 24	10.0	10.8	8.7	11.1	8.8
Aged 25 to 34	13.2	11.9	12.9	15.7	19.8
Aged 35 to 44	13.3	10.9	14.3	16.6	21.8
Aged 45 to 64	26.4	22.4	33.1	29.2	30.2
Aged 45 to 54	14.5	12.4	17.4	17.5	18.0
Aged 55 to 59	6.4	5.5	8.2	6.4	6.7
Aged 60 to 61	2.3	2.0	3.1	2.2	2.4
Aged 62 to 64	3.2	2.6	4.5	3.2	3.1
Aged 65 to 74	7.1	5.7	10.1	6.0	7.1
Aged 75 or older	6.0	5.1	8.5	4.5	5.3

Source: Bureau of the Census, 2010 American Community Survey, Internet site http://factfinder2.census.gov/faces/nav/jsf/pages/index.xhtml; calculations by New Strategist

Table 8.8 Foreign-Born Population by Age and World Region of Birth, 2010

(number and percent distribution of foreign-born by age and world region of birth, 2010; numbers in thousands)

	total	Asian	Europe	Latin America total	Latin America Mexico
Total foreign-born, number	39,956	11,284	4,817	21,224	11,711
Total foreign-born, percent	100.0%	100.0%	100.0%	100.0%	100.0%
Under age 5	0.7	0.9	0.5	0.5	0.5
Aged 5 to 17	6.4	6.0	5.1	6.7	7.4
Aged 18 to 24	8.8	7.7	5.5	10.1	11.1
Aged 25 to 44	41.5	39.9	27.4	46.0	50.1
Aged 45 to 54	18.0	18.7	16.7	17.9	16.2
Aged 55 to 64	12.2	14.1	16.3	10.2	8.4
Aged 65 to 74	7.1	7.8	13.8	5.3	0.4
Aged 75 to 84	3.9	3.7	10.0	2.6	1.7
Aged 85 or older	1.4	1.1	4.6	0.8	0.6
Median age	41.4	42.7	51.7	39.1	37.2

Note: Number of foreign-born by region do not add to total because "other region" is not shown.
Source: Bureau of the Census, 2010 American Community Survey, Internet site http://factfinder2.census.gov/faces/nav/jsf/pages/index.xhtml; calculations by New Strategist

The Middle Aged Are a Substantial Share of Immigrants

Nearly one in five immigrants in 2010 was aged 45 to 64.

The number of legal immigrants admitted to the United States in 2011 surpassed 1 million. Nearly 200,000 were aged 45 to 64, accounting for 19 percent of the total.

Within the 45-to-64 age group, the immigrant share declines steadily with age. Six percent of immigrants admitted to the United States in 2011 were aged 45 to 49. Only 3 percent were aged 60 to 64.

■ Because most immigrants are children and young adults, immigration has a much greater impact on the diversity of younger Americans than on the middle-aged or older population.

Immigrants aged 45 to 64 account for 19 percent of the 2011 total

(percent distribution of 2011 immigrants by age)

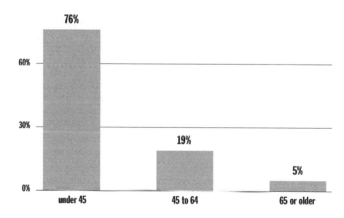

Table 8.9 Immigrants by Age, 2011

(number and percent distribution of immigrants by age, 2011)

	number	percent distribution
Total immigrants	**1,062,040**	**100.0%**
Under age 1	4,361	0.4
Aged 1 to 4	34,017	3.2
Aged 5 to 9	52,828	5.0
Aged 10 to 14	70,295	6.6
Aged 15 to 19	88,970	8.4
Aged 20 to 24	110,144	10.4
Aged 25 to 29	122,128	11.5
Aged 30 to 34	130,789	12.3
Aged 35 to 39	112,983	10.6
Aged 40 to 44	84,394	7.9
Aged 45 to 64	197,995	18.6
Aged 45 to 49	68,174	6.4
Aged 50 to 54	52,623	5.0
Aged 55 to 59	42,941	4.0
Aged 60 to 64	34,257	3.2
Aged 65 to 74	39,386	3.7
Aged 75 or older	13,740	1.3

Note: Immigrants are those granted legal permanent residence in the United States. They either arrive in the United States with immigrant visas issued abroad or adjust their status in the United States from temporary to permanent residence. Numbers may not sum to total because "age not stated" is not shown.
Source: Department of Homeland Security, 2011 Yearbook of Immigration Statistics, Internet site http://www.dhs.gov/files/ statistics/publications/yearbook.shtm

Many Working-Age Adults Do Not Speak English at Home

Most are Spanish speakers, and half have trouble speaking English.

Sixty million residents of the United States speak a language other than English at home, according to the Census Bureau's 2010 American Community Survey—21 percent of the population aged 5 or older. The 62 percent majority of those who do not speak English at home are Spanish speakers.

Among working-age adults (aged 18 to 64), 22 percent do not speak English at home, and 62 percent of those who do not speak English at home are Spanish speakers. Among the Spanish speakers, 50 percent say they speak English less than very well.

■ The language barrier is a problem for many working-age adults.

Half of adults who speak Spanish at home cannot speak English very well

(percent of people aged 18 to 64 who speak a language other than English at home who speak English less than very well, by language spoken at home, 2010)

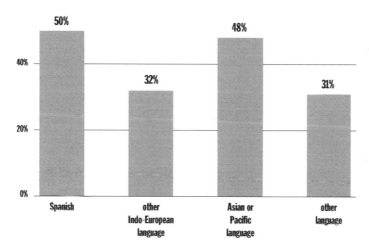

Table 8.10 Language Spoken at Home by People Aged 18 to 64, 2010

(number and percent distribution of people aged 5 or older and aged 18 to 64 who speak a language other than English at home by language spoken at home and ability to speak English very well, 2010; numbers in thousands)

	total		aged 18 to 64	
	number	percent distribution	number	percent distribution
Total, aged 5 or older	**289,216**	**100.0%**	**194,751**	**100.0%**
Speak only English at home	229,673	79.4	152,732	78.4
Speak a language other than English at home	59,542	20.6	42,018	21.6
Speak English less than "very well"	21,853	7.6	19,149	9.8
Total who speak a language other than English at home	**59,542**	**100.0**	**42,018**	**100.0**
Speak Spanish at home	36,996	62.1	25,934	61.7
Speak other Indo-European language at home	10,666	17.9	7,268	17.3
Speak Asian or Pacific Island language at home	9,340	15.7	6,943	16.5
Speak other language at home	2,540	4.3	1,873	4.5
Speak Spanish at home	36,996	100.0	25,934	100.0
Speak English less than very well	16,523	44.7	12,882	49.7
Speak other Indo-European language at home	10,666	100.0	7,268	100.0
Speak English less than very well	3,440	32.3	2,333	32.1
Speak Asian or Pacific Island language at home	9,340	100.0	6,943	100.0
Speak English less than very well	4,471	47.9	3,348	48.2
Speak other language at home	2,540	100.0	1,873	100.0
Speak English less than very well	786	30.9	586	31.3

Source: Bureau of the Census, 2010 American Community Survey, Internet site http://factfinder2.census.gov/faces/nav/jsf/pages/index.xhtml; calculations by New Strategist

Largest Share of Baby Boomers Lives in the South

Millennials outnumber Boomers in many states.

The South is home to the largest share of the population, and consequently to the largest share of the Baby-Boom generation. According to the Census Bureau's 2010 population estimates, 37 percent of Boomers live in the South, where they account for 25 percent of the population.

By state, the smallest proportion of Boomers is found in Utah, at 19 percent. Millennials outnumber Boomers in a number of states, many of them with large Hispanic populations such as Arizona, California, and Texas. In Maine, New Hampshire, and Vermont, the Baby-Boom generation accounts for 29 percent of the population, the highest share among the states.

■ As younger generations enter middle age, the diversity of the population will grow in every state and region.

The Northeast is home to just 19 percent of Boomers

(percent distribution of the Baby-Boom generation by region, 2010)

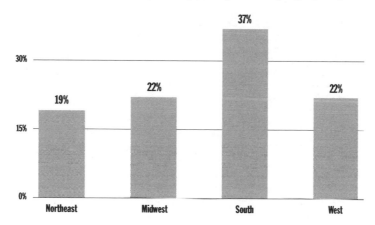

Table 8.11 Population by Age and Region, 2010

(number of people by age and region, 2010; numbers in thousands)

	total	Northeast	Midwest	South	West
Total people	**309,350**	**55,361**	**66,976**	**114,866**	**72,147**
Under age 5	20,201	3,219	4,329	7,680	4,973
Aged 5 to 9	20,382	3,339	4,432	7,691	4,921
Aged 10 to 14	20,694	3,498	4,520	7,711	4,965
Aged 15 to 19	21,959	3,873	4,781	8,062	5,243
Aged 20 to 24	21,668	3,830	4,595	8,038	5,205
Aged 25 to 29	21,153	3,623	4,427	7,861	5,243
Aged 30 to 34	20,094	3,433	4,203	7,506	4,952
Aged 35 to 39	20,082	3,487	4,159	7,596	4,840
Aged 40 to 44	20,899	3,888	4,387	7,751	4,872
Aged 45 to 64	81,780	15,342	18,095	30,004	18,339
Aged 45 to 49	22,648	4,261	4,931	8,359	5,096
Aged 50 to 54	22,365	4,225	5,013	8,122	5,005
Aged 55 to 59	19,779	3,691	4,449	7,186	4,453
Aged 60 to 64	16,987	3,165	3,702	6,335	3,785
Aged 65 to 69	12,515	2,298	2,702	4,789	2,726
Aged 70 to 74	9,326	1,718	2,046	3,571	1,992
Aged 75 to 79	7,313	1,416	1,638	2,730	1,530
Aged 80 to 84	5,750	1,191	1,335	2,039	1,184
Aged 85 or older	5,533	1,206	1,328	1,836	1,162

Source: Bureau of the Census, State Population Estimates, Internet site http://www.census.gov/popest/data/intercensal/state/state2010.html; calculations by New Strategist

Table 8.12 Regional Distribution of Population by Age, 2010

(regional distribution of people by age, 2010)

	total	Northeast	Midwest	South	West
Total people	**100.0%**	**17.9%**	**21.7%**	**37.1%**	**23.3%**
Under age 5	100.0	15.9	21.4	38.0	24.6
Aged 5 to 9	100.0	16.4	21.7	37.7	24.1
Aged 10 to 14	100.0	16.9	21.8	37.3	24.0
Aged 15 to 19	100.0	17.6	21.8	36.7	23.9
Aged 20 to 24	100.0	17.7	21.2	37.1	24.0
Aged 25 to 29	100.0	17.1	20.9	37.2	24.8
Aged 30 to 34	100.0	17.1	20.9	37.4	24.6
Aged 35 to 39	100.0	17.4	20.7	37.8	24.1
Aged 40 to 44	100.0	18.6	21.0	37.1	23.3
Aged 45 to 64	100.0	18.8	22.1	36.7	22.4
Aged 45 to 49	100.0	18.8	21.8	36.9	22.5
Aged 50 to 54	100.0	18.9	22.4	36.3	22.4
Aged 55 to 59	100.0	18.7	22.5	36.3	22.5
Aged 60 to 64	100.0	18.6	21.8	37.3	22.3
Aged 65 to 69	100.0	18.4	21.6	38.3	21.8
Aged 70 to 74	100.0	18.4	21.9	38.3	21.4
Aged 75 to 79	100.0	19.4	22.4	37.3	20.9
Aged 80 to 84	100.0	20.7	23.2	35.5	20.6
Aged 85 or older	100.0	21.8	24.0	33.2	21.0

Source: Bureau of the Census, State Population Estimates, Internet site http://www.census.gov/popest/data/intercensal/state/state2010.html; calculations by New Strategist

Table 8.13 Age Distribution of Population by Region, 2010

(age distribution of people by region, 2010)

	total	Northeast	Midwest	South	West
Total people	**100.0%**	**100.0%**	**100.0%**	**100.0%**	**100.0%**
Under age 5	6.5	5.8	6.5	6.7	6.9
Aged 5 to 9	6.6	6.0	6.6	6.7	6.8
Aged 10 to 14	6.7	6.3	6.7	6.7	6.9
Aged 15 to 19	7.1	7.0	7.1	7.0	7.3
Aged 20 to 24	7.0	6.9	6.9	7.0	7.2
Aged 25 to 29	6.8	6.5	6.6	6.8	7.3
Aged 30 to 34	6.5	6.2	6.3	6.5	6.9
Aged 35 to 39	6.5	6.3	6.2	6.6	6.7
Aged 40 to 44	6.8	7.0	6.6	6.7	6.8
Aged 45 to 64	26.4	27.7	27.0	26.1	25.4
Aged 45 to 49	7.3	7.7	7.4	7.3	7.1
Aged 50 to 54	7.2	7.6	7.5	7.1	6.9
Aged 55 to 59	6.4	6.7	6.6	6.3	6.2
Aged 60 to 64	5.5	5.7	5.5	5.5	5.2
Aged 65 to 69	4.0	4.2	4.0	4.2	3.8
Aged 70 to 74	3.0	3.1	3.1	3.1	2.8
Aged 75 to 79	2.4	2.6	2.4	2.4	2.1
Aged 80 to 84	1.9	2.2	2.0	1.8	1.6
Aged 85 or older	1.8	2.2	2.0	1.6	1.6

Source: Bureau of the Census, State Population Estimates, Internet site http://www.census.gov/popest/data/intercensal/state/ state2010.html; calculations by New Strategist

Table 8.14 Population by Generation and Region, 2010

(number and percent distribution of people by generation and region, 2010; numbers in thousands)

	total	Northeast	Midwest	South	West
Total people	**309,350**	**55,361**	**66,976**	**114,866**	**72,147**
iGeneration (under 16)	65,669	10,831	14,236	24,695	15,907
Millennial (16 to 33)	76,464	13,297	16,209	28,353	18,604
Generation X (34 to 45)	49,530	8,914	10,373	18,521	11,722
Baby Boom (46 to 64)	77,250	14,489	17,109	28,332	17,320
Older Americans (65 or older)	40,438	7,829	9,049	14,965	8,595
PERCENT DISTRIBUTION BY GENERATION					
Total people	**100.0%**	**100.0%**	**100.0%**	**100.0%**	**100.0%**
iGeneration (under 16)	21.2	19.6	21.3	21.5	22.0
Millennial (16 to 33)	24.7	24.0	24.2	24.7	25.8
Generation X (34 to 45)	16.0	16.1	15.5	16.1	16.2
Baby Boom (46 to 64)	25.0	26.2	25.5	24.7	24.0
Older Americans (65 or older)	13.1	14.1	13.5	13.0	11.9
PERCENT DISTRIBUTION BY REGION					
Total people	**100.0%**	**17.9%**	**21.7%**	**37.1%**	**23.3%**
iGeneration (under 16)	100.0	16.5	21.7	37.6	24.2
Millennial (16 to 33)	100.0	17.4	21.2	37.1	24.3
Generation X (34 to 45)	100.0	18.0	20.9	37.4	23.7
Baby Boom (46 to 64)	100.0	18.8	22.1	36.7	22.4
Older Americans (65 or older)	100.0	19.4	22.4	37.0	21.3

Source: Bureau of the Census, State Population Estimates, Internet site http://www.census.gov/popest/data/intercensal/state/state2010.html; calculations by New Strategist

Table 8.15 State Populations by Age, 2010

(total number of people and number aged 45 to 64 by state, 2010; numbers in thousands)

| | total population | aged 45 to 64 | | | | |
		total	45 to 49	50 to 54	55 to 59	60 to 64
United States	**309,350**	**81,780**	**22,648**	**22,365**	**19,779**	**16,987**
Alabama	4,785	1,286	345	348	314	279
Alaska	714	198	55	57	50	36
Arizona	6,414	1,577	427	417	378	355
Arkansas	2,922	761	205	202	185	169
California	37,349	9,328	2,687	2,573	2,217	1,851
Colorado	5,049	1,348	371	373	331	272
Connecticut	3,577	1,022	290	285	241	205
Delaware	900	245	67	66	58	54
District of Columbia	604	140	38	37	34	30
Florida	18,843	5,100	1,398	1,345	1,210	1,147
Georgia	9,713	2,472	721	671	577	502
Hawaii	1,364	371	96	98	94	83
Idaho	1,571	390	103	105	98	84
Illinois	12,843	3,352	937	933	812	671
Indiana	6,491	1,721	472	474	421	354
Iowa	3,050	814	216	224	205	170
Kansas	2,859	740	201	205	184	150
Kentucky	4,346	1,186	322	320	290	253
Louisiana	4,544	1,195	324	331	295	246
Maine	1,328	411	107	111	103	90
Maryland	5,786	1,604	461	442	380	321
Massachusetts	6,557	1,821	514	498	435	374
Michigan	9,878	2,765	740	766	686	573
Minnesota	5,311	1,441	405	403	352	282
Mississippi	2,970	766	208	209	187	162
Missouri	5,996	1,617	443	445	392	337
Montana	991	289	71	79	76	63
Nebraska	1,830	473	128	131	118	96
Nevada	2,705	694	193	183	165	152
New Hampshire	1,317	405	113	112	97	83
New Jersey	8,802	2,432	702	676	568	485
New Mexico	2,066	552	145	148	138	122
New York	19,392	5,195	1,454	1,423	1,243	1,076
North Carolina	9,562	2,519	697	672	605	544
North Dakota	674	179	46	50	46	36
Ohio	11,536	3,200	851	888	790	671
Oklahoma	3,762	970	261	265	238	207
Oregon	3,839	1,053	262	277	275	238
Pennsylvania	12,710	3,570	951	986	883	750
Rhode Island	1,053	293	81	81	71	60
South Carolina	4,636	1,249	332	328	305	284

	total population	aged 45 to 64				
		total	45 to 49	50 to 54	55 to 59	60 to 64
South Dakota	816	215	57	60	55	44
Tennessee	6,357	1,718	465	461	418	375
Texas	25,257	6,071	1,762	1,685	1,434	1,189
Utah	2,776	551	155	153	134	108
Vermont	626	193	50	52	49	42
Virginia	8,025	2,179	620	595	516	448
Washington	6,744	1,831	492	497	456	386
West Virginia	1,854	542	132	143	140	126
Wisconsin	5,691	1,577	436	437	388	316
Wyoming	564	157	39	44	41	33

Source: Bureau of the Census, State Population Estimates, Internet site http://www.census.gov/popest/data/intercensal/state/state2010.html; calculations by New Strategist

Table 8.16 Distribution of State Populations by Age, 2010

(percent distribution of people by state and age, 2010)

| | total population | aged 45 to 64 | | | | |
		total	45 to 49	50 to 54	55 to 59	60 to 64
United States	**100.0%**	**26.4%**	**7.3%**	**7.2%**	**6.4%**	**5.5%**
Alabama	100.0	26.9	7.2	7.3	6.6	5.8
Alaska	100.0	27.7	7.7	7.9	7.1	5.1
Arizona	100.0	24.6	6.7	6.5	5.9	5.5
Arkansas	100.0	26.0	7.0	6.9	6.3	5.8
California	100.0	25.0	7.2	6.9	5.9	5.0
Colorado	100.0	26.7	7.4	7.4	6.6	5.4
Connecticut	100.0	28.6	8.1	8.0	6.7	5.7
Delaware	100.0	27.2	7.5	7.3	6.5	6.0
District of Columbia	100.0	23.2	6.4	6.2	5.7	5.0
Florida	100.0	27.1	7.4	7.1	6.4	6.1
Georgia	100.0	25.4	7.4	6.9	5.9	5.2
Hawaii	100.0	27.2	7.0	7.2	6.9	6.1
Idaho	100.0	24.8	6.6	6.7	6.2	5.4
Illinois	100.0	26.1	7.3	7.3	6.3	5.2
Indiana	100.0	26.5	7.3	7.3	6.5	5.5
Iowa	100.0	26.7	7.1	7.3	6.7	5.6
Kansas	100.0	25.9	7.0	7.2	6.4	5.3
Kentucky	100.0	27.3	7.4	7.4	6.7	5.8
Louisiana	100.0	26.3	7.1	7.3	6.5	5.4
Maine	100.0	30.9	8.0	8.4	7.7	6.8
Maryland	100.0	27.7	8.0	7.6	6.6	5.6
Massachusetts	100.0	27.8	7.8	7.6	6.6	5.7
Michigan	100.0	28.0	7.5	7.8	6.9	5.8
Minnesota	100.0	27.1	7.6	7.6	6.6	5.3
Mississippi	100.0	25.8	7.0	7.0	6.3	5.5
Missouri	100.0	27.0	7.4	7.4	6.5	5.6
Montana	100.0	29.2	7.1	8.0	7.7	6.4
Nebraska	100.0	25.9	7.0	7.1	6.5	5.3
Nevada	100.0	25.7	7.1	6.8	6.1	5.6
New Hampshire	100.0	30.7	8.6	8.5	7.3	6.3
New Jersey	100.0	27.6	8.0	7.7	6.5	5.5
New Mexico	100.0	26.7	7.0	7.2	6.7	5.9
New York	100.0	26.8	7.5	7.3	6.4	5.5
North Carolina	100.0	26.3	7.3	7.0	6.3	5.7
North Dakota	100.0	26.5	6.8	7.5	6.9	5.4
Ohio	100.0	27.7	7.4	7.7	6.9	5.8
Oklahoma	100.0	25.8	6.9	7.1	6.3	5.5
Oregon	100.0	27.4	6.8	7.2	7.2	6.2
Pennsylvania	100.0	28.1	7.5	7.8	6.9	5.9
Rhode Island	100.0	27.9	7.7	7.7	6.7	5.7
South Carolina	100.0	26.9	7.2	7.1	6.6	6.1

	total population	aged 45 to 64				
		total	45 to 49	50 to 54	55 to 59	60 to 64
South Dakota	100.0%	26.4%	7.0%	7.3%	6.7%	5.4%
Tennessee	100.0	27.0	7.3	7.2	6.6	5.9
Texas	100.0	24.0	7.0	6.7	5.7	4.7
Utah	100.0	19.8	5.6	5.5	4.8	3.9
Vermont	100.0	30.8	8.0	8.4	7.8	6.6
Virginia	100.0	27.2	7.7	7.4	6.4	5.6
Washington	100.0	27.2	7.3	7.4	6.8	5.7
West Virginia	100.0	29.2	7.1	7.7	7.6	6.8
Wisconsin	100.0	27.7	7.7	7.7	6.8	5.6
Wyoming	100.0	27.9	7.0	7.8	7.3	5.8

Source: Bureau of the Census, State Population Estimates, Internet site http://www.census.gov/popest/data/intercensal/state/state2010.html; calculations by New Strategist

Table 8.17 State Populations by Generation, 2010

(number of people by state and generation, 2010; numbers in thousands)

	total population	iGeneration (under 16)	Millennial (16 to 33)	Generation X (34 to 45)	Baby Boom (46 to 64)	Older Americans (65 or older)
United States	**309,350**	**65,669**	**76,464**	**49,530**	**77,250**	**40,438**
Alabama	4,785	1,001	1,162	746	1,217	660
Alaska	714	167	191	114	187	55
Arizona	6,414	1,454	1,590	991	1,491	887
Arkansas	2,922	633	704	443	720	421
California	37,349	8,208	9,845	6,236	8,790	4,270
Colorado	5,049	1,096	1,281	845	1,273	553
Connecticut	3,577	715	809	582	963	508
Delaware	900	182	216	140	232	130
District of Columbia	604	92	211	100	133	69
Florida	18,843	3,531	4,288	2,930	4,820	3,274
Georgia	9,713	2,216	2,459	1,673	2,327	1,037
Hawaii	1,364	269	332	213	352	198
Idaho	1,571	383	390	233	370	195
Illinois	12,843	2,757	3,224	2,082	3,165	1,615
Indiana	6,491	1,425	1,581	1,014	1,626	844
Iowa	3,050	647	734	444	771	454
Kansas	2,859	648	711	422	700	377
Kentucky	4,346	908	1,040	696	1,121	580
Louisiana	4,544	993	1,173	688	1,130	560
Maine	1,328	240	281	206	389	211
Maryland	5,786	1,192	1,411	960	1,512	711
Massachusetts	6,557	1,251	1,614	1,069	1,719	906
Michigan	9,878	2,052	2,310	1,535	2,617	1,364
Minnesota	5,311	1,136	1,300	829	1,360	685
Mississippi	2,970	669	742	453	725	381
Missouri	5,996	1,261	1,456	909	1,528	841
Montana	991	198	232	138	275	147
Nebraska	1,830	410	456	269	448	248
Nevada	2,705	590	674	459	656	326
New Hampshire	1,317	251	290	215	382	179
New Jersey	8,802	1,812	2,020	1,487	2,292	1,190
New Mexico	2,066	461	505	303	523	274
New York	19,392	3,801	4,911	3,149	4,904	2,627
North Carolina	9,562	2,033	2,320	1,589	2,379	1,240
North Dakota	674	134	180	92	170	98
Ohio	11,536	2,403	2,696	1,781	3,030	1,626
Oklahoma	3,762	831	942	561	918	509
Oregon	3,839	769	932	603	1,000	536
Pennsylvania	12,710	2,452	2,967	1,946	3,380	1,965
Rhode Island	1,053	198	261	165	277	152
South Carolina	4,636	962	1,134	724	1,182	635

	total population	iGeneration (under 16)	Millennial (16 to 33)	Generation X (34 to 45)	Baby Boom (46 to 64)	Older Americans (65 or older)
South Dakota	816	181	200	114	204	117
Tennessee	6,357	1,326	1,523	1,026	1,625	857
Texas	25,257	6,138	6,612	4,169	5,718	2,620
Utah	2,776	788	810	407	520	251
Vermont	626	113	144	95	183	91
Virginia	8,025	1,645	2,005	1,337	2,055	982
Washington	6,744	1,402	1,680	1,097	1,733	833
West Virginia	1,854	343	412	285	515	298
Wisconsin	5,691	1,182	1,360	880	1,490	779
Wyoming	564	121	142	82	149	70

Source: Bureau of the Census, State Population Estimates, Internet site http://www.census.gov/popest/data/intercensal/state/ state2010.html; calculations by New Strategist

Table 8.18 Distribution of State Populations by Generation, 2010

(percent distribution of people by state and generation, 2010)

	total population	iGeneration (under 16)	Millennial (16 to 33)	Generation X (34 to 45)	Baby Boom (46 to 64)	Older Americans (65 or older)
United States	**100.0%**	**21.2%**	**24.7%**	**16.0%**	**25.0%**	**13.1%**
Alabama	100.0	20.9	24.3	15.6	25.4	13.8
Alaska	100.0	23.4	26.7	15.9	26.2	7.7
Arizona	100.0	22.7	24.8	15.5	23.3	13.8
Arkansas	100.0	21.7	24.1	15.2	24.6	14.4
California	100.0	22.0	26.4	16.7	23.5	11.4
Colorado	100.0	21.7	25.4	16.7	25.2	11.0
Connecticut	100.0	20.0	22.6	16.3	26.9	14.2
Delaware	100.0	20.3	24.0	15.6	25.7	14.4
District of Columbia	100.0	15.3	34.9	16.5	21.9	11.4
Florida	100.0	18.7	22.8	15.5	25.6	17.4
Georgia	100.0	22.8	25.3	17.2	24.0	10.7
Hawaii	100.0	19.7	24.3	15.6	25.8	14.5
Idaho	100.0	24.4	24.8	14.8	23.5	12.4
Illinois	100.0	21.5	25.1	16.2	24.6	12.6
Indiana	100.0	22.0	24.4	15.6	25.1	13.0
Iowa	100.0	21.2	24.1	14.5	25.3	14.9
Kansas	100.0	22.7	24.9	14.8	24.5	13.2
Kentucky	100.0	20.9	23.9	16.0	25.8	13.4
Louisiana	100.0	21.9	25.8	15.1	24.9	12.3
Maine	100.0	18.1	21.2	15.5	29.3	15.9
Maryland	100.0	20.6	24.4	16.6	26.1	12.3
Massachusetts	100.0	19.1	24.6	16.3	26.2	13.8
Michigan	100.0	20.8	23.4	15.5	26.5	13.8
Minnesota	100.0	21.4	24.5	15.6	25.6	12.9
Mississippi	100.0	22.5	25.0	15.3	24.4	12.8
Missouri	100.0	21.0	24.3	15.2	25.5	14.0
Montana	100.0	19.9	23.5	14.0	27.8	14.9
Nebraska	100.0	22.4	24.9	14.7	24.5	13.5
Nevada	100.0	21.8	24.9	17.0	24.2	12.1
New Hampshire	100.0	19.0	22.0	16.4	29.0	13.6
New Jersey	100.0	20.6	23.0	16.9	26.0	13.5
New Mexico	100.0	22.3	24.5	14.7	25.3	13.2
New York	100.0	19.6	25.3	16.2	25.3	13.5
North Carolina	100.0	21.3	24.3	16.6	24.9	13.0
North Dakota	100.0	19.9	26.7	13.7	25.2	14.5
Ohio	100.0	20.8	23.4	15.4	26.3	14.1
Oklahoma	100.0	22.1	25.1	14.9	24.4	13.5
Oregon	100.0	20.0	24.3	15.7	26.1	14.0
Pennsylvania	100.0	19.3	23.3	15.3	26.6	15.5
Rhode Island	100.0	18.8	24.8	15.7	26.3	14.4
South Carolina	100.0	20.7	24.5	15.6	25.5	13.7

	total population	iGeneration (under 16)	Millennial (16 to 33)	Generation X (34 to 45)	Baby Boom (46 to 64)	Older Americans (65 or older)
South Dakota	100.0%	22.2%	24.5%	14.0%	25.0%	14.3%
Tennessee	100.0	20.9	24.0	16.1	25.6	13.5
Texas	100.0	24.3	26.2	16.5	22.6	10.4
Utah	100.0	28.4	29.2	14.7	18.7	9.0
Vermont	100.0	18.1	23.0	15.1	29.2	14.6
Virginia	100.0	20.5	25.0	16.7	25.6	12.2
Washington	100.0	20.8	24.9	16.3	25.7	12.3
West Virginia	100.0	18.5	22.2	15.4	27.8	16.1
Wisconsin	100.0	20.8	23.9	15.5	26.2	13.7
Wyoming	100.0	21.5	25.1	14.5	26.5	12.4

Source: Bureau of the Census, State Population Estimates, Internet site http://www.census.gov/popest/data/intercensal/state/ state2010.html; calculations by New Strategist

Table 8.19 State Populations by Age, Race Alone or in Combination, and Hispanic Origin, 2010

(total number of people and percent distribution by age, race alone or in combination, and Hispanic origin, by state, 2010; numbers in thousands)

| | total | | | | | non-Hispanic |
	number	percent	Asian	black	Hispanic	white
Total population	**308,746**	**100.0%**	**5.6%**	**13.6%**	**16.3%**	**63.9%**
Under age 5	20,201	100.0	6.5	17.5	25.3	51.0
Aged 5 to 9	20,349	100.0	6.3	16.7	23.5	53.5
Aged 10 to 14	20,677	100.0	5.7	16.8	21.9	55.4
Aged 15 to 19	22,040	100.0	5.6	17.2	20.6	56.2
Aged 20 to 24	21,586	100.0	6.2	15.5	20.0	57.8
Aged 25 to 29	21,102	100.0	6.8	14.1	20.4	58.1
Aged 30 to 34	19,962	100.0	7.1	13.9	20.7	57.8
Aged 35 to 39	20,180	100.0	7.2	13.6	19.1	59.6
Aged 40 to 44	20,891	100.0	6.1	13.3	16.5	63.4
Aged 45 to 49	22,709	100.0	5.2	12.9	13.3	67.8
Aged 50 to 54	22,298	100.0	4.8	12.4	10.9	70.9
Aged 55 to 59	19,665	100.0	4.7	11.5	9.4	73.6
Aged 60 to 64	16,818	100.0	4.4	10.3	8.2	76.3
Aged 65 to 69	12,435	100.0	4.1	9.6	7.6	78.0
Aged 70 to 74	9,278	100.0	4.1	9.4	7.5	78.3
Aged 75 to 79	7,318	100.0	3.7	8.6	7.0	80.2
Aged 80 to 84	5,743	100.0	3.1	7.6	6.1	82.7
Aged 85 or older	5,493	100.0	2.7	7.1	4.9	84.9
Alabama	**4,780**	**100.0**	**1.4**	**26.8**	**3.9**	**67.0**
Under age 5	305	100.0	1.9	32.4	8.2	56.9
Aged 5 to 9	308	100.0	1.8	31.3	6.3	59.8
Aged 10 to 14	320	100.0	1.6	32.0	4.6	60.9
Aged 15 to 19	343	100.0	1.4	33.1	4.2	60.4
Aged 20 to 24	335	100.0	1.7	31.0	6.1	60.5
Aged 25 to 29	311	100.0	2.0	29.0	7.0	61.2
Aged 30 to 34	298	100.0	2.0	28.5	6.3	62.4
Aged 35 to 39	308	100.0	1.9	26.6	4.7	65.9
Aged 40 to 44	311	100.0	1.6	25.5	3.4	68.5
Aged 45 to 49	346	100.0	1.3	25.3	2.3	70.0
Aged 50 to 54	347	100.0	1.1	25.7	1.7	70.3
Aged 55 to 59	312	100.0	1.0	24.7	1.3	72.0
Aged 60 to 64	276	100.0	0.9	20.9	1.0	76.3
Aged 65 to 69	210	100.0	0.7	18.3	0.9	79.2
Aged 70 to 74	161	100.0	0.6	18.0	0.8	79.9
Aged 75 to 79	123	100.0	0.5	17.2	0.7	80.9
Aged 80 to 84	89	100.0	0.4	17.0	0.7	81.4
Aged 85 or older	76	100.0	0.3	18.6	0.6	80.1

| | total | | | | | non-Hispanic |
	number	percent	Asian	black	Hispanic	white
Alaska	**710**	**100.0%**	**7.1%**	**4.7%**	**5.5%**	**64.1%**
Under age 5	54	100.0	8.6	7.5	8.7	51.0
Aged 5 to 9	51	100.0	9.0	7.1	8.1	51.8
Aged 10 to 14	51	100.0	8.8	6.6	7.5	53.1
Aged 15 to 19	52	100.0	8.3	5.8	6.9	54.6
Aged 20 to 24	54	100.0	7.2	5.6	7.1	58.5
Aged 25 to 29	55	100.0	6.7	5.1	6.4	63.4
Aged 30 to 34	48	100.0	6.8	4.7	6.0	65.2
Aged 35 to 39	46	100.0	7.4	4.4	5.6	66.3
Aged 40 to 44	47	100.0	7.1	3.8	5.1	67.5
Aged 45 to 49	55	100.0	6.3	3.5	4.2	69.8
Aged 50 to 54	56	100.0	5.8	3.1	3.5	73.6
Aged 55 to 59	50	100.0	5.5	2.9	2.9	75.5
Aged 60 to 64	36	100.0	5.7	2.3	2.6	76.5
Aged 65 to 69	22	100.0	5.5	2.1	2.4	75.6
Aged 70 to 74	13	100.0	6.3	2.6	2.4	73.0
Aged 75 to 79	9	100.0	6.2	2.2	2.1	71.9
Aged 80 to 84	6	100.0	6.2	2.1	1.6	73.3
Aged 85 or older	5	100.0	4.9	2.1	1.7	77.8
Arizona	**6,392**	**100.0**	**3.6**	**5.0**	**29.6**	**57.8**
Under age 5	456	100.0	4.5	7.3	44.9	39.6
Aged 5 to 9	454	100.0	4.3	6.8	43.9	41.1
Aged 10 to 14	449	100.0	3.9	6.8	42.2	42.8
Aged 15 to 19	462	100.0	3.7	6.7	39.8	44.8
Aged 20 to 24	443	100.0	4.0	6.1	35.9	48.9
Aged 25 to 29	440	100.0	4.5	5.6	34.2	51.1
Aged 30 to 34	417	100.0	4.8	5.3	35.0	50.5
Aged 35 to 39	416	100.0	5.0	5.1	33.0	52.9
Aged 40 to 44	407	100.0	4.2	4.9	29.7	57.2
Aged 45 to 49	427	100.0	3.5	4.6	24.9	62.9
Aged 50 to 54	416	100.0	3.0	4.2	20.9	68.0
Aged 55 to 59	375	100.0	2.8	3.5	17.6	72.6
Aged 60 to 64	351	100.0	2.4	2.8	14.1	77.7
Aged 65 to 69	283	100.0	2.0	2.4	12.1	80.7
Aged 70 to 74	215	100.0	2.0	2.2	11.4	81.7
Aged 75 to 79	162	100.0	1.8	2.0	10.7	83.2
Aged 80 to 84	118	100.0	1.3	1.6	9.9	85.1
Aged 85 or older	103	100.0	1.1	1.5	8.2	87.3

	total		Asian	black	Hispanic	non-Hispanic white
	number	percent				
Arkansas	**2,916**	**100.0%**	**1.5%**	**16.1%**	**6.4%**	**74.5%**
Under age 5	198	100.0	2.1	21.4	12.5	62.7
Aged 5 to 9	197	100.0	2.0	20.2	11.1	65.1
Aged 10 to 14	198	100.0	1.7	20.6	9.3	66.9
Aged 15 to 19	204	100.0	1.7	20.6	8.2	67.8
Aged 20 to 24	200	100.0	2.1	18.9	8.4	69.0
Aged 25 to 29	192	100.0	2.3	17.6	9.2	69.4
Aged 30 to 34	184	100.0	2.2	17.2	9.1	69.9
Aged 35 to 39	184	100.0	2.0	15.5	7.9	73.1
Aged 40 to 44	183	100.0	1.7	15.1	6.3	75.4
Aged 45 to 49	206	100.0	1.3	15.0	4.3	77.8
Aged 50 to 54	202	100.0	1.2	15.2	3.3	78.7
Aged 55 to 59	184	100.0	1.1	14.4	2.4	80.7
Aged 60 to 64	167	100.0	0.9	11.4	1.8	84.6
Aged 65 to 69	133	100.0	0.7	9.2	1.3	87.5
Aged 70 to 74	101	100.0	0.6	8.9	1.2	88.3
Aged 75 to 79	78	100.0	0.5	8.5	0.9	89.1
Aged 80 to 84	56	100.0	0.4	8.8	0.8	89.1
Aged 85 or older	51	100.0	0.3	9.8	0.6	88.6
California	**37,254**	**100.0**	**14.9**	**7.2**	**37.6**	**40.1**
Under age 5	2,531	100.0	14.7	8.5	53.3	25.5
Aged 5 to 9	2,506	100.0	14.6	8.2	51.6	27.0
Aged 10 to 14	2,591	100.0	13.9	8.5	50.3	28.3
Aged 15 to 19	2,824	100.0	13.9	8.7	47.9	30.0
Aged 20 to 24	2,766	100.0	14.7	7.9	44.0	33.4
Aged 25 to 29	2,744	100.0	15.4	6.9	42.6	34.8
Aged 30 to 34	2,573	100.0	16.1	6.7	42.9	33.9
Aged 35 to 39	2,574	100.0	17.1	6.5	41.3	34.7
Aged 40 to 44	2,609	100.0	15.7	6.9	37.6	39.2
Aged 45 to 49	2,690	100.0	14.9	7.2	31.6	45.3
Aged 50 to 54	2,563	100.0	14.8	7.1	27.1	49.9
Aged 55 to 59	2,204	100.0	15.0	6.6	23.5	53.9
Aged 60 to 64	1,832	100.0	14.6	6.1	20.3	57.9
Aged 65 to 69	1,304	100.0	14.1	6.0	19.4	59.5
Aged 70 to 74	972	100.0	15.1	6.2	19.0	58.9
Aged 75 to 79	767	100.0	14.6	5.5	18.0	61.2
Aged 80 to 84	603	100.0	13.1	4.6	16.1	65.4
Aged 85 or older	601	100.0	11.2	4.5	12.6	71.2

	total		Asian	black	Hispanic	non-Hispanic white
	number	percent				
Colorado	**5,029**	**100.0%**	**3.7%**	**5.0%**	**20.7%**	**70.0%**
Under age 5	344	100.0	4.9	7.4	32.8	55.5
Aged 5 to 9	349	100.0	4.9	6.8	31.3	57.1
Aged 10 to 14	333	100.0	4.5	6.7	29.3	59.4
Aged 15 to 19	339	100.0	4.0	6.6	26.8	62.0
Aged 20 to 24	349	100.0	4.1	5.7	24.1	65.2
Aged 25 to 29	372	100.0	4.2	5.0	23.3	66.5
Aged 30 to 34	354	100.0	4.3	4.9	23.9	66.1
Aged 35 to 39	354	100.0	4.6	4.7	22.2	67.6
Aged 40 to 44	346	100.0	3.9	4.6	19.3	71.1
Aged 45 to 49	372	100.0	3.2	4.5	15.9	75.3
Aged 50 to 54	371	100.0	2.7	4.1	13.1	79.0
Aged 55 to 59	328	100.0	2.4	3.6	11.4	81.5
Aged 60 to 64	269	100.0	2.3	3.0	10.6	83.2
Aged 65 to 69	182	100.0	2.3	3.0	10.3	83.5
Aged 70 to 74	127	100.0	2.3	3.1	10.9	82.8
Aged 75 to 79	97	100.0	2.3	3.0	10.1	83.9
Aged 80 to 84	73	100.0	2.0	2.4	8.9	86.2
Aged 85 or older	70	100.0	1.6	1.9	7.1	89.0
Connecticut	**3,574**	**100.0**	**4.4**	**11.3**	**13.4**	**71.2**
Under age 5	202	100.0	7.1	16.5	23.2	55.5
Aged 5 to 9	223	100.0	6.1	14.9	19.7	60.9
Aged 10 to 14	240	100.0	4.7	14.7	18.1	63.7
Aged 15 to 19	251	100.0	4.1	15.2	17.6	64.1
Aged 20 to 24	228	100.0	4.9	14.4	18.3	63.0
Aged 25 to 29	214	100.0	6.9	13.3	19.4	60.8
Aged 30 to 34	206	100.0	7.3	13.1	19.7	60.1
Aged 35 to 39	222	100.0	6.6	12.0	16.5	65.0
Aged 40 to 44	262	100.0	4.7	11.1	13.3	70.9
Aged 45 to 49	291	100.0	3.6	10.0	10.4	75.8
Aged 50 to 54	284	100.0	3.0	9.0	8.3	79.5
Aged 55 to 59	240	100.0	2.8	8.0	7.0	82.1
Aged 60 to 64	203	100.0	2.5	7.7	6.2	83.4
Aged 65 to 69	149	100.0	2.3	7.5	5.6	84.5
Aged 70 to 74	106	100.0	2.2	7.6	5.4	84.6
Aged 75 to 79	89	100.0	1.7	6.2	4.2	87.8
Aged 80 to 84	77	100.0	1.1	4.8	3.1	90.9
Aged 85 or older	85	100.0	0.6	3.9	2.2	93.1

| | total | | | | | non-Hispanic |
	number	percent	Asian	black	Hispanic	white
Delaware	**898**	**100.0%**	**3.8%**	**22.9%**	**8.2%**	**65.3%**
Under age 5	56	100.0	5.2	31.1	16.2	49.3
Aged 5 to 9	56	100.0	4.9	30.4	14.0	52.0
Aged 10 to 14	57	100.0	3.9	30.6	11.4	55.1
Aged 15 to 19	65	100.0	3.7	29.3	10.0	57.7
Aged 20 to 24	63	100.0	3.9	25.1	11.2	60.1
Aged 25 to 29	58	100.0	5.6	23.4	12.8	58.5
Aged 30 to 34	54	100.0	6.0	23.9	12.3	58.0
Aged 35 to 39	55	100.0	5.5	23.9	10.3	60.3
Aged 40 to 44	61	100.0	4.1	24.1	7.8	64.0
Aged 45 to 49	68	100.0	3.3	22.2	5.4	68.8
Aged 50 to 54	66	100.0	2.7	20.6	4.0	72.3
Aged 55 to 59	58	100.0	2.5	18.7	3.3	75.2
Aged 60 to 64	53	100.0	2.3	16.4	2.6	78.3
Aged 65 to 69	42	100.0	2.3	14.5	2.1	80.7
Aged 70 to 74	31	100.0	2.3	14.0	2.1	81.2
Aged 75 to 79	24	100.0	1.6	12.6	1.7	83.7
Aged 80 to 84	17	100.0	1.2	10.7	1.7	86.0
Aged 85 or older	16	100.0	1.0	10.8	1.4	86.5
District of Columbia	**602**	**100.0**	**4.5**	**52.2**	**9.1**	**34.8**
Under age 5	33	100.0	4.5	59.6	13.8	23.8
Aged 5 to 9	26	100.0	3.2	67.5	12.6	18.3
Aged 10 to 14	25	100.0	2.4	75.5	10.4	12.9
Aged 15 to 19	40	100.0	4.0	63.0	9.0	25.2
Aged 20 to 24	64	100.0	6.3	38.7	9.5	46.1
Aged 25 to 29	70	100.0	6.7	31.4	10.3	51.9
Aged 30 to 34	55	100.0	7.2	35.5	11.5	46.4
Aged 35 to 39	43	100.0	6.2	43.0	11.7	39.7
Aged 40 to 44	38	100.0	4.1	51.5	10.2	34.7
Aged 45 to 49	39	100.0	3.0	60.5	8.5	28.4
Aged 50 to 54	37	100.0	2.7	64.1	7.2	26.5
Aged 55 to 59	34	100.0	2.6	62.2	5.8	29.6
Aged 60 to 64	30	100.0	2.7	58.0	5.3	34.2
Aged 65 to 69	21	100.0	2.3	57.7	4.8	35.3
Aged 70 to 74	15	100.0	2.5	64.1	4.7	29.0
Aged 75 to 79	12	100.0	2.2	67.6	3.6	26.6
Aged 80 to 84	10	100.0	1.8	67.9	3.5	27.0
Aged 85 or older	10	100.0	1.9	63.4	2.5	32.2

| | total | | | | | non-Hispanic |
	number	percent	Asian	black	Hispanic	white
Florida	**18,801**	**100.0%**	**3.0%**	**17.0%**	**22.5%**	**57.9%**
Under age 5	1,074	100.0	4.0	25.4	29.1	43.2
Aged 5 to 9	1,080	100.0	4.0	24.1	27.7	45.4
Aged 10 to 14	1,131	100.0	3.5	23.4	26.9	47.0
Aged 15 to 19	1,228	100.0	3.3	23.7	26.1	47.7
Aged 20 to 24	1,229	100.0	3.5	21.8	26.4	48.9
Aged 25 to 29	1,179	100.0	3.8	20.3	27.0	49.5
Aged 30 to 34	1,110	100.0	4.1	19.3	28.8	48.3
Aged 35 to 39	1,178	100.0	4.1	17.9	28.3	50.1
Aged 40 to 44	1,253	100.0	3.6	16.6	25.8	54.3
Aged 45 to 49	1,401	100.0	2.9	15.6	22.8	58.9
Aged 50 to 54	1,340	100.0	2.7	15.2	18.6	63.4
Aged 55 to 59	1,202	100.0	2.6	13.6	16.6	67.1
Aged 60 to 64	1,135	100.0	2.2	10.9	14.3	72.5
Aged 65 to 69	959	100.0	1.9	9.3	13.7	75.2
Aged 70 to 74	769	100.0	1.7	8.9	14.4	75.1
Aged 75 to 79	616	100.0	1.3	7.7	13.8	77.3
Aged 80 to 84	482	100.0	0.9	6.5	12.6	80.1
Aged 85 or older	434	100.0	0.7	6.0	11.2	82.2
Georgia	**9,688**	**100.0**	**3.8**	**31.5**	**8.8**	**55.9**
Under age 5	687	100.0	4.4	36.5	15.5	44.3
Aged 5 to 9	695	100.0	4.4	35.6	13.4	47.1
Aged 10 to 14	690	100.0	3.9	36.8	10.8	48.7
Aged 15 to 19	710	100.0	3.7	38.3	9.7	48.4
Aged 20 to 24	680	100.0	4.0	34.7	11.6	49.9
Aged 25 to 29	674	100.0	4.6	32.6	13.4	49.7
Aged 30 to 34	662	100.0	4.8	32.7	13.2	49.4
Aged 35 to 39	698	100.0	5.1	31.8	10.6	52.6
Aged 40 to 44	699	100.0	4.2	31.3	8.2	56.1
Aged 45 to 49	723	100.0	3.5	30.7	5.9	59.6
Aged 50 to 54	669	100.0	3.2	29.6	4.4	62.4
Aged 55 to 59	574	100.0	2.9	28.1	3.3	65.3
Aged 60 to 64	496	100.0	2.6	24.5	2.5	70.0
Aged 65 to 69	356	100.0	2.5	22.2	2.2	72.7
Aged 70 to 74	250	100.0	2.3	21.5	2.1	73.7
Aged 75 to 79	183	100.0	1.9	19.9	1.8	76.1
Aged 80 to 84	129	100.0	1.4	18.7	1.7	77.9
Aged 85 or older	114	100.0	1.0	19.3	1.4	78.1

	total		Asian	black	Hispanic	non-Hispanic white
	number	percent				
Hawaii	**1,360**	**100.0%**	**57.4%**	**2.9%**	**8.9%**	**22.7%**
Under age 5	87	100.0	58.4	5.4	16.9	14.7
Aged 5 to 9	83	100.0	61.4	4.9	15.3	13.0
Aged 10 to 14	82	100.0	63.0	4.4	13.6	12.4
Aged 15 to 19	86	100.0	61.9	3.8	12.6	13.7
Aged 20 to 24	96	100.0	49.0	4.3	11.5	25.7
Aged 25 to 29	97	100.0	49.3	4.0	10.7	26.5
Aged 30 to 34	88	100.0	52.2	3.6	10.2	24.3
Aged 35 to 39	87	100.0	55.8	3.1	9.0	22.5
Aged 40 to 44	90	100.0	57.4	2.6	7.7	22.9
Aged 45 to 49	96	100.0	57.1	2.0	6.8	24.2
Aged 50 to 54	98	100.0	56.6	1.7	5.8	26.7
Aged 55 to 59	93	100.0	55.3	1.4	4.7	30.2
Aged 60 to 64	82	100.0	54.7	1.1	3.9	32.3
Aged 65 to 69	59	100.0	57.4	0.9	3.9	29.7
Aged 70 to 74	41	100.0	62.5	0.7	3.7	25.5
Aged 75 to 79	35	100.0	67.6	0.6	3.3	21.8
Aged 80 to 84	30	100.0	71.8	0.5	2.5	20.1
Aged 85 or older	30	100.0	73.4	0.4	2.1	20.6
Idaho	**1,568**	**100.0**	**1.9**	**1.0**	**11.2**	**84.0**
Under age 5	122	100.0	2.4	2.0	18.8	75.1
Aged 5 to 9	121	100.0	2.4	1.8	17.1	76.7
Aged 10 to 14	117	100.0	2.3	1.7	16.1	77.9
Aged 15 to 19	115	100.0	2.2	1.6	15.2	78.7
Aged 20 to 24	108	100.0	2.3	1.4	14.2	79.9
Aged 25 to 29	107	100.0	2.4	1.1	14.1	80.4
Aged 30 to 34	102	100.0	2.3	1.0	13.2	81.6
Aged 35 to 39	97	100.0	2.4	0.9	12.6	82.1
Aged 40 to 44	95	100.0	2.0	0.8	10.8	84.4
Aged 45 to 49	104	100.0	1.7	0.6	8.5	87.2
Aged 50 to 54	105	100.0	1.4	0.5	6.4	89.6
Aged 55 to 59	97	100.0	1.3	0.4	5.0	91.4
Aged 60 to 64	83	100.0	1.1	0.3	4.0	92.9
Aged 65 to 69	63	100.0	1.0	0.2	3.5	93.7
Aged 70 to 74	46	100.0	0.8	0.2	3.1	94.4
Aged 75 to 79	34	100.0	0.9	0.1	2.8	94.9
Aged 80 to 84	26	100.0	0.9	0.2	2.1	95.8
Aged 85 or older	25	100.0	0.9	0.2	1.7	96.5

	total					non-Hispanic
	number	percent	Asian	black	Hispanic	white
Illinois	**12,831**	**100.0%**	**5.2%**	**15.4%**	**15.8%**	**63.7%**
Under age 5	836	100.0	6.3	18.7	25.5	50.4
Aged 5 to 9	859	100.0	5.9	18.2	24.1	52.4
Aged 10 to 14	879	100.0	5.0	19.2	21.9	54.4
Aged 15 to 19	922	100.0	4.6	20.3	19.7	55.7
Aged 20 to 24	879	100.0	5.8	17.1	19.2	58.1
Aged 25 to 29	910	100.0	6.7	14.6	19.6	59.1
Aged 30 to 34	866	100.0	7.0	14.5	20.7	57.8
Aged 35 to 39	856	100.0	6.9	14.9	19.5	58.7
Aged 40 to 44	870	100.0	5.6	14.4	16.0	63.9
Aged 45 to 49	940	100.0	4.4	14.3	11.9	69.1
Aged 50 to 54	931	100.0	4.1	14.3	9.8	71.6
Aged 55 to 59	808	100.0	4.4	13.4	8.3	73.6
Aged 60 to 64	665	100.0	4.5	12.6	7.1	75.5
Aged 65 to 69	485	100.0	4.4	12.5	6.3	76.6
Aged 70 to 74	364	100.0	3.9	12.7	5.8	77.4
Aged 75 to 79	289	100.0	3.0	11.7	5.2	79.9
Aged 80 to 84	235	100.0	2.3	9.8	4.0	83.6
Aged 85 or older	235	100.0	1.8	8.5	2.8	86.8
Indiana	**6,484**	**100.0**	**2.0**	**10.1**	**6.0**	**81.5**
Under age 5	434	100.0	2.7	15.0	11.6	70.6
Aged 5 to 9	445	100.0	2.5	13.8	10.2	73.3
Aged 10 to 14	452	100.0	2.1	13.4	8.3	75.8
Aged 15 to 19	476	100.0	2.2	12.8	7.2	77.4
Aged 20 to 24	452	100.0	3.1	11.0	7.3	78.2
Aged 25 to 29	420	100.0	2.9	10.8	8.4	77.6
Aged 30 to 34	408	100.0	2.7	10.7	8.7	77.6
Aged 35 to 39	417	100.0	2.6	10.0	7.2	79.7
Aged 40 to 44	424	100.0	2.1	9.2	5.5	82.7
Aged 45 to 49	474	100.0	1.5	8.6	3.9	85.3
Aged 50 to 54	473	100.0	1.2	8.5	3.2	86.5
Aged 55 to 59	419	100.0	1.1	7.7	2.5	88.0
Aged 60 to 64	351	100.0	1.1	6.7	2.1	89.6
Aged 65 to 69	259	100.0	0.9	6.5	1.7	90.3
Aged 70 to 74	193	100.0	0.8	6.2	1.6	91.0
Aged 75 to 79	152	100.0	0.7	6.0	1.6	91.3
Aged 80 to 84	122	100.0	0.5	5.2	1.4	92.5
Aged 85 or older	115	100.0	0.3	4.8	1.0	93.5

	total					non-Hispanic
	number	percent	Asian	black	Hispanic	white
Iowa	**3,046**	**100.0%**	**2.1%**	**3.7%**	**5.0%**	**88.7%**
Under age 5	202	100.0	2.9	7.6	10.3	78.8
Aged 5 to 9	201	100.0	2.9	6.8	9.1	80.8
Aged 10 to 14	201	100.0	2.5	6.1	7.8	83.0
Aged 15 to 19	217	100.0	2.6	5.6	6.8	84.4
Aged 20 to 24	213	100.0	3.7	4.8	6.6	84.3
Aged 25 to 29	198	100.0	3.3	4.2	6.7	85.2
Aged 30 to 34	185	100.0	3.0	4.0	6.6	85.7
Aged 35 to 39	177	100.0	3.0	3.7	6.1	86.6
Aged 40 to 44	187	100.0	2.3	3.0	4.9	89.2
Aged 45 to 49	216	100.0	1.6	2.6	3.3	92.0
Aged 50 to 54	223	100.0	1.2	2.2	2.4	93.7
Aged 55 to 59	204	100.0	1.1	1.8	1.8	94.8
Aged 60 to 64	168	100.0	1.0	1.5	1.5	95.6
Aged 65 to 69	124	100.0	0.9	1.3	1.2	96.2
Aged 70 to 74	100	100.0	0.8	1.2	1.0	96.7
Aged 75 to 79	83	100.0	0.6	1.0	0.8	97.3
Aged 80 to 84	70	100.0	0.4	0.9	0.7	97.8
Aged 85 or older	75	100.0	0.2	0.7	0.6	98.4
Kansas	**2,853**	**100.0**	**2.9**	**7.1**	**10.5**	**78.2**
Under age 5	205	100.0	4.0	11.1	19.1	65.3
Aged 5 to 9	202	100.0	3.9	9.9	17.5	67.9
Aged 10 to 14	199	100.0	3.3	9.5	15.4	70.5
Aged 15 to 19	204	100.0	3.1	9.4	13.6	72.4
Aged 20 to 24	204	100.0	3.9	8.4	12.7	73.5
Aged 25 to 29	198	100.0	3.9	7.6	13.2	73.9
Aged 30 to 34	180	100.0	3.9	7.2	13.7	73.8
Aged 35 to 39	172	100.0	4.2	6.6	12.7	74.9
Aged 40 to 44	174	100.0	3.3	6.3	10.5	78.2
Aged 45 to 49	202	100.0	2.3	6.2	7.3	82.7
Aged 50 to 54	204	100.0	2.0	5.9	5.6	85.1
Aged 55 to 59	183	100.0	1.9	4.9	4.4	87.4
Aged 60 to 64	149	100.0	1.8	4.5	3.7	88.7
Aged 65 to 69	108	100.0	1.7	4.2	3.3	89.7
Aged 70 to 74	83	100.0	1.4	4.2	3.0	90.3
Aged 75 to 79	69	100.0	1.0	3.6	2.7	91.8
Aged 80 to 84	57	100.0	0.7	3.1	2.4	93.1
Aged 85 or older	59	100.0	0.5	2.6	1.7	94.6

	total					non-Hispanic
	number	percent	Asian	black	Hispanic	white
Kentucky	**4,339**	**100.0%**	**1.4%**	**8.7%**	**3.1%**	**86.3%**
Under age 5	282	100.0	2.2	13.0	6.6	78.0
Aged 5 to 9	283	100.0	2.2	11.8	5.2	80.4
Aged 10 to 14	284	100.0	1.7	11.3	3.8	82.7
Aged 15 to 19	297	100.0	1.4	11.5	3.5	83.1
Aged 20 to 24	290	100.0	1.7	10.5	4.5	82.8
Aged 25 to 29	285	100.0	2.0	9.2	5.0	83.3
Aged 30 to 34	281	100.0	2.1	9.1	4.5	83.9
Aged 35 to 39	285	100.0	2.0	8.2	3.8	85.5
Aged 40 to 44	291	100.0	1.6	7.8	2.7	87.4
Aged 45 to 49	324	100.0	1.1	7.6	2.0	88.6
Aged 50 to 54	319	100.0	0.9	7.6	1.3	89.4
Aged 55 to 59	288	100.0	0.8	6.9	1.0	90.7
Aged 60 to 64	251	100.0	0.8	5.7	0.8	92.1
Aged 65 to 69	186	100.0	0.7	5.0	0.8	92.9
Aged 70 to 74	140	100.0	0.6	4.9	0.7	93.2
Aged 75 to 79	105	100.0	0.5	4.9	0.7	93.4
Aged 80 to 84	78	100.0	0.4	4.8	0.6	93.7
Aged 85 or older	69	100.0	0.3	5.1	0.5	93.7
Louisiana	**4,533**	**100.0**	**1.9**	**32.8**	**4.2**	**60.3**
Under age 5	314	100.0	2.1	40.4	6.2	50.8
Aged 5 to 9	306	100.0	2.1	39.8	4.8	52.6
Aged 10 to 14	307	100.0	1.8	39.2	4.1	53.9
Aged 15 to 19	327	100.0	1.8	40.3	4.2	52.8
Aged 20 to 24	338	100.0	2.3	36.6	5.7	54.7
Aged 25 to 29	333	100.0	2.5	33.8	6.3	56.8
Aged 30 to 34	296	100.0	2.4	33.4	6.1	57.4
Aged 35 to 39	276	100.0	2.5	30.9	5.4	60.4
Aged 40 to 44	288	100.0	2.0	31.0	4.3	61.7
Aged 45 to 49	325	100.0	1.6	30.6	3.5	63.3
Aged 50 to 54	329	100.0	1.6	30.3	2.9	64.4
Aged 55 to 59	293	100.0	1.6	29.3	2.6	65.8
Aged 60 to 64	243	100.0	1.4	26.5	2.3	69.0
Aged 65 to 69	178	100.0	1.2	24.4	2.2	71.5
Aged 70 to 74	134	100.0	1.1	23.7	2.3	72.3
Aged 75 to 79	103	100.0	0.9	21.9	2.1	74.4
Aged 80 to 84	77	100.0	0.7	20.0	2.0	76.7
Aged 85 or older	66	100.0	0.6	20.9	1.8	76.2

	total					non-Hispanic
	number	percent	Asian	black	Hispanic	white
Maine	**1,328**	**100.0%**	**1.4%**	**1.6%**	**1.3%**	**94.4%**
Under age 5	70	100.0	2.4	5.0	2.9	88.1
Aged 5 to 9	74	100.0	2.3	3.8	2.4	89.9
Aged 10 to 14	79	100.0	2.1	3.3	2.0	91.1
Aged 15 to 19	88	100.0	2.3	2.9	2.1	91.1
Aged 20 to 24	80	100.0	1.9	2.5	2.0	92.0
Aged 25 to 29	73	100.0	1.9	1.9	1.8	92.8
Aged 30 to 34	72	100.0	1.8	1.7	1.7	93.4
Aged 35 to 39	80	100.0	1.8	1.6	1.2	94.1
Aged 40 to 44	91	100.0	1.4	1.2	1.1	94.9
Aged 45 to 49	108	100.0	1.0	0.9	0.9	95.9
Aged 50 to 54	111	100.0	0.9	0.7	0.7	96.4
Aged 55 to 59	102	100.0	0.8	0.6	0.6	96.9
Aged 60 to 64	90	100.0	0.6	0.4	0.5	97.4
Aged 65 to 69	65	100.0	0.5	0.4	0.4	97.7
Aged 70 to 74	48	100.0	0.6	0.4	0.4	97.8
Aged 75 to 79	39	100.0	0.4	0.3	0.4	98.3
Aged 80 to 84	30	100.0	0.3	0.2	0.3	98.6
Aged 85 or older	29	100.0	0.2	0.3	0.3	98.8
Maryland	**5,774**	**100.0**	**6.4**	**30.9**	**8.2**	**54.7**
Under age 5	364	100.0	8.0	36.6	13.8	42.8
Aged 5 to 9	367	100.0	7.6	35.7	11.2	46.3
Aged 10 to 14	379	100.0	6.6	36.1	9.5	48.4
Aged 15 to 19	406	100.0	6.1	36.5	8.9	48.9
Aged 20 to 24	394	100.0	6.4	33.5	11.1	49.3
Aged 25 to 29	394	100.0	7.3	31.3	12.8	48.8
Aged 30 to 34	368	100.0	8.4	31.8	13.2	46.8
Aged 35 to 39	377	100.0	8.5	32.1	10.8	48.7
Aged 40 to 44	418	100.0	6.9	31.9	8.2	53.0
Aged 45 to 49	462	100.0	5.8	30.4	6.0	57.5
Aged 50 to 54	441	100.0	5.5	28.9	4.7	60.7
Aged 55 to 59	378	100.0	5.2	27.3	3.8	63.5
Aged 60 to 64	318	100.0	5.1	25.8	3.0	65.7
Aged 65 to 69	227	100.0	5.0	24.3	2.7	67.7
Aged 70 to 74	160	100.0	5.3	24.0	2.6	67.9
Aged 75 to 79	125	100.0	4.3	21.9	2.4	71.2
Aged 80 to 84	99	100.0	3.2	18.2	2.0	76.4
Aged 85 or older	98	100.0	2.3	16.3	1.5	79.7

	total		Asian	black	Hispanic	non-Hispanic white
	number	percent				
Massachusetts	**6,548**	**100.0%**	**6.0%**	**7.8%**	**9.6%**	**76.1%**
Under age 5	367	100.0	8.5	11.8	17.2	62.6
Aged 5 to 9	386	100.0	7.8	10.7	14.7	67.2
Aged 10 to 14	406	100.0	6.2	10.3	13.7	69.9
Aged 15 to 19	463	100.0	6.5	10.6	13.6	69.3
Aged 20 to 24	476	100.0	7.9	9.5	12.8	69.4
Aged 25 to 29	442	100.0	8.8	8.5	12.6	69.0
Aged 30 to 34	404	100.0	8.9	8.7	13.0	68.2
Aged 35 to 39	418	100.0	8.5	8.1	11.0	71.5
Aged 40 to 44	469	100.0	6.1	7.4	9.1	76.5
Aged 45 to 49	515	100.0	4.9	6.7	7.3	80.3
Aged 50 to 54	497	100.0	4.2	6.3	5.9	82.9
Aged 55 to 59	433	100.0	3.9	5.6	5.0	85.0
Aged 60 to 64	371	100.0	3.4	5.0	4.3	86.8
Aged 65 to 69	264	100.0	3.3	4.9	3.9	87.5
Aged 70 to 74	192	100.0	3.6	4.8	3.7	87.5
Aged 75 to 79	163	100.0	2.9	4.1	2.9	89.5
Aged 80 to 84	138	100.0	2.1	3.3	2.1	92.0
Aged 85 or older	145	100.0	1.5	2.9	1.5	93.7
Michigan	**9,884**	**100.0**	**2.9**	**15.2**	**4.4**	**76.6**
Under age 5	596	100.0	4.2	20.8	8.8	65.8
Aged 5 to 9	638	100.0	4.1	18.9	7.8	68.6
Aged 10 to 14	675	100.0	3.4	18.9	6.6	70.2
Aged 15 to 19	740	100.0	3.1	20.1	5.7	70.3
Aged 20 to 24	669	100.0	3.8	17.5	5.4	72.4
Aged 25 to 29	590	100.0	4.0	15.8	5.8	73.5
Aged 30 to 34	575	100.0	4.3	16.0	5.9	72.9
Aged 35 to 39	612	100.0	4.1	16.5	5.1	73.3
Aged 40 to 44	665	100.0	3.2	14.6	3.9	77.3
Aged 45 to 49	745	100.0	2.4	12.9	3.0	80.6
Aged 50 to 54	765	100.0	1.9	13.0	2.4	81.8
Aged 55 to 59	683	100.0	1.7	12.5	2.1	82.8
Aged 60 to 64	569	100.0	1.8	12.0	1.9	83.5
Aged 65 to 69	419	100.0	1.7	10.7	1.6	85.2
Aged 70 to 74	306	100.0	1.6	10.1	1.5	86.1
Aged 75 to 79	244	100.0	1.2	10.2	1.5	86.6
Aged 80 to 84	201	100.0	0.9	9.2	1.3	88.2
Aged 85 or older	192	100.0	0.6	8.8	1.0	89.1

	total		Asian	black	Hispanic	non-Hispanic white
	number	percent				
Minnesota	**5,304**	**100.0%**	**4.7%**	**6.2%**	**4.7%**	**83.1%**
Under age 5	356	100.0	7.5	12.0	9.5	69.3
Aged 5 to 9	356	100.0	7.0	10.5	8.4	72.5
Aged 10 to 14	352	100.0	6.2	9.2	6.9	75.9
Aged 15 to 19	368	100.0	6.3	8.7	6.1	77.1
Aged 20 to 24	356	100.0	6.7	7.9	6.1	77.5
Aged 25 to 29	373	100.0	6.5	7.3	6.5	78.2
Aged 30 to 34	343	100.0	6.1	6.9	6.9	78.7
Aged 35 to 39	328	100.0	6.1	6.8	6.0	79.8
Aged 40 to 44	353	100.0	4.4	5.7	4.3	84.2
Aged 45 to 49	406	100.0	3.0	4.3	2.9	88.4
Aged 50 to 54	402	100.0	2.4	3.8	2.1	90.4
Aged 55 to 59	350	100.0	2.2	3.1	1.7	91.9
Aged 60 to 64	280	100.0	2.1	2.5	1.3	92.9
Aged 65 to 69	203	100.0	2.0	2.2	1.1	93.8
Aged 70 to 74	152	100.0	1.8	1.9	1.0	94.5
Aged 75 to 79	122	100.0	1.5	1.6	0.9	95.4
Aged 80 to 84	100	100.0	1.2	1.2	0.6	96.6
Aged 85 or older	107	100.0	0.9	0.9	0.5	97.4
Mississippi	**2,967**	**100.0**	**1.1**	**37.6**	**2.7**	**58.0**
Under age 5	211	100.0	1.2	45.8	4.7	47.8
Aged 5 to 9	206	100.0	1.3	44.3	3.6	50.2
Aged 10 to 14	208	100.0	1.1	44.9	2.8	50.7
Aged 15 to 19	225	100.0	1.1	45.8	2.8	49.8
Aged 20 to 24	211	100.0	1.3	41.9	4.2	52.1
Aged 25 to 29	199	100.0	1.5	40.5	4.8	52.8
Aged 30 to 34	188	100.0	1.4	40.0	4.4	53.6
Aged 35 to 39	187	100.0	1.5	37.4	3.5	57.1
Aged 40 to 44	188	100.0	1.3	36.3	2.7	59.2
Aged 45 to 49	208	100.0	1.0	35.3	2.0	61.1
Aged 50 to 54	209	100.0	0.9	35.5	1.5	61.4
Aged 55 to 59	187	100.0	0.9	33.7	1.1	63.8
Aged 60 to 64	161	100.0	0.7	28.6	0.9	69.3
Aged 65 to 69	121	100.0	0.6	25.5	0.9	72.6
Aged 70 to 74	94	100.0	0.5	24.8	0.7	73.5
Aged 75 to 79	70	100.0	0.5	22.9	0.7	75.6
Aged 80 to 84	52	100.0	0.4	22.5	0.6	76.1
Aged 85 or older	44	100.0	0.3	25.1	0.5	73.8

	total		Asian	black	Hispanic	non-Hispanic
	number	percent				white
Missouri	**5,989**	**100.0%**	**2.1%**	**12.5%**	**3.5%**	**81.0%**
Under age 5	390	100.0	2.8	17.2	6.9	72.4
Aged 5 to 9	390	100.0	2.7	16.2	6.0	74.4
Aged 10 to 14	397	100.0	2.3	16.0	4.9	75.9
Aged 15 to 19	424	100.0	2.2	16.8	4.5	75.4
Aged 20 to 24	413	100.0	2.9	14.5	4.8	76.9
Aged 25 to 29	403	100.0	2.9	13.0	4.8	78.4
Aged 30 to 34	372	100.0	3.0	12.9	4.8	78.5
Aged 35 to 39	368	100.0	2.9	12.8	4.2	79.1
Aged 40 to 44	381	100.0	2.3	12.1	3.3	81.3
Aged 45 to 49	445	100.0	1.6	11.2	2.4	83.7
Aged 50 to 54	444	100.0	1.3	11.0	1.9	84.6
Aged 55 to 59	390	100.0	1.3	10.0	1.6	86.1
Aged 60 to 64	333	100.0	1.2	8.8	1.3	87.7
Aged 65 to 69	257	100.0	1.1	8.1	1.1	88.8
Aged 70 to 74	193	100.0	1.0	7.8	1.1	89.3
Aged 75 to 79	155	100.0	0.8	7.4	1.0	90.2
Aged 80 to 84	119	100.0	0.6	6.7	0.9	91.3
Aged 85 or older	114	100.0	0.4	6.1	0.8	92.2
Montana	**989**	**100.0**	**1.1**	**0.8**	**2.9**	**87.8**
Under age 5	62	100.0	1.6	2.0	5.5	78.2
Aged 5 to 9	61	100.0	1.5	1.8	5.1	79.7
Aged 10 to 14	61	100.0	1.5	1.5	4.7	81.8
Aged 15 to 19	67	100.0	1.6	1.4	4.4	82.4
Aged 20 to 24	67	100.0	1.7	1.3	4.1	83.7
Aged 25 to 29	64	100.0	1.3	0.9	3.5	85.9
Aged 30 to 34	59	100.0	1.3	0.8	3.2	86.8
Aged 35 to 39	56	100.0	1.2	0.6	3.0	87.5
Aged 40 to 44	57	100.0	1.1	0.5	2.6	88.7
Aged 45 to 49	71	100.0	0.8	0.4	2.2	89.9
Aged 50 to 54	79	100.0	0.7	0.4	1.7	91.2
Aged 55 to 59	76	100.0	0.6	0.3	1.5	92.8
Aged 60 to 64	63	100.0	0.6	0.2	1.3	93.6
Aged 65 to 69	47	100.0	0.4	0.2	1.1	94.3
Aged 70 to 74	34	100.0	0.4	0.2	1.1	94.2
Aged 75 to 79	26	100.0	0.4	0.2	1.0	95.0
Aged 80 to 84	20	100.0	0.3	0.1	0.8	96.5
Aged 85 or older	20	100.0	0.3	0.1	0.7	97.3

	total		Asian	black	Hispanic	non-Hispanic white
	number	percent				
Nebraska	**1,826**	**100.0%**	**2.2%**	**5.4%**	**9.2%**	**82.1%**
Under age 5	132	100.0	3.1	9.2	17.2	69.2
Aged 5 to 9	129	100.0	3.0	8.2	15.6	71.8
Aged 10 to 14	123	100.0	2.6	7.7	13.9	74.4
Aged 15 to 19	129	100.0	2.5	7.3	12.1	76.7
Aged 20 to 24	129	100.0	3.2	6.4	11.3	77.9
Aged 25 to 29	129	100.0	3.2	6.0	11.6	78.1
Aged 30 to 34	116	100.0	3.0	5.7	12.0	78.1
Aged 35 to 39	110	100.0	3.1	5.4	11.2	79.3
Aged 40 to 44	110	100.0	2.5	4.9	9.3	82.1
Aged 45 to 49	128	100.0	1.6	4.5	6.1	86.7
Aged 50 to 54	130	100.0	1.3	4.0	4.7	89.0
Aged 55 to 59	118	100.0	1.2	3.4	3.6	90.8
Aged 60 to 64	95	100.0	1.2	3.0	3.0	92.0
Aged 65 to 69	69	100.0	1.1	2.7	2.5	93.0
Aged 70 to 74	54	100.0	0.9	2.6	2.1	93.7
Aged 75 to 79	46	100.0	0.6	2.3	1.8	94.8
Aged 80 to 84	38	100.0	0.5	1.8	1.4	96.0
Aged 85 or older	39	100.0	0.3	1.3	1.0	97.0
Nevada	**2,701**	**100.0**	**9.0**	**9.4**	**26.5**	**54.1**
Under age 5	187	100.0	9.2	12.6	41.5	37.8
Aged 5 to 9	183	100.0	9.3	12.0	40.3	38.9
Aged 10 to 14	183	100.0	9.3	11.8	38.4	40.4
Aged 15 to 19	183	100.0	9.0	12.5	35.7	42.3
Aged 20 to 24	178	100.0	9.4	10.9	33.0	45.7
Aged 25 to 29	197	100.0	9.4	9.7	31.3	48.4
Aged 30 to 34	191	100.0	9.7	9.4	31.8	48.0
Aged 35 to 39	192	100.0	10.2	9.2	30.4	49.2
Aged 40 to 44	191	100.0	9.5	9.0	26.6	53.6
Aged 45 to 49	194	100.0	8.9	8.8	21.3	59.4
Aged 50 to 54	183	100.0	8.8	8.1	17.0	64.5
Aged 55 to 59	165	100.0	8.8	7.3	13.8	68.5
Aged 60 to 64	151	100.0	8.4	6.5	10.7	72.9
Aged 65 to 69	116	100.0	7.9	6.4	9.7	74.5
Aged 70 to 74	82	100.0	7.9	6.7	9.2	74.9
Aged 75 to 79	58	100.0	7.3	6.0	8.6	77.0
Aged 80 to 84	39	100.0	5.8	5.1	7.6	80.4
Aged 85 or older	30	100.0	4.1	4.8	6.5	83.6

	total					non-Hispanic
	number	percent	Asian	black	Hispanic	white
New Hampshire	**1,316**	**100.0%**	**2.6%**	**1.7%**	**2.8%**	**92.3%**
Under age 5	70	100.0	4.9	3.9	6.0	84.8
Aged 5 to 9	78	100.0	4.2	3.3	5.0	87.0
Aged 10 to 14	85	100.0	3.2	2.8	4.1	89.2
Aged 15 to 19	94	100.0	2.7	2.4	4.0	90.2
Aged 20 to 24	85	100.0	3.1	2.4	3.8	90.0
Aged 25 to 29	73	100.0	3.9	2.0	4.1	89.4
Aged 30 to 34	71	100.0	4.5	2.0	3.9	88.8
Aged 35 to 39	82	100.0	4.1	1.7	3.2	90.3
Aged 40 to 44	97	100.0	2.7	1.4	2.6	92.6
Aged 45 to 49	114	100.0	1.9	1.2	2.0	94.2
Aged 50 to 54	112	100.0	1.5	0.9	1.5	95.4
Aged 55 to 59	96	100.0	1.5	0.7	1.2	96.0
Aged 60 to 64	82	100.0	1.3	0.6	1.0	96.6
Aged 65 to 69	57	100.0	1.2	0.6	0.9	96.9
Aged 70 to 74	40	100.0	0.9	0.5	0.9	97.3
Aged 75 to 79	32	100.0	0.9	0.4	0.8	97.5
Aged 80 to 84	25	100.0	0.6	0.4	0.6	98.0
Aged 85 or older	25	100.0	0.4	0.2	0.5	98.5
New Jersey	**8,792**	**100.0**	**9.0**	**14.8**	**17.7**	**59.3**
Under age 5	541	100.0	11.5	18.0	25.6	47.1
Aged 5 to 9	565	100.0	10.7	17.3	22.5	51.4
Aged 10 to 14	587	100.0	9.3	17.6	20.5	54.1
Aged 15 to 19	598	100.0	8.1	18.8	21.1	53.3
Aged 20 to 24	541	100.0	8.5	17.9	24.1	50.7
Aged 25 to 29	553	100.0	11.6	15.8	24.6	49.0
Aged 30 to 34	557	100.0	13.2	15.5	24.1	48.1
Aged 35 to 39	588	100.0	12.6	15.2	21.3	51.7
Aged 40 to 44	650	100.0	9.9	14.8	18.1	57.8
Aged 45 to 49	705	100.0	8.4	14.1	15.2	62.8
Aged 50 to 54	675	100.0	7.8	13.2	12.8	66.6
Aged 55 to 59	566	100.0	7.4	12.2	11.3	69.4
Aged 60 to 64	481	100.0	7.1	11.6	10.0	71.4
Aged 65 to 69	351	100.0	6.8	11.6	9.5	72.3
Aged 70 to 74	260	100.0	6.4	11.8	9.4	72.6
Aged 75 to 79	216	100.0	4.6	10.2	7.9	77.5
Aged 80 to 84	179	100.0	3.1	8.1	6.1	82.7
Aged 85 or older	180	100.0	2.2	6.8	4.5	86.4

	total					non-Hispanic
	number	percent	Asian	black	Hispanic	white
New Mexico	**2,059**	**100.0%**	**2.0%**	**2.8%**	**46.3%**	**40.5%**
Under age 5	145	100.0	2.4	4.3	59.6	24.8
Aged 5 to 9	143	100.0	2.3	3.8	58.9	25.6
Aged 10 to 14	142	100.0	2.2	3.7	57.8	26.9
Aged 15 to 19	150	100.0	2.0	3.6	55.0	28.6
Aged 20 to 24	142	100.0	2.2	3.5	51.4	32.2
Aged 25 to 29	140	100.0	2.4	3.1	50.5	34.3
Aged 30 to 34	128	100.0	2.6	2.8	50.1	35.0
Aged 35 to 39	123	100.0	2.5	2.7	49.4	36.3
Aged 40 to 44	125	100.0	2.3	2.5	47.1	39.3
Aged 45 to 49	145	100.0	1.9	2.4	43.3	43.9
Aged 50 to 54	147	100.0	1.7	2.2	39.0	49.5
Aged 55 to 59	137	100.0	1.5	2.0	34.3	55.3
Aged 60 to 64	120	100.0	1.4	1.6	32.3	58.6
Aged 65 to 69	88	100.0	1.2	1.5	31.1	60.2
Aged 70 to 74	66	100.0	1.1	1.5	32.8	58.6
Aged 75 to 79	50	100.0	1.0	1.5	31.9	60.1
Aged 80 to 84	36	100.0	1.0	1.4	30.9	62.0
Aged 85 or older	32	100.0	0.7	1.3	27.1	66.4
New York	**19,378**	**100.0**	**8.2**	**17.2**	**17.6**	**58.3**
Under age 5	1,156	100.0	8.7	20.7	24.6	48.8
Aged 5 to 9	1,164	100.0	8.4	20.2	22.5	51.1
Aged 10 to 14	1,211	100.0	7.8	20.5	21.2	52.4
Aged 15 to 19	1,366	100.0	7.7	21.0	21.3	51.8
Aged 20 to 24	1,411	100.0	9.3	19.1	21.3	52.0
Aged 25 to 29	1,380	100.0	10.4	17.3	21.5	52.3
Aged 30 to 34	1,279	100.0	10.7	17.3	22.0	51.4
Aged 35 to 39	1,254	100.0	10.2	17.0	20.6	53.4
Aged 40 to 44	1,356	100.0	8.7	17.2	18.2	56.9
Aged 45 to 49	1,459	100.0	8.0	17.0	15.5	60.4
Aged 50 to 54	1,420	100.0	7.7	16.1	13.4	63.6
Aged 55 to 59	1,237	100.0	7.3	14.9	12.2	66.4
Aged 60 to 64	1,066	100.0	6.8	14.1	11.3	68.5
Aged 65 to 69	773	100.0	6.2	14.6	11.0	68.9
Aged 70 to 74	587	100.0	6.2	14.3	11.0	69.3
Aged 75 to 79	475	100.0	5.2	12.3	9.6	73.5
Aged 80 to 84	392	100.0	3.9	10.6	7.7	78.2
Aged 85 or older	391	100.0	3.1	9.8	6.2	81.3

	total		Asian	black	Hispanic	non-Hispanic white
	number	percent				
North Carolina	**9,535**	**100.0%**	**2.6%**	**22.6%**	**8.4%**	**65.3%**
Under age 5	632	100.0	3.7	26.8	16.9	51.9
Aged 5 to 9	636	100.0	3.6	25.9	14.4	55.3
Aged 10 to 14	631	100.0	3.1	27.1	11.4	57.1
Aged 15 to 19	660	100.0	2.8	28.6	9.7	57.6
Aged 20 to 24	662	100.0	3.1	25.1	11.2	59.6
Aged 25 to 29	627	100.0	3.7	22.4	13.3	59.6
Aged 30 to 34	620	100.0	3.7	22.4	13.4	59.4
Aged 35 to 39	660	100.0	3.5	21.9	10.4	62.9
Aged 40 to 44	667	100.0	2.9	22.1	7.6	66.2
Aged 45 to 49	699	100.0	2.2	22.0	5.3	69.2
Aged 50 to 54	670	100.0	1.9	21.9	3.8	71.1
Aged 55 to 59	601	100.0	1.7	21.0	2.6	73.4
Aged 60 to 64	538	100.0	1.4	18.3	1.9	77.1
Aged 65 to 69	403	100.0	1.3	16.5	1.7	79.4
Aged 70 to 74	295	100.0	1.2	16.2	1.5	80.0
Aged 75 to 79	224	100.0	1.0	15.4	1.3	81.4
Aged 80 to 84	165	100.0	0.7	14.7	1.1	82.8
Aged 85 or older	147	100.0	0.5	15.2	0.9	82.8
North Dakota	**673**	**100.0**	**1.4**	**1.6**	**2.0**	**88.9**
Under age 5	45	100.0	1.8	4.2	4.5	79.0
Aged 5 to 9	40	100.0	1.7	3.2	3.8	80.9
Aged 10 to 14	40	100.0	1.4	2.7	3.1	83.4
Aged 15 to 19	47	100.0	1.6	2.3	2.9	84.8
Aged 20 to 24	59	100.0	2.9	2.8	2.8	85.1
Aged 25 to 29	50	100.0	2.2	2.3	2.7	86.4
Aged 30 to 34	41	100.0	1.9	2.0	2.5	86.8
Aged 35 to 39	37	100.0	1.9	1.5	2.0	88.1
Aged 40 to 44	38	100.0	1.4	1.1	1.6	89.6
Aged 45 to 49	46	100.0	0.9	0.7	1.2	91.7
Aged 50 to 54	50	100.0	0.6	0.6	1.0	93.4
Aged 55 to 59	46	100.0	0.5	0.5	0.7	94.7
Aged 60 to 64	36	100.0	0.7	0.4	0.6	95.0
Aged 65 to 69	26	100.0	0.6	0.3	0.5	95.5
Aged 70 to 74	21	100.0	0.4	0.2	0.4	96.3
Aged 75 to 79	18	100.0	0.3	0.1	0.4	97.0
Aged 80 to 84	16	100.0	0.3	0.1	0.3	97.9
Aged 85 or older	17	100.0	0.1	0.1	0.3	98.7

	total					non-Hispanic
	number	percent	Asian	black	Hispanic	white
Ohio	**11,537**	**100.0%**	**2.1%**	**13.4%**	**3.1%**	**81.1%**
Under age 5	721	100.0	3.0	19.7	6.2	71.3
Aged 5 to 9	748	100.0	2.8	17.7	5.2	74.2
Aged 10 to 14	775	100.0	2.2	17.1	4.3	76.1
Aged 15 to 19	824	100.0	2.1	17.4	3.9	76.2
Aged 20 to 24	763	100.0	2.7	15.4	4.1	77.5
Aged 25 to 29	719	100.0	3.1	14.1	4.3	78.2
Aged 30 to 34	691	100.0	3.1	13.7	4.1	78.7
Aged 35 to 39	718	100.0	2.9	13.2	3.4	80.0
Aged 40 to 44	761	100.0	2.2	12.1	2.7	82.4
Aged 45 to 49	855	100.0	1.7	11.7	2.1	83.9
Aged 50 to 54	887	100.0	1.3	11.5	1.7	84.8
Aged 55 to 59	787	100.0	1.3	10.7	1.4	86.1
Aged 60 to 64	665	100.0	1.2	9.6	1.3	87.4
Aged 65 to 69	479	100.0	1.2	9.1	1.1	88.1
Aged 70 to 74	371	100.0	1.1	9.2	1.0	88.3
Aged 75 to 79	298	100.0	0.8	9.0	1.0	88.8
Aged 80 to 84	244	100.0	0.6	8.0	0.8	90.2
Aged 85 or older	230	100.0	0.4	7.2	0.7	91.5
Oklahoma	**3,751**	**100.0**	**2.2**	**8.7**	**8.9**	**68.7**
Under age 5	264	100.0	2.9	12.8	16.8	53.0
Aged 5 to 9	259	100.0	2.7	11.9	15.0	55.3
Aged 10 to 14	254	100.0	2.5	11.6	12.6	57.6
Aged 15 to 19	264	100.0	2.6	11.5	11.3	59.8
Aged 20 to 24	269	100.0	3.0	10.3	11.8	62.9
Aged 25 to 29	266	100.0	3.0	9.2	12.0	64.0
Aged 30 to 34	241	100.0	2.8	9.0	11.8	64.6
Aged 35 to 39	233	100.0	2.9	8.4	10.2	66.9
Aged 40 to 44	228	100.0	2.5	8.0	8.5	70.0
Aged 45 to 49	261	100.0	1.9	7.7	6.2	73.5
Aged 50 to 54	264	100.0	1.7	7.6	4.6	76.1
Aged 55 to 59	236	100.0	1.6	6.8	3.6	78.6
Aged 60 to 64	205	100.0	1.4	5.8	2.8	81.1
Aged 65 to 69	159	100.0	1.2	5.1	2.3	83.0
Aged 70 to 74	121	100.0	1.1	4.7	2.0	84.4
Aged 75 to 79	95	100.0	0.9	4.4	1.7	86.1
Aged 80 to 84	69	100.0	0.7	4.0	1.5	88.0
Aged 85 or older	62	100.0	0.5	4.0	1.3	89.1

	total					non-Hispanic
	number	percent	Asian	black	Hispanic	white
Oregon	**3,831**	**100.0%**	**4.9%**	**2.6%**	**11.7%**	**78.5%**
Under age 5	238	100.0	6.6	4.7	23.3	63.2
Aged 5 to 9	237	100.0	6.6	4.2	21.8	65.0
Aged 10 to 14	243	100.0	6.0	4.1	19.5	67.7
Aged 15 to 19	255	100.0	5.9	3.8	16.9	70.4
Aged 20 to 24	253	100.0	6.0	3.2	15.1	72.8
Aged 25 to 29	265	100.0	5.5	2.8	15.0	74.1
Aged 30 to 34	259	100.0	5.8	2.7	15.3	73.8
Aged 35 to 39	251	100.0	6.4	2.5	14.3	74.4
Aged 40 to 44	248	100.0	5.4	2.3	11.5	78.2
Aged 45 to 49	263	100.0	4.6	2.1	8.3	82.4
Aged 50 to 54	276	100.0	3.8	1.9	5.9	85.9
Aged 55 to 59	273	100.0	3.2	1.5	4.3	88.8
Aged 60 to 64	236	100.0	2.8	1.3	3.4	90.4
Aged 65 to 69	170	100.0	2.6	1.1	2.9	91.5
Aged 70 to 74	120	100.0	2.7	1.1	2.7	91.8
Aged 75 to 79	92	100.0	2.5	0.9	2.2	92.9
Aged 80 to 84	74	100.0	2.3	0.8	1.9	94.0
Aged 85 or older	78	100.0	1.7	0.7	1.5	95.3
Pennsylvania	**12,702**	**100.0**	**3.2**	**11.9**	**5.7**	**79.5**
Under age 5	730	100.0	4.5	17.9	10.9	67.9
Aged 5 to 9	754	100.0	4.2	16.3	9.6	70.8
Aged 10 to 14	791	100.0	3.5	15.8	8.5	72.8
Aged 15 to 19	905	100.0	3.4	16.1	7.9	73.1
Aged 20 to 24	874	100.0	4.3	14.5	7.7	73.9
Aged 25 to 29	782	100.0	4.8	12.9	7.8	74.7
Aged 30 to 34	730	100.0	4.8	12.9	7.9	74.7
Aged 35 to 39	764	100.0	4.5	12.0	6.7	76.9
Aged 40 to 44	851	100.0	3.4	11.4	5.6	79.7
Aged 45 to 49	956	100.0	2.7	10.6	4.3	82.3
Aged 50 to 54	985	100.0	2.2	9.9	3.3	84.4
Aged 55 to 59	879	100.0	2.1	9.0	2.7	86.0
Aged 60 to 64	743	100.0	2.0	8.2	2.4	87.3
Aged 65 to 69	553	100.0	1.8	7.7	2.1	88.2
Aged 70 to 74	427	100.0	1.7	7.5	1.8	88.9
Aged 75 to 79	362	100.0	1.3	7.0	1.4	90.1
Aged 80 to 84	312	100.0	0.8	5.9	1.1	92.0
Aged 85 or older	306	100.0	0.6	5.6	0.8	92.9

	total		Asian	black	Hispanic	non-Hispanic white
	number	percent				
Rhode Island	**1,053**	**100.0%**	**3.5%**	**7.4%**	**12.4%**	**76.4%**
Under age 5	57	100.0	5.2	13.4	23.2	59.2
Aged 5 to 9	60	100.0	4.6	11.7	20.7	63.4
Aged 10 to 14	64	100.0	3.9	10.8	19.1	66.3
Aged 15 to 19	80	100.0	4.6	10.3	17.3	67.8
Aged 20 to 24	82	100.0	5.6	9.1	15.3	69.7
Aged 25 to 29	66	100.0	5.7	8.7	16.9	68.3
Aged 30 to 34	61	100.0	4.9	8.5	16.7	69.3
Aged 35 to 39	64	100.0	4.0	7.7	14.7	73.1
Aged 40 to 44	73	100.0	3.1	6.7	12.3	77.2
Aged 45 to 49	81	100.0	2.6	5.9	9.4	81.4
Aged 50 to 54	81	100.0	2.3	5.6	7.5	83.9
Aged 55 to 59	71	100.0	2.1	4.8	6.2	86.3
Aged 60 to 64	60	100.0	1.9	3.8	5.2	88.5
Aged 65 to 69	43	100.0	1.7	3.4	4.8	89.4
Aged 70 to 74	31	100.0	1.8	3.7	4.4	89.3
Aged 75 to 79	27	100.0	1.2	3.3	3.4	91.3
Aged 80 to 84	25	100.0	0.9	2.6	2.3	93.5
Aged 85 or older	27	100.0	0.6	1.8	1.6	95.2
South Carolina	**4,625**	**100.0**	**1.6**	**28.8**	**5.1**	**64.1**
Under age 5	302	100.0	2.2	35.7	9.9	52.2
Aged 5 to 9	296	100.0	2.2	34.0	8.0	55.7
Aged 10 to 14	297	100.0	1.9	34.4	6.0	57.4
Aged 15 to 19	329	100.0	1.7	35.6	5.6	56.7
Aged 20 to 24	332	100.0	1.8	32.2	7.5	58.2
Aged 25 to 29	304	100.0	2.2	29.8	9.0	58.7
Aged 30 to 34	288	100.0	2.2	29.2	8.4	59.8
Aged 35 to 39	297	100.0	2.2	27.5	6.5	63.3
Aged 40 to 44	305	100.0	1.8	27.8	4.9	64.9
Aged 45 to 49	333	100.0	1.5	27.8	3.3	66.7
Aged 50 to 54	327	100.0	1.3	27.9	2.5	67.6
Aged 55 to 59	303	100.0	1.2	26.8	1.8	69.6
Aged 60 to 64	281	100.0	1.0	23.1	1.4	74.0
Aged 65 to 69	216	100.0	0.9	20.6	1.2	76.8
Aged 70 to 74	153	100.0	0.9	20.3	1.1	77.4
Aged 75 to 79	113	100.0	0.7	19.4	1.0	78.6
Aged 80 to 84	79	100.0	0.5	18.9	0.9	79.4
Aged 85 or older	71	100.0	0.4	20.0	0.8	78.6

	total		Asian	black	Hispanic	non-Hispanic white
	number	percent				
South Dakota	**814**	**100.0%**	**1.3%**	**1.8%**	**2.7%**	**84.7%**
Under age 5	60	100.0	1.8	4.2	5.4	72.7
Aged 5 to 9	56	100.0	1.7	3.5	4.7	74.5
Aged 10 to 14	54	100.0	1.7	2.9	4.0	76.8
Aged 15 to 19	58	100.0	1.6	2.4	3.6	78.6
Aged 20 to 24	58	100.0	2.1	2.4	3.7	80.3
Aged 25 to 29	56	100.0	1.7	2.5	3.7	81.4
Aged 30 to 34	50	100.0	1.7	2.0	3.7	82.7
Aged 35 to 39	46	100.0	1.7	1.9	3.0	83.8
Aged 40 to 44	47	100.0	1.3	1.5	2.6	85.4
Aged 45 to 49	58	100.0	1.0	1.1	1.9	88.4
Aged 50 to 54	59	100.0	0.8	0.8	1.3	90.6
Aged 55 to 59	54	100.0	0.6	0.6	0.9	92.3
Aged 60 to 64	44	100.0	0.6	0.4	0.8	92.9
Aged 65 to 69	32	100.0	0.4	0.3	0.7	93.9
Aged 70 to 74	26	100.0	0.4	0.3	0.6	94.4
Aged 75 to 79	22	100.0	0.3	0.2	0.5	95.8
Aged 80 to 84	18	100.0	0.2	0.2	0.4	96.8
Aged 85 or older	19	100.0	0.1	0.2	0.5	97.6
Tennessee	**6,346**	**100.0**	**1.8**	**17.4**	**4.6**	**75.6**
Under age 5	408	100.0	2.5	23.1	9.6	64.6
Aged 5 to 9	412	100.0	2.5	21.7	7.7	67.8
Aged 10 to 14	419	100.0	2.0	22.2	5.8	69.5
Aged 15 to 19	437	100.0	1.9	23.0	5.2	69.4
Aged 20 to 24	426	100.0	2.0	21.0	6.8	69.7
Aged 25 to 29	418	100.0	2.4	18.9	7.8	70.4
Aged 30 to 34	406	100.0	2.5	18.2	7.3	71.5
Aged 35 to 39	424	100.0	2.4	17.2	5.5	74.3
Aged 40 to 44	431	100.0	2.0	16.6	4.0	76.7
Aged 45 to 49	467	100.0	1.5	16.2	2.8	78.7
Aged 50 to 54	459	100.0	1.3	16.2	2.1	79.7
Aged 55 to 59	415	100.0	1.2	15.1	1.5	81.4
Aged 60 to 64	371	100.0	1.0	12.2	1.2	84.8
Aged 65 to 69	281	100.0	0.9	10.3	1.0	87.1
Aged 70 to 74	207	100.0	0.8	10.1	0.9	87.7
Aged 75 to 79	155	100.0	0.7	9.9	0.8	88.1
Aged 80 to 84	112	100.0	0.5	9.4	0.7	88.9
Aged 85 or older	100	100.0	0.3	9.6	0.6	89.1

	total		Asian	black	Hispanic	non-Hispanic white
	number	percent				
Texas	**25,146**	**100.0%**	**4.4%**	**12.6%**	**37.6%**	**45.3%**
Under age 5	1,928	100.0	4.7	14.2	50.6	31.7
Aged 5 to 9	1,928	100.0	4.7	13.8	49.1	33.2
Aged 10 to 14	1,882	100.0	4.2	14.1	46.9	35.2
Aged 15 to 19	1,883	100.0	4.0	14.6	44.9	36.7
Aged 20 to 24	1,817	100.0	4.5	13.5	42.8	39.2
Aged 25 to 29	1,853	100.0	5.1	12.7	41.8	40.3
Aged 30 to 34	1,760	100.0	5.5	12.8	42.1	39.6
Aged 35 to 39	1,764	100.0	5.9	12.6	40.1	41.2
Aged 40 to 44	1,695	100.0	5.2	12.7	36.7	45.0
Aged 45 to 49	1,760	100.0	4.3	12.7	31.7	50.7
Aged 50 to 54	1,675	100.0	3.9	12.4	27.8	55.3
Aged 55 to 59	1,423	100.0	3.9	11.6	25.2	58.7
Aged 60 to 64	1,175	100.0	3.6	10.2	23.2	62.3
Aged 65 to 69	853	100.0	3.3	9.2	21.6	65.2
Aged 70 to 74	619	100.0	3.1	8.8	21.5	66.0
Aged 75 to 79	477	100.0	2.5	8.5	20.5	68.1
Aged 80 to 84	347	100.0	2.0	7.7	19.4	70.4
Aged 85 or older	305	100.0	1.5	7.8	16.4	73.9
Utah	**2,764**	**100.0**	**2.8**	**1.6**	**13.0**	**80.4**
Under age 5	264	100.0	2.9	2.5	17.2	74.9
Aged 5 to 9	250	100.0	2.9	2.4	16.6	75.6
Aged 10 to 14	228	100.0	2.9	2.3	16.1	76.0
Aged 15 to 19	221	100.0	3.1	2.1	15.3	76.5
Aged 20 to 24	227	100.0	3.4	1.8	14.1	78.1
Aged 25 to 29	230	100.0	3.2	1.4	13.7	79.2
Aged 30 to 34	216	100.0	2.9	1.3	14.3	79.4
Aged 35 to 39	178	100.0	3.2	1.3	15.4	77.9
Aged 40 to 44	154	100.0	3.2	1.3	14.3	79.0
Aged 45 to 49	155	100.0	2.8	1.2	11.2	82.6
Aged 50 to 54	152	100.0	2.4	1.0	8.7	85.9
Aged 55 to 59	133	100.0	2.3	0.8	7.0	88.1
Aged 60 to 64	107	100.0	2.2	0.7	6.0	89.6
Aged 65 to 69	79	100.0	1.8	0.5	5.2	91.0
Aged 70 to 74	59	100.0	1.7	0.5	4.8	91.8
Aged 75 to 79	46	100.0	1.6	0.4	4.2	92.9
Aged 80 to 84	34	100.0	1.6	0.4	3.6	93.6
Aged 85 or older	31	100.0	1.6	0.5	2.9	94.2

	total					non-Hispanic
	number	percent	Asian	black	Hispanic	white
Vermont	**626**	**100.0%**	**1.7%**	**1.5%**	**1.5%**	**94.3%**
Under age 5	32	100.0	2.7	3.9	2.5	89.9
Aged 5 to 9	35	100.0	2.7	3.3	2.3	90.7
Aged 10 to 14	38	100.0	2.4	2.8	2.0	91.6
Aged 15 to 19	46	100.0	2.7	2.6	2.6	91.2
Aged 20 to 24	44	100.0	2.6	2.2	2.6	91.6
Aged 25 to 29	35	100.0	2.4	2.0	2.0	92.5
Aged 30 to 34	34	100.0	2.3	1.7	1.8	93.1
Aged 35 to 39	36	100.0	2.4	1.3	1.5	93.7
Aged 40 to 44	42	100.0	1.7	1.0	1.2	95.0
Aged 45 to 49	50	100.0	1.2	0.8	1.1	95.7
Aged 50 to 54	52	100.0	0.9	0.7	0.8	96.3
Aged 55 to 59	49	100.0	0.8	0.6	0.7	96.7
Aged 60 to 64	41	100.0	0.7	0.4	0.7	97.1
Aged 65 to 69	29	100.0	0.5	0.4	0.6	97.5
Aged 70 to 74	20	100.0	0.6	0.3	0.5	97.9
Aged 75 to 79	16	100.0	0.5	0.3	0.7	97.8
Aged 80 to 84	13	100.0	0.4	0.2	0.6	98.1
Aged 85 or older	13	100.0	0.3	0.3	0.7	98.4
Virginia	**8,001**	**100.0**	**6.5**	**20.7**	**7.9**	**64.8**
Under age 5	510	100.0	8.6	24.9	13.4	53.9
Aged 5 to 9	512	100.0	8.3	24.4	11.3	56.6
Aged 10 to 14	511	100.0	7.1	24.7	9.8	58.7
Aged 15 to 19	551	100.0	6.3	25.8	9.0	59.0
Aged 20 to 24	572	100.0	6.5	22.9	10.5	60.1
Aged 25 to 29	564	100.0	7.8	20.8	11.7	59.7
Aged 30 to 34	526	100.0	8.8	20.2	12.1	58.8
Aged 35 to 39	540	100.0	9.1	19.5	10.1	61.2
Aged 40 to 44	569	100.0	7.3	20.1	8.0	64.3
Aged 45 to 49	621	100.0	5.9	20.2	6.0	67.5
Aged 50 to 54	593	100.0	5.2	19.8	4.7	69.8
Aged 55 to 59	513	100.0	4.8	18.6	3.6	72.5
Aged 60 to 64	442	100.0	4.5	16.1	2.8	76.1
Aged 65 to 69	320	100.0	4.3	15.4	2.4	77.4
Aged 70 to 74	230	100.0	4.2	15.9	2.2	77.4
Aged 75 to 79	174	100.0	3.5	15.5	1.9	78.8
Aged 80 to 84	131	100.0	2.6	14.3	1.6	81.2
Aged 85 or older	122	100.0	1.8	14.2	1.4	82.3

	total		Asian	black	Hispanic	non-Hispanic white
	number	percent				
Washington	**6,725**	**100.0%**	**9.0%**	**4.8%**	**11.2%**	**72.5%**
Under age 5	440	100.0	11.3	8.2	21.7	57.0
Aged 5 to 9	430	100.0	10.9	7.5	19.6	59.8
Aged 10 to 14	438	100.0	9.8	7.1	17.4	62.9
Aged 15 to 19	462	100.0	10.0	6.5	15.5	65.0
Aged 20 to 24	462	100.0	10.2	5.8	14.9	66.3
Aged 25 to 29	480	100.0	10.5	5.3	14.5	67.0
Aged 30 to 34	453	100.0	10.9	5.0	14.4	67.0
Aged 35 to 39	449	100.0	11.2	4.7	12.9	68.6
Aged 40 to 44	460	100.0	9.5	4.5	10.2	73.3
Aged 45 to 49	493	100.0	8.1	4.1	7.4	77.7
Aged 50 to 54	495	100.0	7.3	3.8	5.7	80.7
Aged 55 to 59	453	100.0	6.8	3.1	4.3	83.4
Aged 60 to 64	382	100.0	6.3	2.6	3.6	85.5
Aged 65 to 69	270	100.0	6.0	2.2	3.2	86.7
Aged 70 to 74	187	100.0	6.5	2.1	2.9	86.6
Aged 75 to 79	142	100.0	6.1	1.9	2.5	87.9
Aged 80 to 84	111	100.0	5.2	1.7	2.1	89.9
Aged 85 or older	117	100.0	4.0	1.5	1.5	92.3
West Virginia	**1,853**	**100.0**	**0.9**	**4.2**	**1.2**	**93.2**
Under age 5	104	100.0	1.3	7.2	2.4	88.8
Aged 5 to 9	106	100.0	1.2	6.2	2.0	90.2
Aged 10 to 14	109	100.0	1.0	5.8	1.7	90.9
Aged 15 to 19	120	100.0	1.0	5.9	1.7	90.8
Aged 20 to 24	117	100.0	1.4	5.6	1.8	90.7
Aged 25 to 29	108	100.0	1.4	4.7	1.7	91.5
Aged 30 to 34	112	100.0	1.2	4.5	1.6	92.2
Aged 35 to 39	117	100.0	1.1	3.8	1.3	93.2
Aged 40 to 44	120	100.0	0.9	3.5	1.1	93.9
Aged 45 to 49	133	100.0	0.7	3.5	0.9	94.1
Aged 50 to 54	143	100.0	0.6	3.5	0.7	94.4
Aged 55 to 59	139	100.0	0.6	3.2	0.6	94.9
Aged 60 to 64	125	100.0	0.6	2.6	0.5	95.6
Aged 65 to 69	92	100.0	0.6	2.2	0.5	95.9
Aged 70 to 74	72	100.0	0.5	2.1	0.5	96.3
Aged 75 to 79	55	100.0	0.4	2.1	0.4	96.6
Aged 80 to 84	43	100.0	0.2	2.4	0.4	96.4
Aged 85 or older	36	100.0	0.2	2.5	0.4	96.4

	total		Asian	black	Hispanic	non-Hispanic white
	number	percent				
Wisconsin	**5,687**	**100.0%**	**2.7%**	**7.1%**	**5.9%**	**83.3%**
Under age 5	358	100.0	4.6	12.5	12.3	69.9
Aged 5 to 9	369	100.0	4.1	11.1	10.9	72.9
Aged 10 to 14	376	100.0	3.7	10.8	9.0	75.5
Aged 15 to 19	399	100.0	3.8	10.3	7.6	77.0
Aged 20 to 24	387	100.0	4.2	8.6	7.5	78.5
Aged 25 to 29	372	100.0	4.1	8.0	8.4	78.4
Aged 30 to 34	349	100.0	3.5	7.8	8.6	79.1
Aged 35 to 39	345	100.0	3.1	7.5	7.4	80.9
Aged 40 to 44	380	100.0	2.3	6.3	5.3	84.9
Aged 45 to 49	438	100.0	1.7	5.4	3.6	88.2
Aged 50 to 54	436	100.0	1.3	5.0	2.8	89.8
Aged 55 to 59	386	100.0	1.2	4.5	2.2	91.2
Aged 60 to 64	314	100.0	1.1	3.9	1.9	92.3
Aged 65 to 69	227	100.0	1.0	3.4	1.6	93.2
Aged 70 to 74	173	100.0	1.0	3.2	1.4	93.7
Aged 75 to 79	141	100.0	0.8	2.8	1.2	94.6
Aged 80 to 84	117	100.0	0.6	2.2	1.0	95.9
Aged 85 or older	119	100.0	0.5	1.6	0.7	96.8
Wyoming	**564**	**100.0**	**1.2**	**1.3**	**8.9**	**85.9**
Under age 5	40	100.0	1.5	2.5	14.8	77.5
Aged 5 to 9	37	100.0	1.5	2.0	13.9	78.8
Aged 10 to 14	36	100.0	1.5	2.0	12.7	80.1
Aged 15 to 19	38	100.0	1.4	2.0	11.1	81.9
Aged 20 to 24	40	100.0	2.1	2.2	11.0	81.8
Aged 25 to 29	41	100.0	1.6	1.3	11.0	83.3
Aged 30 to 34	36	100.0	1.4	1.2	10.7	84.0
Aged 35 to 39	34	100.0	1.5	1.1	9.9	84.6
Aged 40 to 44	33	100.0	1.2	1.0	8.4	86.4
Aged 45 to 49	39	100.0	0.9	0.9	6.9	88.7
Aged 50 to 54	44	100.0	0.8	0.8	5.6	90.6
Aged 55 to 59	41	100.0	0.8	0.6	4.7	91.9
Aged 60 to 64	33	100.0	0.6	0.5	4.4	92.4
Aged 65 to 69	23	100.0	0.5	0.4	4.0	93.2
Aged 70 to 74	17	100.0	0.5	0.5	4.3	92.9
Aged 75 to 79	12	100.0	0.5	0.6	4.2	93.1
Aged 80 to 84	9	100.0	0.4	0.5	3.7	94.3
Aged 85 or older	9	100.0	0.4	0.6	3.0	95.1

Note: Asians and blacks are those who identify themselves as being of the race alone and those who identify themselves as being of the race in combination with other races. Numbers do not add to total because not all races are shown, some mixed-race individuals are counted more than once, and Hispanics may be of any race. Non-Hispanic whites are those who identify themselves as being white alone and not Hispanic.
Source: Bureau of the Census, 2010 Census, American Factfinder, Population Estimates, Internet site http:// factfinder2.census.gov/faces/nav/jsf/pages/index.xhtml; calculations by New Strategist

9

Spending

■ Average household spending fell in nearly every age group between 2006 (the year overall household spending peaked) and 2010, after adjusting for inflation. Households headed by Boomers, ranging in age from 45 to 64, cut their spending by 7 percent between 2006 and 2010.

■ Households headed by people aged 45 to 54 spent an average of $57,788 in 2010, 20 percent more than the average household and more than any other age group.

■ Households headed by people aged 55 to 64 spent an average of $50,900 in 2010. After adjusting for inflation, this was 2 percent more than the age group spent in 2000—despite the Great Recession. Behind the small increase during the decade was the growing number of two-income couples in the age group.

Boomer Spending Has Declined

Discretionary items have taken the biggest hit.

Spanning the ages of 46 to 64 in 2010, the younger members of the Baby-Boom generation are in their peak-spending years. Unfortunately, the Great Recession has reduced the income and spending of nearly every age group, and the peak spenders are no exception.

Householders aged 45 to 54 spent $57,788 in 2010, more than any other age group. But this figure was 7 percent less than householders aged 45 to 54 spent in 2006 (the year overall household spending peaked), after adjusting for inflation. The spending of 45-to-54-year-olds in 2010 was even below (by 1 percent) the spending of their counterparts in 2000. Since 2006, spending by householders aged 45 to 54 fell sharply on many discretionary items such as food away from home (down 20 percent), alcoholic beverages (down 37 percent), and fees and admissions to entertainment events (down 5 percent). Meanwhile, spending on health insurance increased by 23 percent and spending on education was up 12 percent.

Householders aged 55 to 64 spent $50,900 in 2010, down 7 percent from what households in the age group spent in 2006, after adjusting for inflation. As with householders aged 45 to 54, those aged 55 to 64 cut their spending on a variety of discretionary items. They reduced their spending on food away from home by 16 percent between 2006 and 2010, and cut their spending on alcoholic beverages by 22 percent. Spending on furniture diminished 19 percent, and spending on the entire category of entertainment declined 7 percent. Health insurance spending increased 16 percent, however, as did spending on vehicle insurance. Education spending by these householders—many of whom have children or grandchildren in college—grew by a substantial 28 percent.

■ The spending of householders aged 55 to 64 should climb in the years ahead because a growing proportion of households will be headed by two-earner couples.

Household spending peaks in the 45-to-54 age group

(average annual household spending by age of householder, 2010)

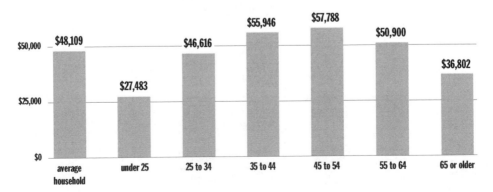

Table 9.1 Average Household Spending, 2000 to 2010

(average annual spending of consumer units on products and services, 2000 to 2010; percent change for selected years; in 2010 dollars)

	average spending			percent change		
	2010	2006	2000	2006–10	2000–06	2000–10
Number of consumer units (in 000s)	121,107	118,843	109,367	1.9%	8.7%	10.7%
Average annual spending of consumer units	$48,109	$52,349	$48,176	–8.1	8.7	–0.1
FOOD	**6,129**	**6,610**	**6,532**	**–7.3**	**1.2**	**–6.2**
Food at home	**3,624**	**3,696**	**3,825**	**–1.9**	**–3.4**	**–5.3**
Cereals and bakery products	502	482	574	4.1	–15.9	–12.5
Cereals and cereal products	165	155	198	6.7	–21.7	–16.5
Bakery products	337	329	376	2.5	–12.6	–10.4
Meats, poultry, fish, and eggs	784	862	1,007	–9.1	–14.4	–22.1
Beef	217	255	301	–15.0	–15.3	–28.0
Pork	149	170	211	–12.3	–19.7	–29.5
Other meats	117	114	128	3.0	–11.2	–8.5
Poultry	138	153	184	–9.5	–16.9	–24.8
Fish and seafood	117	132	139	–11.3	–5.3	–16.0
Eggs	46	40	43	14.9	–7.0	6.8
Dairy products	380	398	412	–4.5	–3.3	–7.7
Fresh milk and cream	141	151	166	–6.9	–8.7	–15.0
Other dairy products	240	247	244	–2.7	0.9	1.8
Fruits and vegetables	679	640	660	6.0	–2.9	2.9
Fresh fruits	232	211	206	10.0	2.2	12.4
Fresh vegetables	210	209	201	0.6	3.7	4.3
Processed fruits	113	118	146	–4.2	–19.0	–22.4
Processed vegetables	124	103	106	20.7	–3.4	16.6
Other food at home	1,278	1,311	1,174	–2.5	11.7	8.9
Sugar and other sweets	132	135	148	–2.4	–8.7	–10.9
Fats and oils	103	93	105	10.7	–11.5	–2.0
Miscellaneous foods	667	678	553	–1.6	22.6	20.5
Nonalcoholic beverages	333	359	317	–7.3	13.4	5.2
Food prepared by consumer unit on trips	43	47	51	–7.5	–8.2	–15.1
Food away from home	**2,505**	**2,914**	**2,706**	**–14.0**	**7.7**	**–7.4**
ALCOHOLIC BEVERAGES	**412**	**538**	**471**	**–23.4**	**14.1**	**–12.5**
HOUSING	**16,557**	**17,702**	**15,599**	**–6.5**	**13.5**	**6.1**
Shelter	**9,812**	**10,463**	**9,008**	**–6.2**	**16.1**	**8.9**
Owned dwellings	6,277	7,048	5,827	–10.9	20.9	7.7
Mortgage interest and charges	3,351	4,059	3,342	–17.4	21.5	0.3
Property taxes	1,814	1,784	1,442	1.7	23.7	25.8
Maintenance, repair, insurance, other expenses	1,112	1,206	1,045	–7.8	15.4	6.4
Rented dwellings	2,900	2,801	2,576	3.5	8.8	12.6
Other lodging	635	613	605	3.5	1.3	4.9
Utilities, fuels, and public services	**3,660**	**3,674**	**3,152**	**–0.4**	**16.6**	**16.1**
Natural gas	440	551	389	–20.1	41.6	13.2
Electricity	1,413	1,369	1,154	3.2	18.7	22.5
Fuel oil and other fuels	140	149	123	–6.2	21.5	14.0

	average spending			percent change		
	2010	**2006**	**2000**	**2006–10**	**2000–06**	**2000–10**
Telephone	$1,178	$1,176	$1,111	0.2%	5.9%	6.1%
Water and other public services	489	429	375	13.9	14.6	30.5
Household services	**1,007**	**1,025**	**866**	**−1.8**	**18.4**	**16.3**
Personal services	340	425	413	−20.0	3.0	−17.6
Other household services	667	600	453	11.1	32.4	47.1
Housekeeping supplies	**612**	**692**	**610**	**−11.6**	**13.4**	**0.3**
Laundry and cleaning supplies	150	163	166	−8.2	−1.5	−9.6
Other household products	329	357	286	−7.8	24.7	15.0
Postage and stationery	132	172	160	−23.2	7.8	−17.3
Household furnishings and equipment	**1,467**	**1,847**	**1,961**	**−20.6**	**−5.8**	**−25.2**
Household textiles	102	167	134	−38.8	24.1	−24.0
Furniture	355	501	495	−29.1	1.1	−28.3
Floor coverings	36	52	56	−30.7	−6.8	−35.4
Major appliances	209	261	239	−19.8	8.9	−12.7
Small appliances and miscellaneous housewares	107	118	110	−9.2	7.0	−2.9
Miscellaneous household equipment	657	750	926	−12.3	−19.0	−29.0
APPAREL AND RELATED SERVICES	**1,700**	**2,027**	**2,350**	**−16.1**	**−13.8**	**−27.7**
Men and boys	**382**	**480**	**557**	**−20.5**	**−13.8**	**−31.4**
Men, aged 16 or older	304	382	436	−20.4	−12.3	−30.2
Boys, aged 2 to 15	78	98	122	−20.8	−19.0	−35.8
Women and girls	**663**	**812**	**918**	**−18.4**	**−11.5**	**−27.8**
Women, aged 16 or older	562	680	769	−17.4	−11.5	−26.9
Girls, aged 2 to 15	101	132	149	−23.5	−11.7	−32.4
Children under age 2	**91**	**104**	**104**	**−12.4**	**0.0**	**−12.4**
Footwear	**303**	**329**	**434**	**−7.9**	**−24.3**	**−30.2**
Other apparel products and services	**261**	**303**	**337**	**−13.8**	**−10.1**	**−22.5**
TRANSPORTATION	**7,677**	**9,202**	**9,392**	**−16.6**	**−2.0**	**−18.3**
Vehicle purchases	**2,588**	**3,700**	**4,328**	**−30.1**	**−14.5**	**−40.2**
Cars and trucks, new	1,219	1,945	2,032	−37.3	−4.3	−40.0
Cars and trucks, used	1,318	1,696	2,241	−22.3	−24.3	−41.2
Gasoline and motor oil	**2,132**	**2,409**	**1,635**	**−11.5**	**47.3**	**30.4**
Other vehicle expenses	**2,464**	**2,547**	**2,888**	**−3.3**	**−11.8**	**−14.7**
Vehicle finance charges	243	322	415	−24.6	−22.4	−41.5
Maintenance and repairs	787	744	790	5.8	−5.8	−0.4
Vehicle insurance	1,010	958	985	5.4	−2.7	2.5
Vehicle rentals, leases, licenses, other charges	423	521	698	−18.9	−25.3	−39.4
Public transportation	**493**	**546**	**541**	**−9.7**	**1.0**	**−8.8**
HEALTH CARE	**3,157**	**2,992**	**2,616**	**5.5**	**14.4**	**20.7**
Health insurance	1,831	1,585	1,245	15.6	27.3	47.1
Medical services	722	725	719	−0.4	0.8	0.4
Drugs	485	556	527	−12.8	5.5	−7.9
Medical supplies	119	127	125	−6.0	0.9	−5.1
ENTERTAINMENT	**2,504**	**2,570**	**2,359**	**−2.6**	**8.9**	**6.1**
Fees and admissions	581	655	652	−11.4	0.5	−10.9
Television, radio, and sound equipment	954	980	788	−2.6	24.4	21.1
Pets, toys, and playground equipment	606	446	423	36.0	5.4	43.3
Other entertainment products and services	364	488	498	−25.4	−2.0	−26.9

	average spending			percent change		
	2010	2006	2000	2006–10	2000–06	2000–10
PERSONAL CARE PRODUCTS, SERVICES	**$582**	**$633**	**$714**	**−8.0%**	**−11.4%**	**−18.5%**
READING	**100**	**127**	**185**	**−21.0**	**−31.5**	**−45.9**
EDUCATION	**1,074**	**960**	**800**	**11.8**	**20.0**	**34.2**
TOBACCO PRODUCTS, SMOKING SUPPLIES	**362**	**354**	**404**	**2.3**	**−12.4**	**−10.4**
MISCELLANEOUS	**849**	**915**	**983**	**−7.2**	**−6.9**	**−13.6**
CASH CONTRIBUTIONS	**1,633**	**2,022**	**1,509**	**−19.2**	**33.9**	**8.2**
PERSONAL INSURANCE AND PENSIONS	**5,373**	**5,700**	**4,261**	**−5.7**	**33.8**	**26.1**
Life and other personal insurance	318	348	505	−8.7	−31.1	−37.1
Pensions and Social Security*	5,054	5,352	–	−5.6	–	–
PERSONAL TAXES	**1,769**	**2,631**	**3,947**	**−32.8**	**−33.4**	**−55.2**
Federal income taxes	1,136	1,851	3,051	−38.6	−39.3	−62.8
State and local income taxes	482	561	712	−14.1	−21.1	−32.3
Other taxes	151	218	185	−30.9	18.2	−18.3
GIFTS FOR PEOPLE IN OTHER HOUSEHOLDS	**1,029**	**1,248**	**1,371**	**−17.6**	**−9.0**	**−25.0**

Because of changes in methodology, the 2006 and 2010 data on pensions and Social Security are not comparable with earlier years.

Note: The Bureau of Labor Statistics uses consumer unit rather than household as the sampling unit in the Consumer Expenditure Survey. For the definition of consumer unit, see the glossary. Spending on gifts is also included in the preceding product and service categories.

Source: Bureau of Labor Statistics, 2000, 2006, and 2010 Consumer Expenditure Surveys, Internet site http://www.bls.gov/cex/; calculations by New Strategist

Table 9.2 Average Spending by Householders Aged 45 to 54, 2000 to 2010

(average annual spending of consumer units (CUs) headed by people aged 45 to 54, 2000 to 2010; percent change for selected years; in 2010 dollars)

	average spending			percent change		
	2010	2006	2000	2006–10	2000–06	2000–10
Number of CUs aged 45 to 54 (in 000s)	25,054	24,696	21,874	1.4%	12.9%	14.5%
Average annual spending of consumer units	$57,788	$62,262	$58,452	–7.2	6.5	–1.1
FOOD	7,230	7,926	7,971	–8.8	–0.6	–9.3
Food at home	4,369	4,365	4,631	0.1	–5.7	–5.7
Cereals and bakery products	600	552	709	8.8	–22.2	–15.4
Cereals and cereal products	199	175	228	13.6	–23.1	–12.7
Bakery products	401	376	481	6.5	–21.8	–16.7
Meats, poultry, fish, and eggs	966	1,051	1,228	–8.1	–14.4	–21.4
Beef	263	333	375	–21.1	–11.1	–29.8
Pork	182	209	251	–12.8	–16.7	–27.4
Other meats	147	143	153	3.0	–6.8	–4.1
Poultry	174	172	214	1.2	–19.6	–18.7
Fish and seafood	144	154	185	–6.2	–16.9	–22.1
Eggs	55	42	51	30.4	–16.7	8.6
Dairy products	453	454	477	–0.3	–4.8	–5.1
Fresh milk and cream	164	163	185	0.4	–11.7	–11.3
Other dairy products	289	290	294	–0.3	–1.3	–1.6
Fruits and vegetables	819	739	793	10.9	–6.8	3.3
Fresh fruits	274	243	237	12.6	2.8	15.7
Fresh vegetables	251	253	255	–0.8	–0.6	–1.4
Processed fruits	134	128	168	5.0	–24.2	–20.4
Processed vegetables	159	115	133	38.7	–13.8	19.6
Other food at home	1,532	1,569	1,423	–2.4	10.3	7.6
Sugar and other sweets	162	169	181	–4.0	–6.8	–10.5
Fats and oils	124	105	129	18.2	–18.8	–4.0
Miscellaneous foods	780	791	669	–1.3	18.3	16.7
Nonalcoholic beverages	419	447	380	–6.2	17.6	10.3
Food prepared by consumer unit on trips	48	57	66	–16.3	–12.9	–27.1
Food away from home	2,861	3,561	3,340	–19.7	6.6	–14.4
ALCOHOLIC BEVERAGES	414	662	528	–37.5	25.4	–21.6
HOUSING	18,900	19,877	17,955	–4.9	10.7	5.3
Shelter	11,517	11,785	10,506	–2.3	12.2	9.6
Owned dwellings	8,163	8,679	7,552	–5.9	14.9	8.1
Mortgage interest and charges	4,667	5,211	4,505	–10.4	15.7	3.6
Property taxes	2,295	2,198	1,863	4.4	18.0	23.2
Maintenance, repair, insurance, other expenses	1,200	1,271	1,184	–5.6	7.3	1.4
Rented dwellings	2,493	2,232	2,044	11.7	9.2	22.0
Other lodging	861	873	910	–1.4	–4.1	–5.4
Utilities, fuels, and public services	4,213	4,231	3,618	–0.4	17.0	16.5
Natural gas	506	647	436	–21.8	48.5	16.2
Electricity	1,578	1,563	1,323	1.0	18.1	19.2
Fuel oil and other fuels	150	162	138	–7.5	17.5	8.7

	average spending			percent change		
	2010	**2006**	**2000**	**2006–10**	**2000–06**	**2000–10**
Telephone	$1,428	$1,373	$1,275	4.0%	7.6%	12.0%
Water and other public services	551	486	446	13.5	9.0	23.6
Household services	**935**	**858**	**738**	**9.0**	**16.2**	**26.7**
Personal services	192	208	186	−7.5	11.6	3.1
Other household services	743	650	551	14.3	18.0	34.9
Housekeeping supplies	**650**	**786**	**674**	**−17.3**	**16.7**	**−3.5**
Laundry and cleaning supplies	165	173	173	−4.7	−0.2	−4.9
Other household products	344	399	313	−13.8	27.6	10.0
Postage and stationery	140	214	186	−34.6	15.1	−24.8
Household furnishings and equipment	**1,585**	**2,217**	**2,420**	**−28.5**	**−8.4**	**−34.5**
Household textiles	109	189	158	−42.4	19.6	−31.1
Furniture	325	615	596	−47.2	3.2	−45.5
Floor coverings	37	52	65	−28.7	−19.6	−42.7
Major appliances	220	308	282	−28.6	9.2	−22.1
Small appliances and miscellaneous housewares	112	161	160	−30.5	1.0	−29.8
Miscellaneous household equipment	783	891	1,159	−12.1	−23.1	−32.4
APPAREL AND RELATED SERVICES	**1,966**	**2,354**	**3,002**	**−16.5**	**−21.6**	**−34.5**
Men and boys	**469**	**582**	**731**	**−19.4**	**−20.4**	**−35.8**
Men, aged 16 or older	390	475	610	−17.9	−22.2	−36.1
Boys, aged 2 to 15	79	108	120	−27.0	−10.1	−34.3
Women and girls	**838**	**988**	**1,237**	**−15.1**	**−20.2**	**−32.3**
Women, aged 16 or older	722	846	1,076	−14.6	−21.4	−32.9
Girls, aged 2 to 15	116	142	160	−18.1	−11.2	−27.3
Children under age 2	**59**	**78**	**68**	**−24.2**	**13.9**	**−13.7**
Footwear	**360**	**371**	**555**	**−3.0**	**−33.1**	**−35.1**
Other apparel products and services	**241**	**336**	**412**	**−28.4**	**−18.3**	**−41.4**
TRANSPORTATION	**9,255**	**10,936**	**11,178**	**−15.4**	**−2.2**	**−17.2**
Vehicle purchases	**3,041**	**4,308**	**4,892**	**−29.4**	**−11.9**	**−37.8**
Cars and trucks, new	1,480	2,257	2,140	−34.4	5.5	−30.8
Cars and trucks, used	1,522	1,959	2,695	−22.3	−27.3	−43.5
Gasoline and motor oil	**2,575**	**2,913**	**2,016**	**−11.6**	**44.5**	**27.7**
Other vehicle expenses	**3,023**	**3,049**	**3,632**	**−0.9**	**−16.0**	**−16.8**
Vehicle finance charges	298	361	495	−17.5	−27.0	−39.8
Maintenance and repairs	947	937	1,014	1.1	−7.7	−6.6
Vehicle insurance	1,262	1,195	1,269	5.6	−5.8	−0.5
Vehicle rentals, leases, licenses, other charges	516	556	853	−7.2	−34.9	−39.5
Public transportation	**616**	**666**	**639**	**−7.5**	**4.2**	**−3.7**
HEALTH CARE	**3,261**	**2,982**	**2,786**	**9.4**	**7.0**	**17.1**
Health insurance	1,747	1,417	1,236	23.3	14.6	41.4
Medical services	879	863	885	1.8	−2.5	−0.7
Drugs	497	540	515	−7.9	4.7	−3.6
Medical supplies	137	163	149	−16.1	9.3	−8.3
ENTERTAINMENT	**3,088**	**2,996**	**2,825**	**3.1**	**6.1**	**9.3**
Fees and admissions	780	819	807	−4.7	1.5	−3.3
Audio and visual equipment and services	1,025	1,103	881	−7.1	25.2	16.3
Pets, toys, hobbies, and playground equipment	736	538	486	36.9	10.6	51.4
Other entertainment products and services	548	535	651	2.4	−17.7	−15.8

	average spending			percent change		
	2010	2006	2000	2006–10	2000–06	2000–10
PERSONAL CARE PRODUCTS, SERVICES	$673	$753	$864	–10.6%	–12.8%	–22.1%
READING	104	144	225	–27.7	–36.2	–53.9
EDUCATION	2,094	1,878	1,451	11.5	29.4	44.3
TOBACCO PRODUCTS, SMOKING SUPPLIES	449	468	476	–4.1	–1.6	–5.7
MISCELLANEOUS	938	1,050	1,174	–10.7	–10.5	–20.1
CASH CONTRIBUTIONS	1,747	2,291	1,946	–23.7	17.7	–10.2
PERSONAL INSURANCE AND PENSIONS	7,668	7,946	6,072	–3.5	30.9	26.3
Life and other personal insurance	441	447	695	–1.3	–35.7	–36.6
Pensions and Social Security*	7,227	7,499	–	–3.6	–	–
PERSONAL TAXES	3,323	3,634	6,002	–8.6	–39.5	–44.6
Federal income taxes	2,309	2,592	4,694	–10.9	–44.8	–50.8
State and local income taxes	831	787	1,074	5.5	–26.7	–22.6
Other taxes	183	255	234	–28.3	9.0	–21.9
GIFTS FOR PEOPLE IN OTHER HOUSEHOLDS	1,623	1,962	2,183	–17.3	–10.1	–25.7

* Because of changes in methodology, the 2006 and 2010 data on pensions and Social Security are not comparable with earlier years.
The Bureau of Labor Statistics uses consumer unit rather than household as the sampling unit in the Consumer Expenditure Survey. For the definition of consumer unit, see the glossary. Spending on gifts is also included in the preceding product and service categories.
Source: Bureau of Labor Statistics, 2000, 2006, and 2010 Consumer Expenditure Surveys, Internet site http://www.bls.gov/cex/; calculations by New Strategist

Table 9.3 Average Spending by Householders Aged 55 to 64, 2000 to 2010

(average annual spending of consumer units (CUs) headed by people aged 55 to 64, 2000 to 2010; percent change for selected years; in 2010 dollars)

	average spending			percent change		
	2010	2006	2000	2006–10	2000–06	2000–10
Number of CUs aged 55 to 64 (in 000s)	21,359	18,952	14,161	12.7%	33.8%	50.8%
Average annual spending of consumer units	$50,900	$54,935	$49,816	−7.3	10.3	2.2
FOOD	**6,068**	**6,633**	**6,544**	**−8.5**	**1.3**	**−7.3**
Food at home	**3,681**	**3,805**	**3,889**	**−3.3**	**−2.2**	**−5.3**
Cereals and bakery products	507	490	558	3.5	−12.3	−9.2
Cereals and cereal products	159	146	177	8.9	−17.6	−10.3
Bakery products	347	344	381	0.9	−9.8	−9.0
Meats, poultry, fish, and eggs	792	866	1,054	−8.6	−17.8	−24.8
Beef	223	243	308	−8.4	−20.9	−27.5
Pork	153	171	236	−10.5	−27.4	−35.0
Other meats	117	108	125	8.2	−13.7	−6.7
Poultry	123	150	185	−18.2	−18.7	−33.5
Fish and seafood	132	149	146	−11.6	2.5	−9.4
Eggs	44	43	54	1.7	−20.5	−19.2
Dairy products	378	400	406	−5.5	−1.5	−7.0
Fresh milk and cream	138	138	160	−0.3	−13.2	−13.5
Other dairy products	240	262	247	−8.3	6.0	−2.8
Fruits and vegetables	692	710	707	−2.5	0.4	−2.1
Fresh fruits	243	249	234	−2.3	6.2	3.7
Fresh vegetables	218	237	219	−8.0	8.1	−0.5
Processed fruits	112	116	146	−3.2	−20.5	−23.1
Processed vegetables	119	109	110	8.9	−0.8	8.0
Other food at home	1,312	1,339	1,162	−2.0	15.2	12.9
Sugar and other sweets	138	131	146	5.4	−10.1	−5.2
Fats and oils	109	107	114	1.8	−6.0	−4.4
Miscellaneous foods	649	672	504	−3.4	33.3	28.8
Nonalcoholic beverages	360	370	333	−2.7	11.1	8.1
Food prepared by consumer unit on trips	56	59	66	−5.9	−9.7	−15.0
Food away from home	**2,387**	**2,826**	**2,655**	**−15.5**	**6.4**	**−10.1**
ALCOHOLIC BEVERAGES	**402**	**516**	**470**	**−22.1**	**9.8**	**−14.4**
HOUSING	**16,673**	**17,878**	**15,654**	**−6.7**	**14.2**	**6.5**
Shelter	**9,397**	**9,950**	**8,341**	**−5.6**	**19.3**	**12.7**
Owned dwellings	6,777	7,426	6,053	−8.7	22.7	12.0
Mortgage interest and charges	3,198	3,538	2,885	−9.6	22.7	10.9
Property taxes	2,216	2,076	1,851	6.8	12.1	19.7
Maintenance, repair, insurance, other expenses	1,362	1,813	1,317	−24.9	37.7	3.4
Rented dwellings	1,689	1,579	1,422	7.0	11.0	18.8
Other lodging	931	944	867	−1.4	8.9	7.3
Utilities, fuels, and public services	**3,979**	**3,937**	**3,490**	**1.1**	**12.8**	**14.0**
Natural gas	456	609	432	−25.1	41.0	5.6
Electricity	1,546	1,473	1,327	4.9	11.0	16.5
Fuel oil and other fuels	194	181	143	7.4	26.2	35.6

	average spending			percent change		
	2010	2006	2000	2006–10	2000–06	2000–10
Telephone	$1,224	$1,206	$1,151	1.5%	4.8%	6.3%
Water and other public services	558	468	437	19.1	7.2	27.7
Household services	**882**	**1,010**	**686**	**–12.7**	**47.2**	**28.5**
Personal services	72	239	118	–69.9	103.0	–38.9
Other household services	810	772	569	4.9	35.8	42.5
Housekeeping supplies	**717**	**799**	**741**	**–10.3**	**7.9**	**–3.2**
Laundry and cleaning supplies	157	178	233	–12.0	–23.4	–32.6
Other household products	403	399	332	1.0	20.3	21.5
Postage and stationery	157	222	176	–29.2	26.0	–10.8
Household furnishings and equipment	**1,698**	**2,182**	**2,395**	**–22.2**	**–8.9**	**–29.1**
Household textiles	138	224	158	–38.4	41.5	–12.8
Furniture	406	500	457	–18.8	9.3	–11.2
Floor coverings	51	87	71	–41.1	22.0	–28.1
Major appliances	249	319	280	–22.0	14.0	–11.0
Small appliances and miscellaneous housewares	149	120	134	24.1	–10.6	11.0
Miscellaneous household equipment	705	932	1,294	–24.4	–28.0	–45.5
APPAREL AND RELATED SERVICES	**1,571**	**2,046**	**2,145**	**–23.2**	**–4.6**	**–26.8**
Men and boys	**370**	**433**	**500**	**–14.5**	**–13.5**	**–26.0**
Men, aged 16 or older	331	383	446	–13.6	–14.1	–25.7
Boys, aged 2 to 15	39	50	53	–21.6	–6.4	–26.7
Women and girls	**614**	**903**	**870**	**–32.0**	**3.8**	**–29.4**
Women, aged 16 or older	564	836	798	–32.5	4.8	–29.3
Girls, aged 2 to 15	50	67	72	–25.4	–7.1	–30.7
Children under age 2	**54**	**71**	**67**	**–24.4**	**6.4**	**–19.5**
Footwear	**292**	**312**	**380**	**–6.3**	**–18.0**	**–23.1**
Other apparel products and services	**241**	**328**	**328**	**–26.5**	**–0.1**	**–26.5**
TRANSPORTATION	**8,111**	**9,384**	**9,930**	**–13.6**	**–5.5**	**–18.3**
Vehicle purchases	**2,584**	**3,423**	**4,588**	**–24.5**	**–25.4**	**–43.7**
Cars and trucks, new	1,452	2,019	2,655	–28.1	–24.0	–45.3
Cars and trucks, used	1,053	1,375	1,910	–23.4	–28.0	–44.9
Gasoline and motor oil	**2,215**	**2,475**	**1,708**	**–10.5**	**44.9**	**29.7**
Other vehicle expenses	**2,763**	**2,853**	**3,007**	**–3.2**	**–5.1**	**–8.1**
Vehicle finance charges	248	323	442	–23.3	–26.8	–43.9
Maintenance and repairs	894	864	851	3.4	1.6	5.1
Vehicle insurance	1,181	1,018	1,008	16.0	1.0	17.2
Vehicle rentals, leases, licenses, other charges	440	648	708	–32.1	–8.5	–37.8
Public transportation	**548**	**632**	**627**	**–13.2**	**0.8**	**–12.6**
HEALTH CARE	**3,859**	**3,846**	**3,176**	**0.3**	**21.1**	**21.5**
Health insurance	2,110	1,813	1,433	16.4	26.5	47.2
Medical services	943	1,058	913	–10.9	15.9	3.3
Drugs	665	821	681	–19.0	20.5	–2.4
Medical supplies	142	155	148	–8.2	4.4	–4.2
ENTERTAINMENT	**2,683**	**2,884**	**2,476**	**–7.0**	**16.5**	**8.4**
Fees and admissions	545	654	645	–16.7	1.5	–15.4
Audio and visual equipment and services	1,061	980	736	8.3	33.2	44.2
Pets, toys, hobbies, and playground equipment	705	519	453	35.8	14.5	55.5
Other entertainment products and services	372	730	642	–49.0	13.7	–42.1

	average spending			percent change		
	2010	2006	2000	2006–10	2000–06	2000–10
PERSONAL CARE PRODUCTS, SERVICES	**$599**	**$634**	**$721**	**–5.5%**	**–12.0%**	**–16.9%**
READING	**126**	**159**	**227**	**–20.8**	**–29.9**	**–44.4**
EDUCATION	**917**	**716**	**481**	**28.1**	**48.8**	**90.6**
TOBACCO PRODUCTS, SMOKING SUPPLIES	**450**	**400**	**442**	**12.4**	**–9.4**	**1.8**
MISCELLANEOUS	**1,146**	**1,195**	**1,043**	**–4.1**	**14.5**	**9.8**
CASH CONTRIBUTIONS	**1,893**	**2,451**	**1,647**	**–22.8**	**48.8**	**14.9**
PERSONAL INSURANCE AND PENSIONS	**6,403**	**6,193**	**4,860**	**3.4**	**27.4**	**31.7**
Life and other personal insurance	471	495	743	–4.9	–33.4	–36.6
Pensions and Social Security*	5,932	5,697	–	4.1	–	–
PERSONAL TAXES	**2,295**	**3,819**	**5,064**	**–39.9**	**–24.6**	**–54.7**
Federal income taxes	1,520	2,817	3,877	–46.0	–27.4	–60.8
State and local income taxes	529	711	889	–25.6	–20.1	–40.5
Other taxes	247	292	298	–15.4	–1.9	–17.0
GIFTS FOR PEOPLE IN OTHER HOUSEHOLDS	**1,484**	**1,646**	**1,703**	**–9.9**	**–3.3**	**–12.9**

* Because of changes in methodology, the 2006 and 2010 data on pensions and Social Security are not comparable with earlier years.
Note: The Bureau of Labor Statistics uses consumer unit rather than household as the sampling unit in the Consumer Expenditure Survey. For the definition of consumer unit, see the glossary. Spending on gifts is also included in the preceding product and service categories.
Source: Bureau of Labor Statistics, 2000, 2006, and 2010 Consumer Expenditure Surveys, Internet site http://www.bls.gov/cex/; calculations by New Strategist

Householders Aged 45 to 54 Are the Biggest Spenders

Their spending patterns reflect the fact that many are empty-nesters.

Householders aged 45 to 54 spent $57,788 on average in 2010, more than any other age group and 20 percent more than the $48,109 spent by the average household. The age group controls 25 percent of household spending, a larger share than any other age group.

Because most householders aged 45 to 54 are either empty-nesters or have older children at home, their spending patterns differ considerably from householders aged 35 to 44. They spend much less than average, for example, on household personal services (day care expenses). But they spend 36 percent more than average on other lodging (hotels, motels, and college dorms). They spend 28 percent more than average on men's and women's clothes, 58 percent more on gifts for people in other households, and 95 percent more on education. The 45-to-54 age group controls more than 40 percent of household spending on education. Surprisingly, however, they spend less than average on furniture and out-of-pocket health insurance costs.

■ Far from being big spenders, the baby-boom generation is finding ways to cut expenses while many costs rise.

Householders aged 45 to 54 spend nearly twice as much as the average household on education

(indexed spending of householders aged 45 to 54 on selected items; 2010)

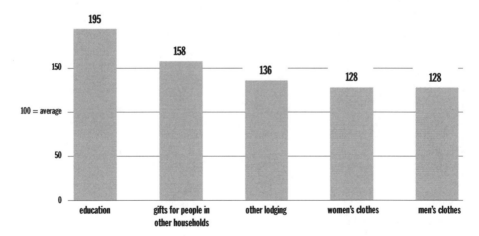

Table 9.4 Average, Indexed, and Market Share of Spending by Householders Aged 45 to 54, 2010

(average annual spending of total consumer units and average annual, indexed, and market share of spending by consumer units headed by people aged 45 to 54, 2010)

	total consumer units	consumer units headed by 45-to-54-year-olds		
		average spending	indexed spending	market share
Number of consumer units (in 000s)	121,107	25,054	–	20.7%
Average annual spending	$48,109	$57,788	120	24.8
FOOD	6,129	7,230	118	24.4
Food at home	3,624	4,369	121	24.9
Cereals and bakery products	502	600	120	24.7
Cereals and cereal products	165	199	121	25.0
Bakery products	337	401	119	24.6
Meats, poultry, fish, and eggs	784	966	123	25.5
Beef	217	263	121	25.1
Pork	149	182	122	25.3
Other meats	117	147	126	26.0
Poultry	138	174	126	26.1
Fish and seafood	117	144	123	25.5
Eggs	46	55	120	24.7
Dairy products	380	453	119	24.7
Fresh milk and cream	141	164	116	24.1
Other dairy products	240	289	120	24.9
Fruits and vegetables	679	819	121	25.0
Fresh fruits	232	274	118	24.4
Fresh vegetables	210	251	120	24.7
Processed fruits	113	134	119	24.5
Processed vegetables	124	159	128	26.5
Other food at home	1,278	1,532	120	24.8
Sugar and other sweets	132	162	123	25.4
Fats and oils	103	124	120	24.9
Miscellaneous foods	667	780	117	24.2
Nonalcoholic beverages	333	419	126	26.0
Food prepared by consumer unit on trips	43	48	112	23.1
Food away from home	2,505	2,861	114	23.6
ALCOHOLIC BEVERAGES	412	414	100	20.8
HOUSING	16,557	18,900	114	23.6
Shelter	9,812	11,517	117	24.3
Owned dwellings	6,277	8,163	130	26.9
Mortgage interest and charges	3,351	4,667	139	28.8
Property taxes	1,814	2,295	127	26.2
Maintenance, repair, insurance, other expenses	1,112	1,200	108	22.3
Rented dwellings	2,900	2,493	86	17.8
Other lodging	635	861	136	28.1
Utilities, fuels, and public services	3,660	4,213	115	23.8
Natural gas	440	506	115	23.8
Electricity	1,413	1,578	112	23.1
Fuel oil and other fuels	140	150	107	22.2

	total consumer units	consumer units headed by 45-to-54-year-olds		
		average spending	indexed spending	market share
Telephone	$1,178	$1,428	121	25.1%
Water and other public services	489	551	113	23.3
Household services	**1,007**	**935**	**93**	**19.2**
Personal services	340	192	56	11.7
Other household services	667	743	111	23.0
Housekeeping supplies	**612**	**650**	**106**	**22.0**
Laundry and cleaning supplies	150	165	110	22.8
Other household products	329	344	105	21.6
Postage and stationery	132	140	106	21.9
Household furnishings and equipment	**1,467**	**1,585**	**108**	**22.4**
Household textiles	102	109	107	22.1
Furniture	355	325	92	18.9
Floor coverings	36	37	103	21.3
Major appliances	209	220	105	21.8
Small appliances and miscellaneous housewares	107	112	105	21.7
Miscellaneous household equipment	657	783	119	24.7
APPAREL AND RELATED SERVICES	**1,700**	**1,966**	**116**	**23.9**
Men and boys	**382**	**469**	**123**	**25.4**
Men, aged 16 or older	304	390	128	26.5
Boys, aged 2 to 15	78	79	101	21.0
Women and girls	**663**	**838**	**126**	**26.1**
Women, aged 16 or older	562	722	128	26.6
Girls, aged 2 to 15	101	116	115	23.8
Children under age 2	**91**	**59**	**65**	**13.4**
Footwear	**303**	**360**	**119**	**24.6**
Other apparel products and services	**261**	**241**	**92**	**19.1**
TRANSPORTATION	**7,677**	**9,255**	**121**	**24.9**
Vehicle purchases	**2,588**	**3,041**	**118**	**24.3**
Cars and trucks, new	1,219	1,480	121	25.1
Cars and trucks, used	1,318	1,522	115	23.9
Gasoline and motor oil	**2,132**	**2,575**	**121**	**25.0**
Other vehicle expenses	**2,464**	**3,023**	**123**	**25.4**
Vehicle finance charges	243	298	123	25.4
Maintenance and repairs	787	947	120	24.9
Vehicle insurance	1,010	1,262	125	25.8
Vehicle rentals, leases, licenses, other charges	423	516	122	25.2
Public transportation	**493**	**616**	**125**	**25.8**
HEALTH CARE	**3,157**	**3,261**	**103**	**21.4**
Health insurance	1,831	1,747	95	19.7
Medical services	722	879	122	25.2
Drugs	485	497	102	21.2
Medical supplies	119	137	115	23.8
ENTERTAINMENT	**2,504**	**3,088**	**123**	**25.5**
Fees and admissions	581	780	134	27.8
Audio and visual equipment and services	954	1,025	107	22.2
Pets, toys, hobbies, and playground equipment	606	736	121	25.1
Other entertainment products and services	364	548	151	31.1

	total consumer units	consumer units headed by 45-to-54-year-olds		
		average spending	indexed spending	market share
PERSONAL CARE PRODUCTS AND SERVICES	**$582**	**$673**	**116**	**23.9%**
READING	**100**	**104**	**104**	**21.5**
EDUCATION	**1,074**	**2,094**	**195**	**40.3**
TOBACCO PRODUCTS AND SMOKING SUPPLIES	**362**	**449**	**124**	**25.7**
MISCELLANEOUS	**849**	**938**	**110**	**22.9**
CASH CONTRIBUTIONS	**1,633**	**1,747**	**107**	**22.1**
PERSONAL INSURANCE AND PENSIONS	**5,373**	**7,668**	**143**	**29.5**
Life and other personal insurance	318	441	139	28.7
Pensions and Social Security	5,054	7,227	143	29.6
PERSONAL TAXES	**1,769**	**3,323**	**188**	**38.9**
Federal income taxes	1,136	2,309	203	42.0
State and local income taxes	482	831	172	35.7
Other taxes	151	183	121	25.1
GIFTS FOR PEOPLE IN OTHER HOUSEHOLDS	**1,029**	**1,623**	**158**	**32.6**

Note: The Bureau of Labor Statistics uses consumer unit rather than household as the sampling unit in the Consumer Expenditure Survey. For the definition of consumer unit, see the glossary. Spending on gifts is also included in the preceding product and service categories. "–" means not applicable.
Source: Bureau of Labor Statistics, 2010 Consumer Expenditure Survey, Internet site http://www.bls.gov/cex/; calculations by New Strategist

Householders Aged 55 to 64 Spend Slightly More than Average

The Great Recession has crimped the spending of Boomers as they approach retirement.

The spending of householders aged 55 to 64 fell 7 percent between 2006 (the year overall household spending peaked) and 2010, after adjusting for inflation. Households headed by 55-to-64-year-olds spent $50,900 in 2010—or only 6 percent more than the average household. The age group's spending fell because many lost their jobs during the Great Recession and had to make do on one income or retire earlier than they had once planned.

Typically, householders aged 55 to 64 are the biggest spenders on travel. In 2010, households in the age group spent 47 percent more than average on other lodging, a category that includes hotels and motels. They spent 11 percent more on public transportation, much of which is airfare. They spend well more than average on gifts for people in other households and on household furnishings, many of them helping their grown children outfit their homes. Health care expenses rise in this age group, and 55-to-64-year-olds spend 37 percent more than the average household on drugs and 31 percent more on medical services.

■ The spending of householders aged 55 to 64 is likely to rise as the economy recovers from the Great Recession.

Householders aged 55 to 64 spend 47 percent more than average on other lodging

(indexed spending of householders aged 55 to 64 on selected items, 2010)

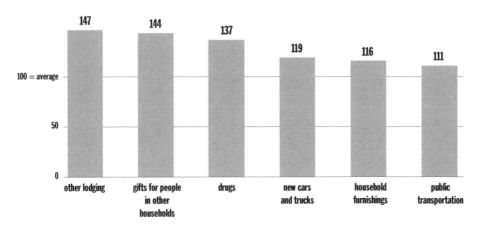

Table 9.5 Average, Indexed, and Market Share of Spending by Householders Aged 55 to 64, 2010

(average annual spending of total consumer units and average annual, indexed, and market share of spending by consumer units headed by people aged 55 to 64, 2010)

	total consumer units	consumer units headed by 55-to-64-year-olds		
		average spending	indexed spending	market share
Number of consumer units (in 000s)	121,107	21,359	–	17.6%
Average annual spending	$48,109	$50,900	106	18.7
FOOD	6,129	6,068	99	17.5
Food at home	3,624	3,681	102	17.9
Cereals and bakery products	502	507	101	17.8
Cereals and cereal products	165	159	96	17.0
Bakery products	337	347	103	18.2
Meats, poultry, fish, and eggs	784	792	101	17.8
Beef	217	223	103	18.1
Pork	149	153	103	18.1
Other meats	117	117	100	17.6
Poultry	138	123	89	15.7
Fish and seafood	117	132	113	19.9
Eggs	46	44	96	16.9
Dairy products	380	378	99	17.5
Fresh milk and cream	141	138	98	17.3
Other dairy products	240	240	100	17.6
Fruits and vegetables	679	692	102	18.0
Fresh fruits	232	243	105	18.5
Fresh vegetables	210	218	104	18.3
Processed fruits	113	112	99	17.5
Processed vegetables	124	119	96	16.9
Other food at home	1,278	1,312	103	18.1
Sugar and other sweets	132	138	105	18.4
Fats and oils	103	109	106	18.7
Miscellaneous foods	667	649	97	17.2
Nonalcoholic beverages	333	360	108	19.1
Food prepared by consumer unit on trips	43	56	130	23.0
Food away from home	2,505	2,387	95	16.8
ALCOHOLIC BEVERAGES	412	402	98	17.2
HOUSING	16,557	16,673	101	17.8
Shelter	9,812	9,397	96	16.9
Owned dwellings	6,277	6,777	108	19.0
Mortgage interest and charges	3,351	3,198	95	16.8
Property taxes	1,814	2,216	122	21.5
Maintenance, repair, insurance, other expenses	1,112	1,362	122	21.6
Rented dwellings	2,900	1,689	58	10.3
Other lodging	635	931	147	25.9
Utilities, fuels, and public services	3,660	3,979	109	19.2
Natural gas	440	456	104	18.3
Electricity	1,413	1,546	109	19.3
Fuel oil and other fuels	140	194	139	24.4

	total consumer units	consumer units headed by 55-to-64-year-olds		
		average spending	indexed spending	market share
Telephone	$1,178	$1,224	104	18.3%
Water and other public services	489	558	114	20.1
Household services	**1,007**	**882**	**88**	**15.4**
Personal services	340	72	21	3.7
Other household services	667	810	121	21.4
Housekeeping supplies	**612**	**717**	**117**	**20.7**
Laundry and cleaning supplies	150	157	105	18.5
Other household products	329	403	122	21.6
Postage and stationery	132	157	119	21.0
Household furnishings and equipment	**1,467**	**1,698**	**116**	**20.4**
Household textiles	102	138	135	23.9
Furniture	355	406	114	20.2
Floor coverings	36	51	142	25.0
Major appliances	209	249	119	21.0
Small appliances and miscellaneous housewares	107	149	139	24.6
Miscellaneous household equipment	657	705	107	18.9
APPAREL AND RELATED SERVICES	**1,700**	**1,571**	**92**	**16.3**
Men and boys	**382**	**370**	**97**	**17.1**
Men, aged 16 or older	304	331	109	19.2
Boys, aged 2 to 15	78	39	50	8.8
Women and girls	**663**	**614**	**93**	**16.3**
Women, aged 16 or older	562	564	100	17.7
Girls, aged 2 to 15	101	50	50	8.7
Children under age 2	**91**	**54**	**59**	**10.5**
Footwear	**303**	**292**	**96**	**17.0**
Other apparel products and services	**261**	**241**	**92**	**16.3**
TRANSPORTATION	**7,677**	**8,111**	**106**	**18.6**
Vehicle purchases	**2,588**	**2,584**	**100**	**17.6**
Cars and trucks, new	1,219	1,452	119	21.0
Cars and trucks, used	1,318	1,053	80	14.1
Gasoline and motor oil	**2,132**	**2,215**	**104**	**18.3**
Other vehicle expenses	**2,464**	**2,763**	**112**	**19.8**
Vehicle finance charges	243	248	102	18.0
Maintenance and repairs	787	894	114	20.0
Vehicle insurance	1,010	1,181	117	20.6
Vehicle rentals, leases, licenses, other charges	423	440	104	18.3
Public transportation	**493**	**548**	**111**	**19.6**
HEALTH CARE	**3,157**	**3,859**	**122**	**21.6**
Health insurance	1,831	2,110	115	20.3
Medical services	722	943	131	23.0
Drugs	485	665	137	24.2
Medical supplies	119	142	119	21.0
ENTERTAINMENT	**2,504**	**2,683**	**107**	**18.9**
Fees and admissions	581	545	94	16.5
Audio and visual equipment and services	954	1,061	111	19.6
Pets, toys, hobbies, and playground equipment	606	705	116	20.5
Other entertainment products and services	364	372	102	18.0

	total consumer units	consumer units headed by 55-to-64-year-olds		
		average spending	indexed spending	market share
PERSONAL CARE PRODUCTS AND SERVICES	$582	$599	103	18.2%
READING	100	126	126	22.2
EDUCATION	1,074	917	85	15.1
TOBACCO PRODUCTS AND SMOKING SUPPLIES	362	450	124	21.9
MISCELLANEOUS	849	1,146	135	23.8
CASH CONTRIBUTIONS	1,633	1,893	116	20.4
PERSONAL INSURANCE AND PENSIONS	5,373	6,403	119	21.0
Life and other personal insurance	318	471	148	26.1
Pensions and Social Security	5,054	5,932	117	20.7
PERSONAL TAXES	1,769	2,295	130	22.9
Federal income taxes	1,136	1,520	134	23.6
State and local income taxes	482	529	110	19.4
Other taxes	151	247	164	28.8
GIFTS FOR PEOPLE IN OTHER HOUSEHOLDS	1,029	1,484	144	25.4

Note: The Bureau of Labor Statistics uses consumer unit rather than household as the sampling unit in the Consumer Expenditure Survey. For the definition of consumer unit, see the glossary. Spending on gifts is also included in the preceding product and service categories. "—" means not applicable.
Source: Bureau of Labor Statistics, 2010 Consumer Expenditure Survey, Internet site http://www.bls.gov/cex/; calculations by New Strategist

10

Time Use

■ Men aged 45 to 54 spend an average of 4.82 hours per day working, 32 percent more than the 3.65 hours spent working by the average man. Men aged 55 to 64 spend 4 percent more time working than the average man.

■ Women aged 45 to 54 spend 3.68 hours per day working, 38 percent more than the 2.66 hours spent working by the average woman. Women aged 55 to 64 spend 16 percent more time working than the average woman.

■ People aged 55 to 64 spend 20 percent more time than the average person caring for animals and pets.

■ Women aged 55 to 64 spend 63 percent more time than the average woman caring for children in other households—mostly their grandchildren.

The Middle Aged Spend More Time at Work than at Play

Men aged 45 to 54 spend 32 percent more time than the average man at work.

Time use varies sharply by age. The middle aged are the ones who spend the most time at work and the least time at play, according to the Bureau of Labor Statistics' American Time Use Survey. On an average day, men aged 45 to 54 spend 4.82 hours working versus the 3.65 hours spent working by all men aged 15 or older. Time at work declines in the 55-to-64 age group, men of that age spending only 4 percent more time working than the average man because some men in the age group are retired.

Women aged 45 to 54 spend 38 percent more time working on an average day than all women aged 15 or older, while those aged 55 to 64 spend 16 percent more. Women aged 55 to 64 spend much more time than the average woman caring for people in other households—mostly their grandchildren and elderly parents.

■ As Boomers age, they may have less leisure time than today's elderly because many will have to postpone retirement.

Time at work peaks in middle age

(average number of hours per day men spend working, by age, 2010)

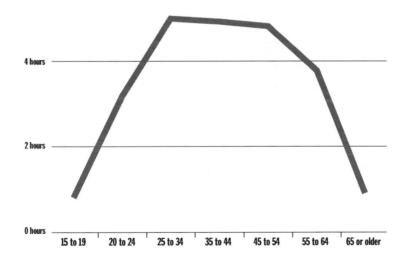

Table 10.1 Detailed Time Use of People Aged 45 to 54, 2010

(hours per day spent in primary activities by total people aged 15 or older and people aged 45 to 54, index of age group to total, and number and percent of people aged 45 to 54 participating in activity on an average day, 2010)

	average hours per day for total people	average hours per day for people aged 45 to 54	index, 45 to 54 to total	people aged 45 to 54 participating in activity number (in 000s)	percent
Total, all activities	**24.00**	**24.00**	**100**	**44,302**	**100.0%**
Personal care activities	9.45	9.00	95	44,302	100.0
Sleeping	8.67	8.26	95	44,286	100.0
Grooming	0.69	0.67	97	35,406	79.9
Health-related self-care	0.09	0.06	67	2,580	5.8
Household activities	1.82	2.04	112	36,455	82.3
Housework	0.57	0.64	112	16,890	38.1
Food preparation and cleanup	0.56	0.59	105	26,142	59.0
Lawn, garden, and houseplants	0.21	0.25	119	5,306	12.0
Animals and pets	0.10	0.12	120	8,378	18.9
Vehicles	0.04	0.04	100	1,087	2.5
Household management	0.19	0.22	116	12,621	28.5
Financial management	0.03	0.05	167	2,395	5.4
Household and personal organization and planning	0.09	0.10	111	6,460	14.6
Household and personal mail and messages (except email)	0.02	0.02	100	2,851	6.4
Household and personal email and messages	0.05	0.05	100	3,578	8.1
Caring for and helping household members	0.43	0.29	67	10,481	23.7
Caring for and helping household children	0.36	0.21	58	8,061	18.2
Caring for household adults	0.01	–	–	1,208	2.7
Helping household adults	0.01	0.02	200	1,823	4.1
Caring for and helping people in other households	0.15	0.20	133	5,497	12.4
Caring for and helping children in other households	0.07	0.10	143	2,447	5.5
Caring for adults in other households	0.01	–	–	476	1.1
Helping adults in other households	0.07	0.08	114	3,118	7.0
Working and work-related activities	3.22	4.35	135	25,184	56.8
Working	3.14	4.24	135	23,956	54.1
Job search and interviewing	0.05	0.05	100	969	2.2
Educational activities	0.45	0.09	20	938	2.1
Taking class	0.28	0.03	11	402	0.9
Homework and research	0.16	0.06	38	676	1.5
Consumer purchases	0.37	0.38	103	16,892	38.1
Grocery shopping	0.10	0.10	100	6,165	13.9
Shopping (except groceries, food, and gas)	0.24	0.25	104	9,881	22.3
Professional and personal care services	0.08	0.08	100	3,925	8.9
Medical and care services	0.05	0.04	80	1,506	3.4
Eating and drinking	1.13	1.11	98	42,412	95.7
Socializing, relaxing, and leisure	4.63	4.22	91	41,644	94.0
Socializing and communicating	0.63	0.59	94	15,267	34.5
Attending or hosting social events	0.08	0.07	88	1,021	2.3

	average hours per day for total people	average hours per day for people aged 45 to 54	index, 45 to 54 to total	people aged 45 to 54 participating in activity	
				number (in 000s)	percent
Relaxing and leisure	3.84	3.49	91	39,716	89.6%
Television and movies	2.73	2.63	96	34,792	78.5
Playing games	0.21	0.08	38	1,860	4.2
Computer use for leisure (except games)	0.20	0.14	70	4,384	9.9
Reading for personal interest	0.30	0.25	83	9,264	20.9
Arts and entertainment (other than sports)	0.08	0.06	75	1,169	2.6
Attending movies	0.03	0.01	33	169	0.4
Sports, exercise, and recreation	0.33	0.26	79	7,184	16.2
Participating in sports, exercise, and recreation	0.31	0.24	77	6,902	15.6
Attending sporting or recreational events	0.03	0.02	67	308	0.7
Religious and spiritual activities	0.16	0.18	113	4,322	9.8
Volunteer activities	0.15	0.15	100	3,095	7.0
Telephone calls	0.10	0.09	90	5,772	13.0
Traveling	1.19	1.24	104	38,447	86.8

Note: Primary activities are those respondents identified as their main activity. Other activities done simultaneously are not included. Travel related to activities is reported separately. Numbers do not sum to total because not all activities are shown. The index is calculated by dividing time spent by age group by time spent by the average person and multiplying by 100. "—" means sample is too small to make a reliable estimate.
Source: Bureau of Labor Statistics, unpublished tables from the 2010 American Time Use Survey, Internet site http://www.bls .gov/tus/home.htm; calculations by New Strategist

Table 10.2 Detailed Time Use of People Aged 55 to 64, 2010

(hours per day spent in primary activities by total people aged 15 or older and people aged 55 to 64, index of age group to total, and number and percent of people aged 55 to 64 participating in activity on an average day, 2010)

	average hours per day for total people	average hours per day for people aged 55 to 64	index, 55 to 64 to total	people aged 55 to 64 participating in activity number (in 000s)	percent
Total, all activities	24.00	24.00	100	35,890	100.0%
Personal care activities	9.45	9.36	99	35,873	100.0
Sleeping	8.67	8.50	98	35,832	99.8
Grooming	0.69	0.65	94	28,211	78.6
Health-related self-care	0.09	0.19	211	3,449	9.6
Household activities	1.82	2.12	116	29,422	82.0
Housework	0.57	0.58	102	12,876	35.9
Food preparation and cleanup	0.56	0.63	113	21,208	59.1
Lawn, garden, and houseplants	0.21	0.32	152	4,930	13.7
Animals and pets	0.10	0.12	120	7,240	20.2
Vehicles	0.04	0.02	50	671	1.9
Household management	0.19	0.25	132	11,014	30.7
Financial management	0.03	0.04	133	1,876	5.2
Household and personal organization and planning	0.09	0.10	111	5,557	15.5
Household and personal mail and messages (except email)	0.02	0.03	150	3,134	8.7
Household and personal email and messages	0.05	0.07	140	3,449	9.6
Caring for and helping household members	0.43	0.09	21	3,429	9.6
Caring for and helping household children	0.36	0.05	14	1,627	4.5
Caring for household adults	0.01	0.03	300	905	2.5
Helping household adults	0.01	0.01	100	1,099	3.1
Caring for and helping people in other households	0.15	0.19	127	4,891	13.6
Caring for and helping children in other households	0.07	0.10	143	1,953	5.4
Caring for adults in other households	0.01	0.02	200	392	1.1
Helping adults in other households	0.07	0.07	100	3,017	8.4
Working and work-related activities	3.22	3.53	110	17,753	49.5
Working	3.14	3.42	109	16,669	46.4
Job search and interviewing	0.05	0.05	100	617	1.7
Educational activities	0.45	0.05	11	507	1.4
Taking class	0.28	0.01	4	190	0.5
Homework and research	0.16	0.04	25	366	1.0
Consumer purchases	0.37	0.41	111	14,310	39.9
Grocery shopping	0.10	0.12	120	6,093	17.0
Shopping (except groceries, food, and gas)	0.24	0.26	108	7,751	21.6
Professional and personal care services	0.08	0.09	113	3,018	8.4
Medical and care services	0.05	0.06	120	1,514	4.2
Eating and drinking	1.13	1.18	104	34,679	96.6
Socializing, relaxing, and leisure	4.63	4.75	103	34,278	95.5
Socializing and communicating	0.63	0.54	86	12,110	33.7
Attending or hosting social events	0.08	0.05	63	681	1.9

	average hours per day for total people	average hours per day for people aged 55 to 64	index, 55 to 64 to total	people aged 55 to 64 participating in activity	
				number (in 000s)	percent
Relaxing and leisure	3.84	4.09	107	33,532	93.4%
Television and movies	2.73	3.03	111	30,361	84.6
Playing games	0.21	0.15	71	2,653	7.4
Computer use for leisure (except games)	0.20	0.16	80	3,588	10.0
Reading for personal interest	0.30	0.37	123	10,177	28.4
Arts and entertainment (other than sports)	0.08	0.07	88	947	2.6
Attending movies	0.03	0.02	67	287	0.8
Sports, exercise, and recreation	0.33	0.27	82	6,473	18.0
Participating in sports, exercise, and recreation	0.31	0.26	84	6,194	17.3
Attending sporting or recreational events	0.03	0.02	67	254	0.7
Religious and spiritual activities	0.16	0.18	113	3,937	11.0
Volunteer activities	0.15	0.16	107	2,412	6.7
Telephone calls	0.10	0.10	100	5,414	15.1
Traveling	1.19	1.20	101	29,742	82.9

Note: Primary activities are those respondents identified as their main activity. Other activities done simultaneously are not included. Travel related to activities is reported separately. Numbers do not sum to total because not all activities are shown. The index is calculated by dividing time spent by age group by time spent by the average person and multiplying by 100. "–" means sample is too small to make a reliable estimate.
Source: Bureau of Labor Statistics, unpublished tables from the 2010 American Time Use Survey, Internet site http://www.bls .gov/tus/home.htm; calculations by New Strategist

Table 10.3 Detailed Time Use of Men Aged 45 to 54, 2010

(hours per day spent in primary activities by total men aged 15 or older and men aged 45 to 54, index of age group to total, and number and percent of men aged 45 to 54 participating in activity on an average day, 2010)

	average hours per day for total men	average hours per day for men aged 45 to 54	index, 45 to 54 to total	men aged 45 to 54 participating in activity number (in 000s)	percent
Total, all activities	**24.00**	**24.00**	**100**	**21,715**	**100.0%**
Personal care activities	9.24	8.78	95	21,715	100.0
Sleeping	8.56	8.15	95	21,707	100.0
Grooming	0.58	0.56	97	16,456	75.8
Health-related self-care	0.08	–	–	917	4.2
Household activities	1.44	1.63	113	16,451	75.8
Housework	0.26	0.28	108	4,731	21.8
Food preparation and cleanup	0.32	0.37	116	10,159	46.8
Lawn, garden, and houseplants	0.31	0.37	119	3,266	15.0
Animals and pets	0.08	0.11	138	3,443	15.9
Vehicles	0.08	0.07	88	889	4.1
Household management	0.16	0.16	100	4,741	21.8
Financial management	0.02	0.03	150	767	3.5
Household and personal organization and planning	0.07	0.08	114	2,192	10.1
Household and personal mail and messages (except email)	0.01	0.01	100	1,000	4.6
Household and personal email and messages	0.05	0.04	80	1,424	6.6
Caring for and helping household members	0.28	0.22	79	4,143	19.1
Caring for and helping household children	0.23	0.18	78	3,323	15.3
Caring for household adults	0.01	0.00	0	270	1.2
Helping household adults	0.01	–	–	659	3.0
Caring for and helping people in other households	0.14	0.15	107	2,067	9.5
Caring for and helping children in other households	0.05	0.06	120	772	3.6
Caring for adults in other households	–	0.00		94	0.4
Helping adults in other households	0.08	0.08	100	1,323	6.1
Working and work-related activities	3.75	4.94	132	13,607	62.7
Working	3.65	4.82	132	12,785	58.9
Job search and interviewing	0.06	0.08	133	699	3.2
Educational activities	0.44	–	–	234	1.1
Taking class	0.30	0.00	0	154	0.7
Homework and research	0.13	0.00	0	61	0.3
Consumer purchases	0.30	0.29	97	7,069	32.6
Grocery shopping	0.08	0.08	100	2,106	9.7
Shopping (except groceries, food, and gas)	0.19	0.19	100	4,086	18.8
Professional and personal care services	0.06	0.06	100	1,393	6.4
Medical and care services	0.04	0.04	100	425	2.0
Eating and drinking	1.17	1.16	99	21,007	96.7
Socializing, relaxing, and leisure	4.88	4.45	91	20,501	94.4
Socializing and communicating	0.61	0.51	84	6,743	31.1
Attending or hosting social events	0.07	0.08	114	492	2.3

	average hours per day for total men	average hours per day for men aged 45 to 54	index, 45 to 54 to total	men aged 45 to 54 participating in activity	
				number (in 000s)	percent
Relaxing and leisure	4.11	3.79	92	19,586	90.2%
Television and movies	2.94	2.95	100	17,199	79.2
Playing games	0.27	0.08	30	769	3.5
Computer use for leisure (except games)	0.20	0.14	70	1,954	9.0
Reading for personal interest	0.25	0.21	84	3,817	17.6
Arts and entertainment (other than sports)	0.09	0.06	67	514	2.4
Attending movies	0.03	0.00	0	18	0.1
Sports, exercise, and recreation	0.45	0.34	76	3,941	18.1
Participating in sports, exercise, and recreation	0.42	0.32	76	3,774	17.4
Attending sporting or recreational events	0.03	0.02	67	167	0.8
Religious and spiritual activities	0.13	0.16	123	1,812	8.3
Volunteer activities	0.12	0.15	125	1,437	6.6
Telephone calls	0.07	0.04	57	1,612	7.4
Traveling	1.22	1.23	101	18,793	86.5

Note: Primary activities are those respondents identified as their main activity. Other activities done simultaneously are not included. Travel related to activities is reported separately. Numbers do not sum to total because not all activities are shown. The index is calculated by dividing time spent by age group by time spent by the average man and multiplying by 100. "–" means sample is too small to make a reliable estimate.
Source: Bureau of Labor Statistics, unpublished tables from the 2010 American Time Use Survey, Internet site http://www.bls .gov/tus/home.htm; calculations by New Strategist

Table 10.4 Detailed Time Use of Men Aged 55 to 64, 2010

(hours per day spent in primary activities by total men aged 15 or older and men aged 55 to 64, index of age group to total, and number and percent of men aged 55 to 64 participating in activity on an average day, 2010)

	average hours per day for total men	average hours per day for men aged 55 to 64	index, 55 to 64 to total	men aged 55 to 64 participating in activity number (in 000s)	percent
Total, all activities	**24.00**	**24.00**	**100**	**17,293**	**100.0%**
Personal care activities	9.24	9.20	100	17,293	100.0
Sleeping	8.56	8.51	99	17,293	100.0
Grooming	0.58	0.55	95	12,773	73.9
Health-related self-care	0.08	–	–	1,390	8.0
Household activities	1.44	1.72	119	13,074	75.6
Housework	0.26	0.26	100	3,688	21.3
Food preparation and cleanup	0.32	0.39	122	7,657	44.3
Lawn, garden, and houseplants	0.31	0.46	148	2,853	16.5
Animals and pets	0.08	0.11	138	2,772	16.0
Vehicles	0.08	0.04	50	586	3.4
Household management	0.16	0.19	119	4,272	24.7
Financial management	0.02	0.03	150	600	3.5
Household and personal organization and planning	0.07	0.07	100	1,972	11.4
Household and personal mail and messages (except email)	0.01	0.03	300	1,149	6.6
Household and personal email and messages	0.05	0.06	120	1,309	7.6
Caring for and helping household members	0.28	0.08	29	1,531	8.9
Caring for and helping household children	0.23	0.05	22	849	4.9
Caring for household adults	0.01	–	–	252	1.5
Helping household adults	0.01	0.01	100	520	3.0
Caring for and helping people in other households	0.14	0.16	114	1,842	10.7
Caring for and helping children in other households	0.05	0.05	100	588	3.4
Caring for adults in other households	–	0.00	–	36	0.2
Helping adults in other households	0.08	0.10	125	1,243	7.2
Working and work-related activities	3.75	3.96	106	9,343	54.0
Working	3.65	3.78	104	8,629	49.9
Job search and interviewing	0.06	0.08	133	432	2.5
Educational activities	0.44	0.06	14	246	1.4
Taking class	0.30	0.00	0	73	0.4
Homework and research	0.13	0.05	38	201	1.2
Consumer purchases	0.30	0.30	100	6,187	35.8
Grocery shopping	0.08	0.09	113	2,524	14.6
Shopping (except groceries, food, and gas)	0.19	0.19	100	3,035	17.6
Professional and personal care services	0.06	0.07	117	1,001	5.8
Medical and care services	0.04	0.05	125	380	2.2
Eating and drinking	1.17	1.26	108	16,863	97.5
Socializing, relaxing, and leisure	4.88	4.95	101	16,605	96.0
Socializing and communicating	0.61	0.46	75	5,069	29.3
Attending or hosting social events	0.07	–	–	170	1.0

	average hours per day for total men	average hours per day for men aged 55 to 64	index, 55 to 64 to total	men aged 55 to 64 participating in activity	
				number (in 000s)	percent
Relaxing and leisure	4.11	4.37	106	16,184	93.6%
Television and movies	2.94	3.34	114	14,911	86.2
Playing games	0.27	0.14	52	950	5.5
Computer use for leisure (except games)	0.20	0.16	80	1,641	9.5
Reading for personal interest	0.25	0.32	128	4,482	25.9
Arts and entertainment (other than sports)	0.09	0.09	100	441	2.6
Attending movies	0.03	0.00	0	127	0.7
Sports, exercise, and recreation	0.45	0.38	84	3,580	20.7
Participating in sports, exercise, and recreation	0.42	0.35	83	3,406	19.7
Attending sporting or recreational events	0.03	–	–	174	1.0
Religious and spiritual activities	0.13	0.14	108	1,502	8.7
Volunteer activities	0.12	0.12	100	768	4.4
Telephone calls	0.07	0.06	86	1,833	10.6
Traveling	1.22	1.25	102	14,583	84.3

Note: Primary activities are those respondents identified as their main activity. Other activities done simultaneously are not included. Travel related to activities is reported separately. Numbers do not sum to total because not all activities are shown. The index is calculated by dividing time spent by age group by time spent by the average man and multiplying by 100. "–" means sample is too small to make a reliable estimate.
Source: Bureau of Labor Statistics, unpublished tables from the 2010 American Time Use Survey, Internet site http://www.bls.gov/tus/home.htm; calculations by New Strategist

Table 10.5 Detailed Time Use of Women Aged 45 to 54, 2010

(hours per day spent in primary activities by total women aged 15 or older and women aged 45 to 54, index of age group to total, and number and percent of women aged 45 to 54 participating in activity on an average day, 2010)

	average hours per day for total women	average hours per day for women aged 45 to 54	index, 45 to 54 to total	women aged 45 to 54 participating in activity	
				number (in 000s)	percent
Total, all activities	**24.00**	**24.00**	**100**	**22,587**	**100.0%**
Personal care activities	9.66	9.21	95	22,587	100.0
Sleeping	8.76	8.36	95	22,578	100.0
Grooming	0.79	0.77	97	18,951	83.9
Health-related self-care	0.10	–	–	1,662	7.4
Household activities	2.18	2.43	111	20,004	88.6
Housework	0.87	0.99	114	12,159	53.8
Food preparation and cleanup	0.79	0.81	103	15,984	70.8
Lawn, garden, and houseplants	0.12	0.13	108	2,040	9.0
Animals and pets	0.11	0.14	127	4,935	21.8
Vehicles	0.01	–	–	198	0.9
Household management	0.22	0.29	132	7,880	34.9
Financial management	0.04	0.07	175	1,628	7.2
Household and personal organization and planning	0.11	0.12	109	4,269	18.9
Household and personal mail and messages (except email)	0.03	0.03	100	1,850	8.2
Household and personal email and messages	0.05	0.06	120	2,153	9.5
Caring for and helping household members	0.58	0.36	62	6,338	28.1
Caring for and helping household children	0.48	0.24	50	4,738	21.0
Caring for household adults	0.02	–	–	938	4.2
Helping household adults	0.01	0.02	200	1,164	5.2
Caring for and helping people in other households	0.16	0.26	163	3,430	15.2
Caring for and helping children in other households	0.08	0.13	163	1,675	7.4
Caring for adults in other households	0.02	–	–	382	1.7
Helping adults in other households	0.06	0.08	133	1,795	7.9
Working and work-related activities	2.73	3.78	138	11,577	51.3
Working	2.66	3.68	138	11,171	49.5
Job search and interviewing	0.03	0.03	100	270	1.2
Educational activities	0.45	0.15	33	704	3.1
Taking class	0.26	0.04	15	248	1.1
Homework and research	0.18	0.11	61	615	2.7
Consumer purchases	0.44	0.47	107	9,823	43.5
Grocery shopping	0.13	0.13	100	4,060	18.0
Shopping (except groceries, food, and gas)	0.28	0.30	107	5,795	25.7
Professional and personal care services	0.10	0.10	100	2,531	11.2
Medical and care services	0.06	0.05	83	1,081	4.8
Eating and drinking	1.09	1.05	96	21,406	94.8
Socializing, relaxing, and leisure	4.39	4.00	91	21,143	93.6
Socializing and communicating	0.65	0.68	105	8,524	37.7
Attending or hosting social events	0.08	0.06	75	529	2.3

	average hours per day for total women	average hours per day for women aged 45 to 54	index, 45 to 54 to total	women aged 45 to 54 participating in activity	
				number (in 000s)	percent
Relaxing and leisure	3.59	3.19	89	20,130	89.1%
Television and movies	2.52	2.33	92	17,593	77.9
Playing games	0.15	0.08	53	1,090	4.8
Computer use for leisure (except games)	0.19	0.14	74	2,429	10.8
Reading for personal interest	0.35	0.29	83	5,447	24.1
Arts and entertainment (other than sports)	0.08	0.07	88	655	2.9
Attending movies	0.03	0.01	33	150	0.7
Sports, exercise, and recreation	0.23	0.18	78	3,242	14.4
Participating in sports, exercise, and recreation	0.20	0.16	80	3,128	13.8
Attending sporting or recreational events	0.03	0.02	67	140	0.6
Religious and spiritual activities	0.18	0.19	106	2,510	11.1
Volunteer activities	0.18	0.14	78	1,658	7.3
Telephone calls	0.13	0.13	100	4,160	18.4
Traveling	1.16	1.25	108	19,654	87.0

Note: Primary activities are those respondents identified as their main activity. Other activities done simultaneously are not included. Travel related to activities is reported separately. Numbers do not sum to total because not all activities are shown. The index is calculated by dividing time spent by age group by time spent by the average woman and multiplying by 100. "–" means sample is too small to make a reliable estimate.
Source: Bureau of Labor Statistics, unpublished tables from the 2010 American Time Use Survey, Internet site http://www.bls.gov/tus/home.htm; calculations by New Strategist

Table 10.6 Detailed Time Use of Women Aged 55 to 64, 2010

(hours per day spent in primary activities by total women aged 15 or older and women aged 55 to 64, index of age group to total, and number and percent of women aged 55 to 64 participating in activity on an average day, 2010)

	average hours per day for total women	average hours per day for women aged 55 to 64	index, 55 to 64 to total	women aged 55 to 64 participating in activity number (in 000s)	percent
Total, all activities	**24.00**	**24.00**	**100**	**18,597**	**100.0%**
Personal care activities	9.66	9.51	98	18,580	99.9
Sleeping	8.76	8.49	97	18,539	99.7
Grooming	0.79	0.76	96	15,438	83.0
Health-related self-care	0.10	0.26	260	2,059	11.1
Household activities	2.18	2.50	115	16,348	87.9
Housework	0.87	0.88	101	9,188	49.4
Food preparation and cleanup	0.79	0.85	108	13,551	72.9
Lawn, garden, and houseplants	0.12	0.20	167	2,077	11.2
Animals and pets	0.11	0.14	127	4,468	24.0
Vehicles	0.01	0.00	0	85	0.5
Household management	0.22	0.30	136	6,742	36.3
Financial management	0.04	0.05	125	1,275	6.9
Household and personal organization and planning	0.11	0.13	118	3,585	19.3
Household and personal mail and messages (except email)	0.03	0.03	100	1,985	10.7
Household and personal email and messages	0.05	0.08	160	2,139	11.5
Caring for and helping household members	0.58	0.11	19	1,898	10.2
Caring for and helping household children	0.48	0.05	10	778	4.2
Caring for household adults	0.02	0.04	200	652	3.5
Helping household adults	0.01	0.01	100	579	3.1
Caring for and helping people in other households	0.16	0.22	138	3,049	16.4
Caring for and helping children in other households	0.08	0.13	163	1,365	7.3
Caring for adults in other households	0.02	0.03	150	356	1.9
Helping adults in other households	0.06	0.05	83	1,773	9.5
Working and work-related activities	2.73	3.13	115	8,411	45.2
Working	2.66	3.08	116	8,040	43.2
Job search and interviewing	0.03	0.03	100	186	1.0
Educational activities	0.45	0.05	11	261	1.4
Taking class	0.26	0.00	0	117	0.6
Homework and research	0.18	0.03	17	164	0.9
Consumer purchases	0.44	0.51	116	8,123	43.7
Grocery shopping	0.13	0.14	108	3,569	19.2
Shopping (except groceries, food, and gas)	0.28	0.33	118	4,716	25.4
Professional and personal care services	0.10	0.12	120	2,017	10.8
Medical and care services	0.06	0.08	133	1,134	6.1
Eating and drinking	1.09	1.11	102	17,816	95.8
Socializing, relaxing, and leisure	4.39	4.57	104	17,672	95.0
Socializing and communicating	0.65	0.62	95	7,041	37.9
Attending or hosting social events	0.08	0.07	88	511	2.7

	average hours per day for total women	average hours per day for women aged 55 to 64	index, 55 to 64 to total	women aged 55 to 64 participating in activity	
				number (in 000s)	percent
Relaxing and leisure	3.59	3.83	107	17,348	93.3%
Television and movies	2.52	2.74	109	15,450	83.1
Playing games	0.15	0.16	107	1,704	9.2
Computer use for leisure (except games)	0.19	0.16	84	1,947	10.5
Reading for personal interest	0.35	0.42	120	5,696	30.6
Arts and entertainment (other than sports)	0.08	0.05	63	506	2.7
Attending movies	0.03	0.02	67	161	0.9
Sports, exercise, and recreation	0.23	0.18	78	2,893	15.6
Participating in sports, exercise, and recreation	0.20	0.17	85	2,788	15.0
Attending sporting or recreational events	0.03	0.00	0	80	0.4
Religious and spiritual activities	0.18	0.22	122	2,435	13.1
Volunteer activities	0.18	0.20	111	1,645	8.8
Telephone calls	0.13	0.14	108	3,581	19.3
Traveling	1.16	1.14	98	15,159	81.5

Note: Primary activities are those respondents identified as their main activity. Other activities done simultaneously are not included. Travel related to activities is reported separately. Numbers do not sum to total because not all activities are shown. The index is calculated by dividing time spent by age group by time spent by the average woman and multiplying by 100. Source: Bureau of Labor Statistics, unpublished tables from the 2010 American Time Use Survey, Internet site http://www.bls .gov/tus/home.htm; calculations by New Strategist

11

Wealth

■ Median household net worth peaks among householders aged 55 to 64—at $222,300 in 2009. This figure is 14 percent below the $257,700 of 2007. The median net worth of householders aged 45 to 54 fell by an even larger 26 percent during those years.

■ The median financial assets of householders ranging in age from 45 to 64 fell by 7 to 9 percent between 2007 and 2009, after adjusting for inflation. Losses in the stock market and in the value of retirement accounts were behind the decline.

■ Householders aged 55 to 64 have more nonfinancial assets than any other age group—a median of $308,000 in 2009. The median value of their nonfinancial assets fell 15 percent between 2007 and 2009, after adjusting for inflation.

■ Boomers reduced their debt between 2007 and 2009. The median amount owed by householders aged 45 to 64 fell 3 to 4 percent during those years, after adjusting for inflation. The percentage of Boomer households with debt also fell slightly.

■ Boomers are worried about retirement. In 2012, only 12 to 16 percent of workers aged 45 or older were "very confident" they would have enough money to live comfortably throughout retirement.

Net Worth Fell Sharply during the Great Recession

Every age group lost ground during the economic downturn.

Net worth is what remains when a household's debts are subtracted from its assets. During the Great Recession, which officially lasted from December 2007 until June 2009, the value of houses, stocks, and retirement accounts fell sharply. At the same time, debt increased. Consequently, net worth fell 23 percent between 2007 and 2009, after adjusting for inflation. These data come from a unique follow-up to the 2007 Survey of Consumer Finances. The survey is taken only every three years. Because of the severity of the Great Recession, however, the Federal Reserve Board arranged for the 2007 respondents to be re-interviewed in 2009 to determine the impact of the Great Recession on household assets, debt, and net worth.

The impact was severe. Net worth fell in every age group. It declined the most—by 37 percent—among householders under age 35, many of them recent homebuyers who bought at the peak. It fell by the smallest percentage, 12 percent, among householders aged 65 to 74, many of whom bought their house decades ago.

■ Net worth typically rises with age as people pay off their debts. That pattern has not changed. In 2009, median household net worth peaked in the 55-to-64 age group at $222,300.

Net worth peaks among householders aged 55 to 64

(median household net worth by age of householder, 2009)

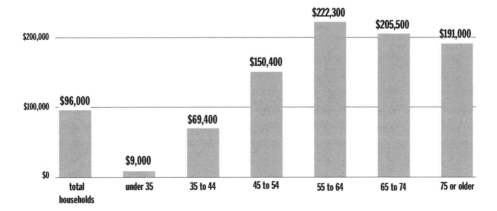

Table 11.1 Net Worth of Households, 2007 and 2009

(median net worth of households by age of householder, 2007 and 2009; percent change, 2007–09; in 2009 dollars)

	2009	2007	percent change
Total households	**$96,000**	**$125,400**	**–23.4%**
Under age 35	9,000	14,200	–36.6
Aged 35 to 44	69,400	97,100	–28.5
Aged 45 to 54	150,400	203,000	–25.9
Aged 55 to 64	222,300	257,700	–13.7
Aged 65 to 74	205,500	232,700	–11.7
Aged 75 or older	191,000	228,900	–16.6

Source: Federal Reserve Board, 2007–09 Panel Survey of Consumer Finances, Internet site http://www.federalreserve.gov/econresdata/scf/scf_2009p.htm; calculations by New Strategist

Financial Asset Value Declined in Most Age Groups

Householders aged 35 to 44 gained ground, however.

Most households own financial assets, which range from transaction accounts (checking and saving) to stocks, mutual funds, retirement accounts, and life insurance. The median value of the financial assets owned by the average household stood at $29,600 in 2009, down by a relatively modest 5 percent since 2007 after adjusting for inflation. Householders aged 35 to 44 were the only ones to make gains in the value of their financial assets between 2007 and 2009.

Transaction accounts, the most commonly owned financial asset, are held by 92 percent of households. Their median value was just $4,000 in 2009—slightly lower than the $4,100 of 2007. Retirement accounts are the second most commonly owned financial asset, with 56 percent of households having one. Most retirement accounts are not large, however, with an overall median value of just $48,000 in 2009. This figure is 5 percent lower than the $50,600 of 2007, after adjusting for inflation.

Only 18.5 percent of households owned stock directly in 2009 (outside of a retirement account). The median value of stock owned by stockholding households was just $12,000 in 2009, 35 percent less than the value in 2007 after adjusting for inflation.

■ The median value of household financial assets peaks in the 55-to-64 age group, at $72,500.

The value of retirement accounts is modest, even in the older age groups

(median value of retirement accounts owned by households, by age of householder, 2009)

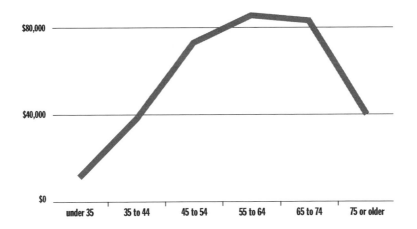

Table 11.2 Ownership and Value of Financial Assets, 2007 and 2009

(percentage of households owning any financial asset and median value of financial assets for owners, by age of householder, 2007 and 2009; percentage point change in ownership and percent change in value, 2007–09; in 2009 dollars)

	2009	2007	percentage point change
PERCENT OWNING			
Total households	**94.6%**	**94.3%**	**0.3**
Under age 35	91.4	90.2	1.2
Aged 35 to 44	92.3	93.5	–1.2
Aged 45 to-54	96.0	94.1	1.9
Aged 55 to 64	97.0	97.9	–0.9
Aged 65 to 74	97.8	96.1	1.7
Aged 75 or older	95.8	98.1	–2.3

	2009	2007	percent change
MEDIAN VALUE			
Total households	**$29,600**	**$31,300**	**–5.4%**
Under age 35	7,400	7,400	0.0
Aged 35 to 44	27,500	25,500	7.8
Aged 45 to 54	58,500	64,300	–9.0
Aged 55 to 64	72,500	78,200	–7.3
Aged 65 to 74	48,000	63,900	–24.9
Aged 75 or older	39,000	41,400	–5.8

Source: Federal Reserve Board, 2007–09 Panel Survey of Consumer Finances, Internet site http://www.federalreserve.gov/econresdata/scf/scf_2009p.htm; calculations by New Strategist

Table 11.3 Households Owning Transaction Accounts, Life Insurance, and CDs, 2007 and 2009

(percentage of households owning transaction accounts, cash value life insurance, and certificates of deposit, and median value for owners, by age of householder, 2007 and 2009; percentage point change in ownership and percent change in value, 2007–09; in 2009 dollars)

	transaction accounts			cash value life insurance			certificates of deposit		
	2009	2007	percentage point change	2009	2007	percentage point change	2009	2007	percentage point change
PERCENT OWNING									
Total households	**92.3%**	**92.6%**	**−0.3**	**24.3%**	**23.2%**	**1.1**	**15.9%**	**15.4%**	**0.5**
Under age 35	88.5	88.0	0.5	13.1	12.4	0.7	7.9	6.5	1.4
Aged 35 to 44	89.8	91.8	−2.0	16.8	17.1	−0.3	9.4	8.9	0.5
Aged 45 to 54	94.1	92.8	1.3	25.3	22.0	3.3	13.9	14.5	−0.6
Aged 55 to 64	95.3	96.5	−1.2	33.4	35.7	−2.3	20.2	19.5	0.7
Aged 65 to 74	95.0	95.0	0.0	36.3	34.6	1.7	24.8	23.0	1.8
Aged 75 or older	94.2	95.1	−0.9	34.2	29.2	5.0	35.2	36.8	−1.6

	transaction accounts			cash value life insurance			certificates of deposit		
	2009	2007	percent change	2009	2007	percent change	2009	2007	percent change
MEDIAN VALUE									
Total households	**$4,000**	**$4,100**	**−2.4%**	**$7,300**	**$8,300**	**−12.0%**	**$20,000**	**$20,700**	**−3.4%**
Under age 35	2,300	2,600	−11.5	2,500	3,600	−30.6	9,000	4,900	83.7
Aged 35 to 44	3,000	3,500	−14.3	7,000	8,300	−15.7	10,000	5,200	92.3
Aged 45 to 54	5,000	4,800	4.2	8,000	10,400	−23.1	18,000	18,600	−3.2
Aged 55 to 64	5,500	5,600	−1.8	10,000	10,400	−3.8	25,000	20,700	20.8
Aged 65 to 74	5,500	7,000	−21.4	10,000	10,600	−5.7	27,700	22,800	21.5
Aged 75 or older	7,000	6,200	12.9	8,000	5,200	53.8	31,400	31,100	1.0

Source: Federal Reserve Board, 2007–09 Panel Survey of Consumer Finances, Internet site http://www.federalreserve.gov/econresdata/scf/scf_2009p.htm; calculations by New Strategist

Table 11.4 Households Owning Retirement Accounts and Stocks, 2007 and 2009

(percentage of households owning retirement accounts and stocks, and median value for owners, by age of householder, 2007 and 2009; percentage point change in ownership and percent change in value, 2007–09; in 2009 dollars)

	retirement accounts			stocks		
	2009	2007	percentage point change	2009	2007	percentage point change
PERCENT OWNING						
Total households	**56.2%**	**55.6%**	**0.6**	**18.5%**	**18.4%**	**0.1**
Under age 35	48.4	44.9	3.5	12.6	14.6	−2.0
Aged 35 to 44	61.2	59.4	1.8	18.9	17.0	1.9
Aged 45 to 54	68.2	68.0	0.2	20.3	18.4	1.9
Aged 55 to 64	62.7	64.3	−1.6	21.3	21.2	0.1
Aged 65 to 74	51.8	53.3	−1.5	21.9	21.0	0.9
Aged 75 or older	29.5	31.3	−1.8	18.6	22.8	−4.2

	retirement accounts			stocks		
	2009	2007	percent change	2009	2007	percent change
MEDIAN VALUE						
Total households	**$48,000**	**$50,600**	**−5.1%**	**$12,000**	**$18,500**	**−35.1%**
Under age 35	11,400	10,400	9.6	3,000	3,100	−3.2
Aged 35 to 44	38,000	38,300	−0.8	12,000	15,500	−22.6
Aged 45 to 54	73,000	81,400	−10.3	11,700	19,700	−40.6
Aged 55 to 64	85,600	103,600	−17.4	16,000	24,900	−35.7
Aged 65 to 74	83,200	79,700	4.4	25,000	36,200	−30.9
Aged 75 or older	40,000	36,200	10.5	35,000	101,500	−65.5

Note: Stock ownership is direct ownership outside of a retirement account or mutual fund.
Source: Federal Reserve Board, 2007 09 Panel Survey of Consumer Finances, Internet site http://www.federalreserve.gov/ econresdata/scf/scf_2009p.htm; calculations by New Strategist

Table 11.5 Households Owning Pooled Investment Funds and Bonds, 2007 and 2009

(percentage of households owning pooled investment funds and bonds, and median value for owners, by age of householder, 2007 and 2009; percentage point change in ownership and percent change in value, 2007–09; in 2009 dollars)

	pooled investment funds			bonds		
	2009	2007	percentage point change	2009	2007	percentage point change
PERCENT OWNING						
Total households	**10.8%**	**11.5%**	**–0.7**	**2.6%**	**1.7%**	**0.9**
Under age 35	5.4	5.8	–0.4	0.5	0.2	0.3
Aged 35 to 44	10.0	11.7	–1.7	1.3	0.7	0.6
Aged 45 to 54	13.2	12.6	0.6	2.4	1.1	1.3
Aged 55 to 64	14.5	14.1	0.4	3.3	2.4	0.9
Aged 65 to 74	11.5	13.8	–2.3	6.2	4.5	1.7
Aged 75 or older	12.6	15.1	–2.5	5.5	3.9	1.6

	pooled investment funds			bonds		
	2009	2007	percent change	2009	2007	percent change
MEDIAN VALUE						
Total households	**$47,000**	**$58,700**	**–19.9%**	**$50,000**	**$62,100**	**–19.5%**
Under age 35	10,000	15,000	–33.3	–	–	–
Aged 35 to 44	35,000	27,300	28.2	5,000	103,600	–95.2
Aged 45 to 54	35,000	51,800	–32.4	27,000	127,600	–78.8
Aged 55 to 64	70,400	115,000	–38.8	65,000	82,800	–21.5
Aged 65 to 74	100,000	155,300	–35.6	86,000	51,600	66.7
Aged 75 or older	70,000	77,700	–9.9	37,400	96,500	–61.2

Note: "Pooled investment funds" exclude money market funds and indirectly held mutual funds. They include open-end and closed-end mutual funds, real estate investment trusts, and hedge funds. "–" means sample is too small to make a reliable estimate.
Source: Federal Reserve Board, 2007–09 Panel Survey of Consumer Finances, Internet site http://www.federalreserve.gov/econresdata/scf/scf_2009p.htm; calculations by New Strategist

Nonfinancial Assets Are the Basis of Household Wealth

The average household saw the value of its nonfinancial assets fall during the Great Recession.

The median value of the nonfinancial assets owned by the average American household stood at $204,000 in 2009, far surpassing the $29,600 median in financial assets. Between 2007 and 2009, the value of the nonfinancial assets owned by the average household fell 13 percent, after adjusting for inflation. Nearly every age group saw its nonfinancial assets fall in value, primarily because of the decline in housing values. Householders under age 35 were the only ones who made gains.

Eighty-seven percent of households own a vehicle, the most commonly held nonfinancial asset. The value of the vehicles owned by the average household fell steeply (down 26 percent) between 2007 and 2009, after adjusting for inflation. Behind the decline was the reluctance of households to buy new vehicles during the Great Recession.

The second most commonly owned nonfinancial asset is a home, owned by 70 percent. Homes are by far the most valuable asset owned by Americans, and they account for the largest share of net worth. In 2009, the median value of the average owned home was $176,000, 15 percent below the median of $207,100 in 2007 (in 2009 dollars). Housing prices have continued to decline, driving median home values even lower than the numbers shown here.

■ The continuing decline in housing values may have reduced average household net worth below the 2009 figure.

Median housing value peaks in the 45-to-54 age group

(median value of the primary residence among homeowners, by age of householder, 2009)

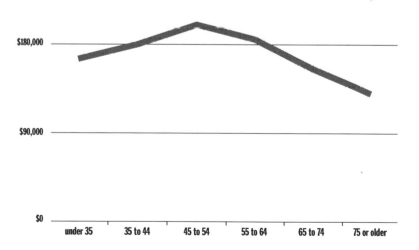

Table 11.6 Ownership and Value of Nonfinancial Assets, 2007 and 2009

(percentage of households owning any nonfinancial asset and median value of nonfinancial assets for owners, by age of householder, 2007 and 2009; percentage point change in ownership and percent change in value, 2007–09; in 2009 dollars)

	2009	2007	percentage point change
PERCENT OWNING			
Total households	**92.6%**	**92.7%**	**–0.1**
Under age 35	89.5	88.1	1.4
Aged 35 to 44	92.3	91.8	0.5
Aged 45 to 54	95.0	95.2	–0.2
Aged 55 to 64	95.5	96.1	–0.6
Aged 65 to 74	96.0	95.3	0.7
Aged 75 or older	86.2	90.4	–4.2

	2009	2007	percent change
MEDIAN VALUE			
Total households	**$204,000**	**$234,800**	**–13.1%**
Under age 35	52,800	44,400	18.9
Aged 35 to 44	196,500	232,000	–15.3
Aged 45 to 54	289,500	326,600	–11.4
Aged 55 to 64	308,000	361,900	–14.9
Aged 65 to 74	253,000	306,200	–17.4
Aged 75 or older	193,100	238,900	–19.2

Source: Federal Reserve Board, 2007–09 Panel Survey of Consumer Finances, Internet site http://www.federalreserve.gov/econresdata/scf/scf_2009p.htm; calculations by New Strategist

Table 11.7 Households Owning Primary Residence, Other Residential Property, and Nonresidential Property, 2007 and 2009

(percentage of households owning primary residence, other residential property, and nonresidential property, and median value for owners, by age of householder, 2007 and 2009; percentage point change in ownership and percent change in value, 2007–09; in 2009 dollars)

	primary residence			other residential property			nonresidential property		
	2009	2007	percentage point change	2009	2007	percentage point change	2009	2007	percentage point change
PERCENT OWNING									
Total households	**70.3%**	**68.9%**	**1.4**	**13.0%**	**13.9%**	**−0.9**	**7.6%**	**8.3%**	**−0.7**
Under age 35	44.6	40.5	4.1	7.1	5.3	1.8	3.1	3.1	0.0
Aged 35 to 44	68.9	66.6	2.3	11.4	12.5	−1.1	7.0	7.9	−0.9
Aged 45 to 54	78.1	77.3	0.8	14.4	15.5	−1.1	9.5	10.0	−0.5
Aged 55 to 64	81.9	82.2	−0.3	18.6	21.0	−2.4	10.9	11.5	−0.6
Aged 65 to 74	86.8	85.5	1.3	17.9	19.2	−1.3	11.1	10.9	0.2
Aged 75 or older	77.2	79.2	−2.0	11.2	14.3	−3.1	5.7	9.0	−3.3

	primary residence			other residential property			nonresidential property		
	2009	2007	percent change	2009	2007	percent change	2009	2007	percent change
MEDIAN VALUE									
Total households	**$176,000**	**$207,100**	**−15.0%**	**$150,000**	**$141,700**	**5.9%**	**$69,000**	**$78,800**	**−12.4%**
Under age 35	165,000	186,400	−11.5	100,000	62,100	61.0	30,000	51,800	−42.1
Aged 35 to 44	180,000	212,300	−15.2	155,700	155,300	0.3	28,600	59,000	−51.5
Aged 45 to 54	200,000	238,200	−16.0	176,000	163,800	7.4	90,000	79,000	13.9
Aged 55 to 64	185,000	207,100	−10.7	150,000	155,300	−3.4	100,000	103,600	−3.5
Aged 65 to 74	155,000	191,600	−19.1	149,500	139,800	6.9	100,000	103,600	−3.5
Aged 75 or older	130,000	155,300	−16.3	160,000	103,600	54.4	60,000	103,600	−42.1

Source: Federal Reserve Board, 2007–09 Panel Survey of Consumer Finances, Internet site http://www.federalreserve.gov/econresdata/scf/scf_2009p.htm; calculations by New Strategist

Table 11.8 Households Owning Vehicles and Business Equity, 2007 and 2009

(percentage of households owning vehicles and business equity, and median value for owners, by age of householder, 2007 and 2009; percentage point change in ownership and percent change in value, 2007–09; in 2009 dollars)

	vehicles			business equity		
	2009	2007	percentage point change	2009	2007	percentage point change
PERCENT OWNING						
Total households	**86.8%**	**87.9%**	**−1.1**	**11.9%**	**12.4%**	**−0.5**
Under age 35	87.2	85.8	1.4	7.7	7.1	0.6
Aged 35 to 44	87.6	87.9	−0.3	15.4	15.8	−0.4
Aged 45 to 54	90.6	91.1	−0.5	15.0	15.1	−0.1
Aged 55 to 64	90.5	92.5	−2.0	15.9	17.2	−1.3
Aged 65 to 74	88.3	90.8	−2.5	9.1	10.1	−1.0
Aged 75 or older	67.6	74.3	−6.7	3.8	5.4	−1.6

	vehicles			business equity		
	2009	2007	percent change	2009	2007	percent change
MEDIAN VALUE						
Total households	**$12,000**	**$16,200**	**−25.9%**	**$94,500**	**$103,600**	**−8.8%**
Under age 35	10,500	14,500	−27.6	41,300	46,600	−11.4
Aged 35 to 44	15,000	18,100	−17.1	70,000	98,700	−29.1
Aged 45 to 54	15,000	18,600	−19.4	80,000	103,600	−22.8
Aged 55 to 64	15,000	17,800	−15.7	150,000	152,500	−1.6
Aged 65 to 74	12,000	15,200	−21.1	500,000	517,800	−3.4
Aged 75 or older	7,900	9,700	−18.6	250,000	258,900	−3.4

Source: Federal Reserve Board, 2007–09 Panel Survey of Consumer Finances, Internet site http://www.federalreserve.gov/ econresdata/scf/scf_2009p.htm; calculations by New Strategist

Most Households Are in Debt

Among households with debt, the amount owed increased between 2007 and 2009.

Seventy-eight percent of households have debt, owing a median of $75,600 in 2009. The median amount of debt owed by the average debtor household increased by 7.5 percent between 2007 and 2009, after adjusting for inflation. The percentage of households in debt fell slightly, however.

Householders aged 35 to 54 are most likely to be in debt, with 87 to 88 percent owing money. Debt declines with age, falling to a low of 35 percent among householders aged 75 or older.

Four types of debt are most common—debt secured by the primary residence (mortgages), which is held by 47 percent of households; credit card debt (43 percent); vehicle loans (34 percent); and education loans (18 percent). Mortgages account for the largest share of debt. The median amount owed by the average homeowner for the primary residence stood at $113,500 in 2009. Education loans are second in size, the average household with this type of debt owing a median of $15,000—more than the $12,400 owed by (the more-numerous) households with vehicle loans. Credit card debt is tiny by comparison, the average household with a credit card balance owing only $3,300.

■ Americans are attempting to pay down their debts, reducing consumer demand.

Education loans are common among young and middle-aged householders

(percent of households with education loans, by age of householder, 2009)

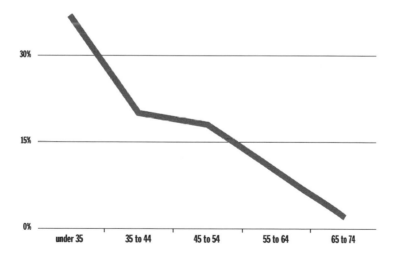

Table 11.9 Debt of Households, 2007 and 2009

(percentage of households with debt and median amount of debt for debtors, by age of householder, 2007 and 2009; percentage point change in households with debt and percent change in amount of debt, 2007–09; in 2009 dollars)

	2009	2007	percentage point change
PERCENT WITH DEBT			
Total households	**77.5%**	**79.7%**	**–2.2**
Under age 35	84.6	85.4	–0.8
Aged 35 to 44	87.7	87.3	0.4
Aged 45 to 54	86.6	88.1	–1.5
Aged 55 to 64	77.7	83.4	–5.7
Aged 65 to 74	62.1	68.5	–6.4
Aged 75 or older	35.0	36.2	–1.2

	2009	2007	percent change
MEDIAN AMOUNT OWED			
Total households	**$75,600**	**$70,300**	**7.5%**
Under age 35	51,000	37,800	34.9
Aged 35 to 44	109,500	113,700	–3.7
Aged 45 to 54	100,200	103,500	–3.2
Aged 55 to 64	62,000	64,300	–3.6
Aged 65 to 74	48,100	41,800	15.1
Aged 75 or older	8,200	20,000	–59.0

Source: Federal Reserve Board, 2007–09 Panel Survey of Consumer Finances, Internet site http://www.federalreserve .gov/'econresdata/scf/scf_2009p.htm; calculations by New Strategist

Table 11.10 Households with Residential Debt, 2007 and 2009

(percentage of households with residential debt, and median amount of debt for debtors, by age of householder, 2007 and 2009; percentage point change in households with debt and percent change in amount of debt, 2007–09; in 2009 dollars)

| | secured by residential property | | | | | | | | |
| | secured by primary residence | | | home equity line of credit | | | other residential debt | | |
	2009	2007	percentage point change	2009	2007	percentage point change	2009	2007	percentage point change
PERCENT WITH DEBT									
Total households	**46.6%**	**47.8%**	**−1.2**	**10.5%**	**8.7%**	**1.8**	**5.1%**	**5.7%**	**−0.6**
Under age 35	39.8	37.4	2.4	4.3	3.7	0.6	3.3	3.2	0.1
Aged 35 to 44	60.0	60.0	0.0	10.2	8.5	1.7	6.0	7.0	−1.0
Aged 45 to 54	62.2	64.3	−2.1	14.0	12.3	1.7	6.7	7.7	−1.0
Aged 55 to 64	46.8	51.9	−5.1	17.1	12.8	4.3	6.6	8.3	−1.7
Aged 65 to 74	34.9	37.4	−2.5	11.9	10.3	1.6	4.7	4.3	0.4
Aged 75 or older	11.5	13.4	−1.9	4.3	3.8	0.5	0.9	0.6	0.3

| | secured by residential property | | | | | | | | |
| | secured by primary residence | | | home equity line of credit | | | other residential debt | | |
	2009	2007	percent change	2009	2007	percent change	2009	2007	percent change
MEDIAN AMOUNT OWED									
Total households	**$113,500**	**$113,900**	**−0.4%**	**$21,500**	**$22,800**	**−5.7%**	**$130,000**	**$98,400**	**32.1%**
Under age 35	144,600	140,100	3.2	20,000	20,300	1.5	118,000	80,800	46.0
Aged 35 to 44	127,800	128,300	−0.4	20,000	24,900	−19.7	150,000	110,600	35.6
Aged 45 to 54	111,600	113,900	−2.0	30,000	25,900	15.8	115,000	86,000	33.7
Aged 55 to 64	95,000	93,200	1.9	20,000	21,900	−8.7	155,000	110,900	39.8
Aged 65 to 74	80,000	81,800	−2.2	28,000	15,500	80.6	115,000	116,000	−0.9
Aged 75 or older	49,000	33,900	44.5	13,000	25,900	−49.8	23,000	51,800	−55.6

Source: Federal Reserve Board, 2007–09 Panel Survey of Consumer Finances, Internet site http://www.federalreserve.gov/ econresdata/scf/scf_2009p.htm; calculations by New Strategist

Table 11.11 Households with Credit Card Debt, Vehicle Loans, and Education Loans, 2007 and 2009

(percentage of households with credit card, vehicle, and education debt, and median amount of debt for debtors, by age of householder, 2007 and 2009; percentage point change in households with debt and percent change in amount of debt, 2007–09; in 2009 dollars)

	credit card balances			vehicle loans			education loans		
	2009	2007	percentage point change	2009	2007	percentage point change	2009	2007	percentage point change
PERCENT WITH DEBT									
Total households	**43.2%**	**47.8%**	**–4.6**	**33.9%**	**36.0%**	**–2.1**	**17.7%**	**16.3%**	**1.4**
Under age 35	42.8	50.6	–7.8	43.1	46.0	–2.9	36.8	35.7	1.1
Aged 35 to 44	49.6	52.6	–3.0	44.7	44.1	0.6	19.7	15.7	4.0
Aged 45 to 54	50.5	54.1	–3.6	35.5	38.3	–2.8	18.0	14.8	3.2
Aged 55 to 64	44.6	50.4	–5.8	30.8	35.5	–4.7	9.9	11.3	–1.4
Aged 65 to 74	35.0	38.7	–3.7	21.3	21.9	–0.6	1.9	1.9	0.0
Aged 75 or older	20.2	21.8	–1.6	5.5	7.2	–1.7	0.0	0.5	–0.5

	credit card balances			vehicle loans			education loans		
	2009	2007	percent change	2009	2007	percent change	2009	2007	percent change
MEDIAN AMOUNT OWED									
Total households	**$3,300**	**$3,100**	**6.5%**	**$12,400**	**$11,200**	**10.7%**	**$15,000**	**$12,400**	**21.0%**
Under age 35	3,000	1,900	57.9	12,200	11,300	8.0	15,000	14,500	3.4
Aged 35 to 44	3,000	3,600	–16.7	13,000	12,300	5.7	16,000	12,400	29.0
Aged 45 to 54	4,000	3,700	8.1	13,000	10,900	19.3	15,000	10,700	40.2
Aged 55 to 64	4,500	4,100	9.8	12,000	9,600	25.0	12,000	7,300	64.4
Aged 65 to 74	2,900	3,200	–9.4	10,000	12,500	–20.0	–	–	–
Aged 75 or older	2,000	800	150.0	9,500	7,600	25.0	–	–	–

Note: "–" means sample is too small to make a reliable estimate.
Source: Federal Reserve Board, 2007–09 Panel Survey of Consumer Finances, Internet site http://www.federalreserve.gov/econresdata/scf/scf_2009p.htm; calculations by New Strategist

Retirement Worries Are Growing

Few workers are "very confident" in having enough money for a comfortable retirement.

Only 14 percent of workers are very confident in their ability to afford a comfortable retirement, according to the 2012 Retirement Confidence Survey. The 14 percent figure is well below the 23 percent who felt very confident in 2002. There is little variation in retirement confidence by age.

Reality may be dawning on many workers. Since 2002, the expected age of retirement has climbed. The percentage of all workers expecting to retire at age 65 or older (including those who say they will never retire) increased from 52 to 70 percent between 2002 and 2012. Among workers aged 55 or older, fully 74 percent expect to retire at age 65 or older.

One reason so many are putting off retirement is that they have little in the way of retirement savings. Among workers approaching retirement—those aged 55 or older—the 60 percent majority has saved less than $100,000 for retirement (not counting the value of their home).

■ Nearly one-third of workers aged 55 or older have saved less than $10,000 for retirement.

Most workers are not planning on an early retirement

(percent of workers aged 25 or older who expect to retire at age 65 or older, by age, 2012)

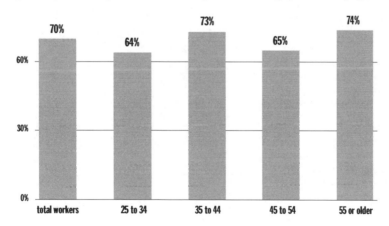

Table 11.12 Retirement Confidence, 2002 and 2012

(percentage of workers aged 25 or older who are "very confident" in financial aspects of retirement, by age, 2002 and 2012; percentage point change, 2002–12)

	total workers	25 to 34	35 to 44	45 to 54	55 or older
You will have enough money to live comfortably throughout your retirement years					
2012	14%	13%	16%	12%	16%
2002	23	26	20	21	25
You will have enough money to take care of basic expenses during retirement					
2012	26	26	27	25	27
2002	38	40	38	39	32
You are doing a good job of preparing financially for retirement					
2012	19	22	21	14	18
2002	23	26	23	21	24
You will have enough money to take care of medical expenses during retirement					
2012	13	14	15	11	14
2002	20	19	17	19	26
You will have enough money to pay for long-term care during retirement					
2012	9	10	11	8	8
2002	13	15	14	10	14
The Social Security system will continue to provide benefits of at least equal value to the benefits received by retirees today					
2012	6	4	4	4	12
2002	6	1	4	7	16
The Medicare system will continue to provide benefits of at least equal value to the benefits received by retirees today					
2012	4	2	3	6	7
2002	5	3	4	5	15

Source: Employee Benefit Research Institute, Retirement Confidence Surveys, Internet site http://www.ebri.org/surveys/rcs/2012/

Table 11.13 Expected Age of Retirement, 2002 and 2012

(expected age of retirement among workers aged 25 or older, by age, 2002 and 2012; percentage point change, 2002–12)

	2012	2002	percentage point change
ALL WORKERS			
Before age 60	8%	17%	−9
Aged 60 to 64	16	22	−6
Age 65	26	29	−3
Aged 66 or older	37	18	19
Never retire	7	5	2
Don't know/refused	5	9	−4
AGED 25 TO 34			
Before age 60	15	21	−6
Aged 60 to 64	16	20	−4
Age 65	27	33	−6
Aged 66 or older	34	17	17
Never retire	3	4	−1
Don't know/refused	4	5	−1
AGED 35 TO 44			
Before age 60	5	16	−11
Aged 60 to 64	15	27	−12
Age 65	29	30	−1
Aged 66 or older	35	14	21
Never retire	9	6	3
Don't know/refused	6	8	−2
AGED 45 TO 54			
Before age 60	10	21	−11
Aged 60 to 64	18	17	1
Age 65	22	28	−6
Aged 66 or older	34	21	13
Never retire	9	7	2
Don't know/refused	6	6	0
AGED 55 OR OLDER			
Before age 60	1	6	−5
Aged 60 to 64	15	25	−10
Age 65	23	23	0
Aged 66 or older	44	26	18
Never retire	7	2	5
Don't know/refused	8	18	−10

Source: Employee Benefit Research Institute, Retirement Confidence Surveys, Internet site http://www.ebri.org/surveys/rcs/2012/

Table 11.14 Retirement Savings by Age, 2012

(percent distribution of workers aged 25 or older by savings and investments, not including value of primary residence, by age, 2012)

	total	25 to 34	35 to 44	45 to 54	55 or older
Total workers	**100%**	**100%**	**100%**	**100%**	**100%**
Less than $10,000	48	57	51	46	31
$10,000 to $24,999	12	19	10	8	9
$25,000 to $49,999	10	12	11	9	8
$50,000 to $99,999	10	6	14	9	12
$100,000 or more	20	6	15	29	40
$100,000 to $249,999	10	5	12	12	18
$250,000 or more	10	1	3	17	22

Source: Employee Benefit Research Institute, 2012 Retirement Confidence Survey, Internet site http://www.ebri.org/surveys/rcs/2012/

Glossary

adjusted for inflation Income or a change in income that has been adjusted for the rise in the cost of living, or the consumer price index (CPI-U-RS).

age Classification by age is based on the age of the person at his/her last birthday.

American Community Survey The ACS is an ongoing nationwide survey of 250,000 households per month, providing detailed demographic data at the community level. Designed to replace the census long-form questionnaire, the ACS includes more than 60 questions that formerly appeared on the long form, such as language spoken at home, income, and education. ACS data are available for areas as small as census tracts.

American Housing Survey The AHS collects national and metropolitan-level data on the nation's housing, including apartments, single-family homes, and mobile homes. The nationally representative survey, with a sample of 55,000 homes, is conducted by the Census Bureau for the Department of Housing and Urban Development every other year.

American Indians Include Alaska Natives (Eskimos and Aleuts) unless those groups are shown separately.

American Time Use Survey Under contract with the Bureau of Labor Statistics, the Census Bureau collects ATUS information, revealing how people spend their time. The ATUS sample is drawn from U.S. households that have completed their final month of interviews for the Current Population Survey. One individual from each selected household is chosen to participate in the ATUS. Respondents are interviewed by telephone only once about their time use on the previous day.

Asian Includes Native Hawaiians and other Pacific Islanders unless those groups are shown separately.

Baby Boom Americans born between 1946 and 1964.

Baby Bust Americans born between 1965 and 1976, also known as Generation X.

Behavioral Risk Factor Surveillance System The BRFSS is a collaborative project of the Centers for Disease Control and Prevention and U.S. states and territories. It is an ongoing data collection program designed to measure behavioral risk factors in the adult population aged 18 or older. All 50 states, three territories, and the District of Columbia take part in the survey, making the BRFSS the primary source of information on the health-related behaviors of Americans.

black The black racial category includes those who identified themselves as "black" or "African American."

Consumer Expenditure Survey The CEX is an ongoing study of the day-to-day spending of American households administered by the Bureau of Labor Statistics. The CEX includes an interview survey and a diary survey. The average spending figures shown in this book are the integrated data from both the diary and interview components of the survey. Two separate, nationally representative samples are used for the interview and diary surveys. For the interview survey, about 7,500 consumer units are interviewed on a rotating panel basis each quarter for five consecutive quarters. For the diary survey, 7,500 consumer units keep weekly diaries of spending for two consecutive weeks.

consumer unit *(on spending tables only)* For convenience, the term consumer unit and households are used interchangeably in the spending section of this book, although consumer units are somewhat different from the Census Bureau's households. Consumer units are all related members of a household, or financially independent members of a household. A household may include more than one consumer unit.

Current Population Survey The CPS is a nationally representative survey of the civilian noninstitutional population aged 15 or older. It is taken monthly by the Census Bureau for the Bureau of Labor Statistics, collecting information from more than 50,000 households on employment and unemployment. In March of each year, the survey includes the Annual Social and Economic Supplement, which is the source of most national data on the characteristics of Americans, such as educational attainment, living arrangements, and incomes.

disability As defined by the National Health Interview Survey, respondents aged 18 or older are asked whether they have difficulty in physical functioning, probing whether respondents can perform nine activities by themselves without using special equipment. The categories are walking a quarter mile; standing for two hours; sitting for two hours; walking up 10 steps without resting; stooping, bending, kneeling; reaching over one's head; grasping or handling small objects; carrying a 10-pound object; and pushing/pulling a large object. Adults who report that any of these activities is very difficult or they cannot do it at all are defined as having physical difficulties.

dual-earner couple A married couple in which both the householder and the householder's spouse are in the labor force.

earnings A type of income, earnings is the amount of money a person receives from his or her job. *See also* Income.

employed All civilians who did any work as a paid employee or farmer/self-employed worker, or who worked 15 hours or more as an unpaid farm worker or in a family-owned business, during the reference period. All those who have jobs but who are temporarily absent from their jobs due to illness, bad weather, vacation, labor management dispute, or personal reasons are considered employed.

expenditure The transaction cost including excise and sales taxes of goods and services acquired during the survey period. The full cost of each purchase is recorded even though full payment may not have been made at the date of purchase. Average expenditure figures may be artificially low for infrequently purchased items such as cars because figures are calculated using all consumer units within a demographic segment rather than just purchasers. Expenditure estimates include money spent on gifts for others.

family A group of two or more people (one of whom is the householder) related by birth, marriage, or adoption and living in the same household.

family household A household maintained by a householder who lives with one or more people related to him or her by blood, marriage, or adoption.

female/male householder A woman or man who maintains a household without a spouse present. May head family or nonfamily households.

foreign-born population People who are not U.S. citizens at birth.

full-time employment Thirty-five or more hours of work per week during a majority of the weeks worked.

full-time, year-round Fifty or more weeks of full-time employment during the previous calendar year.

Generation X Americans born between 1965 and 1976, also known as the baby-bust generation.

Hispanic Because Hispanic is an ethnic origin rather than a race, Hispanics may be of any race. While most Hispanics are white, there are black, Asian, and American Indian Hispanics.

household All the persons who occupy a housing unit. A household includes the related family members and all the unrelated persons, if any, such as lodgers, foster children, wards, or employees who share the housing unit. A person living alone is counted as a household. A group of unrelated people who share a housing unit as roommates or unmarried partners is also counted as a household. Households do not include group quarters such as college dormitories, prisons, or nursing homes.

household, race/ethnicity of Households are categorized according to the race or ethnicity of the householder only.

householder The person (or one of the persons) in whose name the housing unit is owned or rented or, if there is no such person, any adult member. With married couples, the householder may be either the husband or wife. The householder is the reference person for the household.

householder, age of Used to categorize households into age groups such as those used in this book. Married couples, for example, are classified according to the age of either the husband or wife, depending on which one identified him or herself as the householder.

housing unit A house, an apartment, a group of rooms, or a single room occupied or intended for occupancy as separate living quarters. Separate living quarters are those in which the occupants do not live and eat with any other persons in the structure and that have direct access from the outside of the building or through a common hall that is used or intended for use by the occupants of another unit or by the general public. The occupants may be a single family, one person living alone, two or more families living together, or any other group of related or unrelated persons who share living arrangements.

Housing Vacancy Survey The HVS is a supplement to the Current Population Survey, providing quarterly and annual data on rental and homeowner vacancy rates, characteristics of units available for occupancy, and homeownership rates by age, household type, region, state, and metropolitan area. The Current Population Survey sample includes 72,000 housing units—61,200 occupied and 10,800 vacant.

housing value The respondent's estimate of how much his or her house and lot would sell for if it were for sale.

iGeneration Americans born from 1995 to the present. Also known as the Plurals.

immigration The relatively permanent movement (change of residence) of people into the country of reference.

in-migration The relatively permanent movement (change of residence) of people into a subnational geographic entity, such as a region, division, state, metropolitan area, or county.

income Money received in the preceding calendar year by each person aged 15 or older from each of the following sources: (1) earnings from longest job (or self-employment), (2) earnings from jobs other than longest job, (3) unemployment compensation, (4) workers' compensation, (5) Social Security, (6) Supplemental Security income, (7) public assistance, (8) veterans' payments, (9) survivor benefits, (10) disability benefits, (11) retirement pensions, (12) interest, (13) dividends, (14) rents and royalties or estates and trusts, (15) educational assistance, (16) alimony, (17) child support, (18) financial assistance from outside the household, and other periodic income. Income is reported in several ways in this book. Household income is the combined income of all household members. Income of persons is all income accruing to a person from all sources. Earnings are the money a person receives from his or her job.

industry The industry in which a person worked longest in the preceding calendar year.

job tenure The length of time a person has been employed continuously by the same employer.

labor force The labor force tables in this book show the civilian labor force only. The labor force includes both the employed and the unemployed (people who are looking for work). People are counted as in the labor force if they were working or looking for work during the reference week in which the Census Bureau fields the Current Population Survey.

labor force participation rate The percent of the civilian noninstitutional population that is in the civilian labor force, which includes both the employed and the unemployed.

married couples with or without children under age 18 Refers to married couples with or without own children under age 18 living in the same household. Couples without children under age 18 may be parents of grown children who live elsewhere, or they could be childless couples.

median The amount that divides the population or households into two equal portions: one below and one above the median. Medians can be calculated for income, age, and many other characteristics.

median income The amount that divides the income distribution into two equal groups, half having incomes above the median, half having incomes below the median. The medians for households or families are based on all households or families. The median for persons are based on all persons aged 15 or older with income.

Medical Expenditure Panel Survey MEPS is a nationally representative survey that collects detailed information on the health status, access to care, health care use and expenses and health insurance coverage of the civilian noninstitutionalized population of the U.S. and nursing home residents. MEPS comprises four component surveys: the Household Component, the Medical Provider Component, the Insurance Component, and the Nursing Home Component. The Household Component is the core survey, is conducted each year, and includes 15,000 households and 37,000 people.

metropolitan statistical To be defined as a metropolitan statistical area (or MSA), an area must include a city with 50,000 or more inhabitants, or a Census Bureau-defined urbanized area of at least 50,000 inhabitants and a total metropolitan population of at least 100,000 (75,000 in New England). The county (or counties) that contains the largest city becomes the "central county" (counties), along with any adjacent counties that have at least 50 percent of their population in the urbanized area surrounding the largest city. Additional "outlying counties" are included in the MSA if they meet specified requirements of commuting to the central counties and other selected requirements of metropolitan character (such as population density and percent urban). In New England, MSAs are defined in terms of cities and towns rather than counties. For this reason, the concept of NECMA is used to define metropolitan areas in the New England division.

Millennial generation Americans born between 1977 and 1994.

mobility status People are classified according to their mobility status on the basis of a comparison between their place of residence at the time of the March Current Population Survey and their place of residence in March of the previous year. Nonmovers are people living in the same house at the end of the period as at the beginning of the period. Movers are people living in a different house at the end of the period than at the beginning of the period. Movers from abroad are either citizens or aliens whose place of residence is outside the United States at the beginning of the period, that is, in an outlying area under the jurisdiction of the United States or in a foreign country. The mobility status for children is fully allocated from the mother if she is in the household; otherwise it is allocated from the householder.

National Ambulatory Medical Care Survey The NAMCS is an annual survey of visits to nonfederally employed office-based physicians who are primarily engaged in direct patient care. Data are collected from physicians rather than patients, with each physician assigned a one-week reporting period. During that week, a systematic random sample of visit characteristics are recorded by the physician or office staff.

National Compensation Survey The Bureau of Labor Statistics' NCS examines the incidence and detailed provisions of selected employee benefits in private sector establishments and state and local governments. Each year BLS economists visit a representative sample of establishments across the country, asking questions about the establishment, its employees, and their benefits.

National Health and Nutrition Examination Survey The NHANES is a continuous survey of a representative sample of the U.S. civilian noninstitutionalized population. Respondents are interviewed at home about their health and nutrition, and the interview is followed up by a physical examination that measures such things as height and weight in mobile examination centers.

National Health Interview Survey The NHIS is a continuing nationwide sample survey of the civilian noninstitutional population of the U.S. conducted by the Census Bureau for the National Center for Health Statistics. Each year, data are collected from more than 100,000 people about their illnesses, injuries, impairments, chronic and acute conditions, activity limitations, and the use of health services.

National Hospital Ambulatory Medical Care Survey The NHAMCS, sponsored by the National Center for Health Statistics, is an annual national probability sample survey of visits to emergency departments and outpatient departments at non-Federal, short stay and general hospitals. Data are collected by hospital staff from patient records.

National Household Education Survey The NHES, sponsored by the National Center for Education Statistics, provides descriptive data on the educational activities of the U.S. population, including after-school care and adult education. The NHES is a system of telephone surveys of a representative sample of 45,000 to 60,000 households in the U.S.

National Survey of Family Growth The 2002 NSFG, sponsored by the National Center for Health Statistics, is a nationally representative survey of the civilian noninstitutional population aged 15 to 44. In-person interviews were completed with 12,571 men and women, collecting data on marriage, divorce, contraception, and infertility. The 2002 survey updates previous NSFG surveys taken in 1973, 1976, 1988, and 1995.

National Survey on Drug Use and Health Formerly called the National Household Survey on Drug Abuse, this survey, sponsored by the Substance Abuse and Mental Health Services Administration, has been conducted since 1971. It is the primary source of information on the use of illegal drugs by the U.S. population. Each year, a nationally representative sample of about 70,000 individuals aged 12 or older are surveyed in the 50 states and the District of Columbia.

Native Hawaiian and other Pacific Islander Beginning with the 2000 census, this group was identified as a racial category separate from Asians. In most survey data, however, the population is included with Asians.

net migration Net migration is the result of subtracting out-migration from in-migration for an area. Another way to derive net migration is to subtract natural increase (births minus deaths) from total population change in an area.

net worth The amount of money left over after a household's debts are subtracted from its assets.

nonfamily household A household maintained by a householder who lives alone or who lives with people to whom he or she is not related.

nonfamily householder A householder who lives alone or with nonrelatives.

non-Hispanic People who do not identify themselves as Hispanic are classified as non-Hispanic. Non-Hispanics may be of any race.

non-Hispanic white People who identify their race as white and who do not indicate a Hispanic origin.

nonmetropolitan area Counties that are not classified as metropolitan areas.

occupation Occupational classification is based on the kind of work a person did at his or her job during the previous calendar year. If a person changed jobs during the year, the data refer to the occupation of the job held the longest during that year.

occupied housing units A housing unit is classified as occupied if a person or group of people is living in it or if the occupants are only temporarily absent—on vacation, example. By definition, the count of occupied housing units is the same as the count of households.

outside principal cities The portion of a metropolitan county or counties that falls outside of the principal city or cities; generally regarded as the suburbs.

own children Sons and daughters, including stepchildren and adopted children, of the householder. The totals include never-married children living away from home in college dormitories.

owner occupied A housing unit is "owner occupied" if the owner lives in the unit, even if it is mortgaged or not fully paid for. A cooperative or condominium unit is "owner occupied" only if the owner lives in it. All other occupied units are classified as "renter occupied."

part-time employment Less than 35 hours of work per week in a majority of the weeks worked during the year.

percent change The change (either positive or negative) in a measure that is expressed as a proportion of the starting measure. When median income changes from $20,000 to $25,000, for example, this is a 25 percent increase.

percentage point change The change (either positive or negative) in a value which is already expressed as a percentage. When a labor force participation rate changes from 70 percent of 75 percent, for example, this is a 5 percentage point increase.

poverty level The official income threshold below which families and people are classified as living in poverty. The threshold rises each year with inflation and varies depending on family size and age of householder.

primary activity In the time use tables, primary activities are those respondents identify as their main activity. Other activities done simultaneously are not included.

proportion or share The value of a part expressed as a percentage of the whole. If there are 4 million people aged 25 and 3 million of them are white, then the white proportion is 75 percent.

race Race is self-reported and can be defined in three ways. The "race alone" population comprises people who identify themselves as only one race. The "race in combination" population comprises people who identify themselves as more than one race, such as white and black. The "race, alone or in combination" population includes both those who identify themselves as one race and those who identify themselves as more than one race.

regions The four major regions and nine census divisions of the United States are the state groupings as shown below:

Northeast:
—New England: Connecticut, Maine, Massachusetts, New Hampshire, Rhode Island, and Vermont
—Middle Atlantic: New Jersey, New York, and Pennsylvania

Midwest:
—East North Central: Illinois, Indiana, Michigan, Ohio, and Wisconsin
—West North Central: Iowa, Kansas, Minnesota, Missouri, Nebraska, North Dakota, and South Dakota

South:

—South Atlantic: Delaware, District of Columbia, Florida, Georgia, Maryland, North Carolina, South Carolina, Virginia, and West Virginia

—East South Central: Alabama, Kentucky, Mississippi, and Tennessee

—West South Central: Arkansas, Louisiana, Oklahoma, and Texas

West:

—Mountain: Arizona, Colorado, Idaho, Montana, Nevada, New Mexico, Utah, and Wyoming

—Pacific: Alaska, California, Hawaii, Oregon, and Washington

renter occupied *See* Owner occupied.

Retirement Confidence Survey The RCS, sponsored by the Employee Benefit Research Institute (EBRI), the American Savings Education Council (ASEC), and Mathew Greenwald & Associates (Greenwald), is an annual survey of a nationally representative sample of 1,000 people aged 25 or older. Respondents are asked a core set of questions that have been asked since 1996, measuring attitudes and behavior towards retirement. Additional questions are also asked about current retirement issues.

rounding Percentages are rounded to the nearest tenth of a percent; therefore, the percentages in a distribution do not always add exactly to 100.0 percent. The totals, however, are always shown as 100.0. Moreover, individual figures are rounded to the nearest thousand without being adjusted to group totals, which are independently rounded; percentages are based on the unrounded numbers.

self-employment A person is categorized as self-employed if he or she was self-employed in the job held longest during the reference period. Persons who report self-employment from a second job are excluded, but those who report wage-and-salary income from a second job are included. Unpaid workers in family businesses are excluded. Self-employment statistics include only nonagricultural workers and exclude people who work for themselves in incorporated business.

sex ratio The number of men per 100 women.

suburbs *See* Outside central city.

Survey of Consumer Finances A triennial survey taken by the Federal Reserve Board. It collects data on the assets, debts, and net worth of American households. For the 2007 survey, the Federal Reserve Board interviewed a representative sample of 6,500 households.

unemployed Those who, during the survey period, had no employment but were available and looking for work. Those who were laid off from their jobs and were waiting to be recalled are also classified as unemployed.

white The "white" racial category includes many Hispanics (who may be of any race) unless the term "non-Hispanic white" is used.

Youth Risk Behavior Surveillance System The YRBSS was created by the Centers for Disease Control to monitor health risks being taken by young people at the national, state, and local level. The national survey is taken every two years based on a nationally representative sample of 16,000 students in 9th through 12th grade in public and private schools.

Bibliography

Agency for Healthcare Research and Quality
Internet site http://www.ahrq.gov/
—Medical Expenditure Panel Survey, Internet site http://meps.ahrq.gov/mepsweb/ survey_comp/household.jsp

Bureau of the Census
Internet site http://www.census.gov
—2010 American Community Survey, American FactFinder, Internet site http://factfinder2 .census.gov/faces/nav/jsf/pages/index.xhtml
—2010 Census, American Factfinder, Internet site http://factfinder2.census.gov/faces/nav/ jsf/pages/index.xhtml
—2010 Census, Internet site http://2010.census.gov/2010census/data/
—A Child's Day: 2009, Internet site http://www.census.gov/hhes/socdemo/children/data/ sipp/well2009/tables.html
—American Housing Survey National Tables: 2009, Internet site http://www.census.gov/ housing/ahs/data/ahs2009.html
—Educational Attainment, CPS Historical Time Series Tables, Internet site http://www .census.gov/hhes/socdemo/education/data/cps/historical/index.html
—Educational Attainment, Internet site http://www.census.gov/hhes/socdemo/education/
—Families and Living Arrangements, Internet site http://www.census.gov/population/www/ socdemo/hh-fam.html
—Fertility of American Women: 2010, Detailed Tables, Internet site http://www.census .gov/hhes/fertility/data/cps/2010.html
—Geographical Mobility, Internet site http://www.census.gov/hhes/migration
—Health Insurance, Internet site http://www.census.gov/hhes/www/hlthins/
—Historical Health Insurance Tables, Current Population Survey Annual Social and Economic Supplements, Internet site http://www.census.gov/hhes/www/hlthins/data/ historical/HIB_tables.html
—Historical Income Tables, Internet site http://www.census.gov/hhes/www/income/data/ historical/index.html
—Housing Vacancies and Homeownership Survey, Internet site http://www.census.gov/ hhes/www/housing/hvs/hvs.html
—Income, Current Population Survey, Internet site http://www.census.gov/hhes/www/ income/data/index.html
—Number, Timing, and Duration of Marriages and Divorces: 2009, Current Population Reports P70-125, 2011, Internet site http://www.census.gov/hhes/socdemo/marriage/data/ sipp/index.html
—Population Estimates, Internet site http://www.census.gov/popest/data/index.html
—Poverty, Current Population Survey, Internet site http://www.census.gov/hhes/www/ poverty/index.html
—School Enrollment, Historical Tables, Current Population Survey Annual Social and Economic Supplements, Internet site http://www.census.gov/population/www/socdemo/ school/.html
—School Enrollment, Internet site http://www.census.gov/hhes/school/

Bureau of Labor Statistics

Internet site http://www.bls.gov

> —Consumer Expenditure Surveys, various years, Internet site http://www.bls.gov/cex/home.htm
>
> —2010 American Time Use Survey, Internet site http://www.bls.gov/tus/home.htm
>
> —Characteristics of Minimum Wage Workers, 2011, Internet site http://www.bls.gov/cps/minwage2011tbls.htm
>
> —College Enrollment and Work Activity of 2010 High School Graduates, Internet site http://www.bls.gov/news.release/hsgec.nr0.htm
>
> —Employee Tenure, Internet site http://www.bls.gov/news.release/tenure.toc.htm
>
> —Employment Projections, Internet site http://www.bls.gov/emp/
>
> —Employment and Unemployment among Youth Summary, Internet site http://bls.gov/news.release/youth.nr0.htm
>
> —Employment Characteristics of Families, Internet site http://www.bls.gov/news.release/famee.toc.htm
>
> —Labor Force Statistics from the Current Population Survey—Annual Averages, Internet site http://www.bls.gov/cps/tables.htm#empstat
>
> —National Compensation Survey, Internet site http://www.bls.gov/ncs/ebs/home.htm
>
> —Table 15. Employed persons by detailed occupation, sex, and age, Annual Average 2011 (Source: Current Population Survey), unpublished table received from the BLS by special request

Centers for Disease Control and Prevention

Internet site http://www.cdc.gov

> —Behavioral Risk Factor Surveillance System, Prevalence Data, Internet site http://apps.nccd.cdc.gov/brfss/
>
> —Cases of HIV/AIDS and AIDS in the United States and Dependent Areas, 2009, Internet site http://www.cdc.gov/hiv/surveillance/resources/reports/2009report/
>
> —Youth Risk Behavior Surveillance–United States, 2009, Internet site http://www.cdc.gov/HealthyYouth/yrbs/index.htm

Employee Benefit Research Institute

Internet site http://www.ebri.org/

> —Retirement Confidence Surveys, Internet site http://www.ebri.org/surveys/rcs/

Federal Interagency Forum on Child and Family Statistics

Internet site http://childstats.gov

> —America's Children: Key National Indicators of Well-Being, 2011, Internet site http://www.childstats.gov/

Federal Reserve Board

Internet site http://www.federalreserve.gov/econresdata/scf/scfindex.htm

> —*Surveying the Aftermath of the Storm: Changes in Family Finances from 2007 to 2009*, Appendix tables, Internet site http://www.federalreserve.gov/econresdata/scf/scf_2009p.htm

Homeland Security
Internet site http://www.dhs.gov/index.shtm
 —Yearbook of Immigration Statistics, Internet site http://www.dhs.gov/files/statistics/
 publications/yearbook.shtm

National Center for Education Statistics
Internet site http://nces.ed.gov
 —*The Condition of Education 2011*, Internet site http://nces.ed.gov/programs/coe/
 —*Digest of Education Statistics: 2011*, Internet site http://nces.ed.gov/programs/digest
 —National Household Education Survey, Internet site http://nces.ed.gov/nhes/

National Center for Health Statistics
Internet site http://www.cdc.gov/nchs
 —*Anthropometric Reference Data for Children and Adults: United States, 2003–2006*,
 National Health Statistics Reports, Number 10, 2008, Internet site http://www.cdc.gov/nchs/
 products/pubs/pubd/nhsr/nhsr.htm
 —Birth Data, Internet site http://www.cdc.gov/nchs/births.htm
 —*Complementary and Alternative Medicine Use Among Adults and Children: United States,
 2007*, National Health Statistics Report, No. 12, 2008, Internet site http://www.cdc.gov/nchs/
 products/nhsr.htm
 —*Health Characteristics of Adults 55 Years of Age and Over: United States, 2004–2007*,
 National Health Statistics Reports, No. 16, 2009, Internet site http://www.cdc.gov/nchs/nhis
 .htm
 —Mortality Data, Internet site http://www.cdc.gov/nchs/deaths.htm
 —*National Ambulatory Medical Care Survey: 2009 Summary Tables,* Internet site http://
 www.cdc.gov/nchs/ahcd/web_tables.htm#2009
 —*National Hospital Ambulatory Medical Care Survey: 2008 Emergency Department
 Summary,* Internet site http://www.cdc.gov/nchs/ahcd/web_tables.htm#2009
 —*National Hospital Ambulatory Medical Care Survey: 2008 Outpatient Department
 Summary,* Internet site http://www.cdc.gov/nchs/ahcd/web_tables.htm#2009
 —*Health, United States,* various editions, Internet site http://www.cdc.gov/nchs/hus.htm
 —*Sexual Behavior, Sexual Attraction, and Sexual Identity in the United States: Data
 from the 2006–2008 National Survey of Family Growth,* National Health Statistics Reports,
 No. 36, 2011, Internet site http://www.cdc.gov/nchs/nsfg/new_nsfg.htm
 —*Summary Health Statistics for U.S. Adults: National Health Interview Survey, 2010,*
 Series 10, No. 252, 2012, Internet site http://www.cdc.gov/nchs/nhis.htm
 —*Summary Health Statistics for U.S. Children: National Health Interview Survey, 2010,*
 Series 10, No. 250, 2011, Internet site http://www.cdc.gov/nchs/nhis.htm
 —*Summary Health Statistics for the U.S. Population: National Health Interview Survey,
 2010*, Series 10, No. 251, 2011, Internet site http://www.cdc.gov/nchs/nhis.htm

National Sporting Goods Association
Internet site http://www.nsga.org
 —Sports Participation, Internet site http://www.nsga.org

Substance Abuse and Mental Health Services Administration
Internet site http://www.samhsa.gov

   National Survey on Drug Use and Health, 2010, Internet site http://www.samhsa.gov/data/
   NSDUH/2k10ResultsTables/Web/HTML/TOC.htm

University of California, Berkeley, Survey Documentation and Analysis, Computer-assisted Survey Methods Program
Internet site http://sda.berkeley.edu/

   —General Social Surveys 1972-2010 Cumulative Data Files, Internet site http://sda.berkeley
   .edu/cgi-bin/hsda?harcsda+gss10

University of Michigan, Monitoring the Future Study
Internet site http://monitoringthefuture.org

   —Monitoring the Future Study, Data Tables and Figures, Internet site http://
   monitoringthefuture.org/data/data.html

Index

abortion, attitude toward, 31
accidents, as cause of death, 86
accounts, transaction, 304
AIDS, 79
alcoholic beverages
    consumption of, 58
    spending on, 267–283
alternative medicine, 84
American Dream, attitude toward, 13–14
apartments, living in, 99
apparel, spending on, 267–283
arthritis, health condition, 68–70
Asia, place of birth, 220
Asian Americans
    by state, 238–263
    educational attainment, 43, 45
    employment status, 149, 152
    full-time workers, 125, 131
    homeownership of, 97
    household income, 109
    household type, 185, 193
    households with children, 193
    in poverty, 141
    marital status, 203
    men's income, 125
    population, 215–217, 238–263
    women's income, 131
Asian language speakers, 224
assets. *See also* Net worth.
    financial, 303–306
    nonfinancial, 308–310
asthma, health condition, 68–70
attitudes
    toward abortion, 31
    toward Bible, 22
    toward death penalty, 30
    toward euthanasia, 32
    toward evolution, 20
    toward finances, 11, 316
    toward gay marriage, 25
    toward government role in health care, 18
    toward gun control, 30
    toward health, 53
    toward health care received, 83–84
    toward homosexuality, 24
    toward ideal number of children, 16
    toward income, 10
    toward job, 11
    toward life, 5–6
    toward marijuana legalization, 31
    toward marriage, 5
    toward Medicare, 316
    toward politics, 27–28
    toward premarital sex, 24
    toward retirement, 316
    toward science, 20
    toward sex roles, 17
    toward social class membership, 10
    toward Social Security, 316
    toward spanking, 16
    toward standard of living, 13–14
    toward success, 8
    toward working mothers, 17

back pain, health condition, 68–70
Bible, attitude toward, 22
birth, place of, 219
Black Americans
    by state, 238–263
    educational attainment, 43, 45
    employment status, 149, 152
    full-time workers, 126, 132
    homeownership of, 97
    household income, 110
    household type, 186, 194
    households with children, 194
    in poverty, 141
    marital status, 204
    men's income, 126
    population, 215–217, 238–263
    women's income, 132
blood pressure, high, 68–71
bonds, 306
bronchitis, health condition, 68–70
business equity, 310

cancer
    as cause of death, 86
    health condition, 68–70
cash contributions, spending on, 267–283
Catholic, 21
cerebrovascular disease, as cause of death, 86
certificates of deposit, 304
children
    age of in household, 192–197
    average number per household, 190
    ideal number of, 16
    presence of in household, 192–197
    spanking, attitude toward, 16
    standard of living, 14
    time spent caring for, 287–298
    with AIDS, 79
cholesterol, high, 72

chronic liver disease and cirrhosis, as cause of death, 86
chronic lower respiratory disease, as cause of death, 86
cigarette smoking, 58. *See also* Tobacco products.
class membership, 10
climate, as reason for moving, 102
college enrollment, 49
computer, time spent on, 287–298
conservative political leanings, 27
coronary, health condition, 68–70
cost of living. *See* Standard of living.
credit card debt, 314

death
    causes of, 86
    penalty, attitude toward, 30
debt, household, 312–314
Democratic party affiliation, 28
diabetes
    as cause of death, 86
    health condition, 68–70, 72
disability, by type, 78
divorce, 201, 203–206, 208
doctor visits. *See* Physician visits.
drinking, alcoholic beverages, 58
drugs. *See also* Marijuana.
    illicit, use of, 59
    prescription, 74–76
    spending on, 75–76, 267–283
dual-income couples, 155

earnings. *See also* Income.
    by educational attainment, 136–139
    minimum wage, 174
eating, time spent, 287–298
education
    debt, 314
    spending on, 267–283
    time spent, 287–298
educational attainment
    by generation/age, 35, 37
    by race and Hispanic origin, 43, 45
    by sex, 39, 41
    earnings by, 136–139
emergency department services. *See* Hospital
    emergency services.
emphysema, health condition, 68–70
employment. *See also* Labor force.
    as reason for moving, 102
    based health insurance, 63
    long-term, 172
English language speakers, 224
entertainment, spending on, 267–283
Europe, place of birth, 220
evolution, attitude toward, 20
exercise, 56

face pain, health condition, 68–70
families. *See* Households.
family, as a reason for moving, 102
female-headed household. *See* Households,
    female-headed.
finances, attitude towards, 11, 316
food
    preparation and cleanup, time spent, 287–298
    spending on, 267–283
foreclosure, as reason for moving, 102
foreign-born. *See also* Immigrants.
    by region of birth, 220
    population, 219–220
full-time workers, 124–128, 130–134, 166
furnishings and equipment, spending on, 267–283

gardening and lawn care, time spent, 287–298
gasoline, spending on, 267–283. *See also*
    Transportation.
gay and lesbian relationships, attitude toward, 24–25
geographic mobility. *See* Mobility, geographic.
gifts, spending on, 267–283
government health insurance, 62, 64–66. *See also*
    Medicaid and Medicare.
grooming, time spent, 287–298
gun control, attitude toward, 30

happiness, 5
hay fever, health condition, 68–70
headaches, health condition, 68–70
health, as reason for moving, 102
health care
    government role in, attitude toward, 18
    rating of, 83–84
    spending on, 65–66, 267–283
    time spent, 287–298
health care visits. *See* Physician visits, Hospital
    outpatient services, and Hospital emergency
    services.
health conditions, 68–72
health insurance
    coverage, 62–64
    spending on, 267–283
health status, 53
hearing impairments, health condition, 68–70
heart disease
    as cause of death, 86
    health condition, 68–70
high blood pressure, health condition, 68–71
high cholesterol, health condition, 72
Hispanic Americans
    by state, 238–263
    educational attainment, 43, 45
    employment status, 149, 152
    full-time workers, 127, 133

homeownership of, 97
household income, 111
household type, 187, 195
households with children, 195
in poverty, 141
marital status, 205
men's income, 127
population, 215–217, 238–263
women's income, 133
homeopathic medicine, use of, 84
homeowners
    by household type, 95
    by race and Hispanic origin, 97
    by region, 95
    by type of structure, 99
    number of, 93
    trends in, 91
homes, as nonfinancial assets, 309
home-secured debt, 313
homosexuality, attitude toward, 24–25
hospital emergency services, use of, 82
hospital inpatient services, use of, 83
hospital outpatient services, use of, 82
household services, spending on, 267–283
households. *See also* Households, female-headed,
        Households, male-headed, Households,
        married-couple, and Households,
        single-person.
    assets of, 303–310
    by race and Hispanic origin, 185–188, 193–196
    by type, 183, 185–188, 199
    debt of, 312–314
    homeownership of, 91, 93, 95, 97, 99, 309
    income of, 105, 107, 109–112, 114–119
    size, 190, 199
    wealth of, 301
    with children, 192–197
households, female-headed
    by race and Hispanic origin, 185–188, 193–196
    homeownership of, 95
    income of, 114–119
    living alone, 183, 185–188, 199
    with children, 192–196
households, male-headed
    by race and Hispanic origin, 185–188, 193–196
    homeownership of, 95
    income of, 114–119
    living alone, 183, 185–188, 199
    with children, 192–196
households, married-couple
    by race and Hispanic origin, 185–188, 193–196
    dual-income, 155
    homeownership of, 95
    income of, 114–119
    with children, 192–196

households, single-person
    by race and Hispanic origin, 185–188
    by sex, 183, 185–188, 199
    homeownership of, 95
    income of, 114–119
housekeeping supplies, spending on, 267–283
housework, time spent, 287–298
housing. *See also* Shelter, Homeowners, and Renters.
    as a reason for moving, 102
    by type of structure, 99
    spending on, 267–283
hypertension, health condition, 68–71

immigrants, 222. *See also* Foreign-born.
income. *See also* Earnings.
    by race and Hispanic origin, 109–112, 125–128,
        131–134
    household, 105, 107, 109–112, 114–119
    men's, 121, 124–128
    of full-time workers, 124–128, 130–134
    relative to others, 10
    trends in, 105, 121–122
    women's, 122, 130–134
insurance, personal, spending on, 267–283. *See also*
        Life insurance, Health insurance, and
        Property insurance.
Interest, mortgage, spending on, 267–283
Internet, as source of news, 27

Jewish, 21
job. *See also* Labor Force, Occupation, and Workers.
    as a reason for moving, 102
    long-term, 172
    satisfaction, 11
    tenure, 171

kidney disease, health condition, 68–70

labor force. *See also* Job and Workers.
    by occupation, 157–164
    by race and Hispanic origin, 149–150, 152–153
    by sex, 145, 147, 149–150, 152–153, 166–167, 169,
        176, 178–179
    full-time, 124–128, 130–134, 166
    participation, 145, 147, 149–150, 152–153, 179
    part-time, 166–167
    projections, 178–179
    self-employed, 169
    status of married couples, 155
    trends, 145, 178–179
    unemployed, 147, 149–150, 152–153
    unionized, 176
language spoken at home, 224
Latin America, place of birth, 220
leisure time, 287–298

liberal political leanings, 27
life expectancy, 87
life insurance
    as financial asset, 304
    spending on, 267–283
liver disease
    as cause of death, 86
    health condition, 68–70
living alone. *See* Households, single–person.
lower class membership, 10

male-headed households. *See* Households,
        male-headed.
marijuana
    attitude toward legalization, 31
    use, 60
marital history, 208
marital status. See also Marriage.
    by race and Hispanic origin, 203–206
    by sex, 201, 203–206, 208
marriage. *See also* Marital status.
    gay, attitude toward, 25
    happiness of, 5
married couples. *See* Households, married-couple.
Medicaid, 64–66, 75–76
Medicare, 64–66, 75–76, 316
men
    AIDS, number with, 79
    earnings of, 136–137
    educational attainment, 39, 43, 136–137
    high blood pressure, 71
    high cholesterol, 72
    income, 121, 124–128
    job tenure, 171–172
    labor force characteristics, 145, 147, 149–150,
        166–167
    labor force projections, 178–179
    life expectancy, 87
    living alone, 183, 185–188, 199
    marital status, 201, 203–206, 208
    physician visits, 81
    physical activity, 56
    population, 212
    prescription drug use, 74
    school enrollment, 47
    self-employed, 169
    time use, 291–294
    union representation, 176
    weight, 55
Mexico, place of birth, 220
middle-class membership, 10
migraines. *See* Headaches.
military health insurance, 64, 75–76
minimum wage workers, 174
mobile homes, living in, 99

mobility, geographic
    rate, 101
    reason for, 102
    since age 16, 8
moderate political leanings, 27
mortgage
    debt, 313
    interest, spending on, 267–283
movers. *See* Mobility, geographic.
multi-racial Americans, 215

neck pain, health condition, 68–70
nephritis, as cause of death, 86
net worth, household, 301
never-married, 201, 203–206, 208
news, sources of, 27
newspapers, as source of news, 27
non-Hispanic whites. *See* White, Non-Hispanic
        Americans.

obesity. *See* Weight.
occupation, 157–164
outpatient department. *See* Hospital outpatient services.
overweight. *See* Weight.

parents' standard of living, 13
part-time workers, 166–167
pensions, spending on, 267–283
personal care products and services, spending on,
        267–283
pet care, time spent, 287–298
physical activity, 56
physician visits
    frequency of, 81
    rating of health care received, 83
political leanings, 27
population
    by generation, 211, 217, 229, 234–237
    by place of birth, 219–220
    by race and Hispanic origin, 215–217, 238–263
    by region, 226–229
    by sex, 212
    by state, 230–263
    foreign-born, 219–220
    trends, 213
poverty, 141
prescription drugs
    spending on, 75–76
    use of, 74
private health insurance, 62–63, 65–66, 75–76
projections, labor force, 178–179
property
    as nonfinancial asset, 309
    taxes, spending on, 267–283

Protestant, 21
public transportation, spending on, 267–283

race. *See* Asian Americans, Black Americans,
        Hispanic Americans, Multi-racial
        Americans, and White non-Hispanic
        Americans.
radio, as source of news, 27
reading
    spending on, 267–283
    time spent, 287–298
regions
    homeownership by, 95
    moving between, 101
    population of, 226–229
religious. *See also* Bible.
    activities, time spent on, 287–298
    preferences, 21
renters. *See also* Shelter.
    by type of structure, 99
    number of, 93
Republican party affiliation, 28
respiratory disease, as cause of death, 86
retirement
    accounts, 305
    age of, expected, 317
    as reason for moving, 102
    attitude toward, 316
    savings, 318

savings, 304–306, 318
school. *See also* Education.
    attitude toward Bible in, 22
    enrollment, 47, 49
science, attitude toward, 20
self-employment, 169
septicemia, as cause of death, 86
sex
    homosexuality, attitude toward, 24–25
    premarital, attitude toward, 24
    roles, attitude toward, 17
shelter, spending on, 267–283
shopping, time spent, 287–298
single-family homes, living in, 99
single-person households. *See* Households,
        single-person.
singles. *See* Never-married.
sinusitis, health condition, 68–70
sleeping, time spent, 287–298
smoking, 58
Social Security, attitude toward, 316
Spanish language speakers, 224
spending. *See also* individual product categories.
    by category, 267–283
    trends, 267–275

sports, time spent playing, 287–298
standard of living, 13–14
states
    moving between, 101
    place of birth, 219
    population of, 230–263
stock ownership, 305–306
stroke, health condition, 68–70
student loan debt, 214
suicide
    as cause of death, 86
    doctor-assisted, attitude toward, 32

taxes, personal, spending on, 267–283. *See also*
        Property taxes.
teeth, absence of, health condition, 68–70
telephone, time spent on, 287–298
television
    as source of news, 27
    time spent watching, 287–298
tobacco products, spending on, 267–283. *See also*
        Cigarette smoking.
transportation, spending on, 267–283
traveling, time spent, 287–298
trust in others, 6

ulcers, health condition, 68–70
unemployment, 147, 149–150, 152–153
union representation, 176
upper class membership, 10
utilities, fuels, and public services, spending on,
        267–283

vehicle purchases, spending on, 267–283
vehicles, as nonfinancial assets, 310
visual impairments, health condition, 68–70
volunteering, time spent, 287–298

wealth, household, 301
weight, 55
White Americans, employment status, 150, 153
White non-Hispanic Americans
    by state, 238–263
    educational attainment, 43, 45
    full-time workers, 128, 134
    homeownership, 97
    household income, 112
    household type, 188, 196
    households with children, 196
    in poverty, 141
    marital status, 206
    men's income, 128
    population, 215–217, 238–263
    women's income, 134

widowhood, 201, 203–206, 208
women
    AIDS, number with, 79
    earnings, 138–139
    educational attainment, 41, 45, 138–139
    high blood pressure, 71
    high cholesterol, 72
    income, 122, 130–134
    job tenure, 171–172
    labor force characteristics, 145, 147, 152–153,
        166–167
    labor force projections, 178–179
    life expectancy, 87
    living alone, 183, 185–188, 199
    marital status, 201, 203–206, 208
    physical activity, 56
    physician visits, 81
    population, 212
    prescription drug use, 74
    school enrollment, 47
    self-employed, 169
    time use, 295–298
    weight, 55
    working, attitude toward, 17
work, time spent at, 287–298. *See also* Job, Labor
        force, and Occupation.
workers. *See also* Job, Labor force and Occupation.
    full-time, 124–128, 130–134, 166
    in unions, 176
    minimum wage, 174
    part-time, 166–167
    self-employed, 169
    unemployed, 147, 149–150, 152–153
working class membership, 10